Technological
competitiveness

TECHNOLOGICAL COMPETITIVENESS

Contemporary and Historical Perspectives on the Electrical, Electronics, and Computer Industries

Edited by

William Aspray

IEEE Center for the History of Electrical Engineering

NEW ENGLAND INSTITUTE
OF TECHNOLOGY
LEARNING RESOURCES CENTER

IEEE
PRESS

The Institute of Electrical and Electronics Engineers, Inc., New York

Cover photo: Engineering Research Associates Laboratory, St. Paul, Minnesota, c. 1950. Courtesy of the Charles Babbage Institute, University of Minnesota.

Technical Reviewer

Melvin Kranzberg
Georgia Institute of Technology

This book may be purchased at a discount from the publisher when ordered in bulk quantities. For more information contact:

IEEE PRESS Marketing
Attn: Special Sales
PO Box 1331
445 Hoes Lane
Piscataway, NJ 08855-1331
Fax: (908) 981-8062

Printed in the United States of America

10 9 8 7 6 5 4 3 2 1

ISBN 0-7803-0427-6
IEEE Order Number: PC0324-4

Library of Congress Cataloging-in-Publication Data

Technological competitiveness : contemporary and historical
    perspectives on the electrical, electronics, and computer industries
    [edited by] William Aspray.
        p.   cm.
    Proceedings of a conference held Oct. 10–11, 1991 at Rutgers
University.
    Includes bibliographical references and index.
    ISBN-0-7803-0427-6
    1. Computer industry—Congresses.   2. Electronic industries—
Congresses.   3. Electric industries—Congresses.   4. Competition,
international—Congresses.   I. Aspray, William.
    HD9696.C62T39 1993   92-30772
    338.4'76213—dc20   CIP

Dedicated to Eric Herz,
who appreciates the value of history to engineering

Contents

Preface

"Competition, we have now learnt, is neither good nor evil in itself; it is a force which has to be studied and controlled; it may be compared to a stream whose strength and direction have to be observed, that embankments may be thrown up within which it may do its work harmlessly and beneficially." (Arnold Toynbee, *Lectures on the Industrial Revolution in England,* 1884)

Although technological competitiveness was a familiar concept by the nineteenth century, it only became an important public issue in the United States in the 1980s.[1] The Reagan administration believed that if businesses could improve themselves in various ways and if the federal government could lower taxes and remove onerous regulation, American industry could once again fend off challenges from other nations, especially Japan, and America could resume its position as world economic leader. The Reagan administration, together with many of America's journalists and business school faculty, thus defined technological competitiveness as a competition among nations for technical prowess that was assumed to translate into economic advantage.

We use the term "technological competitiveness" in this way and in three others in this book. Besides competition among nations there is, most obviously, competition *among* firms to use technology to provide products or services that compare favorably with those of competing firms in order to gain customers, profits, or markets. There is also competition *within* firms *among* different technologies, or among products or services based upon these technologies. Finally, there is competition among technologies themselves to become the dominant technology for a particular application.

According to conservative Republican principles as practiced over the past dozen years, competitiveness must be achieved without reliance upon a national technology policy targeting specific industries for special treatment, given that such a policy would smack of social planning. Despite this philosophy, several technologies involving electronics, such as high-definition television, supercomputers, and semiconductors, came in for special attention from the Reagan and Bush administrations.

There were at least two reasons for this apparent contradiction of policy. One was that the government did not believe it could afford to ignore electronics and computing, which represented the largest and most dynamic area of technology in the second half of the twentieth century. Moreover, these technologies are central to so-called "high technology," which itself is the mainstay of the American government's strategy for national competitiveness. High technologies depend critically upon a skilled professional labor force, extensive research and development, and advanced manufacturing technologies. The Reagan and Bush administrations assumed that the nation had its greatest competitive advantages over other nations in these areas through its superior educational and research infrastructure and its wide availability of venture capital. Therefore, plans for the nation's economic well-being were built on strong performance of high-tech industries. Because electronics and computing are among the highest of high technologies in the late twentieth century and because so many other high-technology fields involve the use of electronic components or computers, the administration believed it must attend to them carefully to protect national competitiveness.

Technological competitiveness has come under close scrutiny from the professional engineering, business, and public policy communities in recent years.[2] The IEEE U.S. Activities Office, for example, formed the Committee on U.S. Competitiveness in the 1980s to identify key factors and suggest solutions for national competitiveness. This committee has recommended greater attention to the manufacturing process and quality control, the need for more accessible and lower cost capital, educational improvements especially at the K–12 levels, refocusing of research and development on more practical areas, modifications to antitrust laws that will encourage joint research-and-development operations, trade policy that will strengthen the nation's industries, tort reform to avoid liability in cases where products conform to highest known scientific and engineering standards, and a coherent national technology policy that addresses the commercial as well as the military sector. Other bodies, such as the Harvard Business School, the MIT Sloan School of Management, the Sloan Foundation, the Council on Competitiveness, and the Office of Technology Assessment, have organized similar studies, which together have led to many useful suggestions for improved technological competitiveness at the firm and national levels.

What possibly can historians add to this discussion? Competitiveness was of course not a new concept in the 1980s. By the end of the nineteenth century, at the latest, companies at the cutting edge of technology were competing fiercely in international markets for business viability. The contested technologies were somewhat different then: fine chemicals, metallurgy, business machines, automobiles, electrical power and appliances, and telecommunications. But many of the factors were the same as they are today: research and development, venture capital, university-industry relations, patents, etc. Thus there is a century of experience with technological competitiveness among firms, among nations, and among technologies upon which historians might draw to bring greater understanding to today's situation.

The potential for increased understanding of contemporary competitiveness through historical examination seemed patently obvious to the staff of the IEEE-Rutgers Center for the History of Electrical Engineering. We knew that a number of historians of technology had investigated such factors as research and development, manufacturing, management, marketing, government regulation, and trade policies in both successful and unsuccessful technological businesses of the past. We also knew that many business leaders, government policy analysts, and academics were studying similar issues concerning today's firms and nation-states. It quickly became apparent to us, however, that few, if any people held a strong grasp of both the contemporary and the historical perspectives of technological competitiveness. We decided, therefore, to convene a conference that would bring together these two perspectives, as represented, respectively, by business-oriented historians of technology and engineers/engineering managers experienced in global competition.

We restricted the conference to electrotechnology, i.e. electrical, electronic, and computer technologies in keeping with the interests of our center. Because electrotechnology has been in the vanguard of competitiveness for more than a century, it has received considerable historical attention, so there exists an ample body of historical literature upon which to draw. By restricting our attention to technological competitiveness within this one set of technologies, we were also able to provide greater coherence in our discussions. A generous grant from the Alfred P. Sloan Foundation enhanced the conference by enabling us to bring together a distinguished group of engineers and historians from around the world.

The conference was held October 10–13, 1991 at Rutgers University in New Brunswick, New Jersey. Thirty-two invited speakers and commentators attended from nine countries of North America, Europe, and Asia. (See the program listing in the appendix.) The historians presented case studies, upon which the engineers commented. Seventeen of the case studies and commentaries are published in this volume. To leave more room for outside viewpoints, the center's staff did not make presentations at the conference. In this publication, however, we have included a study by a member of our staff, Eric Schatzberg. All articles have been refereed, and many authors also revised their papers on the basis of the conference discussion, thus this publication represents something more than conference proceedings.

Perhaps the optimal organization for this book would have been according to factors of competitiveness, such as manufacturing methods, venture capital, or government regulation. The state of historical scholarship did not permit this organization, however. Most historical study of technological businesses has been written by historians of technology rather than by historians of business. Historians of technology have traditionally concentrated not on factors of competitiveness, but instead on the technology itself. (The one exception is a literature on the historical development of research and development laboratories.) The book is therefore organized primarily according to type of technology. There is some justification for this practice: competitiveness factors tend to be more similar within a single technology than across technologies; for example, two computer firms are more likely to confront similar issues of competitiveness than, say, a computer firm and a power supplier.

These papers constitute a first attempt to study competitiveness from an historical perspective. No standard literature or standard set of issues existed to inform the writing of these papers. Most of the authors started with their current historical research projects and tried to extract from them information about competitiveness. It would be unrealistic to expect these cases to give direct lessons ready for application to our present situation, or even to give definitive explications of the various aspects of competitiveness. (We have nonetheless drawn out a few lessons from history in the conclusion.) The desired kind of synthesis is possible only after a substantial number of focused analytical case studies have been analyzed and studied for patterns. We should instead accept these papers as pioneering efforts that give some initial insights (together with an indication of how history can inform us about contemporary issues).

This volume does not undertake a thorough needs-and-opportunities assessment for further historical research on technological competitiveness, for it seems premature to do so. As a first step in this direction, however, each section begins with an introduction that not only describes the papers, but also suggests some of the ways in which these papers might be expanded to gain a wider understanding of competitiveness.[3] The introductions should not be construed as identifying all aspects of technological competitiveness, indicating the full range of opportunities for further research, or citing the entire existing literature on this subject. They have the more modest, but hopefully useful goal of giving the reader a place to start in the study of this important subject.

Before turning to the papers, we shall make a few general remarks about the characteristics of technological competitiveness. To a large degree, the factors are the same ones that business historians address: research, development, manufacturing, capital and finance, education, marketing, patents and litigation, strategic planning, organizational structure, etc. The balance and character of these factors, however, differs significantly when one considers technologically competing businesses as compared with typical commercial enterprises or other nontechnology-based businesses.[4] For example, technological businesses are set apart by the rapid obsolescence of products and services, which leads to unrelenting pressure for research and development. To remain competitive, these businesses often have to employ advanced, expensive packaging and manufacturing technologies. Their work requires a generally educated workforce and highly educated management, which often leads to close associations with universities and affects business practices ranging from the siting of plants to the conditions of employment of professional employees. Extensive venture capital is required to turn innovative, often untested technologies into successful businesses, which leads to unusual relationships between company management and its financial backers. Technological businesses often compete in international markets, where national regulation of import-export of advanced technologies may significantly alter market conditions. Many technological products are dependent for their existence on the military for their markets or even for the basic research and development on which they are based, leading to some special conditions for competitiveness. These and many other factors differentiate technological businesses from non-technological ones.

Opportunities for historical research on technological competitiveness abound. We hope that this book will encourage further study that informs both historical scholarship and our understanding of the contemporary world.

Notes

1. For example, in the *Wealth of Nations* Adam Smith stated that "The essence of the Industrial Revolution is the substitution of competition for the mediaeval regulations

which had previously controlled the production and distribution of wealth." Following Smith, Arnold Toynbee wrote in the early 1880s that "Competition, heralded by Adam Smith, and taken for granted by Ricardo and Mill, is still the dominant idea of our time . . ." (See Arnold Toynbee, Lectures on the Industrial Revolution in England, *Toynbee's Industrial Revolution*. New York: Augustus M. Kelley, 1969.)

2. Some of the most perceptive writing on contemporary business and policy issues of technology, such as the work of Michael Porter at the Harvard Business School, is cited in the notes to the chapters by Kenneth Lipartito and James Gover.

3. We will occasionally cite some of the most important literature in the introduction. However, the interested reader might wish to consult Bernard S. Finn, *The History of Electrical Technology: An Annotated Bibliography*, New York: Garland, 1991.

4. Rather than try to characterize all the factors of technological business, I direct the reader's attention to Bruce Bruemmer and Sheldon Hochheiser, *The High-Technology Company: A Historical Research and Archival Guide* (Minneapolis, Charles Babbage Institute, 1989). This book gives an introductory description of industrial activity and documentation in high-technology companies and cites some of the existing literature on high technology and its history.

Acknowledgments

The competitiveness conference on which this volume is based was held in October 1991 to inaugurate the move of the Center for the History of Electrical Engineering from the New York headquarters of the Institute of Electrical and Electronics Engineers, Inc. (IEEE) to the New Brunswick campus of Rutgers University. I am grateful to both the IEEE and Rutgers for their support of electrical engineering history in general and this project in particular.

We are pleased to have received generous support from the Alfred P. Sloan Foundation. Its support enabled us to bring together a distinguished international group of engineers and historians.

James Brittain, Bernard Carlson, Paul Ceruzzi, Bernard Finn, James Gover, Thomas Hughes, and Stuart Leslie were kind enough to help identify speakers for the conference. Michael Ann Ellis and Joseph N. Tatarewicz assisted greatly with conference planning and organization. Andrew Goldstein and Frederik Nebeker helped in many ways with the preparation of this book, including reading and commenting on drafts of the introductions and historical articles.

I would also like to thank all the engineers and historians who were session chairs, speakers, or commentators. A full listing of their names can be found in the appendix.

We are grateful to the organizations listed below, who provide generous support to the Center for the History of Electrical Engineering in the form of operating, endowment, and project funding.

Founding Partners: IEEE
Rutgers University
Alfred P. Sloan Foundation
IEEE Foundation-General Fund
IBM Corp.

Senior Partners: IEEE Foundation-Life Member Fund
National Science Foundation

Associates: Electro-Mechanical Company
Environmental Research Institute of Michigan
KBR Foundation
Sematech
Microwave Theory and Techniques Society

We are also grateful to the hundreds of individuals who have contributed to our Friends Fund.

Introduction

Competitiveness became a fashionable topic during the Reagan presidency. His administration argued that if businesses could improve themselves in various ways and the federal government could lower taxes and remove onerous regulation, American industry could fend off challenges from other countries, especially Japan, and the nation would resecure its position as world leader in business and technology. Competitiveness was supposed to be achieved, however, without benefit of a national technology policy targeting specific industries for special treatment—for this smacked of social planning. Nevertheless, certain technologies, such as high-definition television, supercomputers, and semiconductors, did come in for special attention from the federal government.

Many of these technologies involved electronics or computing. This was to be expected because they are among the most "high-tech." They are ones that could not be developed without a skilled professional labor force, substantial research and development, and advanced manufacturing technologies. And it was in these areas that the United States assumed it had its greatest advantages because of its existing educational and research infrastructure and its general availability of venture capital. Electrotechnology, an embracing term which we use to include electrical, electronic, and computer technologies, was thus at the core of national competitiveness as it came to be understood in the 1980s.

Competitiveness was of course an issue before the 1980s. By the end of the nineteenth century, companies at the cutting edge of technology were competing fiercely in international markets for business viability. The contested technologies were different then: fine chemicals, metallurgy, business machines, automobiles, electrical power and appliances, and telecommunications. But research and development, venture capital, university-industry relations, patents, and many other factors were at that time similar to what they are today in technologically competitive industries. Thus there is a century of experience with technological competitiveness among firms and among nations on which we can draw to understand today's situation.

It was clear to us at the IEEE-Rutgers Center for the History of Electrical Engineering that there was potential for increased understanding if contemporary competitiveness issues were investigated in a historical context. We knew that a number of historians of technology had investigated both successful and unsuccessful technological businesses from the past, and there was every reason to believe that what they had learned about research and development, manufacturing, management, marketing, government regulation, trade policies, and many other issues could give insight into our contemporary situation. We also knew that many business leaders, government policy analysts, and academics had carefully considered these same issues for today's firms and nation-states, and that their insight into contemporary affairs might teach historians about the intricate interplay of many factors of competitiveness and help historians focus their research.

We could hardly identify anybody who had both contemporary and historical perspectives on technological competitiveness. We decided, therefore, to hold a conference bringing together the two perspectives, as represented by business-oriented historians of technology and seasoned engineers and engineering managers with first-hand experience competing in the global marketplace. Electrotechnology has been continuously highly competitive for more than a century. Our decision to restrict the conference to this technology provided a cohesive subject for analysis, but one still large and important enough that there were ample numbers of historians who have studied it and engineers who have experienced it. A generous grant from the Alfred P. Sloan Foundation enabled us to invite to our conference some of the very best engineers and historians from around the world. We believe that the results on electrotechnology can be widely applied to other technical areas where competition occurs.

The conference was held October 10–13, 1991 at and near the Rutgers University campus in New Brunswick, New Jersey. There were thirty-two invited speakers and commentators representing nine countries of North America, Europe, and Asia. (The appendix lists the program.) Historians presented case studies and engineers commented on them. Eighteen of the case studies and commentaries are published in this volume. In order to leave more room for outside viewpoints, we decided not to have staff of the IEEE-Rutgers history center give papers at the conference—even though some of the staff were working on competitiveness issues. But we have included in the published record one paper by staff member Eric Schatzberg. All articles were refereed, and the authors had an opportunity to revise their papers on the basis of the commentaries and the extensive discussion given at the conference. Thus we regard the papers as finished publications rather than conference proceedings.

Because of the different mix of papers, this volume is organized differently from the conference. Both are organized primarily according to type of technology. There are several intellectual and practical reasons for this decision. Competitiveness factors tend to be similar across a given technology; two computer firms are more likely to confront similar issues of competitiveness than a computer firm and a power supplier, for example. Because historians have not traditionally focused their studies on competitiveness (but rather more generally on the history of technology in a business setting), there is not yet much historical literature on specific aspects of technological competitiveness, such as the role of manufacturing technology or of the marketing of technical products and services; the one exception is the well-established body of historical literature on research laboratories. Historians are more likely to identify with other historians who study similar technologies than with those who study similar business aspects. (If we had selected historians who were foremost business historians, this may not have been true; but few business historians have grappled with businesses that are technologically driven. It is instead the historians of technology who have addressed issues that can be categorized as concerning competitiveness.) On a more practical level, in several places we had to retain the conference structure because commentaries referred to specific papers.

The first section of the book addresses issues that are at the heart of contemporary concerns about technological competitiveness. Two papers by academics who are not historians describe aspects of the Japanese system and its tremendous advances in electronics since World War II. The first paper is by Lennart Stenberg, a social scientist at the University of Lund who tracks science and technology policy for the Swedish government. Through a case study of molecular beam epitaxy, Stenberg demonstrates the strengths and weaknesses of the research infrastructure in Japan. He emphasizes the strong role played by the business sector and the relatively weak role of the academic sector in shaping the research infrastructure. He considers such factors as the rigidity and segmentation in the research system based on business and government practices and the importance of knowledge-transfer networks from university professors to their students working in industry. The second paper, by electrical engineering professor Yuzo Takahashi of the Tokyo University of Agriculture and Technology, considers the electronic components industry in Japan since the Second World War. Takahashi argues that, while attention has often focused on Japanese computers and supercomputers, perhaps more can be learned from an examination of the electronic components industry, which enabled Japanese manufacturers to provide quality and reliability in more complicated electronic systems and devices. Takahashi identifies the importance of consumer markets to Japanese electronics firms, and the importance of mechanized manufacturing for improvements in quality, reliability, and cost. He draws comparisons with the American system.

The second section continues this comparison through an examination of the U.S. electronics industry. The first paper, by James Gover, an engineer with Sandia National Laboratory and vice-chairman of the IEEE Competitiveness Council, provides an overview of the U.S. electronics industry and draws many comparisons between the United States and Japan. Of particular interest in his paper are the differences between these two countries in the mix of "upstream" electronics (packaging, software, semiconductor manufacturing, materials, and manufacturing equipment) and "downstream" electronics (communications, manufacturing, data processing, consumer electronics, and defense electronics). In the next paper, Stuart Leslie, a historian of technology at Johns Hopkins University, examines Silicon Valley, the great American success story that serves as a model for virtually every

high-technology regional economic development plan promulgated during the past
two decades. Leslie considers federal spending, industry-university relationships,
corporate strategies, and technological innovation. He concludes that Silicon Valley
was shaped largely by Cold War defense policy and may actually offer little guidance
for peace-time technological development policy. The paper by Robert Smith, a historian at the Smithsonian's National Air and Space Museum and a close student of
NASA, completes the section. Smith investigates the phenomenon of Big Science,
such as space telescopes and superconducting supercolliders, and its relationship to
national competitiveness. He argues that American policy-makers have placed great
hope and huge amounts of money in Big Science projects, but they have not had the
intended payoffs in industrial innovation or productivity which were promised as
part of the justification for such large expenditures.

The third section turns to the closely allied topic of electronic computers. The
first paper is by Martin Campbell-Kelly, a historian and computer scientist at the
University of Warwick who has written the definitive study of ICL, the main British
computer firm. Drawing from that study, Campbell-Kelly investigates British government policies for promoting and defending its indigenous computer industry
from foreign, especially American, competition between 1949 and 1985. He describes British military sponsorship of three computer centers which spun off their
prototype computer systems to the commercial sector, efforts on limited budgets to
guarantee markets for British computer firms, government intervention to rationalize the computer industry through forced consolidation, and actions to protect the
remaining firm (ICL) from market forces so that it would undertake research and
implement long-term strategies. Boelie Elzen, a historian of technology at the University of Nijmegen in the Netherlands, and Donald Mackenzie, a sociologist of science and technology at the University of Edinburgh, prepared the final paper of this
section. It explores the interplay between technical development and social relations
in the American supercomputer industry. It argues against a commonly held view
that U.S. science and engineering lost competitive advantage through insufficient
access for U.S. researchers to supercomputer power. It also argues that the social
networks established between the manufacturers of supercomputers and their customers created a mutual dependency that imposed a barrier on new entrants to the
supercomputer industry and affected the design of subsequent generations of supercomputers, including a diminished value given to computing speed.

The fourth section studies telecommunications. In the first paper, Kenneth
Lipartito, a business historian at the Harvard Business School, notes that the term
"technological competitiveness" is usually applied to companies that compete with
one another for customers, profits, markets, or survival—or more recently to nations
or other geopolitical units that compete to insure wealth for the geopolitical region
through the success of its technological businesses. It is hard to understand, he ac-
knowledges, how this concept applies to industries that are monopolistic or under
public ownership. He extends the notion of competitiveness to include the rivalry
between different groups for the determination of how a technology should be employed, to what aims, and for what benefits. This broader concept of competitiveness
he explores through a case study of telecommunications in the American South between 1880 and 1920. Pascal Griset, a historian of technology at the *Centre national*

de la recherche scientifique in Paris, considers the case of competitiveness in the French telephone industry since 1945. At the beginning of this period, the French telephone system was antiquated and French telephone companies were subsidiaries of foreign companies. A modern national telephone system was needed to improve the competitiveness of France's commerce and industry. But the French government wanted an indigenous telephone industry to develop the new telephone system, in order to reduce France's dependence on foreign technology and to improve its national balance of payments. The tension between these two aims is the main subject of the paper. Amos Joel, a retired Bell Laboratories engineer, the recipient of the 1992 IEEE Medal of Honor, and a leading authority on telephone switching, provides commentary on the Lipartito and Griset papers. His comments are mainly directed at changes in the 1980s caused by competition in interexchange toll service and additional competition that is likely to occur in the near future through the introduction of new technologies.

The fifth section considers electrical technology for the home. In the first paper, Arne Kaijser, a historian of technology in the Royal Institute of Technology in Stockholm, analyzes the fierce competition between three technologies (gas, oil, and electricity) for the domestic lighting and cooking markets in Sweden between 1880 and 1960. Two aspects of his analysis have wider applicability. The first is his analysis of technical performance, pricing, propaganda, and political pressure as factors in technological competitiveness. The second is his analysis of grid-based energy systems (e.g., electricity, gas, and district heating), in which the energy is delivered to users through a special physical network constructed for this purpose, versus nongrid-based systems (e.g., oil, coal, and biomass fuels), where the energy is delivered to users through existing transport systems. Susan Douglas, a historian of technology at Hampshire College, wrote the other paper in this section. Douglas uses the examples of ham radio operators, hi-fi enthusiasts, and FM programmers to exemplify oppositional uses of commercially developed technologies by subcultures of American tinkerers, and explains how they helped to identify underdeveloped or completely neglected technologies. The paper analyzes the competition among three subcultures (youth, engineering tinkerer, and corporate) in determining the future shape of technology.

The sixth section considers electrical technology for industry and commerce. The first paper is by Eric Schatzberg, a historian of technology employed by the IEEE-Rutgers Center. He investigates the competition between three technologies (steam, cable, and electricity) in the last quarter of the nineteenth century to mechanize urban transit in the United States. He argues that electrical technology, which in the end won the competition, was initially not known to be clearly superior on cost. He gives two nontechnical reasons that provided support for electricity in the initial period when costs were uncertain: American enthusiasm for the progressive new electrical technology, and structure of the electrical equipment industry. The second paper is by Anne Millbrooke, a historian of technology at United Technologies, the maker of Otis elevators. She traces the competition within Otis primarily between hydraulic and steam elevator systems in the late nineteenth and twentieth centuries. She also explains how business, technical, and regulatory factors reversed the use of these two technologies in elevators over time. The third paper is by Ulrich

Wengenroth, a historian of technology at the Technical University of Munich. Wengenroth examines the competition of electric motors to replace steam engines in the period 1890 to 1925. Steam engines were better suited for many manufacturing applications, were less expensive per unit of energy produced, and were more frequently customized to specific applications. Electric motors were able to win the competition, however, because they had greater versatility and allowed industrial designers to take a new approach to production technology. W. Bernard Carlson, a historian of technology at the University of Virginia, prepared the section's final paper. By considering events in the American electrical industry that led to the formation of General Electric in 1892, Carlson illuminates the interplay between competition and consolidation in technological industries. While competition can lead to better products and lower prices, it can also engender inefficiency, duplicative effort, and waste. Carlson's study provides insight into the influence of individuals and their personalities on the level of competition and the timing of mergers, the importance of competition between firms for sources of capital, and the value of having the right organizational structure beyond having good products, low prices, and low production costs.

The final section considers electric power. Not unlike telecommunications, power companies tended to be monopolistic or publicly held, so there is some question about what competitiveness means in such an industry. Alain Beltran, a historian at the *Institut d'histoire du temps present*, examines the history of *Electricité de France* since 1946. His story tells of three different kinds of competition at play; competition of nuclear technology with coal, oil, and natural gas; competition of French power companies with other firms in the European Economic Community; and competition of France with other nations through industrial strength. Beltran's paper is interesting for its discussion of how economic competition was simulated in a monopolistic environment, his discussion of how tax laws shape the competitive environment, and his brief consideration of the sociological factors that enabled nuclear power to succeed in France. Gabrielle Hecht, a historian of technology at Stanford University, examines in the volume's final paper the relationship between engineering work and politics, economics, and culture in the French nuclear power industry between 1955 and 1969. Hecht traces three stages of competitiveness: first a period characterized by competition between government agencies (for nuclear weapons and nuclear power) over their conflicting agendas, next a period of economic competition to deliver power from the monopolistic nuclear power industry at as low a price as possible and preferably at competitive prices with conventionally produced power, and finally a period of competition of the French industry against non-French firms and non-French technologies to construct power plants around the world.

The greatest value of the conference was to bring engineers and historians together to discuss an important contemporary issue from their complementary perspectives. The volume includes many good papers, and all of the contributions address some aspect or another of competitiveness; but it is clear that these papers represent only a first attempt to study competitiveness from an historical perspective. No standard literature and no standard set of issues existed when these contributors were preparing their papers, and most of these papers are spin-offs from other historical research projects—none of which focuses specifically on competitiveness. This is not because we invited the wrong set of people to the conference, but rather because this subject has been largely neglected by historians of technology up to this time.

We will not take up the space required to give a thorough needs-and-opportunities assessment for the historical study of technological competitiveness, for it seems premature to do so. A few remarks can be made, however. To a large degree, the factors are the same ones that business historians address: research, development, manufacturing, capital and finance, education, marketing, patents and litigation, strategic planning, organizational structure, etc. The balance and character of these factors, however, is significantly different in technologically competing businesses from commercial enterprises or other nontechnology-based businesses. For example, technological businesses are set apart by the rapid obsolescence of products and services, which leads to unrelenting pressure for research and development. To remain competitive, these businesses often have to employ advanced, expensive packaging and manufacturing technologies. The work requires a generally educated workforce and highly educated key personnel, which often leads to close associations with universities and affects business aspects ranging from the siting of plants to the conditions of employment and professional employees. Extensive venture capital is required to turn innovative, often untested technologies into businesses, which leads to unusual relationships between company management and its financial backers. Technological businesses often compete in international markets, where national regulation of import-export of advanced technologies and other factors may entirely shape market conditions. Many technological products are dependent for their existence on the military for their markets or even for the basic research and development on which they are based, leading to some special conditions for competitiveness. These and many other factors differentiate technological businesses from nontechnological ones.

Rather than try to characterize all the factors of technological business, I direct the reader's attention to Bruce Bruemmer and Sheldon Hochheiser's, *The High-Technology Company: A Historical Research and Archival Guide* (Minneapolis, Charles Babbage Institute, 1989). This book gives an introductory description of industrial activity and documentation in high-technology companies and cites some of the existing literature on high technology and its history. It gives overviews of basic business functions (planning, basic research, research and development, production, marketing sales, product support and enhancement) and support services (financial, legal, and others). An introduction to many of the important factors of technological competitiveness can be abstracted from this account.

There are many good opportunities for research on technological competitiveness. We hope that this book encourages further study that informs both historical scholarship and our contemporary world.

PART I

Japanese Electronics

This section addresses issues currently at the heart of American and European concerns about technological competitiveness. Two papers by academics who were not trained as historians describe aspects of technological development in Japan, focusing in particular on Japan's tremendous advances in electronics since World War II.

The first paper is by Lennart Stenberg, a social scientist at the University of Lund who tracks science and technology policy for the Swedish government. Through a case study of molecular beam epitaxy, Stenberg probes the strengths and weaknesses of the Japanese research infrastructure. He emphasizes the strong role of the business sector and the surprisingly weak role of the academic sector in shaping it. He points to rigidity and segmentation in the research system created by business and government practices and notes the importance of knowledge-transfer networks extending from university professors to their students working in industry.

The author of the second paper is Yuzo Takahashi, an electrical engineering professor at the Tokyo University of Agriculture and Technology and perhaps the most active scholar of the history of electrical engineering in Japan. Takahashi's topic is the electronic components industry in Japan since World War II. He argues that the attention lavished on Japanese computers and supercomputers could perhaps more profitably be directed toward an examination of the electronic components industry, which he claims enabled Japanese manufacturers to provide their legendary quality and reliability in complex electronic systems and devices. Through comparisons with the American system, Takahashi identifies the critical importance of consumer markets to Japanese electronics firms, as well as the importance of mechanized manufacturing for improvements in quality, reliability, and cost.

These two papers provide a springboard for further consideration of Japan's technological system and of technological competitiveness among nations. There has been very little historical scholarship written in the English language about business and technology in modern Japan, so the field is wide open for research.[1]

Further studies would help us to determine how typical is the case of molecular beam epitaxy investigated by Stenberg. Are there variations in the Japanese research structure as one moves from components, to devices, to systems, to software? Which industries have strong research infrastructures, and why? Do Japanese natural resources or particular needs of the Japanese people explain why certain research areas are strong and others are weak? Have these areas developed *laissez faire* or did the government and business consortia take a firm hand in choosing specific technologies and building research infrastructures for them?

American journalists and politicians have frequently cited the actions of the Japanese government, especially MITI, in promulgating a national technology policy. Many Americans have assumed that Japan has been successful because of strong government intervention, and calls for an American national technology policy are based in part on the perceived Japanese success. We have precious little historical evidence, however, that MITI was omniscient in selecting the right technological areas, companies, or technological approaches, or that this system has worked as efficiently as the American press makes it out to be. We know, for example, that the Fifth Generation Computer Project orchestrated by MITI has fallen far short of its lofty goals. Less attention has been given in public discussion to the strong business alliances that exist among companies in Japan and to the important sway the leaders of these business alliances have over government policy. The CEO of Mitsubishi, for example, undoubtedly has more influence on technology and business legislation in Japan than has, say, the CEO of General Electric on the legislation of the U.S. government. It may be that guidance from the business community is behind whatever success the Japanese government has achieved with its technology policy. We cannot tell without looking closely at some historical examples.

Stenberg has noted some surprising weaknesses, such as rigidity and segmentation, in the Japanese research system. It may be fruitful to undertake a comparative historical analysis of a technological area being pursued both in Japan and in the West to see how these and many other factors played out in comparison. Was the venue of research the academic, industrial, or government sector? Did institutions within and across these sectors share information and ideas? Did the locus of research in the academic (or business) sector affect the balance of attention given to research on new technologies, improvement of existing technologies, advances in manufacturing methods or quality control, marketing factors, etc.? One might, for example, extend Margaret Graham's masterful study of RCA and the videodisc[2] by taking a closer look, in comparison, at RCA's Japanese competitors in the videodisc business. Portable radios, television, semiconductors, and computers would also be good subjects for comparative study.

Takahashi's thesis that components are a critical factor in Japan's success with complicated systems and devices deserves serious historical examination. We know that the relationships between Japanese manufacturers and their component suppliers are radically different from these relationships in the United States and Europe. The Japanese manufacturers form a much closer alliance with their suppliers, to a point where they can jointly discuss design, technical specifications, and manufacturing methods and agree to modify the operations of both manufacturer and supplier; whereas in the United States and Europe, manufacturers and suppliers work more independently and rely more on specifications dictated by the manufacturer through formal contractual agreements. The automobile industry would seem to present an ideal case for this comparative analysis, but so would television manufacturing.

Takahashi's article raises a number of other questions that merit historical investigation: How have the Japanese achieved quality and reliability in their products and what difference has it actually made in sales? Are these Japanese methods transferable to the West, or do they depend on the particular Japanese infrastructure?

One test would be to investigate how successful Japanese companies have been at manufacturing in plants outside their own country, such as they have done with automobiles. The Japanese have concentrated on consumer markets, whereas America has spent much of its R&D money on military systems. P. R. Morris has shown how this has led the Japanese and American semiconductor manufacturers to adopt different market strategies and product lines.[3] It would be useful to examine the effect of catering to military or commercial markets in other technical areas such as microwaves, lasers, or mobile communications. It might similarly be interesting to compare MITI and DARPA with regard to their impact on technological advances and business developments in their respective countries, e.g., in the areas of materials or high-definition television.

Another question might be raised about differences between, and effects of, American and Japanese practices on career paths. American technological businesses tend to draw their corporate leaders from the business ranks, while Japanese businesses are more likely to promote from the engineering ranks. Similarly, large American corporations seem historically to have relied more heavily on marketing, advertising, and accounting procedures and less heavily on technical innovation and incessant product improvement to advance their businesses than did their Japanese counterparts. U.S. companies seem to expend relatively more of their resources on basic research, while their Japanese counterparts devote themselves more to directed research. Japanese companies appear to have traditionally paid more attention to manufacturing technologies and the use of robotics and other forms of automation than their U.S. counterparts. These impressions need to be verified and their significance investigated through a set of historical case studies, both for industries as a whole and for specific companies.

Notes

1. Takahashi cites most of the important literature on Japanese technology. Also see Marie Anchordoguy, *Computers, Inc.: Japan's Challenge to IBM*. Cambridge, MA: Harvard University Press, 1989.

2. Margaret Graham, *RCA and the Videodisc: The Business of Research* (New York: Cambridge University Press, 1986).

3. *A History of the World Semiconductor Industry* London: Peter Peregrinus, 1990.

Technological Strength Needs and Feeds a New Research Infrastructure in Japan

Lennart Stenberg

Competition between Research Systems

There are great differences among countries in the efforts of their institutions in the areas of science and technology. In almost all countries we find institutions of higher education doing academic research and firms engaged in product development. Beyond that, however, it becomes very difficult to generalize.

There are some critical differences in how the funding of research and development (R&D) is divided between government and private sources, how government funds are distributed according to social objectives, where governments prefer to spend their R&D funds for a certain objective, and the extent to which firms carry out research of a more fundamental or general kind than that associated with the development of a specific product.

What concerns us here is that part of the total R&D system that functions as a research infrastructure for the development of industrial technology. Organizations belonging to that infrastructure may include research groups at universities, government laboratories, other types of freestanding nonacademic research establishments, and corporate research laboratories.[1] The mix of organizations and their relative weight will vary between countries and fields.

What is the significance of these differences between countries in the institutional makeup of their research infrastructures? Do the differences affect the economic payoff of public investments in industrially related research? Do they affect the ability of a country to benefit from new developments internationally in science and technology? In short, do some countries have research systems that are more competitive than others, in the sense that they provide better support for the development of their domestic industries?

5

There are signs that these questions are becoming increasingly important. There is, for example, a growing concern in the United States, the United Kingdom, and Sweden that publicly funded research, although proving itself on the international scientific scene, does not create the domestic economic benefits sought, but is instead primarily supporting innovation elsewhere.

One could certainly argue that such disappointments are caused by false expectations about the nature of the linkage between scientific research and industrial innovation, and that it disregards the intrinsically international nature of science and technology. Nevertheless, there may still be some structural factors at work that put some countries in a better position than others to translate progress in scientific research to success in the development of industrial technology.

Furthermore, the importance of taking advantage of research at the scientific frontier may be growing. It is often suggested that the link between science and innovation has become more direct. With today's sophistication in technology, specific pieces of research can frequently have direct relevance for the solution of technical problems, while in the past the economic benefits of scientific research were for the most part much more diffuse and achieved mainly indirectly through the general knowledge instilled in graduates from universities or engineering schools. There may consequently be more to win today from an effective linkage between science and innovation, and more to lose from the absence of such a linkage.

Japanese industry is generally considered to be very effective in translating research into commercial success. A popular image has been that in Japan the government and the business sector have contributed little in terms of developing new basic technologies, and instead have concentrated on combining and refining technologies developed elsewhere. Consistent with this view there has been a great deal of criticism, from both inside and outside Japan, of Japanese universities for not maintaining a sufficiently high standard in their research and for not contributing to the international advancement of knowledge to an extent commensurate with the economic stature of Japan. Since universities are highly dependent on governments for the financing of their research, such criticism is ultimately aimed at the Japanese government.

There is little reason to doubt that Japan and its industry have benefitted enormously from the importation or copying of technology developed in the West, and especially in the United States. In most areas, however, Japanese industry has now progressed far beyond the "catch-up" phase and is aggressively pursuing basic technology development of its own. A powerful research infrastructure is being established as an integral part of this development, but it has a different structure than in many other countries, especially in the very strong participation of the corporate sector in long-term research.

The purpose of this paper is to examine the dynamics of the growth of the industrially oriented research infrastructure in Japan with a focus on the changing role of universities in this context.

The leading role of the business sector in the expansion and structural transformation of the Japanese research landscape is first illustrated by presenting some data on the growth of basic research in Japanese industry. This presentation is contrasted with similar data for other types of research institutions. The difficulties Japanese universities encounter in responding to and matching developments in the business sector are discussed on a general level. In order to better understand the institutional dynamics of the Japanese research system, some results from a case study of the field of molecular beam epitaxy (MBE) are reported. The chapter concludes with a discussion of what will determine the future evolution of the institutional structure of the Japanese research system.

The Business Sector Takes a Leading Role in Basic (Technology) Research

During most of the postwar period, Japanese industry has a remarkable record of expansion, which has been interrupted on only a few occasions and then only for short periods. This expansion has gone hand in hand with a continuous upgrading of the technical level of products and production facilities, a process in which investment in research and development has become increasingly important.

The first substantial growth in the establishment of research laboratories in Japanese industry occurred in the early 1960s. In response to liberalization of imports, Japanese firms felt under strong pressure to upgrade their technology to an internationally competitive level. One of the primary functions of the new laboratories was facilitating the importation and adaption of foreign technology.

Government programs for support of industrial R&D were set in place to further support raising the technical level in Japanese industry. Gradually, a system of government-sponsored collaborative research was developed.[2]

The 1970s saw a slowing in R&D growth (Fig. 1). For the Japanese electronics industry this was, however, a crucial period during which it established itself as a serious contender on the international scene. There is evidence that government R&D programs played an important role in this development.[8]

A second boom in laboratory building in Japanese industry occurred during the 1980s. It differed from the one in the 1960s in that now the emphasis was on research for the development of "new, original, basic technologies" and required an environment and management style that would support creative research.

Already around 1980 there emerged a consensus in Japan that the country had to put greater emphasis on basic (technology) research.[9] This idea has since remained the leading theme of Japanese science and technology policy. In the Japanese policy debate three major motives for strengthening basic research in Japan have been put forward. First, it has been suggested that Japan, after having gained from generous access to foreign technology, ought now to do its part and return something to the rest of the world. A second argument has been that now that Japan has caught up with the international frontier in technology, what can be found of new technology abroad is not enough to support the further growth of the Japanese economy. Finally, some have warned that in the future the United States and Europe will be more restrictive in their sharing of technology with Japan. All these arguments have been used to support the thesis that Japan has to take a leading role in the development of new basic technologies.

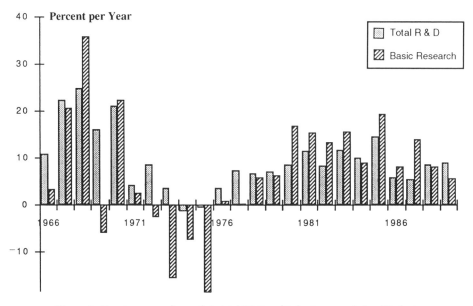

Figure 1. Year-to-year real growth in total R&D and in basic research for all industry in Japan 1965–1989. (*Source:* Statistics Bureau [3–7, 10])

The concern with development of new basic technologies is often translated into a call for a stronger emphasis on basic research. This call is interpreted in very different ways, depending on the vantage point. Some would have it mean that the government now should spend more money on the basic sciences and especially on fields of little interest to industry. Others see it rather as a change in the emphasis of industrially oriented R&D.

As it turns out, the largest share of growth in basic research has occurred in the business sector, which can be seen both in the data on basic research in the available R&D statistics and in the mushrooming of new corporate research laboratories.

In Japan, as in most other countries, it has been very difficult for the public sector to contribute to the strengthening of basic research, due to the generally austere fiscal climate during the 1980s. Within these limitations, however, there has been an increasing emphasis on basic research both in the research carried out in many of the governmental research institutes and in the research supported by the government in the private sector. There have also been significant changes in the organization of research and in the procedures for its funding, which are intended to improve, in particular, the conditions for basic research.

The overall result has nonetheless been that the business sector in Japan has acquired not only a more prominent role in applied R&D than in probably any other country but is also increasingly moving to center stage in a number of fields of rather basic research, simply by outgrowing the research capacity of universities and public research institutes. Figure 2 illustrates a decade's change in the relative weight of basic research in different types of research institutions in Japan.

Basic research in industry is more focused than that in universities, which means that for fields of current or potential industrial interest universities today in all

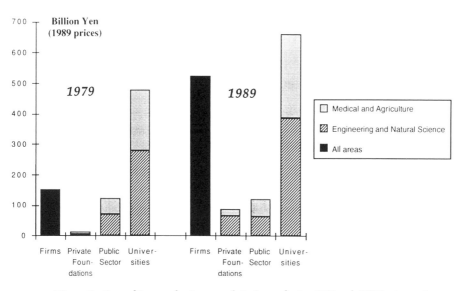

Figure 2. Expenditure on basic research in Japan during 1979 and 1989 by type of research organization. (*Source:* Statistics Bureau [10, 11])

likelihood spend less than industry. It is quite remarkable for this structural reshaping of the Japanese research landscape to have occurred over only a decade.

Basic research is carried out in very different contexts in different types of institutions. In those firms that carry out such research at all, basic research is a small part of their total R&D (for all of Japanese manufacturing industry the fraction was 6.4 percent in 1989) and could be regarded as overhead for more applied R&D. In universities, on the other hand, basic research is a major occupation, representing more than half of all R&D even in engineering departments, and is intimately tied to the function of graduate education. Research institutes vary widely in character, and therefore also in the relative weight of their basic research.

Firms invest in basic research for a number of reasons,[12] though for many Japanese firms diversification has been an important motive. For the electronics industry, however, diversification has not been a major factor because of the huge potential for growth. Thus, the issue in this industry has been to realize this potential by aggressively investing in new generations of products, some of which, one could argue, have been genuinely new.

Growth in the sales base has thus been the main factor behind the electronics industry's growth in R&D (Figs. 3–5). There has also been a 50 percent increase in R&D intensity. Basic research has followed the development of overall R&D very closely. On the other hand, sales growth has been slower in most other industries, which has led firms to allocate a growing portion of their R&D to basic research for the purpose of building a base for future diversification. As a result, basic research has expanded as fast or even faster in these other industries than in the electronics industry.

According to official statistics, the electrical equipment industry increased its basic research expenditure by a factor of around 3 in real terms from 1979 to 1989,

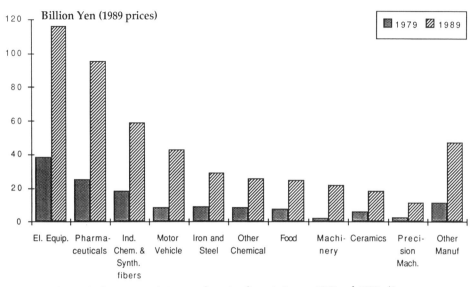

Figure 3. Basic research in manufacturing firms in Japan, 1979 and 1989. (*Source:* Statistics Bureau [10, 11])

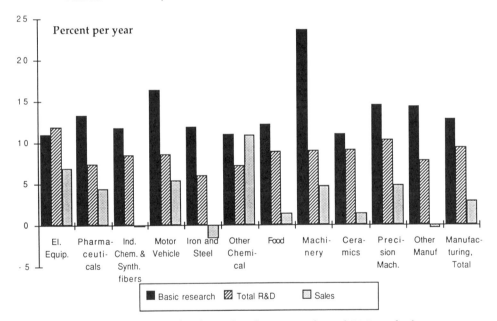

Figure 4. Average annual real growth in basic research, total R&D, and sales in manufacturing firms in Japan 1979–1989. (*Source:* Statistics Bureau [10, 11])

reaching a total amount of ¥116 billion in the latter year. This increase represented a little over 4 percent of overall R&D in that industry. The number of researchers engaged in basic research grew from some 2500 to 5000 during the same period, reflecting the greater resources available to each researcher at the end of the period.[13]

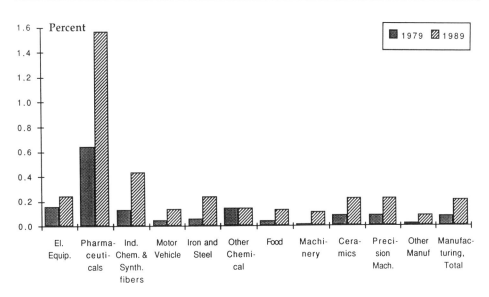

Figure 5. Basic research as a share of sales by industrial sector in Japan, 1979 and 1989. (*Source:* Statistics Bureau [10, 11])

The increase in R&D intensity is comparable to that in the electronics industry in the United States, but the sales growth has been faster in Japan, and there appears to have been a stronger commitment in Japan to expand basic research at the same rate as overall R&D.[14]

Economic Constraints on the Development of Research at Japanese Universities

A rather negative view is often expressed of Japanese universities by Japanese as well as foreign observers, although instances of positive testimony appear to be on the rise. One problem in evaluating the criticism often leveled at the research function of Japanese universities in particular is that, in order to provide arguments for budget requests, representatives of universities as well as public authorities have a stake in painting a picture of Japanese universities as being in a state of disrepair and hopelessly lacking in research funds. It needs to be remembered, however, that universities everywhere complain about a shortage of funds.

The best available source for comparing the amount of resources invested in university research in different countries is a study by Irvine, Martin, and Isard,[15] which looks at government funding of "academic and related research." Although governments dominate university research funding, for our purposes it is a weakness of this study that it does not also include information on private funding. This lack is especially significant for both the United States and Japan inasmuch as these two countries have a large number of private universities, which to an increasing extent rely on private funds in various forms and which in the United States are among the leading universities in terms of research. This weakness and the general problem of accurately distinguishing between resources being spent on education and research notwithstanding, the study provides a valuable basis for some international comparisons.

On a per capita basis, the Japanese university system as a whole does indeed seem to be undersized compared to those of the other countries studied (Fig. 6). There are, however, very large differences between fields. For example, Japan is up to par in engineering sciences, but allocates far fewer resources to other fields, such as the physical sciences, than most other countries.[16] In terms of research infrastructure for industrial technology the Japanese universities must, therefore, be said to be doing better than their reputation in terms of the resources that they command (see Fig. 7).[17]

Another indicator of the research capacity of Japanese universities is the training of research students. This is a role that traditionally has been thought to distinguish universities from other research environments and is therefore of special interest. Comparative data for the United States, Sweden, and Japan for engineering and physics and chemistry, respectively, clearly illustrate the difficulty Japanese universities are having in attracting doctoral students (Fig. 8), while statistics for the last few years show rapid growth in the number of students from other Asian countries enrolling in doctoral degree programs in Japanese engineering schools.

A special feature of the Japanese system is the so-called thesis doctorates, which are usually granted to researchers who have joined a company or research institute immediately after receiving a master's degree and subsequently done research work of a quality deemed sufficient for the award of a doctoral degree.

The research effort in the higher education sector in Japan is concentrated in fewer universities than in the United States. The distribution of granted doctoral degrees between universities can serve as an approximate indicator of the degree of concentration of university research in Japan (Figs. 9 and 10).

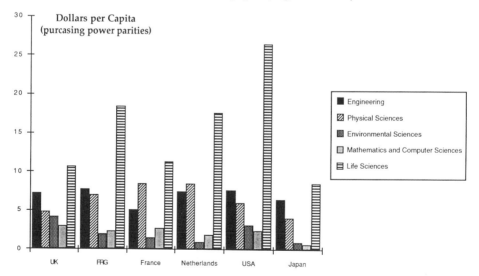

Figure 6. Government funding of research at universities in 1987. (*Source:* Irvine et al.[15])

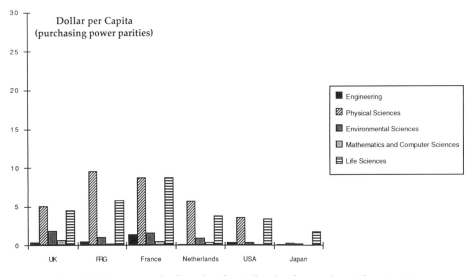

Figure 7. Government funding of academically related research outside universities in 1987. (*Source:* Irvine et al.[15])

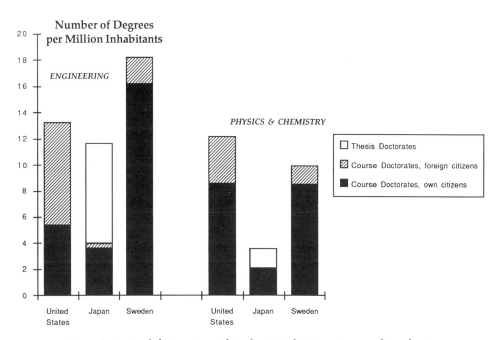

Figure 8. Doctoral degrees granted in the United States, Japan, and Sweden in 1985. (*Sources:* NSF,[18] Monbusho,[19] and Statistics Sweden[20])

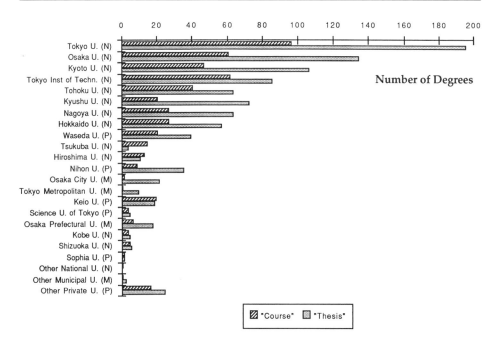

Figure 9. Doctoral degrees in engineering granted in Japan in 1986 by university. (*Sources:* Monbusho[19, 21])

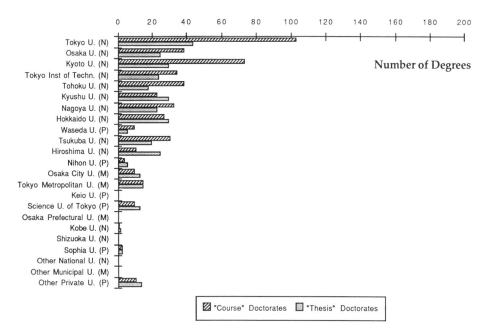

Figure 10. Doctoral degrees in physical sciences granted in Japan in 1986 by university. (*Sources:* Monbusho[19, 21])

The Case of Molecular Beam Epitaxy

In order to arrive at a better understanding of what factors are shaping the evolution of the Japanese research system and how these factors may be changing in their relative importance, a field at the intersection of science and technology was selected for detailed study. Molecular beam epitaxy (MBE), a technique for the highly controlled growth of crystals, represents a suitable case, being a fairly well-delineated field, attracting the attention of researchers in academic circles as well as in industry, and having a research community of manageable size for intensive study.

The approach taken was to study the evolution of the community of MBE researchers in Japan. Using bibliometric data, Japanese researchers active in the MBE field and the organizations for which they worked were identified for different time periods. Similar data were also gathered for other countries so that the institutional structure of the research communities in Japan could be compared with those in other countries. Information on the qualitative aspects of the development of MBE research in the leading Japanese organizations was obtained through interviews.

Research on MBE was started in the United States in the late 1960s by Arthur and Cho at Bell Labs. After technological breakthroughs around 1979 and 1980, which made possible the fabrication of high-quality lasers as well as the realization of the high electron mobility transistor (HEMT), the field grew very rapidly during the 1980s. The appearance of commercial MBE machines around 1980 and the subsequent improvement of their reliability and ease of operation have been crucial factors for the growth of the field. MBE technology, although used today for commercial production of HEMTs, lasers, and certain other devices by some firms, is still mainly used as a "research technology" for explorative studies of new artificially engineered materials and related new types of devices. Its main use is for the growth of semiconductor materials, but there are also examples of applications to high T_c superconducting materials and organic materials. MBE is one of several alternative techniques for epitaxial growth.

Comparing Research Systems Using Bibliometric Data

Figure 11 summarizes MBE publication data for Japanese organizations retrieved on-line from the Inspec database hosted by ESA-QUEST. Shown are the number of researchers who appear at least once, during the indicated three-year periods, as authors of publications considered to belong to the MBE field.[22] Each author was counted only once in each three-year period during which he or she published. The time periods refer to the time when the publications were indexed in the Inspec database.

Assuming that it takes, on average, one year for Inspec to index a publication and one to two years from the actual performance of a certain piece of research until it appears in a publication, Figure 11 can be roughly translated to represent the number of researchers involved in the performance of research during a certain time period by shifting each column one step to the left. Thus interpreted, Figure 11

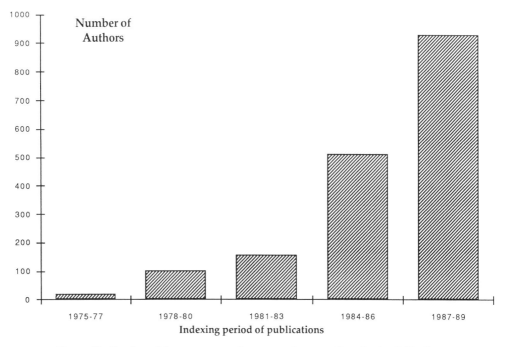

Figure 11. Number of Japanese researchers appearing as authors in the field of MBE. (*Source:* Raw data retrieved from on-line search in Inspec)

suggests that MBE research started in Japan on a very small scale during the period 1972–1974, and then expanded around the mid-1970s. This expansion seems to have run out of steam in the late 1970s, only to be followed by a new period of rapid growth in the early 1980s. Growth has continued after that, but at a slower rate. This development conforms well with the information obtained through interviews.

To give some impression of the variety of publication activity among different authors, Figure 12 distributes authors during each three-year period according to how many times they were published. During the 1980s around half the authors published only once in a three-year period, while around 30 percent published three or more papers during the same time. Combining Figures 11 and 12, it seems a reasonable estimate that in the mid-1980s the Japanese MBE research community comprised about 300 active researchers.

We will soon turn to a comparison of the institutional structure of the Japanese MBE research community with that in other countries. For this comparison we will have to rely on the number of publications instead of the number of authors as a measure of the size of the research effort.[23] This is certainly less than ideal. A comparison of the two types of data for Japanese organizations suggest, however, that there is a fair amount of correlation between the number of authors and the number of publications for the organizations most active in publishing. During the period 1987 to 1989, a weighted average for the ratio between number of authors and number of publications was around 1.5 in Japan. Of the top dozen organizations, ranked by number of authors, all except two had ratios in the range 1.0 to 1.75. The two ex-

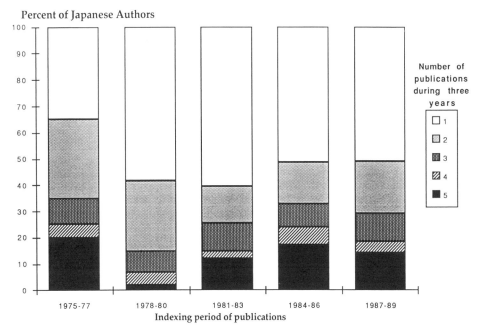

Figure 12. Distribution of Japanese authors in the field of MBE by number of papers published. (*Source:* Raw data retrieved from on-line search in Inspec)

ceptions had ratios of 2.3 and 3.1, respectively. Among organizations with fewer authors the variation was larger (Fig. 13). As long as interpretation of the data is restricted to identifying broad patterns of institutional structure and does not focus too much on individual organizations, data showing the number of publications should be acceptable as a rough proxy for the more direct measure using the number of researchers.

Of a total of some 6500 publications indexed in the Inspec database during the period 1969 to 1989, 48 and 19 percent came from organizations in the United States and Japan, respectively (Fig. 14). Overall, there has been a very rapid growth in MBE publications in all parts of the world. In absolute numbers most of that growth has occurred since the early 1980s. The growth was slower in Japan than elsewhere during the indexing period 1981 to 1983, and more rapid during the next three-year period. As explained earlier, publications indexed 1981–1983 correspond approximately to research done between 1978 and 1980.

In order to broadly compare the evolution of the MBE research communities in Japan, the United States, and the three largest western European countries in terms of R&D, each research organization was categorized into one of the following six groups:

- Telecommunications research organizations
- Three largest industrial firms in terms of total number of MBE publications (excluding those covered in the previous group)
- Other firms

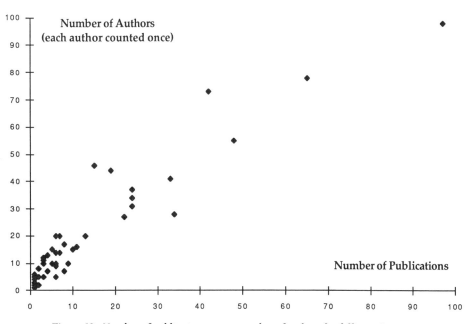

Figure 13. Number of publications versus number of authors for different Japanese organizations in the MBE field for the indexing period 1987–1989. (*Source:* Raw data retrieved from on-line search in Inspec)

- Government research laboratories/institutes and cooperative research organizations
- Three largest universities in terms of total number of MBE publications
- Other universities (and other higher education institutions)

Due to fundamental differences in the organization of research in the different countries, the six categories are not in all respects strictly comparable. As an example, in the United States, Japan, and the United Kingdom telecommunications research organizations have the legal status of companies, while the Bundespost in West Germany and the Centre National pour des Etudes de Telecommunication (CNET) in France are government research organizations. Also, AT&T differs somewhat from the telecommunications research organizations in the other countries in that it has a production arm.

Figures 15 and 16 show how the number of publications developed for each group over three-year periods in the United States and Japan, respectively. It should be noted that the scale for the United States is twice that for Japan, roughly corresponding to the ratio between the two countries' populations.

In the United States, Bell Labs and IBM pioneered the field, while in Japan the same role was played by the Electrotechnical Laboratory (ETL) and Tokyo Institute of Technology (TIT). However, NTT, the Japanese counterpart to Bell Labs, entered the field early on and expanded its activities rapidly to achieve the position of the largest Japanese organization in terms of MBE-related papers published. This is a position similar to that of Bell Labs in the United States. Fujitsu, the largest

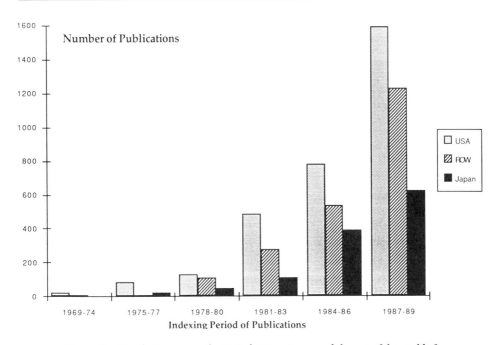

Figure 14. Distribution among the United States, Japan, and the rest of the world of publications in the field of MBE. (*Source:* Raw data retrieved from on-line search in Inspec)

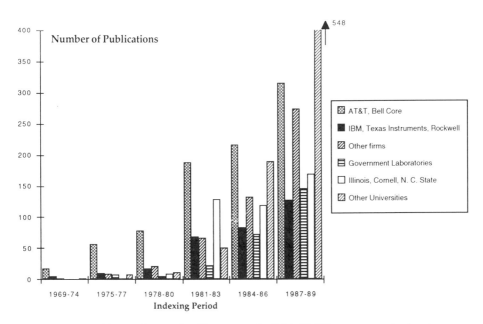

Figure 15. Distribution of publications in the field of MBE among organizations in the United States. (*Source:* Raw data retrieved from on-line search in Inspec)

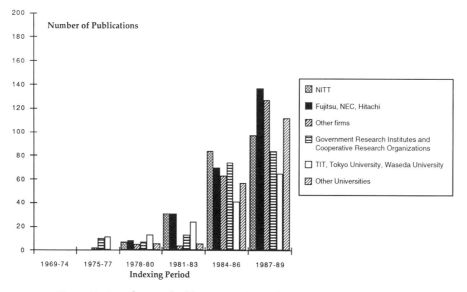

Figure 16. Distribution of publications in the field of MBE among orgfanizations in Japan. (*Source:* Raw data retrieved from on-line search in Inspec)

mainframe producer in Japan, also showed evidence of a strong capability at a fairly early stage, with the number of its papers published approaching that of IBM in the United States.

Judging from the publication data, universities initially played a more marginal role in the United States than in Japan, but developed a stronger presence from the early 1980s, first through a small core group and later including a very large number of universities. At the end of the period the relative role of the three leading universities in the field was similar in Japan and in the United States, while other universities represented a much stronger force in the United States than in Japan. In absolute terms the largest American universities published at more than twice the rate of the largest Japanese universities.

Research outside universities and the corporate sector has in Japan been mainly carried out by ETL and the Joint Optoelectronics Laboratory (OJL), the latter operating for only a six-year period. (Upon the dissolution of OJL, a new research cooperative, of different legal status and with different sources of funding, the Optoelectronics Technology Research Laboratory [OTL], was created.) It appears that ETL and the OJL played a relatively larger role in Japan than did the national laboratories in the United States. In absolute terms, however, the biggest government laboratories in the United States had about the same number of papers published as ETL and OJL during the period 1987 to 1989. No cooperative research organizations have been identified in the United States.

The telecommunications companies (Bell Labs, Bellcore, and NTT) aside, the top industrial companies in Japan almost reach the publication levels of their counterparts in the United States, but the number of companies in the United States is almost twice that of Japan. Predictably a large number of the American companies have their main business outside civilian electronics. Of the two leading manufacturers of MBE equipment in the United States, Varian and Perkin Elmer, Varian in particular had more papers published than their Japanese counterparts, Ulvac and Anelva.

Overall the research communities of the two countries exhibit rather similar development, with a strong concentration of only a few organizations during the 1970s, and then rapid growth in the 1980s in the number of organizations actively pursuing MBE research. On a per capita basis the Japanese business sector has a stronger publication record than its American counterpart, while the university sector is weaker. The leading Japanese industrial firms compare well with American firms even in absolute terms, while the same cannot be said for the universities.

If we compare what has just been described with developments in France, the United Kingdom, and West Germany (Figs. 17–19), the differences between Japan and the United States are in many respects smaller than are each of these countries' differences from the three West European countries.

The university sector in Japan, which among all the sectors exhibited the greatest difference from its counterpart in the United States, compares favorably with that in the European countries, falling somewhere between the United Kingdom and West Germany in terms of per capita publication counts and placing far ahead of France. In absolute numbers of papers published, the three largest Japanese universities had about 50 percent more than their counterparts in the United Kingdom and West Germany. One may therefore conclude that in the field of MBE, American universities are exceptionally strong and Japanese universities at least comparable to universities in the large European countries.

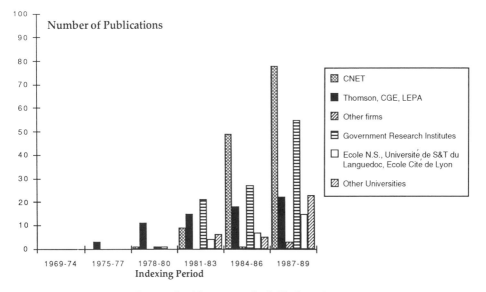

Figure 17. Distribution of publications in the field of MBE among organizations in France. (*Source:* Raw data retrieved from on-line search in Inspec)

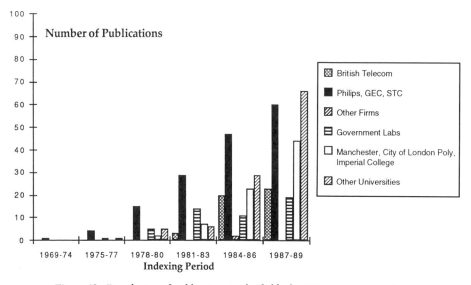

Figure 18. Distribution of publications in the field of MBE among organizations in the United Kingdom. (*Source:* Raw data retrieved from on-line search in Inspec)

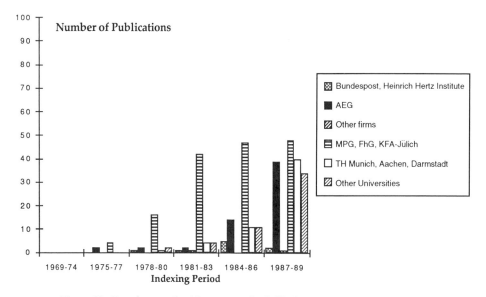

Figure 19. Distribution of publications in the field of MBE among organizations in West Germany. (*Source:* Raw data retrieved from on-line search in Inspec)

The weak showing of French universities is partly balanced by a large activity in government research institutes, most of which belong to the system of CNRS institutes, the major exception being LETI in Grenoble. West Germany also has a large institute sector. Until the latter half of the 1980s this sector was almost totally dominated by the Institute for Solid State Physics in Stuttgart, belonging to the Max

Planck Gesellschaft (MPG). This institute actually dominated the whole MBE research community in West Germany well into the 1980s. More recently the activity has broadened to other Max Planck institutes, some Fraunhofer Gesellschaft (FhG) institutes, and KFA in Jülich. In the United Kingdom only one government laboratory, the Royal Signals and Radar Establishment (RSRE), has published significantly in the MBE field.

Telecommunications research organizations stand out in France through the activities at CNET, which operates several laboratories in different locations. Its publication activity is about four times that of British Telecom, and on a per capita basis is comparable to that of AT&T and Bellcore combined. The Bundespost and the Heinrich Hertz Institute generate very few MBE publications, making West Germany an exception among the countries studied because it does not have a large MBE presence tied to telecommunications research.

The Western European countries most clearly set themselves apart from Japan and the United States by their rather narrow industrial participation in MBE. In West Germany MBE research in industry is concentrated to AEG, which has a strong research program in elemental semiconductor MBE. In France a smaller publication activity is divided rather evenly between Thomson and CGE. In the United Kingdom Philips started MBE research early and has more recently been joined by the GEC, both today publishing quite actively in the MBE field. Riber in France and Vacuum Generator in the United Kingdom are both world-class manufacturers of MBE equipment, but publish only very sporadically in the scientific and technical literature.

Both Japan and the United States thus seem to have better balanced MBE research systems than the large Western European countries in the sense that industrial companies are better represented in Japan and the United States.

If the large European countries have only one or two companies actively pursuing MBE research, smaller countries might be expected to lack significant corporate research altogether. When we compare the situation in the Netherlands, Switzerland, and Sweden (Fig. 20), we find that this expectation is only partly fulfilled, since all three countries have two or three research groups actively publishing in the MBE field. In the Netherlands and in Switzerland there is about equal contribution to the MBE literature from a single company on the one hand, and a number of publicly funded research organizations on the other, while in the Swedish case all the published papers come from technical universities. It is noteworthy that the technical universities in both Switzerland and Sweden reach a publication level only a little below the leading Japanese universities and are well in line with the leading universities in the larger European countries.

Toward a More Integrated Japanese Research System[24]

A striking feature of the evolution of the MBE field is that the early work was done primarily in industry, while the academic world only hesitatingly entered the field and then, with the exception of a small number of university research groups showing a more pioneering spirit, only after technological breakthroughs had been achieved in 1979.

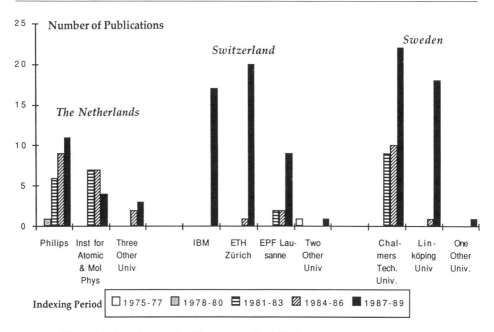

Figure 20. Distribution of publications in the field of MBE among organizations in the Netherlands, Switzerland, and Sweden. (*Source:* Raw data retrieved from on-line search in Inspec)

Also in Japan a handful of firms—Mitsubishi, Matsushita, Hitachi, Fujitsu, and NTT—became involved in MBE research fairly early, although ETL and a group under Professor Takahashi at the Tokyo Institute of Technology were the first to start such research. Around 1978, however, a widespread pessimism had developed in the Japanese MBE research community. The firms had grown increasingly impatient with the lack of substantial progress in making MBE a practical technology, and Mitsubishi and Matsushita were actually soon to discontinue their efforts. The same might also have happened at Fujitsu and Hitachi if the prospects of MBE technology had not suddenly become brighter. As a semipublic organization, NTT was in a special position and it had other main targets for its MBE research, in particular long-wave-length lasers for optical communication, so it is not surprising that it held out longer than the other firms.

Fujitsu played an important role in creating a brighter outlook for MBE through its invention of the HEMT, which was announced in 1980. Fujitsu was one of several organizations in the world working on the development of a new device based on the concept of modulation doping introduced by Dingle at Bell Labs in 1978. Through very effective collaboration between Dr. Mimura, an accomplished device physicist, and Dr. Hiyamizu, who led an MBE group that had accumulated several years of valuable experience in MBE growth of GaAs/GaAlAs heterostructures, Fujitsu was able to beat its competitors and secure a basic patent for the HEMT.

As a result of the HEMT patent, Fujitsu committed itself more strongly than the other Japanese electronics firms, excepting maybe NTT, to MBE technology. In addition to bringing the production of discrete HEMTs to commercial production,

Fujitsu has invested considerable resources in R&D on HEMT ICs, and has also done considerable R&D on optoelectronic ICs (OEICs). In these efforts the company has received strong support from MITI as a participant in three of the latter's R&D programs, all started around 1980.[26]

During the 1970s, MITI encouraged MBE research in Japanese firms, mainly through financial support for the acquisition of MBE equipment. Through the almost simultaneous launching of three large R&D programs, which all had the development of MBE technology as an important component, MITI's involvement in this technology took on a totally different dimension. That the programs started about the time of the crucial breakthroughs in the technology is certainly an example of fortuitous timing.

Through the Superlattices Devices project, which was part of a larger research program[27] that was more exploratory in nature than previous research programs, MITI supported MBE research in three firms—Fujitsu, Hitachi, and Sumitomo Electric—in addition to providing a boost for MBE research at the ETL. The Supercomputer Project included support for MBE research at Fujitsu and Oki. The long-range horizon of both these projects, ten years for the former and eight for the latter, stimulated the participating firms to take a long-term view in the planning of their research, and thereby helped create very favorable working conditions for the researchers.

In the case of the OEIC project, the MBE work was done in the Optoelectronics Joint Research Laboratory (OJRL), which began its operation in 1981. Interest in MBE grew among the firms while the research program for the OJRL was being planned. While most industrial firms other than Fujitsu were still hesitant to invest their own funds heavily in MBE, they found it increasingly attractive to get a window on this technology through participation in joint research sponsored by the government. Soon the OJRL developed into a very well-equipped and productive environment for MBE research, with close links to a large number of firms built into the very structure of the organization.[28]

Together the OJRL and the ETL represented a very strong research infrastructure for the development of MBE research in the individual firms, and research managers at ETL played a decisive role in conceiving and launching the OEIC project and the OJRL. In terms of MBE the OJRL represented a more focused research effort than ETL, which pursued a wider range of topics. The two organizations' research was therefore complementary.

When the OJRL was discontinued upon completion of the OEIC project, 13 firms—all but two of which had been members of the OJRL—set up a new laboratory, the Optoelectronics Technology Research Laboratory (OTL), to continue joint research in largely the same field as the OJRL, including a major effort in MBE. Although this new joint laboratory gets most of its financing from the Japan Technology Center, which is a semigovernmental organization, it is legally a private enterprise.[29]

In retrospect the OJRL represented a crucial step in the development of cooperative research in Japan. By focusing on fundamental research topics it became possible for the OJRL to become a truly joint laboratory with very open communication between researchers from different firms. It was followed by what literally amounted to a wave of joint research laboratories, the OTL being only one of them. It should be noted that while the OJRL was to prove a very effective vehicle for raising the level of MBE research in Japan, its establishment was, at least initially, not favored by the leading semiconductor firms. They would have preferred that the government instead invest the money in the firms' own internal research efforts.

In the early 1980s only Fujitsu and NTT were strongly committed to invest their own funds in MBE research, and the two firms have since remained at the cutting edge of this field in Japan, more precisely the dominating III-V segment of it. In contrast, early research at Hitachi, Sumitomo Electric, and Oki seem to have relied significantly on moral and economic support from MITI, while other firms that began MBE research did so without any direct financial support from MITI. Mitsubishi Electric and Sanyo were among the earliest to start MBE research in "the second wave," focusing, respectively, primarily on III-V and II-VI optical devices. A large number of firms started MBE research around 1982/1984. NEC and Matsushita developed rather diverse research programs, with optical devices representing a minor part, while Sharp, Rohm, and Omron concentrated almost totally on the development of short-wave-length lasers. Sony and Toshiba, although engaging in MBE research, came to favor MOCVD as their technique of choice for high-quality epitaxial growth. In the latter part of the 1980s an additional 5 to 10 firms, some, for example Toyota, outside the electronics industry, have started MBE research for the most part on a limited scale.

Today's research problems are naturally not the same as those of a decade ago, but the spectrum of MBE R&D activities has broadened considerably both in the sense that a wider range of materials systems is being studied today and that R&D extends from very basic research on quantum effect devices to the development of more effective processes for the growth of materials used in the commercial production of devices. Some of the most challenging problems facing MBE researchers today are related to the fabrication of low-dimensional structures such as the so-called quantum wires and quantum dots, which is a field receiving a lot of attention but still waiting for a breakthrough. In some respects the situation resembles that of MBE growth of heterostructures in the late 1970s.

If anything, the commercial payoff is probably more uncertain now than it was then. That half a dozen or more Japanese electronic firms are nevertheless pursuing extensive research in the field of low-dimensional structures can be viewed as a concrete example of the growing commitment to basic research in Japanese industry. It is also an example of how it has become more costly to do leading-edge research. There are now several alternative epitaxial growth processes, and the number seems to continue to grow. Furthermore, the MBE machines are increasingly becoming part of larger and more complex UHV processing systems combining equipment for epitaxy, lithography, etching, implantation, and analysis. Investment in the necessary equipment has thus grown considerably, especially for those firms that are exploring several epitaxial growth techniques in parallel.

The role of government research support has less relative weight today than a decade ago, but is probably still of some importance, especially for the second-tier firms. On the government side, MITI is also less dominant. MITI's instruments remain pretty much the same as before, but on a smaller scale, and are now complemented by initiatives from other ministries, notably the Science and Technology Agency (STA) and the Ministry for Education, Science and Culture (Monbusho). While the operation of joint laboratories was regarded as a daring experiment in 1980, it is today a rather well-established practice, even if the system of their continued financing is still open to question.

As a consequence of trade disputes between Japan and the United States in the semiconductor field, MITI now has to proceed with some caution when providing research support to Japanese semiconductor firms. There is, of course, some research on low-dimensional structures at ETL. Such research is also carried out at the OTL, and on a smaller scale at the Advanced Telecommunications Research Laboratories (ATR), another joint research laboratory. Although OTL has a total of only 20 researchers, they are all looking at the problem of how to fabricate low-dimensional structures from different angles and have at their disposal a very generously and innovatively equipped laboratory. Its member companies, including those lacking significant in-house research in the field, therefore have a good window on the status of relevant technologies.

There will be some direct support for research in individual firms forthcoming under a new 10-year project on Quantum Functional Devices, which represents a follow-up of *two* earlier projects, the Superlattices Devices and the Three-Dimensional ICs projects. In planning this project MITI has been faced with a very different situation than when it planned the Superlattices Devices project 10 years earlier. The international trade frictions, already referred to, have forced MITI to consider the invitation of foreign firms to participate in the program.[30] On the home front STA and Monbusho have already started similar programs, making it harder for MITI to convince the Ministry of Finance that its program is really needed. Finally, the firms themselves are less and less in need of encouragement from MITI.

STA became an active supporter of basic research in the life and materials sciences during the 1980s. It promoted creative research by trying to increase the mobility between research organizations in Japan and by breaking up their rigid boundaries. Exploratory Research for Advanced Technology (ERATO), in operation since 1981 under the auspices of the Research and Development Corporation of Japan (JRDC), an agency under STA, and the Frontier Research Program (FRP), started in 1986 at the Institute of Physical and Chemical Research (RIKEN), are two schemes set up for this purpose. Significant projects on MBE-related research on low-dimensional structures have been started under both programs.

One ERATO project, the Quantum Wave Project, which aims at fabrication of materials and structures that will permit study of quantum wave effects, is conducted under the leadership of one of the foremost academic authorities of MBE in Japan, Professor Sakaki of Tokyo University. This project was started in 1988, with research performed at three locations: the Research Center for Advanced Science and Technology (RCAST) of Tokyo University, NEC's Tsukuba Research Laboratories, and Matsushita Giken, which is also in the Tokyo area. Two other ERATO projects, this time under the direction of Professor Nishizawa of Tohoku University, have also explored advanced epitaxial growth techniques, although in this case procedures other than MBE were used. The Laboratory for Quantum Materials at RIKEN was one of the first laboratories to be established under the FRP, and it has been deeply involved in growing very high-quality crystals using MBE and other advanced epitaxial growth techniques.

In the previously mentioned STA schemes, the research staffs were recruited from different places for temporary assignment to the various projects and laboratories. For researchers from companies this normally means, as in the case of joint research laboratories like the OJRL and the OTL, that the researchers are on leave from their firms for a period, the length of which may be for the whole project or for a shorter period. At the same time, a similar arrangement has been much more difficult to realize for researchers with permanent employment at national universities or national research institutes. Both the ERATO and FRP projects, however, have succeeded in recruiting newly graduated doctorates and have thereby taken the first steps toward establishing a system of postdoctoral appointments that barely existed previously in Japan but is common in many other countries. Special efforts have also been made to recruit foreign researchers.

STA is charged with the responsibility of coordinating the government's science and technology policy, except for those parts relating to the higher education sector. The initiatives mentioned, as well as others, for example, research support through the Special Coordination Funds for Promoting Science and Technology, do indeed appear to serve the useful function of stimulating the expansion of the Japanese research system and increasing the mobility and communication between its different sectors. Traditional career paths and employment practices are definitely hindering an effective integration of the Japanese research system, but barriers are coming down. The practice of lifelong employment, although it obviously limits permanent changes in employment, may in fact present some advantages for the temporary shifting of research staff, as with the dispatching of researchers from firms to joint research laboratories or to universities. So far, this opportunity has not been widely utilized for public sector employees at universities or institutes, but this probably could be changed without tinkering in any fundamental way with the system of lifelong employment.

When comparing the situation before and immediately after the sudden increase in MBE research in the early 1980s with the recent conditions pertaining to research on low-dimensional structures, it appears that universities have strengthened their relative position. For example, the number of university groups involved in research on low-dimensional structures is quite large, while until the mid-1980s only half a dozen universities were doing significant MBE research in Japan. One reason for this increase in academic interest is simply that the research questions have become recognized as scientifically more challenging, and that their exploration requires a broader spectrum of scientific and technical expertise than the problems posed by the desire to grow heterostructures by MBE. Many alternative technologies—each one often drawing on a combination of several basic technologies—for fabrication of low-dimensional structures are still being explored, but so far there is no obvious winning candidate. Device concepts based on the use of low-dimensional structures are likely to represent a radical departure from existing types of devices, necessitating the development of a whole new set of concepts and theories, sometimes referred to as "mesoscopic electronics."

Theoretical work has thus become more important, as has interdisciplinary research, but universities will tend to be in a particularly strong position for the former. Universities also have a great potential for interdisciplinary work, but the realization of this potential usually requires special organizational efforts. Developments in university research funding and organization in Japan during the last decade have been supportive of interdisciplinary research. First there has been a trend, as in many other countries, to concentrate research facilities in "centers" that serve several departments and sometimes even several universities. This arrangement allows a pooling both of economic resources, which makes it easier to acquire costly equipment such as MBE machines and other semiconductor processing and analysis equipment, and of human resources, which increases the breadth of expertise that can be brought to bear on a particular research problem. Second, special research programs focusing on certain problems, but still basic in nature, have been launched with support from Monbusho and have had as their objective the combining of the resources of many research groups. One program, "Basic Studies on Electron Wave Interference Effects in Mesoscopic Structures," begun in 1990 under the leadership of Professor Namba, director of the Research Center for Extreme Materials at Osaka University, is a particularly interesting case in the context of research on low-dimensional structures.

The high cost of purchasing MBE equipment was probably one of the, if not the, most important reasons that MBE research developed more slowly at universities than it did in firms. Although industrial research laboratories still tend to be much better equipped than those at universities, the improvements in university equipment funding that occurred during the 1980s appear to have made the availability of equipment much less of a decisive bottleneck for university research than before. In addition to the previously mentioned trend toward a greater use of research centers and the like, a higher degree of selectivity has also been introduced in the allocation of research grants. For example, under a grants-in-aid program for "specially promoted distinguished research" introduced in the early 1980s, at least four university researchers obtained grants that were used to acquire new MBE systems.[18]

As already indicated, research on low-dimensional structures may require rather complex configurations of epitaxial growing, processing, and analysis equipment. Even if this raises the cost of equipment very significantly in comparison to a stand-alone MBE machine, and is likely to make it difficult for many academic research groups to participate in the research, several groups have already been able to acquire such equipment.

Research staff, and especially doctoral students, may be a scarcer resource for university research than funding. Generally speaking, Japanese universities have experienced great difficulty in attracting doctoral students. This, of course, limits the research capacity of universities and, some may argue, results in an inadequate supply of research manpower to industry. Traditionally universities have been thought to have a unique role in combining research and advanced research training. A closer look at the MBE case, however, presents us with a much more complex picture of alternative ways of training researchers, among which university doctoral studies represent only one possibility.

During the first phase of MBE research at Japanese firms in the 1970s, each company had to develop its own competence internally, since there was no opportunity to hire outside researchers already experienced in the field. There was some exchange of experience at conferences and through an informal group organized by Dr. Gonda at ETL, and there was some input from the scientific literature.

By the time industry expanded its MBE research in the early 1980s the situation had not changed very much. There was still very little university research in this area, and only a few doctoral graduates had taken up research in industry by then, primarily from Professor Takahashi's group at the Tokyo Institute of Technology. Only during the latter part of the 1980s did universities begin to supply doctoral students experienced in MBE to industry in any significant way, but still in rather small numbers and mainly from three groups.

The number of doctoral degrees granted for research in the field of MBE by 1990 was estimated through a combination of bibliometric searches and interviews for six leading and early established university research groups. A total of almost 30 doctoral degrees were granted for MBE research in these groups, just over half of which went to students in the two groups at the Tokyo Institute of Technology; the rest were divided equally between students at Tokyo University and the remaining three universities taken together. Around 20 of these graduates are continuing MBE research, and half of them—about ten researchers—are working in companies. Other universities may have contributed some additional doctoral degrees, but probably very few.

In a new field, such as MBE, wherein universities are actually lagging behind industry in acquiring experience, it becomes very difficult for universities to respond to industry's need for research manpower. In such a situation a joint research laboratory is a very interesting solution to the need to rapidly expand the training of researchers. The OJRL shows that under a small group of experienced scientists it is possible to develop very successful research in a new field, and, in the process of doing so, to train young researchers in that field. None of the researchers recruited by that laboratory had any previous experience with MBE. In 1990 approximately ten researchers were actively pursuing MBE research after having returned to their companies. Twenty researchers are currently working in the OTL, which can be seen as continuing the educational mission of the OJRL. In many respects the laboratories operating under the ERATO and FRP programs serve a similar function.

The rapid growth in the number of thesis doctorates awarded in engineering indicates that a large and growing portion of advanced research training is occurring "on the job" in corporate research laboratories (Fig. 21). In quantitative terms this has been by far the most important mode of research training for industry in the MBE field. The backgrounds of the pioneers of MBE in Japanese industry vary, but most of them already had research experience from some other field and some had previously obtained a course doctorate. It should also be mentioned that it is fairly common for firms to send their young researchers to a Japanese or foreign university for one or two years as special students. Some examples of this were encountered in the MBE field.

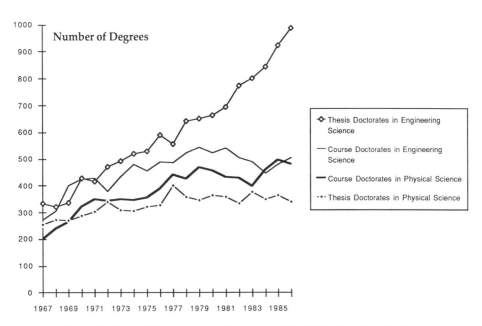

Figure 21. Doctoral degrees granted in Japan in 1967–1986 in the physical sciences and engineering. (*Sources:* Shigen Chosa Sho[32] and Monbusho[19, 21])

There is of course no simple way of comparing the research experience obtained from doctoral studies with that of working in a joint research laboratory or the like, but considering that research at the latter tends to be at the cutting edge, one probably should not assume that research training in the joint laboratories is necessarily inferior to that of doctoral studies. On-the-job research training in a company can be a somewhat more narrow experience, since it takes place in a more homogeneous environment. A period as a special student can counteract this by broadening their horizons. These comments on research training are only suggestions and need further support for any stricter claim to validity. They do show, however, that the whole question of the institutional framework for research training needs to be looked at with fresh eyes.

A recent and very important development is that several of the top MBE researchers in industry and at ETL have been recruited as professors to establish new university research groups. The most striking instance is Osaka University, which during a short period has hired no less than four prominent MBE researchers, one each from Fujitsu, Hitachi/OJRL, NTT, and ETL. Similarly, Tokyo and Hiroshima Universities have hired leading researchers from Hitachi and ETL, respectively. In a very concrete way this illustrates how basic research competence acquired in a new field in industrial laboratories is fed into the university research system, thereby allowing the areas of knowledge opened up by industry to be consolidated and further deepened. This transfer of competence from industry to academe has the effect of both bringing the research level of universities up to par with that of industry and improving the conditions of communication between academic and industrial research. The described development is unique neither to Japan nor to the field of MBE, but appears to apply to much of electronics research in a number of countries.

Conclusions

The Japanese research system has been characterized by a high degree of rigidity and segmentation. Career systems, employment practices, and anxious guarding of jurisdictional boundaries between ministries have contributed to limited communication and infrequent mobility of researchers across institutional boundaries. Other factors relating to the nature of the research have further amplified these tendencies. For one thing, each institution has usually learned more from contacts with foreign groups than from domestic contacts. Industry, busy catching up with Western technology, has had limited interest in the research being done at Japanese universities, especially since the latter have themselves been trying to catch up with the West in their more academic realms.

Of course, integrating factors have not been totally absent. National laboratories, especially those under MITI, such as the ETL, have played an important role as focal points and communication centers for the exploration of new technologies first developed abroad. The various R&D programs launched by MITI also served to conserve scarce resources and foster the exchange of technological knowledge among firms. Initially, the conception and management of these programs depended heavily on the technological expertise of the national laboratories. Through the emergence of a system of joint research laboratories, however, the coordinating and focusing role of the national laboratories has been challenged.

Although direct research cooperation between industry and universities has been very limited and still needs to be improved, two types of relations, which appear more advanced in Japan than elsewhere, have existed to support communication between these two arenas. One is the very close relations between university professors and their students, which are usually maintained long after graduation. The other is the firms' practice of sending young researchers as special students to universities in Japan or abroad.

As the relative level of science and technology in Japan has progressed in comparison to the rest of the world, the benefits to be gained from domestic mobility, communication, and cooperation are growing. The fact that Japanese industry is advancing to a leading position in many fields of technology is fostering a stronger commitment to basic research in all parts of the Japanese research system. Japanese firms have shown themselves willing to allocate a small, but valuable, part of their rapidly growing R&D budgets to long-term explorative research. The aggressive investment in new technology by these firms makes it natural for the government to increasingly focus its scarce resources on long-term research and high-risk noncommercial technological development.

As a result, Japanese research organizations that belong to different sectors are developing increasingly overlapping interests at the basic research end of the R&D spectrum. Even within the existing institutional framework, this stimulates competition as well as communication and cooperation between research groups in different sectors. Competition can be expected to enhance the quality level of the research. Efforts to develop cooperation that come up against institutional obstacles will create pressure for institutional reform and innovation to overcome them. Such institutional changes are clearly already underway, but the process has only recently been started, so most of the changes are still to come.

Great uncertainty still remains about the future institutional shape of the Japanese research infrastructure in fields relevant to the development of industrial technology. Thus, the extent to which ministries other than Monbusho will be able to fund research in universities will be of vital importance and will strongly affect the resources available to universities, the extent to which extrauniversity research organizations will be augmented, and the kind of cooperative arrangements that can be reached between these organizations and universities. As long as MITI, STA, and other ministries are effectively barred from providing significant research funds to universities, they have to channel their funds to other organizations such as individual firms, national laboratories, or other nonuniversity organizations.

For some time there has been a cap on personnel growth in national laboratories and there is little reason to believe that this cap will be lifted. If Monbusho retains its virtual monopoly of government funding of university research, research funds from other ministries will have to be channelled to firms or to nongovernmental, nonuniversity laboratories. If, on the other hand, these other ministries were free to fund university research, the picture could change dramatically. In that case, the future development of joint research of the kind currently supported by, for example, the Japan Key Tech Center could also be affected. Reallocation of such research to universities along models common in the United States would then become possible. The long-term sustenance of joint research laboratories is, in any case, open to question, considering that the system for financing them is still in many ways a temporary one.

The ability of universities to attract doctoral students may be the most crucial factor affecting their future position in the Japanese research system. In this respect, universities face a very difficult situation, since there is currently a shortage of researchers in Japan. As a result, firms are forced to outbid each other in trying to recruit fresh masters degree recipients. At the same time, the economic conditions for doctoral students are poor. It would not take enormous resources to change the latter condition, however, and the leading engineering schools are currently trying to convince industry to donate money for stipends for doctoral students. An alternative or a complementary approach being discussed is for companies to encourage researchers to pursue some of their research at the universities and to make this a condition for the granting of thesis doctoral degrees.

The practice of lifelong employment is a key factor behind the readiness of Japanese firms to commit resources to basic research. A very important result of basic research is the development of competence on the part of the researchers. One consequence of lifelong employment is that Japanese firms can be confident that they will be able to reap the full benefit of the competence thus acquired by their researchers. An added result is that the firms are prepared to provide much of the training for their researchers either in-house, or externally in joint research laboratories, or through their assignment to universities as special students. Were the employment system to change in a way that drastically increased the mobility of researchers among organizations, the basis for Japanese firms' heavy investment in long-term research and competence development might well be undercut, leading to a higher value being placed on doctoral-level research training at universities. Even without such a change, the increasing emphasis on "original and creative research" could in itself increase the demand that researchers develop more varied viewpoints by working in a wider range of environments, universities being prime candidates.

The challenges facing Japanese universities differ in intensity rather than in character from those facing academic research elsewhere in the world. This forces Japanese universities, which in many respects are very traditional, to be particularly innovative in defining their unique contribution to the Japanese research system.

Acknowledgments

The author wishes to express his gratitude to several persons and institutions for their support of the research reported in this paper: Professor Jon Sigurdson of the Research Policy Institute at Lund University, Masahiro Kawasaki, former Director General of the National Institute of Science and Technology Policy (NISTEP) in Tokyo, and Professor Ryo Hirasawa of Tokyo University for their encouragement and generous provision of excellent working environments in their respective organizations during different phases of the research, and to the Swedish Board for Technical Development (STU) for providing the financial support. I would also like to thank all the Japanese researchers and research managers who, in interviews, generously shared their experience of the development of MBE in Japan.

Notes

1. The results of long-term research in firms are often shared rather openly with outside researchers, which justifies identifying corporate research, at least partly, as part of the research infrastructure.

2. Jonah D. Levy and Richard J. Samuels, *Institutions and Innovation: Research Collaboration as Technology Strategy in Japan* (Cambridge, Mass.: Dept. of Political Science, M.I.T., April 1989).

3. Statistics Bureau, Management and Coordination Agency, Japan, *Kagaku Gijutsu Kenkyu Chosa Sogo Hokokusho* (Tokyo, March 1986).

4. Statistics Bureau, Management and Coordination Agency, Japan, *Report on the Survey of Research and Development 1985* (Tokyo, March 1986).

5. Statistics Bureau, Management and Coordination Agency, Japan, *Report on the Survey of Research and Development 1986* (Tokyo, March 1987).

6. Statistics Bureau, Management and Coordination Agency, Japan, *Report on the Survey of Research and Development 1987* (Tokyo, March 1988).

7. Statistics Bureau, Management and Coordination Agency, Japan, *Report on the Survey of Research and Development 1988* (Tokyo, March 1989).

8. Kenneth Flamm, *Targeting the Computer* (Washington, D.C.: The Brookings Institution, 1987).

9. This consensus is well articulated by the Council for Science and Technology.

10. Statistics Bureau, Management and Coordination Agency, Japan, *Report on the Survey of Research and Development 1989* (Tokyo, March 1990).

11. Statistics Bureau, Management and Coordination Agency, Japan, *Report on the Survey of Research and Development 1980* (Tokyo, March 1981).

12. Nathan Rosenberg, "Why do firms do basic research (with their own money)?" in *Research Policy*, Vol. 19, 1990, pp. 165–174.

13. These estimates are based on the assumption that R&D expenditure per employed researcher is the same for different types of R&D in the electrical equipment industry.

14. The numbers just quoted should of course only be considered as rough indicators. The definitional problems surrounding basic research in industry are so large that NSF in recent years only reluctantly has published such data for the United States. It seems, however reasonable to assume, that there has at least been some consistency in the way the concept of basic research has been interpreted by those answering surveys of R&D, whatever objections one might have to those interpretations.

15. John Irvine, Ben R. Martin, and Phoebe A. Isard, *Investing in the Future. An International Comparison of Government Funding of Academic and Related Research* (Aldershot, England: Edward Elgar, 1990).

16. It should be noted that the comparisons are based on currency translations using purchasing power parities rather than market exchange rates. For Japan the dollar amounts would be almost 50 percent higher if exchange rates were used instead.

17. Governments also provide funding of basic research at research institutions other than universities. Irvine et al. have selected certain institutions as qualifying for the category of "academically related research." It appears, however, that this selection has a bias against the engineering sciences. For example, none of MITI's institutes are included, although an institution such as the Electrotechnical laboratory (ETL) most definitely must be regarded as performing a large amount of quite basic research. The issue of government funding of basic technology research outside universities is thus not settled by this study. As far as the physical and life sciences are concerned, the inclusion of academically related research outside universities lends further support to the view that government funded research in these fields is smaller in Japan than elsewhere.

18. National Science Foundation (NSF), *Science and Engineering Doctorates: 1960–88* (Washington, D.C., 1989).

19. Monbusho, "Daigaku Shiryo," No. 101 (Tokyo, 1987).

20. Statistics Sweden, *Utbildningsstatistisk årsbok 1986* (Stockholm, 1986).

21. Monbusho, "Daigaku Shiryo," No. 109 (Tokyo, 1988).

22. Molecular beam epitaxial growth was introduced as a "controlled term" in the INSPEC database in 1979. In order to capture MBE publications prior to 1979 the search was designed to include MBE and alternative expressions as "uncontrolled terms." The publication set thus obtained was for the period 1979–1989 in the case of Japan, and was about 40 percent larger than that retrieved using the controlled term and 50 percent larger than for all countries taken together. An additional reason for choosing a generous search strategy was the fact that the data were used to identify as many organizations with any degree of involvement in MBE research as possible.

23. With the search techniques used it was much less time-consuming to count the number of publications per organization than the number of authors.

24. The case is developed in more detail in Stenberg 25.

25. Lennart Stenberg, "Molecular Beam Epitaxy—A Mesoview of Japanese Research Organization," in *Dynamics of Science Based Innovation*, ed. Hariolf Grupp (Heidelberg: Springer-Verlag, 1992).

26. The three programs are "Optical Measurement and Control System" (often referred to as the OEIC project) (1979–1985), "High Speed Computing System for Scientific and Technological Uses" (often referred to as the Supercomputer Project) (1981–1989) and "The Superlattices Devices Project" (1981–1990).

27. "Research and Development Project on Basic Technologies for Future Industries."

28. Fujitsu, Hitachi, Mitsubishi Electric, NEC, Toshiba, Furukawa Electric, Matsushita, Oki, and Sumitomo Electric all sent research staff to the OJRL, and the five first firms, occupying a leading role in the OEIC project, each furnished the OJRL with a research group leader. An additional six firms were members of the OJRL without sending any researchers.

29. The Japan Key Technology Center, operated under the joint supervision of MITI and the Ministry of Post and Telecommunication, was set up in the mid-1980s with a major portion of its capital made up of dividends from government ownership of NTT shares. It invests up to 70 percent of the capital needed by new joint research laboratories.

30. The decision to open MITI's programs to foreign firms has also lead to a transfer of the management responsibility for these programs from the Agency for Industrial Science and Technology (AIST) to a revamped NEDO, a semiprivate organization. As of early 1992, of a total of eight firms applying for participation in the program, two were non-Japanese.

31. In 1990 a total of at least 35 different research groups at 25 to 30 universities in Japan may have actively pursued MBE research.

32. Shigen Chosa Sho (National Institute of Resources), *Kagaku Gijutsu Shihyo no Kaihatsu ni Kansuru Kiso Chosa* (Basic study regarding the development of science and technology indicators) (Tokyo: Science and Technology Agency [STA], October 1987).

33. The Council for Science and Technology, "Recommendation of the Council for Science and Technology on the 11th Inquiry Titled 'Comprehensive Fundamental Policy for Promotion of Science and Technology from the Long-term View' " (Transl.) (Japan, November 1984).

Progress in the Electronic Components Industry in Japan after World War II

Yuzo Takahashi

Introduction

Electronic equipment is composed of active devices (electron tubes, transistors, integrated circuits), as well as various types of components, that is, passive (resistors, capacitors, coils, transformers), functional (speakers, microphones, magnetic heads, micromotors), and electromechanical (tuners, connectors, printed circuit boards). The function of a specific piece of electronic equipment is determined by the active devices used, while components play supporting roles. This does not imply, however, that their role is unimportant; rather, performance depends heavily upon their quality and reliability. As electronic equipment gets more and more complicated, reliable components become indispensable.[1] The components industry is necessary for a sound electronics industry.

The Japanese electronic components industry has achieved a prominent position in the world market. Tables 1 and 2 show, respectively, the changes in production and export of Japanese electronic equipment, devices, and components after World War II. When the war ended, the Japanese electronic industry was said to be more than 10 years behind its Western counterparts. Twenty years later, American manufacturers were accusing the Japanese components industry of "dumping" in America. Another interpretation would be that Japanese components had become competitive in the U.S. market. Many Japanese components companies established offshore production facilities in the late 1960s, and radio components made in other Asian countries began to compete with Japanese components around that time.[2]

For a full understanding of the electronics industry, we need to examine not only the history of such "stars" as semiconductors and computers, but also that of electronic components. This chapter narrates the development of the electronic

TABLE I   Change in Production in the Japanese Electronics Industry[a]

Year	Overall	Consumer Equipment	Industrial Equipment	Electron Tubes	Semi-conductor	Electronic Components
1948	89.4	29	4	22	—	34
1949	78.6	28	5	23	—	23
1950	97.8	15	11	27	—	44
1951	183	46	38	39	—	59
1952	252	97	47	49	—	57
1953	412	184	84	79	—	64
1954	447	171	145	69	—	62
1955	539	253	119	103	—	65
1956	879	410	183	188	—	99
1957	1,349	625	286	254	39	145
1958	1,836	970	321	279	88	177
1959	3,363	1,922	413	512	190	325
1960	4,327	2,414	567	616	257	473
1961	5,089	2,898	752	502	282	655
1962	5,785	3,165	901	618	339	762
1963	5,998	3,228	1,039	569	339	823
1964	7,264	3,894	1,260	588	500	1,022
1965	7,065	3,446	1,243	494	510	1,372
1966	9,292	4,582	1,651	687	567	1,805
1967	12,288	6,156	2,360	913	738	2,121

[a]Value in hundred million yen. Note one dollar was 360 yen in the period 1949–1971.
Source: Denshikogyo Nijunenshi (Twenty Years of the Electronics Industries), Electronic Industries Association of Japan, 1968, pp. 2–3.

components industry in Japan up to the 1960s, with special reference to the history of improving the quality of the components. Fixed resistors are considered as an example of technological competitiveness. Some elements that influenced the development of the Japanese electronics industry are discussed.[3]

Japanese Electronic Components Industry till the Mid-1950s

Radio and Communications Industries before and during World War II

Radio broadcasting was initiated in Japan by a public corporation (present-day NHK) in 1925. Radio shops and importers then began to appear in cities, and domestic production of almost all kinds of radio components became well established by the middle 1930s. About one-third of the contemporary components manufacturers were founded before the end of World War II (see Fig. 1).

Electronic components manufacturers were and are principally classified into two categories: large companies that produce components as a subsidiary business,[4] and smaller (often small-scale) companies that specialize in components manufacturing. Before the war there were several large companies with a long history of telegraph, telephone, and wireless weapons production, but they manufactured the

TABLE II Change in Export in the Japanese Electronics Industry[a]

Year	Overall	Consumer Equipment	Industrial Equipment	Electron Tubes	Semi-conductor	Electronic Components
1948	0.7					
1949	0.8					
1950	2.9					
1951	4.8					
1952	5.1					
1953	6.5					
1954	4.1					
1955	19	3.4	8.6	3.3	—	3.7
1956	38	18.2	7.9	4.3	—	7.9
1957	70	41.5	7.9	5.3	0.05	15.6
1958	171	129.0	10.7	8.4	1.3	21.9
1959	488	407.1	15.0	15.4	11.9	38.6
1960	712	572.3	25.7	28.2	23.1	62.2
1961	908	684.6	49.2	36.2	33.9	104.2
1962	1,140	833.4	67.8	42.1	38.3	149.2
1963	1,378	1,017.7	86.6	49.2	40.9	171.4
1964	1,768	1,258.9	155.1	56.0	48.8	244.8
1965	2,194	1,514.2	284.6	68.8	67.1	328.1
1966	2,998	2,187.1	164.1	101.3	69.5	475.8
1967	3,622	2,669.2	340.4	71.2	55.8	485.6

[a]Value in hundred million yen. Note one dollar was 360 yen in the period 1949–1971.
Source: Denshikogyo Nijunenshi (Twenty Years of the Electronics Industries), Electronic Industries Association of Japan, 1968, pp. 2–3.

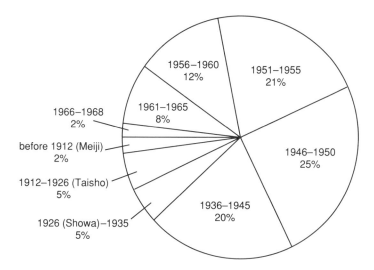

Figure 1. The years Japanese electronic components companies were founded. (*Source: Denshikogyo Sanjunenshi (Thirty Years of the Electronics Industries)*, Electronic Industries Association of Japan, 1979, p. 247)

components for their own use. At that time, components manufacture, like radio manufacture, was labor-intensive, with many kinds produced in small quantities. It was therefore not attractive to large and established companies. Some wholesalers founded subsidiary companies to manufacture radio sets and components, and a number of small manufacturers arose, often as garage factories. One important component market was amateurs, who bought them to construct radio sets. Many small companies were founded and owned by inventor–entrepreneurs who had been amateurs, so it is easy to see why this sector of the radio and components industry was amateurish in nature. It was not until 1960 that these companies began to acquire the characteristics of larger organizations.

The government discovered that radio was a useful tool for communication control. Raw materials were therefore supplied to the radio industry in spite of shortages during the war, though short-wave reception was prohibited for individuals after 1936. During the final stage of the war, all radio and components factories were converted to munitions plants, so when the war ended, the Japanese radio and components industry was virtually nonexistent.

Still, the Japanese made some original contributions to components technology in the area of research and development. In 1931, T. Takei and Y. Kato of the Tokyo Institute of Technology invented ferrite, which was utilized in magnetic cores for high-frequency coils and transformers.[5] The Institute of Physical and Chemical Research (Riken) succeeded in mass-producing carbon film resistors in 1933. The NHK Research Laboratory (founded in 1930) started a department for radio components in 1940 and began basic research on resistors, coils, and capacitors, while stressing the improvement of electrolytic capacitors. During the war, the Japanese army and navy promoted research on radio weapons and military communications in collaboration with national and public laboratories (the Electrotechnical Laboratory, Riken, the NHK Research Laboratory, etc.) and with universities. Methods for impregnating materials for paper capacitors, ceramic dielectrics, and metalized paper were investigated. The Japanese army examined solid carbon resistors used in the equipment in the B-29 bomber. The Electrotechnical Laboratory discovered ferroelectric barium titanate in 1944.[6] The fruits of this and other research provided the basis for the development of components technology after the war.

Postwar Reconstruction of the Japanese Radio and Components Industries

Reconstruction of the Japanese radio industry after the war was rapid because the occupation force needed to restore communications and radio in order to carry out occupation policies. People were eager to have radio sets as a medium of information and entertainment. At the end of 1945, the occupation force gave orders for the production of four million radio sets, thus inaugurating the radio boom. Since the market for industrial products had been drastically reduced, and since all munitions production was prohibited, a lot of companies began radio manufacturing, including both large and prestigious firms (not only electrical companies, but also those in other fields such as petroleum) and small new companies. In 1948, production of radio sets and the number of homes that owned them exceeded the highest prewar numbers for the first time. About eight hundred thousand sets were produced in that year. The radio boom was, at the same time, a components boom, since many radio sets were being constructed by amateurs and by semiprofessionals who bought components at stores. Components manufacturers sold their products mainly to wholesale stores because wholesalers pay cash, whereas set assemblers pay by bank draft, which could take several months to clear. The market for radio components was a seller's market. The components industry was also boosted by problems experienced by the rival finished-radio industry. Tight financial policies and the resulting depression in 1949 were difficult for the radio industry to withstand. Furthermore, the commodity tax was so heavy (around 30 percent for radio sets) that many radio set manufacturers could not survive the depression, which caused their numbers to drop from some 200 to about 20. Since retail sales of electronic components were not taxed as heavily, the boom in amateur-made radios and in components continued. It has been estimated that the number of radio sets constructed by amateurs in 1950 was three times the number made by companies.

The business upturn accompanying the Korean War (1950–1953) and the beginning of commercial broadcasting in 1952 (before then Japan had only public broadcasting, the Nippon Hoso Kyokai/NHK) accelerated the transition from cheap regenerative radio sets to superheterodyne models. In 1953, television broadcasting started, as a result of which numerous amateurs began constructing superheterodyne radio sets and television sets enthusiastically, and television components began selling very well. The quantity of components sold to wholesale stores reached a peak, with a ratio (components sold to wholesale stores/components sold to set makers) of four to one, in 1953/1954. Components manufacturers also began producing television receiver kits for amateur and semiprofessional construction, and their manufacture peaked around 1955.

Production of portable radio sets using battery-supplied miniature tubes began in 1952. These portable radios, which were the immediate predecessor of transistor radios, were produced mainly by small companies, but major appliance makers took them up within a year. Portable radio exports were considerable by 1955.

In the depression period after the Korean War, major companies such as Hitachi and Toshiba began manufacturing home electrical appliances, including radios and television sets. Most of these companies had been manufacturers of receiving tubes, and thus were creditors of the bankrupt radio set makers. When they took over the bankrupt factories, these large companies used their existing networks, which had been developed for the sales and service of motors and pumps, for the distribution and maintenance of radio and television sets. Sales of components to set manufacturers (assemblers) increased rapidly in 1955, and, as the price of manufactured sets decreased, the wave of amateur-made television sets waned. Some components makers began to assemble television and portable radio sets themselves, but failed due to undercapitalization and because they had no sales and maintenance network of their own. Thereafter the market for consumer electronics and home electrical appliances, in particular that for radio and television, has been dominated by the large companies, and components companies have confined themselves almost exclusively to electronic components.[7]

The status of components manufacturers changed substantially. Selling to large assemblers is quite different from selling to wholesalers because assemblers do not pay cash and they continuously press for price reductions and imposed acceptance tests. Many components manufacturers therefore became subcontractors for particular large assemblers.

In the beginning, the quality of Japanese components was poor, with electrolytic capacitors being especially problematic. The NHK Research Laboratory attempted to improve them, and, as a result, the Electrolytic Condenser Investigation Society was founded in 1947 by research workers of the NHK Laboratory together with engineers from the manufacturers.[8] Superheterodyne radios demanded higher-quality components than those of regenerative receivers. A committee for the improvement of radio sets was founded in 1950 by the broadcasting corporations, the Radio Communications Industries Association (now the Electronic Industries Association of Japan), dealers, and electrical power distribution companies, all under the supervision of the occupation force. Contests for amateur-made radio sets took place. As a result, remarkable miniaturization of components for portable radios was achieved.

New components, such as tuners, deflection yoke coils, and flyback transformers, were necessary for television sets. In 1952, the NHK Research Laboratory and components manufacturers started the Television Components Investigation Society for the purpose of promoting amateur construction of television receivers. The association recommended several circuits, which were also used by many professional set makers. Television components were often copied from American designs, and by 1957, more than 57 Japanese companies had become licensees of RCA, Western Electric, EMI, and Philips. RCA's experience was especially helpful for Japanese television components manufacturers.

Quality standards for television components were higher than for radio because the number of components used in a set was several times greater.[9] New conditions also had to be met. For example, temperatures within a vacuum tube television set often exceed 80°C or even 100°C. Furthermore, the components were subjected to very high-frequency, high-voltage, and pulsating conditions. High humidity, which is common in Japan, aggravated the situation and often led to rapid degradation in insulation. To attain uniform quality, television components manufacturers adopted mass-production systems, and incorporated acceptance tests imposed by the assemblers. Even then, some television assemblers purchased resistors made for communications (industrial) use instead of those made for consumer electronics.

Starting in 1953, radio components such as mica capacitors and variable capacitors were exported to Argentina and Brazil. This constituted the first substantial export of Japanese radio components.

Reconstruction of Communications Industry and Components Technology after the War

The occupation force pressed for the reconstruction of the communications network, with technical staff members instructing the Japanese in advanced communications technology and statistical quality control.

Government and public institutions strove to improve the quality of electronic components. A study committee on paper capacitors was founded in the Ministry of Communications in 1947, and the Electrical Communications Laboratory (ECL) (formerly a part of the Electrotechnical Laboratory, the present Laboratories of Nippon Telegraph and Telephone Corporation) began intensive research on resistors and electrolytic capacitors in 1948. Through these activities, and based upon a study carried out before and during World War II, the Paper Condenser Investigation Society was founded in 1948.[10] The Ministry, recognizing that quality and reliable components were indispensable for communications equipment, and receiving the orders from the occupation force, granted the ECL the authority to determine component specifications. The Laboratory carried out sampling tests on items being manufactured and began to set standards for acceptance. The small manufacturers experienced great difficulties in meeting the requirements, so they had to learn new techniques to improve the quality. Since component prices were falling rapidly, they were highly motivated as each manufacturer wanted to secure technological advantage over its competition. The leadership of the Laboratory can therefore be considered effective, with the improvements in carbon variable resistors being one of the Laboratory's most successful contributions. This improved variable resistors technology was very useful for both communications equipment and television receivers.

Standards from America and those imposed by the Japanese government contributed much to the technological improvement: these standards came from the Japanese Industrial Standards (JIS), standards of the Japanese Self-Defense Force (founded in 1950), the American JAN (Joint Army–Navy standards), and MIL (military standards succeeding JAN). The JIS began to be promulgated in 1949, the JIS for electronic components being modeled after JAN and MIL.

After 1950, foreign technology was introduced into Japan by the Foreign Capital Law through license contracts. By 1955, Siemens had introduced techniques for manufacturing polystyrene capacitors and automatic carbon resistors.

The Ministry of International Trade and Industry (MITI) began its Grants-in-Aid Researches for Mining and Industry in 1951. Manufacturers of resistors, capacitors, transformers, and crystal resonators were supported by this system, and more than 40 projects were authorized by 1955.

Growth of Japanese Components Industry and the Foreign Market

The Turning Point

A popular expression in Japan in 1956 was "Mohaya sengo dewa nai" (The reconstruction period is over). Coincidentally, higher economic growth began, with the Japanese electronics and components industry also experiencing a turning point around that time. Tokyo Tsushin Kogyo (now Sony) put transistor radios on sale in 1955. Together with the portable tube-sets that immediately preceded them, they represented the first Japanese electronics goods exported in large quantities to Western markets. The emergence of transistor radios was accompanied by significant miniaturization of components, including those suitable for printed circuit boards.[11] Transistor radios were the driving force of the components industry.

Around 1955 some other important transitions and new trends appeared:

1. The government began to promote the electronics industry. In 1957, "Denshinho" (Electronics Industry Promotion Special Measures Law) was passed. This law stressed the promotion of the manufacture of components such as capacitors and resistors.[12]

2. As mentioned earlier, large companies began to dominate the consumer electronics and home electrical appliances markets.

3. Commercial technical journals specializing in electronics appeared, where previously there had been only professional newsletters and popular magazines for radio fans.[13]

Development and Growth to the 1960s

Along with the boom in home electrical appliances that began in 1953, popular demand for television receivers increased rapidly. Virtually every Japanese housewife dreamed of having a washing machine, a television set, and a refrigerator. Production of television sets in terms of value doubled each year from 1955 to 1958, and the average annual growth rate of consumer electronics from 1955 to 1960 was about 60 percent.

The components industry also grew rapidly, especially after 1957. For example, in 1955 individual factories worth hundreds of millions of yen began to be constructed. The ratio of production in 1959 to production in 1958 was 2.0 for resistors (both in terms of quantity and in terms of value), 2.0 for capacitors (in terms of value), and 2.4 for speakers (in terms of quantity).

Foreign countries, notably the United States, began to buy not only assembled radios and televisions, but also components made in Japan. Significant export of television components started around 1955. In 1958 and 1959, major American radio makers began to purchase large numbers of all kinds of components for transistor radios from Japan. They were soon followed by American components companies. The percentage of production output that went for export was, however, still not high. In 1960 it was a little under 2 percent for fixed carbon film resistors (in terms of quantity), a little over 10 percent for paper capacitors and metalized paper capacitors (in terms of quantity), 3 percent for fixed ceramic capacitors (in terms of quantity), 12 percent for electrolytic capacitors (in terms of quantity), and 20 percent for speakers (in terms of value).

Individual components manufacturers then began to study the foreign market. In 1957, an observation group of components manufacturers (consisting of 12 persons and headed by N. Matsumoto, who was the president of Pioneer Electronic) visited the United States. One of the results of the visit was the first domestic Radio and TV Parts Show in 1958 in Japan. Also in 1958, the Electronic Industries Association of Japan (EIAJ) opened an office in New York in conjunction with the Japan External

Trade Organization (JETRO). The following year, an electronic components show sponsored by the EIAJ was held in New York. Export of Japanese techniques for manufacturing components also began in 1958.[14]

Another milestone was the admission of the previously small-scale components companies to the Tokyo and Osaka stock exchanges in 1961.[15] Admission of these companies, which had previously been ranked second or lower, to the stock market signified a remarkable elevation of power and prestige for the industry. This new status also marked the transition from founder-owned firms to public financing. Around this time there was also a serious labor shortage, so it would not be possible for components companies to remain labor-intensive much longer. Some of them constructed new factories in provinces where it was expected that an ample labor force could still be found. The industry strove to mechanize its manufacturing. Capital expenses for plant mechanization became a significant barrier to entry into the industry. Companies that secured the necessary funds in the stock market continued to grow, becoming increasingly independent of the large assembling companies. The mechanized automatic production systems were often developed by the components companies themselves, and a great many of them introduced statistical quality control and total quality control.[16]

Export of television components was accelerated in 1961. It is notable that Admiral and Zenith, the American protectionist leaders, changed their policy and began to purchase Japanese components in 1963. After 1964, American set makers opened buying offices in Japan, while Japanese components companies had begun establishing local offices in the United States in 1959, where they sold their components under their own brand names. After 1965, many Japanese component makers founded local production facilities in the United States. Export of components to Europe started around 1962, and the number of Japanese components technology and plants exported to Asian and South American countries increased remarkably in 1966.

National and public institutions strove to promote electronic components technology and industry. In addition to the Electrolytic Condenser Research Society and the Condenser Research Society (formerly the Paper Condenser Research Society), the Resistor Research Society was established in 1957. Today these three societies belong to the EIAJ. The introduction of the printed circuit board was motivated by the demand for highly reliable components, since replacement of defective components was difficult. In order to produce some components, however, it was still necessary to learn advanced Western technologies. From 1960 to 1970, Japanese components companies therefore entered into license contracts with American and German companies for ceramic materials, precision resistors, tantalum electrolytic capacitors, metalized paper capacitors, television tuners, transistorized tuners, and connectors.

From about 1963 to about 1965, there was a serious depression in Japan, signaling the end of the era of economic growth. Domestic sales of color television sets did not increase, and the demand for black-and-white sets had almost been satisfied. The consumer electronics and components industries were in depression, too. As a result, a business process of concentration and rationalization occurred in the components industry after 1965.

In Japan, the transistorization of radio sets was almost completed by 1964, and transistorization of television sets increased remarkably after 1965. Color television sales soared in 1966, and notable transistorization of color television sets began around 1969.

On the export scene, the shipment of tape recorders increased remarkably around 1960, and a boom of transceiver exports to the United States occurred about the same time. Exports of black-and-white television sets to the United States grew rapidly in 1962, and of large quantities of color televisions in 1964. In 1966, export of car radios to the United States increased.

In the meantime, production of industrial electronics had been growing, both in absolute terms and in relation to consumer electronics. The ratio reached a peak in 1965, when industrial electronics showed a 45 percent share of the total for production. After that, the growth of consumer electronics accelerated, though the growth rate was higher in consumer electronics. The Japanese components industry grew rapidly under these favorable conditions.

Beginning in 1967, American manufacturers charged the Japanese with "dumping" of fixed resistors and electron tubes. The following year they added transformers, speakers, tuners, capacitors, ferrites, and television sets (both black-and-white and color) to the list.[17] As a consequence, the increase in export of components slowed in the early 1970s. One of the results of the American protectionist action was that Japanese electronic components manufacturers proved that they could still compete successfully because of their high-quality production.

After World War II, the inspection of many industrial products meant for export was made mandatory. The intention of this action was to eliminate the deterioration in quality of export goods resulting from the excessive competition among Japanese manufacturers. When the quality of Japanese electronic components improved substantially, the legal inspection lost its *raison d'etre*. The inspections of interfrequency transformers, variable air capacitors, and composition resistors were therefore abolished in 1969, with nearly all electronic components becoming free from the inspection by 1971.

The Japanese components industry had now become number one in the world. For example, in 1970 Japan was first in the production of capacitors, the United States second: the ratio of production in Japan (in terms of quantity) vs. the United States was 10:1 for aluminum electrolytic capacitors, 4:1 for ceramic capacitors, and 4:1 for film capacitors.

Carbon Composition Resistors and Carbon Film Resistors: An Example of Technological Competitiveness

Carbon film resistors and carbon composition resistors are two major kinds of fixed resistors. Carbon composition resistors were dominant in the United States, while in Japan, carbon film resistors were used extensively. These film resistors were first developed by Germany in the 1920s and introduced into Japan in 1933, after a visit by Dr. T. Akabira of the Riken to Germany. About the time World War II ended, the Japanese "discovered" carbon composition resistors while examining communications equipment on a downed American B-29 bomber, and were surprised by their apparent "marvelous" characteristics. After the war the Japanese made painstaking efforts to produce composition resistors domestically. In the meantime, an increasing demand for precision and transistorization of electronic circuits encouraged the production of carbon film resistors, and in the 1970s, some major Japanese resistor companies stopped manufacturing composition resistors altogether. For the moment it seemed that the effort spent to learn composition resistor technology had been unnecessary, but Japanese resistor technology was improved remarkably by the attempt.

From a technological point of view, carbon composition resistors are suitable for mass-production and they are inexpensive. Their surface is intrinsically insulating, which is advantageous since a metal chassis is used for electronics circuits. Failure of carbon composition resistors is rare, but their resistance value is not precise (the values of produced carbon composition resistors have a wide range) and not stable. One can, of course, sort resistors from a large batch into groups. This is especially so for the E-series where the allowed percent deviations mean that nominal values overlap, and, theoretically speaking, the manufacturer can sell all of the products.[18] In practice, however, a large number of the resistors remain unsold, because the demand is not the same in batch distribution. Furthermore, in carbon composition resistors resistance tends to change, showing large secular variation, and it alters with applied voltage, especially at high temperatures. In the humid Japanese climate, these resistors are especially problematic. In contrast, one can easily produce carbon film resistors of precise resistance, since trimming by helical cutting is possible, and the high-frequency characteristics of carbon film resistors are superior to those of the composition type. The film resistors may suffer from breakdown failures, but these failures are more probable for resistors of high resistance and small size, since the width of their film helix is narrow. The film resistors are comparatively suitable for lower resistance value, though carbon composition resistors as well as carbon film resistors of $0.5 \ \Omega$–$10 \ M\Omega$ can be made without much difficulty. It is also necessary to insulate carbon film resistors with a surface coating of paint.

When the war ended, a large amount of communications components produced for the Japanese army and navy were released into the market. Such resistors were available for the radio boom that occurred just after the war. As a consequence, the price of the resistors remained low, which made the manufacture of resistors unprofitable. The growth of the resistor industry was therefore retarded.

In Japan, the commercial production of carbon composition resistors began around 1951. During the Korean War, a considerable number of Japanese resistors (both carbon film and carbon composition) was exported to the United States. Rumor has it that American companies imported them in haste because of a shortage of resistors for consumer electronics equipment, major production of resistors there having shifted to military applications. Japanese composition resistors were also used for the repair of the U.S. military communication equipment during the Korean War. These sudden demands resulted in the emergence of a number of small-scale, often cottage-level resistor manufacturers in Japan. These factors hampered the rationalization of the resistor industry. Japanese engineers learned a great deal from American technology in the repair service.

At that time, the Japanese believed that carbon composition resistors were superior to the film type. It must be noted, however, that the thinking that "made in America is absolutely far superior to made in Japan" strongly influenced the Japanese engineers. They thought that imminent transition from film resistors to composition resistors was unavoidable. Film resistors were manufactured manually, and were expensive, their mean price being several times higher than that of composition resistors. The Japanese thought that home production of carbon composition resistors was without doubt necessary, and they studied them intensively.[19] Efforts to improve carbon film resistors were made as well. Government and public institutions supported the efforts of industry both for film and composition resistors.[20] A paper by Grisdale et al. published in 1951[21] stimulated basic research on carbon film resistors technology. Siemens's technology of precision carbon film resistors was introduced for communications use around 1954 by Fujitsu. Small-sized carbon film resistors, molded with insulating resin, were developed to compete with carbon composition resistors. Resistors of higher quality were needed for television receivers. Alkaline-free porcelain, introduced in 1953, the year of the beginning of television broadcasting, proved very effective in reducing the breakdown of carbon film resistors. For example, in the direct current field, the breakdown of resistors tended to occur because of the electrolytic corrosion of the carbon layer, which was caused by alkaline ions. New synthetic paints contributed greatly to improving the characteristics of carbon film resistors in high humidity.

The Japanese began to recognize the superior characteristics of carbon film resistors around 1955. In 1960, Riken-type RM carbon film resistors passed the MIL specification test that required operation at 70°C. In the color television boom beginning in 1966, resistors with higher precision were needed, since circuit designers wanted to use resistors with a precision of ±5 percent. Since it was difficult to meet this requirement with carbon composition resistors, makers of color television sets had to use carbon film resistors even though they were more expensive. Resistor manufacturers thus strove to reduce the price of the film resistors by introducing mechanized helical trimming machines. As home production of the automatic machines was successfully achieved, the price of the film resistors sank below that of the composition resistors. Mechanization continued until the first half of the 1970s, by which time the size of carbon film resistors was remarkably reduced. For resistors of 1/4 W, the size of the film resistors became comparable to that of the composition type, while for smaller wattages, they had become smaller than carbon composition resistors. Film resistors of larger wattage remained considerably larger than the composition resistors, because effective surface cooling is low for larger resistors. As the transistorization proceeded, demand shifted to resistors of lower resistance and of smaller wattage, which encouraged the production of carbon film resistors.

During the 1960s the Japanese suspected that carbon film resistors would yet be superseded by carbon composition resistors, so they continued their efforts to mass-produce the composition type. A large quantity of composition resistors was exported to the United States, and the Japanese became the main supplier for the American original equipment manufacturers (OEMs). As a result, production of carbon composition resistors (in terms of quantity) in Japan in 1965 surpassed that of carbon film resistors. Figure 2 illustrates the history of carbon resistor production. In the figure one can see that carbon composition resistors were considerably less expensive than the carbon film type around 1966. During this period, the resistor companies developed in both size and scale.

It then became apparent that carbon film resistors were superior to carbon composition resistors in both quality and in price. The following two episodes highlight the situation.

The JIS (Japanese Industrial Standards) for carbon film resistors had regulations that mandated a resistance allowance of ±20 percent, but these regulations were dropped in the 1961 revision because they had lost their *raison d'etre,* since inexpensive carbon film resistors of ±10 percent were produced without difficulty. In contrast, the standards for carbon composition resistors of ±20 percent tolerance were retained.

In 1961, Tama Electric—a manufacturer that held the highest position in Japanese precision resistor technology—became a licensee of International Resistance Company (IRC), a U.S. manufacturer. Tama introduced various resistor technologies, but carbon composition resistors were not among them. IRC wanted to export the composition resistor technology to Japan, but Tama did not think it necessary. Apparently, the Americans overestimated the future of the composition resistors, while the Japanese had come to realize that it was limited.

Some major Japanese resistor companies stopped manufacturing carbon composition resistors in the 1970s. As a result, the production of carbon composition resistors is now only one small aspect of the production of fixed resistors.

Elements of the Growth of the Japanese Components Industry

Here we explore some of the significant elements that influenced the successful development of the Japanese electronic components industry. First of all, the industry benefited greatly from the advanced Western technology in quality improvement.

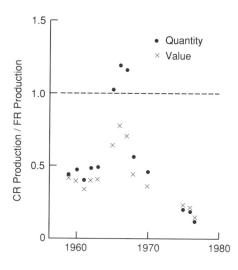

Figure 2. Change in the ratio (production of carbon composition resistors/production of carbon film resistors) in Japan. (*Source:* Based upon the statistics given in *Denshibuhinkogyo Kisochosa Hokoku (Report on the Basic Inquiries of Electronic Components Industry),* 1961 and 1964, Japan Electronics Industry Development Association; and Denshikogyo Nenkan (Yearbook of Electronics Industries), for 1969, 1971–72, and 1979, compiled under the supervision of the Ministry of International Trade and Industry, Dempa Publications, Tokyo)

Japan had been dependent on European and American industrial techniques since the Meiji Restoration in 1868, and people had fallen into the habit of worshiping Western civilization. After World War II the Japanese were especially receptive to the American technology, as they thought their inferior industry and technology were the cause of their defeat. The thinking concerning the carbon resistors was a typical example. Furthermore, the Japanese were obliged by the occupation force to adopt American technology. They were therefore not only receptive, but had no other alternative. The final outcome was very favorable for the Japanese electronics industry.

During World War II, Japanese industry was isolated from Western technology. This isolation hampered Japanese technology; the Japanese had to carry out their research, development, and production during this period almost independently. However, this experience provided the basis of postwar industrial development. The lost war was, in these contexts, virtually the starting point of the successful resurgence of the Japanese electronics industry.

The growth of the components industry proceeded as consumer electronics expanded. In addition to this expanding home market, consumer equipment made in Japan found many overseas outlets. Among these products, transistor radios were a primary force for the miniaturization of components. As Japanese industry grew at a rapid rate, the shortage of labor became a serious problem. Since it was being pushed to become mechanized, the components industry could not remain labor-intensive. Manufacturers who succeeded in this miniaturization and mechanization achieved remarkable growth. One should thus not overlook the significant role played by consumer electronics, since this area is the basis of the country's electronics industry. A substantial domestic market and serious competition among domestic manufacturers were equally necessary for successful growth.

The quality of the Japanese components improved incidentally as a result of mechanization. Besides being reliable and inexpensive, components mass-produced by mechanized systems tend to be of uniform quality. Although this generalization has been true for consumer electronics components, it has not proved to be the case for industrial electronics components, since due to limited demand, they are not mass-produced by mechanized processes. Consequently, their quality is not uniform and their reliability is not necessarily high.[22] Experience shows that a high rate of consumer electronics production is indispensable if one wishes to develop the technology necessary for improving quality.

Although the promotion and support of the Japanese government and other national and public institutions were important to the industry's success, it must be noted that this support was concentrated on components for communications and industrial use, not on those for consumer use. Instead, the success of components for consumer electronics must first of all be attributed to the efforts of the manufacturers themselves.

Competition between U.S. and Japanese electronics is one of the interesting issues of this industry's development. The present study sheds some light on this topic. American electronics laid stress upon the military sector and underestimated the significance of consumer electronics. The Americans seemed to ignore radio and television production while depending strongly upon Japanese suppliers for American OEMs. The growth of the Japanese components industry was therefore due partly, though unintentionally, to this American strategy.

Acknowledgments

In connection with this study, the author interviewed more than 30 people who are involved in the electronic components industry and related work. Thanks are due to their valuable cooperation and discussion.

Notes

1. Since the introduction of integrated circuits, the number of components used in various equipment tended to decrease. Production of components rose, however, as equipment production increased. In recent years, components have been integrated as modules and supplied to equipment assemblers. The necessity of quality components/modules has been increased.

2. Development of the Japanese electronics industry should be discussed in relation not only to the American and European ones but also to the Asian ones. For a global history, especially after the 1960s, see Gene Gregory, *Japanese Electronics Technology—Enterprise and Innovation*, 2nd ed., Chap. 30 (Chichester, England: Wiley, 1986).

3. For Western readers interested in the history of the Japanese electronics industry, the following books will be useful, though they contain little discussion of electronic components. Gregory, see note 2; Ronald Dore, *British Factory-Japanese Factory—The Origins of National Diversity in Industrial Relations* (Berkeley: Univ. California Press, 1973); Chalmers Johnson, *MITI and the Japanese Miracle—The Growth of Industrial Policy, 1925–1975* (Stanford, Calif.: Stanford Univ. Press, 1982).

4. Examples of large companies engaged in the manufacture of communications equipment: NEC, Oki, Toshiba, Japan Radio Co., and Fujitsu. Matsushita and Sharp have been the principal manufacturers of home electrical appliances and consumer electronics, with Sanyo joining them after World War II. Matsushita has also been stressing components production.

5. Ferrite was the key technology of the present TDK.

6. Ferroelectric barium titanate was utilized as material for ceramic capacitors and became the key technology of the present Murata.

7. Pioneer Electronic and Trio (now Kenwood) were exceptions: Pioneer manufactured speakers, Trio, radio coils, and they both turned themselves into hi-fi and stereo equipment makers.

8. The Electrolytic Condenser Investigation Society began issuing its organ *Electrolytic Condenser Review* in 1947.

9. For example, 10 to 20 fixed resistors and one variable resistor are used in a superheterodyne radio, while approximately one hundred fixed resistors and five or six variables exist in a black-and-white television set. A regenerative radio set requires several resistors.

10. The Paper Condenser Investigation Society has published its newsletter *Paper Condenser Review* (later *Condenser Review*) since 1948.

11. The polyethylene-insulated variable capacitors of Mitsumi Electric and the miniature intermediate-frequency transformers of Toko both contributed much to the transistor radio.

12. The MITI had identified electronics as a key sector of the industrial structure already in "Kishinho" (Machinery Industry Promotion Special Measures Law) promulgated in 1956. Kishinho, the model for Denshinho, stressed the importance of electronic components production. Carrying out the policy, MITI established the Japan Electronics Industry Development Association (JEIDA) in 1958. A yearbook of the electronics industry under the supervision of MITI appeared in 1959.

13. *Electronician* (later *Denshikogyo*), the first, appeared in 1953. Publication of *Denshigijutsu* began in 1959. *Denshi*, the newsletter of EIAJ, was started in 1961.

14. Shizuki Electric exported a plant of metalized paper capacitors to Taiwan in 1958.

15. TDK, Mitsumi, Aiwa, Tamura, Nitsuko, Trio (now Kenwood), Noble, Tokyo Cosmos, and Pioneer were all admitted.

16. The waves of mechanization and of statistical quality control came later than in the electronics equipment assembly industry. This lag can be ascribed to the much smaller size of the components manufacturers.

17. See, for example, Chapter 9 of Gregory, in note 2.

18. In the ±20 percent series, for example, nominal resistances, such as 10 kΩ, 15 kΩ, 22 kΩ, 33 kΩ, 47 kΩ, 68 kΩ, and 100 kΩ, are chosen. The lower limit for 15-kΩ resistors is 12 kΩ, a value that is the same as the upper limit for 10-kΩ resistors. Likewise, there is no gap in the boundary between 10-kΩ resistors and 22-kΩ resistors.

19. An investigation committee on resistors in Kansai, consisting of university professors, research workers in national and public research institutes, and engineers with manufacturing companies, began the study in 1949, and published their report, "Kansai-Teikotai-Iinkai Hokoku," in 1952.

20. A contest of resistors (carbon film and carbon composition) was organized by the MITI in 1953 in collaboration with the Electrotechnical Laboratory, the Electrical Communications Laboratory, Research Laboratory of NHK, Radio Communications Industries Association (now EIAJ), and several others.

21. R. O. Grisdale, A. C. Pfister, and W. van Roosbroeck, "Pyrolytic film resistors: Carbon and borocarbon," *Bell Syst. Tech. J.*, Vol. 31, 1951, pp. 271–314.

22. Today it often happens that manufacturers of industrial electronics equipment use quality components made for consumer electronics instead of ordering specific industrial components.

PART II

U.S. Electronics

This part continues the comparison begun in Part I, through an examination of the U.S. electronics industry. The first chapter is by James Gover, an engineer with Sandia National Laboratory who has been active in IEEE's competitiveness activities. Gover provides an overview of the U.S. electronics industry and draws many comparisons between the United States and Japan. Of particular interest in his chapter are the differences between these two countries in their mix of "upstream" electronics (packaging, software, semiconductor manufacturing, materials, and manufacturing equipment) and "downstream" electronics (communications, manufacturing, data processing, consumer electronics, and defense electronics).

In the next chapter, Stuart Leslie, a historian of technology at Johns Hopkins University, examines Silicon Valley, the great American success story that has served as a model for virtually every high-technology regional economic development plan promulgated during the past two decades. Leslie considers federal spending, industry–university relationships, corporate strategies, and technological innovation. He concludes that Silicon Valley was shaped largely by Cold War defense policy and may actually offer little guidance for peace-time technological development policy.

The chapter by Robert Smith, a historian at the Smithsonian Institution's National Air and Space Museum and at Johns Hopkins University, completes the section. In the 1980s, Big Science projects, such as the space telescope and the superconducting supercollider, were publicly defended on the basis that they would lead to improved national competitiveness. Smith contends that at least one common form of this argument—one frequently used in advocacy of public expenditure for science—is based on an erroneous theory of the relation between science and technology. He argues that "what historians of technology do dispute is the notion that basic science runs naturally and in an orderly way to applied science and thence to development and commercial applications and that the process is somehow inevitable."

All three of these chapters present opportunities for further research. Gover's chapter gives informative measures of the competitive situation between Japan and the United States today, makes certain predictions about trends in the electronics industry, and notes certain important issues such as the mix of upstream and downstream electronics and the degree of vertical integration in large electronics companies in the two countries. However, his excellent study is concerned more with the present than the past (only one of his charts goes back as far as 1977); and it would be useful to provide an historical baseline for his observations and, through historical analysis, advance some reasons for the trends he cites.

Gover's chapter suggests many opportunities for the economic historian to compare and explain the U.S. and Japanese electronics industries—especially changes over time—such as the amount of vertical integration in the industry's largest companies, government and total R&D expenditures in upstream and downstream electronics, market share, amount of foreign sales as a percentage of total sales, and capital investment for advanced laboratory and manufacturing equipment.[1] Gover notes how complex and multitiered the electronics industry is; however, no economic historian has yet done justice to this structure or explained its evolution. (Takahashi's chapter in Part I sketches a small part of the evolution of the Japanese electronics industry.) Sound business histories of vertically integrated U.S. companies, such as IBM and General Electric, compared with histories of companies that have not achieved vertical integration might add informative detail to the statistical findings of the economic historians.

Leslie's provocative conclusion that Silicon Valley may not be an appropriate role model for technological competitiveness or regional economic improvement is worth considering in greater detail. His qualitative analysis would be well served by an accompanying quantitative analysis of funding provided by military versus other government and private sources, and amounts of military funding for basic research instead of development of military needs. It would also be useful to compare Silicon Valley with other regional concentrations of high technology.[2] A study of Boston's Route 128 might well confirm Leslie's finding about Silicon Valley because MIT, Lincoln Labs, MITRE, Raytheon, BBN, and many small radar and instrumentation companies, perhaps along with many other companies, have received heavy funding for military R&D. For a high-tech region perhaps not so heavily tied to military funding, one might investigate central New Jersey and its television, pharmaceutical, and telecommunications companies. One might also consider efforts by state governments, such as North Carolina and Ohio, to build up indigenous high-tech industries. Finally, one might gain a new perspective on the value of military funding to national or firm competitiveness by looking at examples such as Texas Instruments, Raytheon, and almost any aerospace company—all of which previously conducted most of their basic research and development for military purposes but now are competing in national and global commercial markets.

Readers might question the practical significance of Smith's thesis, even if correct, if in fact the federal government has received important technological payoffs from Big Science projects it supported. It is beyond the scope of Smith's chapter to provide a cost (technological)-benefit analysis of Big Science. It is too early to consider the cost benefits of the space telescope and supercollider. There have, however, been large expenditures on science in the past that could be studied for their technological return on investment. Smith cites NASA's university program. The national energy laboratories and DARPA's projects in materials science and computer science are other examples. These types of studies may help historians of technology to formulate new ideas about the relation between science and technology because, at the present, historians are more confident in their knowledge of what that relation is not.

Notes

1. A recent article has suggested that U.S. weaknesses are market fit, cycle time, effective implementation, quality, and continuous product improvement. (John D. Trudel, "How to Succeed in Business," *IEEE Spectrum* June 1992, pp. 14–16). It would also be useful to track these factors in the U.S. and Japan with historical economic data.
2. Leslie, himself, is working on a book on American technology during the Cold War era which will consider other regional centers of development. AnnaLee Saxenian of the University of California-Berkeley is near completion of a study of Route 128 in the Boston area.

Review of the Competitive Status of the United States Electronics Industry*

James E. Gover[†]

Leadership in the Electronics Industry is Important to the Nation's Economy

Electronics, the largest manufacturing industry in the world, employs 2.6 million Americans and is the technology building block of most manufacturing and service industries.

> One out of every eight U.S. manufacturing jobs is in electronics. That is three times the size of the auto industry, and nine times that of the basic steel industry.[1]

The worldwide market for electronic goods is over $800 billion. The U.S. share of this market is approximately $200 billion. The world market is expected to approach $2 trillion by the turn of the century. As shown in Figure 1, electronics manufacturing industries have the highest value added of any manufacturing industry. Between 1977 and 1986 value added per production worker hour increased by 150 percent in electronics. Despite our high import of electronics goods, no other U.S. manufacturing industry exports more than does electronics. Twenty-five percent of U.S. electronics industry sales is from exports, and the value of these exports has increased at an average rate of 18 percent a year since 1977.

The U.S. Department of Commerce has identified 12 emerging technologies in four major categories that have a U.S. market potential of $350 billion and a world

*This work was done at Sandia National Laboratories for the U.S. Department of Energy under Contract DE-AC04-76DP00789.

†Dr. James E. Gover, a Fellow of the IEEE, in 1988 served as an IEEE Congressional Fellow. In 1992 and 1993 he is working in the office of Senator Roth as an IEEE Competitiveness Fellow.

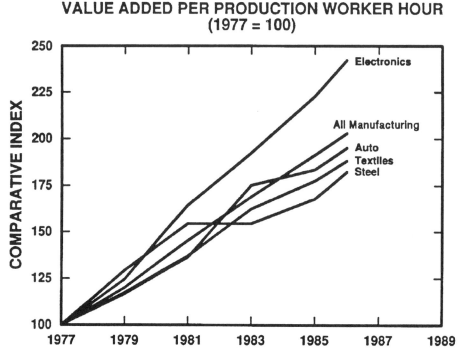

Figure 1. Electronics have the highest value added of the manufacturing industries.

market potential of $1 trillion by the year 2000. Except for superconductors and bio-technology, ten of these emerging technologies are dominated by electronics.[2]

The Structure of the Electronics Industry is Complicated

Electronics industries have a complex, multitiered, fragile structure that begins *up-stream* with materials and equipment for manufacturing semiconductor integrated circuits and chips. These devices form the basic hardware building blocks for five major *downstream* electronics industrial sectors: communications, data processing, manufacturing, consumer products, and defense electronics. The electronics chain is depicted in Figure 2.

Products of the downstream sectors include telephones, fax machines, satellites, PCs, minicomputers, mainframe computers, workstations, word processors, software, CAD, CAM, robotics, auto electronics, VCRs, radios, television sets, clocks, electronic controls, copying machines, and a wide range of defense products.

Note that packaging has been shown as a separate step in the chain. Up until the early 1990s the packaging function was divided between (1) the manufacturing of semiconductors from which a semiconductor device could leave assembled in a connector with multiple pins and (2) the downstream electronics sector in which these

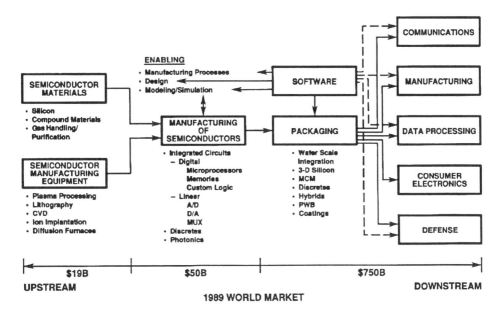

Figure 2. The electronics chain has five major downstream elements, which are fed by upstream sectors comprising packaging, software, semiconductor manufacturing (including enabling capabilities), materials, and manufacturing equipment.

packaged parts could be interconnected on a printed wiring board. As the speed and power density of integrated circuits increases, packaging is developing an identity as a sophisticated discipline for which practices are closely aligned with semiconductor manufacturing. Eventually, for high-performance systems we expect packaging to be absorbed into semiconductor manufacturing and to lose its identity as a separate step in the chain.

Also note that I have shown software as a separate element of the electronics chain located upstream from the downstream electronics sector. Some electronics companies gain competitive advantage by exploiting their excellence in software. However, as competition grows in a downstream sector, core competences in both semiconductor manufacturing technology and software are required as differentiating strengths.

In Japan, most of the companies that are heavily invested in downstream electronics sectors are also vertically integrated and heavily invested in upstream sectors, particularly in semiconductors. Thus these companies may take their profits from sales of upstream manufacturing equipment, midstream semiconductor products, or downstream electronics products. Sony's entry into the entertainment field offers them the option of taking their profits from movies and other entertainment media. If these profits are sufficiently high, they may operate their upstream supporting industries at a loss.

(In Japan) Six firms, all with annual revenues of more than $10 billion and with close links with other major Japanese industries, produce approximately 85 percent of

Japanese semiconductors, 80 percent of Japanese computers, 80 percent of Japanese telecommunications equipment, and 60 percent of Japanese consumer electronics.[3]

There are six major firms or bank-centered societies of business, keiretsu, in Japan. These include Sumitomo, Mitsubishi, Mitsui, Dai Ichi Kangyo, Fuyo, and Sanwa. In addition to these bank-centered keiretsu, Japan has supply-centered keiretsu consisting of groups of companies integrated along a supplier chain dominated by a major manufacturer. Bank-centered keiretsu include 182 companies, or 10 percent of the companies on the Tokyo Stock Exchange that earn 18 percent of Japan's business profits from 17 percent of total Japanese business sales, employ 5 percent of Japan's labor force, and hold over 14 percent of Japan's total paid-up capital.[4] Unlike these bank-centered keiretsu, in which power is distributed among the various member companies, the supply-centered keiretsu are clearly hierarchical with power concentrated in the hands of the major manufacturers.

Charles H. Ferguson, research associate at MIT's Center for Technology, Policy, and Industrial Development, has pointed out that the keiretsu structure benefits Japanese business through both vertical and horizontal linkages.[5]

In the United States, only a few companies, notably IBM, AT&T, Motorola, and Hewlett-Packard, are vertically integrated, but those few primarily use their semiconductor products to their strategic advantage in downstream markets. As Japan's semiconductor companies gain control of semiconductor technology, they can and probably will use that asset to control downstream markets, such as computers. Most U.S.-manufactured semiconductors are built by merchant companies whose only business is semiconductors. If these companies collapse, downstream U.S. electronics manufacturers that rely on the purchase of state-of-the-art microelectronics technology will be at the mercy of foreign suppliers who are competing in the same downstream electronics sector.

Control of a large enough segment of the downstream industries creates the cash flow for upstream research and development (R&D) investment. That in turn permits control of upstream industries, and ultimately control of all the downstream markets. For example, Japan's strength in consumer electronics created a market for semiconductors and resulted in their dominance of DRAM memory chips. Their dominance of the DRAM market created a market for DRAM manufacturing equipment built in Japan and led to severe upstream market loss by the U.S. semiconductor manufacturing equipment industry. Because DRAM processing technology is the most demanding of all integrated circuit types, DRAM dominance carries into other areas of microelectronics.

As concurrent engineering practices are developed so that microelectronics manufacturing equipment, manufacturing processes, semiconductor technology, and circuit design are done simultaneously, the necessity for a nation to be prominent in all these elements will be even more important than it is today. For example, as manufacturing equipment is being developed, competitive microelectronics companies will find it necessary to be simultaneously designing the products and processes that use this equipment. To do this will require close cooperation between the equipment manufacturers and the microelectronics product manufacturers. SEMATECH is developing the linkages between these industries in the United States.

If the United States is to be a major player in the world of electronics, we must be strong throughout the upstream building block segments of electronics and at the same time have enough presence in downstream markets to maintain market pull for the upstream technologies.

The United States is Losing Market Share in Electronics to Japan

The best metric for competitiveness assessment is world market share. The United State's share of world electronics markets decreased steadily throughout the 1980s, with entire electronics sectors such as consumer electronics almost vanishing from U.S.-based and -owned manufacturing facilities. "In electronics, . . . the largest U.S. manufacturing industry, the United States exported $5B to Japan in 1987 but imported $26B."[6]

The U.S. Commerce Department recently reported that Japan could surpass the United States in production of electronic goods by 1994, and emphasized that since 1984 (except for software and medical equipment) the United States lost market share in 35 of 37 electronics categories.[7] Even in fields such as personal computers, supercomputers, and microprocessors, long dominated by the United States, the U.S. market share has declined.[8] Further loss in world market share in most categories continued through 1990. For example, U.S. factories' share of the U.S. market in computers went from 94 percent in 1979 to 66 percent in 1989.[9]

The United States Has Lost Market Share in Semiconductor Manufacturing Equipment

A recent article in the *Far Eastern Economic Review* illustrated the decline in the United States' market share in semiconductor manufacturing equipment with the data shown in Figure 3.[10]

Between 1980 and 1990 the top ten manufacturers of semiconductor manufacturing equipment shifted as shown in Table 1.

It is clear that the loss of a $9 billion industry such as semiconductor manufacturing equipment is not a serious loss to the U.S. economy unless there is a domino or ripple effect into downstream electronics sectors. It is this concern that has prompted so much attention for this relatively small sector of the electronics industry. Even South Korea has expressed concern about their ability to build semiconductors without a competitive presence in semiconductor manufacturing equipment.

> Because of the deepening dependence on imported (semiconductor manufacturing) equipment, we are worried that both the balanced growth of the semiconductor equipment industry and the growth of the memory device industry may suffer in the future. This scenario emphasizes the need to develop the semiconductor equipment industry.[11]

Of most concern is the stepper market, where Japan's firms dominate most of the world market. *Steppers* are a type of lithography equipment that limit the feature

SEMICONDUCTOR EQUIPMENT

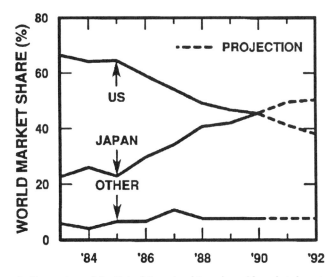

Figure 3. Comparison of the United States' and Japan's world market share in semi-conductor manufacturing equipment points up the rapid decline in the United States' market share in this sector.

size and number of transistors that may be made in an integrated circuit. In 1989 Japanese firms held 74 percent of the world market share in optical steppers with U.S. firms holding 15 percent of market share. In diffusion furnaces, Japanese firms held 60 percent of market share and U.S. firms held 35 percent. In deposition technology, ion implanters, and etching equipment U.S. firms held over 50 percent of market share.[12]

TABLE I Comparison of Semiconductor Manufacturing Equipment Sales in 1980 and 1990

1980 Sales ($million)		1990 Sales ($million)	
Perkin-Elmer	151	Tokyo Electron	706
GCA	116	Nikon	692
Applied Materials	115	Applied Materials	572
Fairchild	105	Advantest	423
Varian	90	Canon	421
Teradyne	83	Hitachi	304
Eaton	79	General Signal (GCA)	286
General Signal	57	Varian	285
Kulicke & Soff	47	Teradyne	215
Advantest	46	Silicon Valley Group (Perkin-Elmer)	204
Top 10 Total	889	Top 10 Total	4,108
		Total 1989 World Sales	9,078

The United States Has Also Lost Market Share in Semiconductors

Between 1979 and 1989 the top ten manufacturers of integrated circuits built with this equipment shifted as shown in Table 2. Note that as we move down the electronics chain the economic stakes dramatically increase with the market share in downstream sectors depending on market share in upstream sectors and vice versa.

In semiconductors a trend similar to manufacturing equipment has been observed in the United States' and Japan's world market shares. This trend is illustrated in Figure 4.

To many, a 1 percent or 2 percent loss in a world market may seem inconsequential. In a recent presentation to the United States's Industrial Competitiveness Committee of the IEEE, Turner Hasty, former Chief Operating Officer of SEMATECH, shed considerable light on this topic with some very conservative estimates of the economic impact of market share in semiconductors.

> The size of the world semiconductor market is about $49.5B so 1 percent of market share equates to $495M. The average U.S. (semiconductor) industry sales per employee is $85K which would give you a total of 5,824 American jobs per each point of market share. . . . You have to take into account that 48.8 percent of the U.S. industry employment is outside this country so we deducted that and came up with the 2,982 jobs you see here (in the U.S.). The corresponding loss in wages to U.S. workers ($130M) and R&D funds ($59M) and tax revenues ($40M) begins to give you a picture of the staggering losses in an industry that is the foundation of America's largest employer, electronics. [13]

Should the United States lose the domestic semiconductor industry, at risk would be the U.S. share of the worldwide electronics industry. Because semiconductors offer the technology leverage for the $800 billion worldwide electronics industry, using the same scaling factors as Turner Hasty used for semiconductors, I conservatively estimate a 1 percent loss in total electronics sales to result in a loss of

TABLE II Comparison of Semiconductor Sales in 1979 and 1989 Illustrates Japan's Gains

1979 Sales ($million)		1989 Sales ($million)	
TI	1,282	NEC	5,015
Motorola	919	Toshiba	4,930
Philips	761	Hitachi	3,974
NEC	595	Motorola	3,319
National	532	Fujitsu	2,963
Fairchild	469	TI	2,787
Hitachi	453	Mitsubishi	2,579
Toshiba	442	Intel	2,430
Intel	440	Matsushita	1,882
Siemens	368	Philips	1,716
Top 10 Total	6,261	Top 10 Total	31,595
		Total 1989 World Sales	55,000

Source: Dataquest.

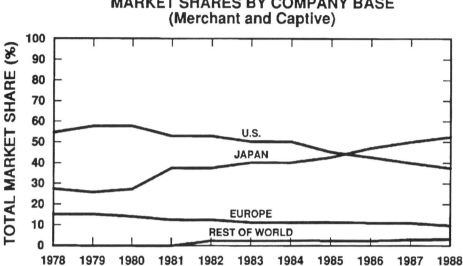

Figure 4. In the world semiconductor market, Japan overtook the United States near the end of 1985, and then rapidly surpassed the United States. (*Source: Dataquest*, January 1989)

over 50,000 jobs for Americans, over $2 billion loss in wages to American workers, over $1 billion reduction in R&D funds, and over $640 million loss in tax revenue.

Furthermore, sustaining market share is more than the financial impact of a 1 or 2 percent loss in market. At stake may be the ability to maintain *any* share of the market. To be competitive, firms must be able to market internationally. United States semiconductor manufacturers have not been very successful in marketing semiconductor products in Japan. In fact, concern for this led to the U.S.-Japan Semiconductor Trade Agreement that was signed in 1986. At that time foreign firms' share of Japan's semiconductor market was only 8.6 percent. By 1990, the share of foreign firms had grown to 13.2 percent of Japan's market, but still fell well short of the 20 percent share that U.S. authorities interpreted the trade agreement to guarantee. Japan's officials have interpreted 20 percent to only be a target. As negotiations for a new trade agreement have progressed to replace the 1986 agreement, which expired in July 1991, Japan's officials have expressed opposition to managed trade and have proposed that the problem would be solved if U.S. manufacturers would improve their competitiveness.[14]

The progress of foreign semiconductor market share in Japan is shown in Figure 5.

The U.S. Market Share in Computers Is Also at Risk

Much has been written about the U.S. loss of market share in consumer electronics. Less known, however, is the loss of market share to Japan in computer sales. The data are shown in Figure 6.

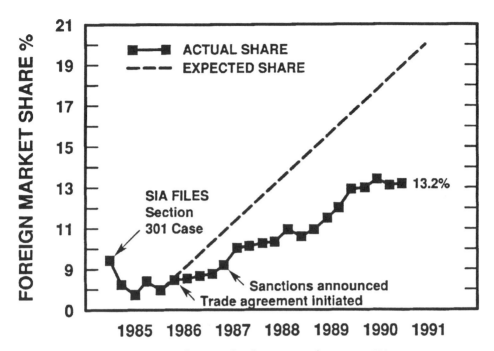

Figure 5. Foreign semiconductor market share in Japan has not met U.S. expectations. (*Source:* Semiconductor Industry Association)

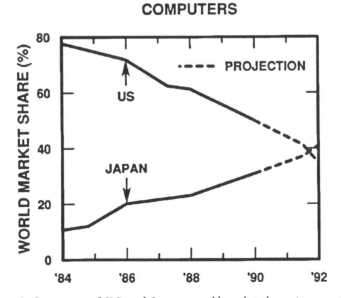

Figure 6. Comparison of U.S. and Japanese world market shares in computers shows the United States is on a rapid downward trend.

Many analysts are predicting that the market for personal computers will rapidly shift to notebook and laptop models, a field in which Japanese-based and -owned companies are expected to dominate sales. To counter this trend, U.S. companies have formed partnerships with Japanese companies. In many, if not most, of these partnerships Japanese firms will provide most of the value-added manufacturing; U.S. firms will market these products with the labels of U.S.-based companies. IBM

has teamed with Toshiba in the manufacture of color LCD screens; Apple is negotiating with Sony to manufacture a laptop computer; AT&T has teamed with Matsushita to build a notebook computer; TI is selling laptops designed with a Japanese partner; and Compaq has long depended on its partnership with Japan's Citizen to provide hardware and packaging of its laptop and notebook computers.

> Citizen subassemblies make up so much of the finished machines (sold by Compaq) that one market researcher counts all LTEs (a Compaq laptop computer) as Japanese imports.[15]

The marketing and service excellence of U.S. companies and their well-established relationship with U.S. consumers will assure that products with U.S. corporation titles maintain a strong presence in the laptop and notebook business. Intel's excellence in microprocessors and flash memories and Conner's excellence in hard disk drives suggest that at least some of the components are built in the United States.

A leading executive of the U.S. electronics industry, Dr. Andrew Grove of Intel, recently tabulated the shift in the top ten computer manufacturers between 1984 and 1989. These data are shown in Table 3.[16] Note how well Hitachi is positioned in computers, equipment, and semiconductors.

Nor should we feel too secure about the United States' strength in software. *The Economist* recently reported that Japan is creating a strong software development capability to support their soaring personal computer business. In many instances, software produced in Japan is selling for less than 10 percent of the selling price for American software.[17]

TABLE III The Shift in Leading Computer Manufacturers between 1984 and 1989 Reflects Japan's Growth in Market Share

	1984	1989
1	IBM	IBM
2	DEC	DEC
3	Burroughs	Fujitsu
4	Control Data	NEC
5	NCR	Unisys
6	Fujitsu	Hitachi
7	Sperry	Hewlett-Packard
8	Hewlett-Packard	Siemens
9	NEC	Olivetti
10	Siemens	NCR

Fujitsu is planning a 200-person R&D center in the U.S. to develop a next-generation version of Unix software, which could make Japanese hardware more competitive.[18]

Already, Japanese software factories churn out programs with half as many defects as comparable American products, according to a study by the Massachusetts Institute of Technology.[19]

One should be aware that even though U.S. market share in software grew from 70 to 72 percent between 1984 and 1987, by 1990 U.S. market share had dropped to 57 percent. In Table 4 we compare world market shares of software.[19]

As Japan takes over an increasing share of the computer laptop market, we can expect this to further pull up their sales of software.

Supercomputers, workstations, telecommunications, and semiconductor markets are at risk. *If present trends continue, U.S.-owned electronics manufacturers could be out of the domestic electronics business early in the twenty-first century. Our economy will suffer, our standard of living will diminish, and modern defense technology will be imported.*

These Market Share Losses Have Resulted in a High-Tech Trade Deficit with Japan

Although only 17 percent of total U.S. trade is with Japan, nearly 45 percent (about $50 billion) of the U.S. trade deficit is with Japan. Between 1987 and 1989 the global U.S. trade deficit went down 29 percent, but the U.S. deficit with Japan went down only 13 percent. While Japan purchases 20 percent of the U.S. agricultural exports, they only purchase 10 percent of the U.S. high-tech exports. About 36 percent of the U.S. imports from Japan are high-tech products. Even though the global U.S. trade balance in high-tech products improved to an $8 billion surplus in 1988, including a surplus with the European Community, the U.S. high-tech trade deficit with Japan remained above $20 billion.[20]

U.S. Semiconductor R&D Performance is Lagging behind Japan's

There are many measures of how competitive an industry is based on sales data. An *estimate* of how competitive an industry will be in the future can be made from their

TABLE IV Software Market Shares by Nation in 1990

Country	Market Share (%)	Total Sales ($Billion)
United States	57	62.7
Japan	13	14.3
France	8	8.8
Germany	7	7.7
Britain	6	6.6
Canada	3	3.3
Others	6	6.6

investment in R&D, the performance of their R&D, and their capital investment. We may think of sales data as a measure of competitiveness and R&D investment and performance as the time derivative of competitiveness. That is, low R&D performance will eventually lead to diminished competitiveness. One way of assessing the R&D performance of an industry is through their presentations at international meetings, particularly those regarded to be highly prestigious and a valuable marketing tool for industry.

In microelectronics the Institute of Electrical and Electronics Engineers (IEEE) sponsors two annual meetings that are highly regarded around the world. These are the International Electron Devices Meeting (IEDM) and the International Solid-State Circuits Conference (ISSCC). Although Japan has domestic electrical engineering societies that are considered by many Japanese to be technically ahead of, or at least equivalent to, the IEEE,[21] in the United States IEEE conferences and publications are considered to be the most prestigious, and they are technically superior to any other presentation or publication opportunity in microelectronics. In fact, unlike other nations, U.S. researchers in electronics and microelectronics have no domestic electrical engineering societies that promote the exchange of R&D information at the national level. That ended in the early 1960s when the IEEE absorbed the American Institute of Electrical Engineers. Of course, at that time the United States dominated electronics technology and it was U.S. policy to share R&D with the world. It was not even conceivable in the early 1960s that the United States could lose this dominant position. Even though the 1990 IEEE Secretary, Dr. Fumio Harashima, Professor of Robotics, Tokyo University, has recommended that IEEE-USA sponsor conferences of specific interest to U.S. institutions, the IEEE has not seen fit to shift away from the 1960s paradigm.[21]

United States researchers in microelectronics consider a presentation at IEDM or ISSCC as a very high measure of peer recognition of their work, and our microelectronics companies consider presentations at these meetings as public evidence that their company is pushing the frontiers of technology. There are definite marketing advantages to presenting work at these two meetings. Thus, not only do scientists and engineers compete as individuals to present their work, their employers encourage, if not demand, it.

I have reviewed the program of the 1990 IEDM,[22] presented December 9 to 12, 1990, in San Francisco and the 1991 ISSCC,[23] held in San Francisco, February 13 to 15, 1991. Between 2000 and 3000 scientists and engineers attended each of these meetings. In Table 5 major categories of the topics are listed along with the affiliations of the authors as U.S. Industry, U.S. Universities and U.S. Government-Owned Laboratories, Japan, Europe, and Other. Even though the European papers are split between university and industry in about the same proportion as U.S. papers, I have not broken down the European papers because there are so few of them. The Japanese papers are written almost exclusively by industry personnel; therefore, I do not separate the few written by nonindustry personnel.

Presentations at these two U.S.-located meetings are critically reviewed, and substantially fewer than 50 percent of those papers submitted for review are accepted for presentation. Reviewers of papers for these meetings take great pride in their objectivity; nevertheless, about 80 percent of the reviewers are from the United States.

TABLE V   The List of First-Author Affiliations of Papers Presented at the 1990
IEDM and 1991 ISSCC Shows Japan and the United States to Be in Close Competition

	Affiliation				
Conference and Topic	U.S. Industry	U.S. Universities and Government	Japan	Europe	Other
IEDM					
1. Integrated Circuits	9	0	14	3	0
2. Device Technology	6	5	18	3	0
3. Solid-State Devices	10	8	16	6	0
4. Detectors, Sensors, and Displays	5	7	8	1	1
5. Quantum Electronics and Compound Semiconductors	10	9	5	1	2
6. Modeling and Simulation	10	16	6	8	0
7. Vacuum Electronics	7	11	1	2	1
ISSCC					
8. Low-Temperature Circuits and Special-Purpose Processors	2	3	2	0	0
9. High-Speed RAM	1	0	6	0	0
10. Oversampling Converters	2	1	1	3	0
11. Microprocessors	3	1	2	0	0
12. High-Density DRAM	0	0	6	0	0
13. Communications	2	1	1	2	0
14. Hard Disk and Data Communications ICs	6	0	1	0	0
15. High-Performance Logic	1	1	4	1	0
16. High-Speed Data Acquisition	5	0	2	0	0
17. Emerging Technologies	4	1	1	0	1
18. Image Sensors and Processors	0	1	5	0	0
19. Telecommunications CKTs	1	0	2	3	0
20. Video Signal Processors	0	0	5	0	0
21. Nonvolatile Memory	1	0	4	0	0
22. Analog Techniques	3	0	0	2	0

Therefore, any minor subconscious bias in paper selection would likely favor U.S. authors. Despite this, conference officials at the ISSCC find the acceptance rate of Japanese papers to be twice that of U.S. papers because of the quality of the work.[24]

At first glance the total U.S. contribution of 153 papers compares favorably to Japan's contribution of 110 papers. If one then deducts from the U.S. total the 65 papers from universities, the comparison favors Japan, but not by a significant margin (about 20 papers). However, closer examination of specific topics from Table 5 presents much cause for U.S. alarm.

- Japanese industrial researchers are starting to pull away from U.S. industrial researchers in most of those areas where there is significant product market:
    1. Integrated Circuits
    2. Device Technology

    3. Solid-State Devices
    4. Detectors, Sensors, and Displays
    9. High-Speed RAM
   12. High-Density DRAM
   15. High-Performance Logic
   18. Image Sensors and Processors
   20. Video Signal Processors
   21. Nonvolatile Memory

- Areas where the market remains strong and the United States will remain competitive, although not dominant, include:

    8. Low-Temperature Circuits and Special-Purpose Processors
   10. Oversampling Converters
   11. Microprocessors
   13. Communications
   19. Telecommunications Circuits

- If one could make a case that U.S. universities and government laboratory research provided an exclusive advantage to U.S. industry, then the United States would also appear to remain competitive in the following areas:

    3. Solid-State Devices
    4. Detectors, Sensors, and Displays

- Areas where the market is strong and the United States appears to remain dominant include:

   14. Hard Disk and Data Communications ICs
   16. High-Speed Data Acquisition
   22. Analog Techniques

- United States universities and government laboratories are important contributors to physics-oriented, microelectronics-device R&D (IEDM), but are practically invisible in engineering-design-oriented, microelectronics-circuit R&D (ISSCC). The latter area, not physics, drives products.
- United States universities, government laboratories, and industry continue to lead in areas where the market future is most uncertain, the area is new (and therefore offers more publishing opportunities), or the area is only supportive to technology; that is, modeling and simulation.

    5. Quantum Electronics and Compound Semiconductors
    6. Modeling and Simulation
    7. Vacuum Electronics
   17. Emerging Technologies

Although we recognize that all crystal balls are speculative, in the absence of a paradigm shift we believe that these data suggest the following disturbing scenarios:

- Continued growth in Japan's share of the worldwide microelectronics market.

- Continued decline in the United States's share of the worldwide microelectronics market.
- Continued superiority of U.S. microelectronics R&D only in those areas of speculative or low market potential.
- Europe and the rest of the world outside the United States and Japan will not be major players in state-of-the-art microelectronics.

As Michael Borrus, director of the University of California's Berkeley Roundtable on the International Economy, has so clearly stated,

> At the present rate of attrition, the U.S. merchant semiconductor industry will be an insignificant factor on world markets in roughly five years. That is the window of opportunity for the industry and government to act. . . . When historians trace the decline of the U.S. electronics industry, they will finger the decade of the 1980s, wondering why the United States never seems able to treat the ills that it endlessly documented and diagnosed.[25]

This decline of the U.S. electronics industry is reflected in a decade-spanning comparison of the number and categories of papers presented by various groups at the international IEDM and ISSCC conferences (Table 6). This comparison can be made for IEDM by categories because they have changed categories very little in the last decade. However, only the total number of papers can be compared for ISSCC because of the many changes in session titles that make categorizing difficult. Note the shift from a preponderance of U.S. papers in 1980 and 1981 to a preponderance of papers from Japan in 1990 and 1991.

United States attendees at last year's Semicon Japan, held in Tokyo the week of October 22, 1990, were surprised to hear the conference's keynote speaker, Tadashi Kubota, Matsushita Senior Managing Director, predict that in 10 years the only U.S. semiconductor manufacturing companies that will survive are IBM, Motorola, and Intel; IBM and Motorola because they have downstream products for their microelectronics and Intel because they have microprocessors as their primary product. (In the case of microprocessors, software is a bigger limiter than manufacturing technology.) Tadashi Kubota predicted that Texas Instruments would be out of semiconductor manufacturing in less than five years because of its lack of downstream commercial products.

To determine the direct economic impact of U.S. loss of the merchant semiconductor industry, one only needs to review the recent rapid growth of this industry. In Table 7 are listed the world trends in semiconductor sales and the investment in manufacturing facilities that is required to support this rapidly expanding industry.

To stay in microelectronics, competition requires great capital investment and great investment in R&D.

> Last year (1988) alone, the U.S. semiconductor industry spent about $3.5B in capital investment. Over the next several product generations, state-of-the-art (semiconductor) manufacturing facilities are expected to cost between $500M and $750M. Such spending strains the resources of even very large companies.[26]

TABLE VI Comparison of First-Author Nationalities for Papers Presented at the IEDM[a] Conference in 1980 and the ISSCC[b] Conference in 1981 to the Same Conferences One Decade Later Shows that Participation of Japanese Authors Has Increased Markedly, Whereas Participation by U.S. Authors Has Declined

Conference and Category	U.S. Industry		U.S. Universities and Government		Japan		Europe		Other	
	1980	1990	1980	1990	1980	1990	1980	1990	1980	1990
IEDM										
Integrated Circuits	15	9	2	0	12	14	0	3	1	0
Device Technology	20	6	6	5	11	18	3	3	1	0
Solid-State Devices	16	10	13	8	7	16	10	6	3	0
Detectors, Sensors, and Displays	17	5	4	7	4	8	3	1	1	1
Quantum Electronics	8	10	10	9	0	5	0	1	2	2
Vacuum Electronics and Electron Tubes	17	7	4	11	0	1	1	2	0	1
	1981	1991	1981	1991	1981	1991	1981	1991	1981	1991
ISSCC										
All Categories	50	31	6	9	23	42	12	11	1	1

[a] International Electron Devices Meeting, sponsored by the Institute of Electrical and Electronics Engineers.

[b] International Solid-State Circuits Conference, sponsored by the Institute of Electrical and Electronics Engineers.

TABLE VII World Data Show the Recent Rapid Growth of Semiconductor
Sales and Facility Investment in $Billions

Year	1986	1987	1988	1989	1990	1991	1992
Semiconductor Sales	29.7	36.5	50.5	55.0	55.4	62.0	81.0
Facility Investment	5.0	6.1	9.3	10.5	10.4	13.7	17.6
Ratio: FI/SS	0.17	0.17	0.18	0.19	0.19	0.22	0.22

Source: Dataquest.

Note that if semiconductor sales sustain through the 1990s the 18 percent
growth rate they achieved during the latter half of the 1980s, by the year 2000 annual
sales will exceed $250 billion. By that time computers will be built on a single chip
and practically all the value added will reside in this chip, the display, and the
software.

Failure of the U.S. merchant semiconductor industry will be of higher consequences than just loss of U.S. market share in microelectronics. Downstream electronics markets will be at risk.

> How do you make a better computer than Hitachi and market it sooner if you are de-
> pendent on Hitachi for computer chips? asks Stephen Cohen of the Berkeley Round-
> table on the International Economy. The answer is: No Way.[27]

In the supercomputer industry Cray Research, a relatively small American
company, attempts to compete for market share with Fujitsu, Hitachi, and NEC.
Cray purchases many of its integrated circuit chips from Fujitsu.

> "We have our own chip divisions," an NEC spokesman told David Sanger, of the New
> York Times. "(We) can custom-make the high speed chips we need. Cray can't."[28]

When semiconductor technology progresses to the point where the system
logic and memory are all contained on a single chip, semiconductor manufacturers
will be positioned to control all of the downstream electronics sectors. Unless there
is a dramatic change in the competitiveness of the U.S. semiconductor industry, by
the turn of the century these electronics companies will be Japanese firms.

Notes

1. Testimony of Mitchell Kertzman, President and CEO of Powersoft Corporations and 1990
   Chairman of the American Electronics Association, to the Senate Subcommittee on Science, Technology, and Space, August 1, 1990.

2. Charles H. Ferguson, "America's high-tech decline," *Foreign Policy*, Spring 1989, p. 136.

3. Leyla Woods, "U.S. trade with Japan in perspective," *Bus. Am.*, July 2, 1990, p. 17.

4. Marie Anchordoguy, "A brief history of Japan's keiretsu," *Harvard Bus. Rev.*, July–August
   1990, pp. 58–59.

5. Charles H. Ferguson, "Computers and the coming of the U.S. keiretsu," *Harvard Bus.
   Rev.*, July–August 1990, p. 63.

6. B. R. Scott, "Competitiveness: Self help for a worsening problem," *Harvard Bus. Rev.*, July–August 1989.

7. U.S. Department of Commerce, International Trade Administration, "The competitive status of the U.S. electronics sector from materials to systems," April 1990, p. 17.

8. *The Wall Street Journal*, "Japan could surpass the U.S. in output of electronics soon, new report says," June 11, 1990, p. B4.

9. *Fortune*, "Is made in USA fading away?" September 24, 1990, p. 62.

10. *Far Eastern Economic Review*, "Reinventing research," May 24, 1990, p. 69.

11. Electronics Components Section, Ministry of Trade and Industry and the Korea Semiconductor Equipment Association, "1990 industrial technology requirements for semiconductor equipment," Seoul, Korea, September 1990.

12. U.S. Department of Commerce, "National security assessment of the U.S. semiconductor wafer processing equipment industry," April 1991, p. 26.

13. Turner Hasty, presentation to the IEEE-USA National Government Activities Committee Colloquium on the IEEE-USA Legislative Initiative, October 20, 1990, Washington, D.C.

14. *Asahi Evening News*, April 18, 1991.

15. *Business Week*, "Laptops take off," March 18, 1991, p. 120.

16. Andrew S. Grove, "The future of the computer industry," *Calif. Manage. Rev.*, Fall 1990, p. 159.

17. *The Economist*, "Revenge of the Nipponerds," August 11, 1990, p. 71.

18. *Business Week*, "Where are computer makers thriving? Hint: It starts with a 'J'," November 19, 1990, p. 63.

19. *Business Week*, "Can the U.S. stay ahead in software?" March 11, 1991, p. 99.

20. U.S. Department of Commerce, Technology Administration, "Emerging Technologies—A Survey of Technical and Economic Opportunities," Spring 1990, p. VII.

21. Personal Communication, Fumio Harashima, Professor of Robotics, Tokyo University, and 1990 Secretary of the IEEE.

22. 1990 International Electron Devices Meeting, Technical Program Book.

23. 1991 IEEE International Solid-State Circuits Conference, Advance Program.

24. Personal Communication, 1991 ISSCC Officials, Frank Hewlett, James Jorgensen, and Charles W. Gwyn.

25. Michael Borrus, "Chips of state," *Issues Sci. Technol.*, Fall 1990, p. 45.

26. National Advisory Committee on Semiconductors, "A strategic industry at risk," *A Report to the President and Congress*, November 1989, p. 5.

27. *Business Week*, 1990, op. cit., p. 63.

28. James Fallows, "Containing Japan," *Atl. Mon.*, May 1989, p. 44.

How the West Was Won

The Military and the Making of Silicon Valley

Stuart W. Leslie

The extraordinary story of Silicon Valley continues to intoxicate American business leaders, policymakers, and politicians alike. Despite its recent ups and downs, Silicon Valley remains a potent symbol of American high-technology competitiveness. In fact, no plan for regional economic development seems complete these days without its version of "silicon plain," "silicon mountain," or "silicon beach" (which at least makes some sense technically!).

Yet those who would emulate the example of Silicon Valley too often overlook a crucial part of the story. Behind the essentially self-serving image of the "new alchemists,"[1] "the big score,"[2] and "silicon valley fever,"[3] behind the triumphant tales of freewheeling entrepreneurs and visionary venture capitalists lies a more unsettling reality about the military's role, unintentional and otherwise, in setting America's past industrial policy, and about the implications of that policy for our future industrial competitiveness.[4]

For better and for worse, Silicon Valley owes its present configuration largely to patterns of federal spending, corporate strategy, industry–university relationships, and technological innovation shaped by the assumptions and priorities of cold war defense policy. Indeed, the name Silicon Valley itself may be something of a misnomer, ignoring as it does the crucial role of microwave electronics and aerospace in providing this archetype for American high-technology industry. Created and sustained in the name of national security, Silicon Valley may offer limited guidance at best for an industrial policy aimed at a very different kind of international competition.[5]

Before World War II

For all its isolation from the centers of East Coast industry, the Santa Clara Valley played a surprisingly significant role in the early days of radio and electronics. Broadcasting pioneer Federal Telegraph (later bought by ITT) got its start in Palo Alto under Stanford graduate Cyril Elwell, with financial backing from Stanford's president and several faculty members.[6] Audion inventor Lee de Forest worked there for a time developing more powerful arc transmitters, and in the process made the crucial observation that an audion could generate continuous waves.[7] Charles Litton, another Stanford graduate, joined Federal's vacuum tube department following a stint at Bell Laboratories, then quit to go into business for himself when Federal moved the laboratory back east in 1932. William Eitel and Jack McCullough similarly left Heintz and Kaufman (cofounded by yet another Stanford graduate, Ralph Heintz) in 1934 to design and build their own tubes for the amateur radio market.[8]

Under Frederick Terman, Stanford University became the leading academic center for radio research on the West Coast. Son of an eminent Stanford psychologist, Terman grew up on campus, took his undergraduate degree there, and then headed off to M.I.T. for graduate training in electrical engineering. He returned to Stanford in 1925 with his doctorate and promptly launched an aggressive, commercially oriented program in radio electronics.[9] Following M.I.T.'s example, he drew his research problems directly from industry and encouraged active collaboration between his students and local electronics companies. Terman did what he could to encourage young radio engineers to stay in the area. He arranged a special fellowship to lure one of his most promising graduate students, David Packard, back from General Electric, and put him to work with another top prospect, William Hewlett. Terman then helped his two students go into business in 1939 making audio oscillators based on ideas the three of them had been exploring in the laboratory. Walt Disney Studies bought the first batch for the *Fantasia* sound track.

Stanford also played a key role in fostering the klystron, perhaps the most important electronics innovation developed on the West Coast before World War II. In 1937 the Varian brothers, working with several Stanford physicists, invented the klystron, an original and extremely flexible microwave receiver and transmitter. Under an unusual contract with the university, the Varians were granted access to faculty, laboratory space, and modest funding for materials in return for a half interest in any resulting patents.[10] A subsequent agreement between the university and Sperry Gyroscope Company provided substantial corporate funding for klystron research and development at Stanford and gave Sperry an exclusive license to make, use, and sell any microwave equipment developed in the university laboratory.[11] To follow up on its investment, Sperry set up a small development and production facility in nearby San Carlos.[12]

The War Years

None of the West Coast companies grew very large before World War II. To survive in an industry still dominated by eastern laboratories and patents, they had to exploit technical niches, either by creating new products, like Hewlett-Packard, or by improving the performance and reliability of traditional ones, like Eitel-McCullough.[13]

Wartime orders gave the infant industry a chance to show what it could do. RCA, GE, Westinghouse, and the other East Coast giants won the lion's share of the defense electronics contracts, but even relatively small orders could make a big difference for the West Coast start-ups. Hewlett-Packard, spurred by massive orders for its line of electronic measuring instruments, jumped from nine employees and $37,000 in sales in 1940,[14] to one hundred employees and $1 million in sales just three years later.[15] Eitel-McCullough, on the strength of huge subcontracts from Western Electric and GE, grew even faster, churning out 100,000 tubes a week at the peak of wartime production.[16] At the same time, it proved that it could still beat the competition in quality as well as quantity, mass-producing tubes that more established firms like GE could never seem to get right even as prototypes.[17] Sperry, recognizing the dangers of too widely separating its research and development (R&D) from production, moved the entire Stanford klystron group out to its Long Island laboratories for the duration.

Terman spent the war directing the Radio Research Laboratory (RRL), a spinoff of the famous Radiation Laboratory housed upriver at Harvard and devoted to radar countermeasures. He brought along a number of Stanford students and colleagues—30 in all served tours of duty at RRL—and together they received a practical education in the art of microwave engineering. Writing to a colleague back at Stanford, Terman said:

> I have learned a tremendous amount, for I had never before realized the amount of work required to make a device ready for manufacture after one had a good working model, such as the number of drawings, the amount of detailed design that is involved to turn out a good job, the problems of how to get stuff to meet specifications, testing and standardization problems, etc.[18]

Post-War Growth in West Coast Industry

Terman returned to Stanford in 1946 with a new title, Dean of Engineering, and a new vision of western industrial leadership:

> The west has long dreamed of an indigenous industry of sufficient magnitude to balance its agricultural resources. The war advanced these hopes and brought to the west the beginnings of a great new era of industrialization. A strong and independent industry must, however, develop its own intellectual resources of science and technology, for industrial activity that depends on imported brains and second-hand ideas cannot hope to be more than a vassal that pays tribute to its overlords, and is permanently condemned to an inferior competitive position.[19]

Yet Terman and his colleagues recognized that the war had advanced more than hopes. By introducing new kinds of tubes and by opening up an entirely new range of the electromagnetic spectrum, it had revolutionized electronics. And since most of that new knowledge had been created under government sponsorship, and would therefore be available to anyone, the East Coast industry would no longer be able to control the field through patents as it had done before the war. More than ever, they all realized, in the postwar world the secret of success was going to be research.

Terman and the core of electronics veterans he brought back with him from RRL and other wartime laboratories were especially well positioned by their wartime experiences to exploit the most recent advances in microwave electronics. Stanford's traveling-wave tube (TWT) program exemplified the new style of postwar electronics. Perfected at Bell Laboratories during the war by a team that included recent Stanford graduate Lester Field, the TWT offered significant improvements in bandwidth and tuning over other microwave tubes, making it ideal for electronic countermeasures applications. Terman knew about Field's work, recognized its implications, and convinced Field to continue his research back at Stanford.[20] With strong military support, Field rapidly established himself as one of the best researchers in one of the most competitive specialties in postwar electronics. Although on a shoestring budget compared with industrial efforts at Bell and RCA, Field and his students, including such future industry leaders as Dean Watkins and Stanley Kaisel, kept pace with the giants, developing new kinds of TWTs, increasing their power, and reducing their noise levels.[21]

The Sperry klystron group also came back to the West Coast after the war, determined to go into business for themselves. Some, like Marvin Chodorow and Edward Ginzton, joined the university faculty. Others, including Russell Varian, took temporary jobs as research associates. In 1948 they founded Varian Associates to design and manufacture klystrons and other advanced microwave tubes. The company literally got its start at Stanford. Its first board meeting was held on campus, its board of directors included several faculty members, and its first successful product, a tiny reflex klystron for guided missiles, was designed by a faculty consultant.[22]

The Korean War transformed Varian and other fledgling electronic enterprises into big business. The sudden demand for microwave tubes for radar, electronic countermeasures, and communications gave these companies the inside track in securing defense contracts, especially the invaluable research and development contracts that could position them for the lucrative production contracts ahead. California's share of prime military contracts doubled during the course of the war, from 13.2 percent to 26 percent. From 1951 to 1953 California received some $13 billion in prime contracts, overtaking longtime defense contract leader New York State.[23] That windfall represented not so much savvy political maneuvering, as some New York congressmen charged, but rather the success of California aerospace and electronics companies in anticipating, and cultivating, the military market. Most of that money went to southern California aerospace contractors in Los Angeles and San Diego, but Santa Clara County companies won their share, and before the end of the decade would be pushing San Diego for second place.[24]

"Varian's growth during the first decade or so was rapid, primarily military based, and tied in closely with the growth of the aerospace industry," the head of its tube division recalled.[25] Its product line expanded into a full range of klystrons, from low-power models for airborne radar and guided missiles through medium-power versions for mobile communications and radar jamming to very-high-power tubes for radar transmitters, all but a tiny fraction destined for the defense industry. To expand its output, Varian arranged a sizable loan through the Defense Production Administration, plus an additional $1.35 million from the air force for a new small tube manufacturing plant.[26] Meanwhile, Varian's sales climbed from $200,000 in 1949 to $1.5 million two years later to $25 million by the end of the decade, with military tubes accounting for all but a small fraction. Employment soared from 325 in 1951 to 1300 by 1958.[27] Varian strengthened its ongoing ties to the university by signing on as the first tenant of the Stanford Industrial Park, negotiating a long-term lease on university-owned land just south of campus for its research laboratories and its expanding tube department.[28]

Litton's growth paralleled Varian's. Litton did a good business before the war designing and building machinery for manufacturing power vacuum tubes, and, like other tube-related companies, grew dramatically during the early war years. Charles Litton himself spent the war back at Federal Telephone's New Jersey plant making radar tubes. Afterwards, he returned to California and reorganized Litton Industries into a power tube manufacturer with a reputation for delivering high-quality magnetrons at prices bigger companies lost money on.[29] He then sold the company in 1953 to an aggressive group of Hughes expatriates led by Charles "Tex" Thorton, who dramatically expanded the operation to meet the sudden demand for tubes in the national air defense program. In just three years the new managers tripled sales (to $6.2 million) and backlog (to $36 million), and quadrupled employment (to 2115).[30] Like Varian, Litton Industries aimed almost exclusively at the military market, with such products as pulse magnetrons and tunable klystrons for radar and tunable continuous-wave magnetrons for jamming and missile guidance systems.

Eimac, though more commercially diversified than either Varian or Litton, also rode the wave of defense appropriations. It supplied high-power klystrons for virtually every major air defense project—the Dew Line, White Alice, and Pole Vault—tubes for missile tracking, and a truly giant klystron, the X626 (with 1.25 million watts of peak power) for ballistic missile detection.[31] On the strength of those contracts, the company grew to 2600 employees and $29 million in sales by 1959.

Stanford's laboratories continued to spawn innovative start-up companies looking for opportunities to commercialize the latest microwave technologies being developed there. Huggins Laboratories got its start in 1948 when founder R. A. Huggins, a former research associate at the university, put the first traveling-wave tube on the market. With a boost from government R&D contracts, Huggins continued to expand, diversifying into backward-wave oscillators, low-noise TWTs, and electrostatic focused tubes, all based on research done at Stanford. By 1961 Huggins was doing $3.5 million of business a year and among the leaders in the TWT field.[32] Ray Stewart, after a peripatetic early career with Litton and Dalmo Victor, joined Lester Field's group in the late 1940s as a technician, building some of the earliest TWTs. Though essentially self-taught, Stewart decided to try his luck in the market, first with vacuum tube furnaces and vacuum pumps, and then in 1952 with the first commercial backward-wave oscillator.[33] William Ayer, a graduate student in Stanford's Radioscience Laboratory, cofounded Granger Associates (with former RRL and Stanford Research Institute [SRI] researcher John Granger) in 1956 to produce ionospheric sounders and military communications equipment based on designs pioneered at the university. By 1962 Granger Associates was doing $5 million a year in sales.[34] In the meantime, Ayer and another Granger engineer spun off Applied Technologies to concentrate on electronic countermeasures and long-range detecting and monitoring equipment.[35] Its 1961 sales topped $1 million. Stanley Kaisel, yet another Field student, spent two years working on TWTs for RCA, returned to Stanford during the Korean War to run a tube laboratory on a classified countermeasures contract, then took a job with Litton. Convinced that he could make more long-lived and reliable TWTs than what was currently on the market, he and another Litton engineer broke away in 1959 to form Microwave Electronics Corporation (MEC). Initially specializing in low-power, low-noise TWTs for electronic countermeasures, MEC built up $5 million-a-year business with 400 employees by the time it sold out to Teledyne in 1965. Like Granger and Applied Technologies, MEC relocated in the Stanford Industrial Park to cement its academic connections.[36]

Watkins-Johnson was undoubtedly the most financially successful of the new Stanford spinoffs. A former student of Lester Field, Dean Watkins had gone on to Hughes, then essentially swapped places with his mentor in 1953. At Stanford, Watkins led the Stanford TWT research to national prominence over the next few years, especially for work on low-noise TWTs. In 1957 he and former Hughes engineer Richard Johnson cofounded Watkins-Johnson to develop and manufacture microwave tubes for surveillance, reconnaissance, countermeasures, and telemetry, all directly based on the TWT technology Watkins had been perfecting at Stanford. Watkins-Johnson secured its initial financing from the Kern County Land Company, a large real estate and oil holding company looking for profitable investment outlets.[37] Watkins-Johnson immediately started returning money on that investment, turning a profit its first year. Sales rose from $500,000 in 1958 to $4.6 million in 1961 to $9.5 million in 1963 to $16.8 million in 1966, with consistently strong earnings.[38] Watkins-Johnson later acquired both Stewart Engineering and Granger Associates. By the early 1960s a third of the nation's TWT business, and a substantial share of the klystron and magnetron business as well, was located in the Santa Clara Valley, most of it a stone's throw from Stanford.

Response from the East Coast Industrial Establishment

That kind of success naturally attracted the attention of established East Coast companies ready to cash in on the burgeoning military electronics market. By East Coast standards, the West Coast start-ups were still puny. Industry leaders GE and RCA posted 1956 sales of $725 million each. Admiral, Sylvania, Philco, Zenith, Westinghouse, and a dozen other companies had sales of over $100 million. But with half of all electronics sales going to the military that year—$3 billion a year in all—and an increasing share of that going for high-technology equipment for missiles, avionics, and the like, even the most myopic component maker could read the writing on the wall.[39] On average, military electronics was about the same or slightly less profitable than commercial business, about 10 percent on sales. But as *Fortune* pointed out, military electronics nonetheless represented "a whale of a good business," both because the defense market was generally steadier than its commercial counterpart and because military R&D contracts offered an inexpensive entry into new fields and enticing prospects for commercial spin-off.

Sylvania, primarily a manufacturer of television and radio tubes, got its chance to break into the military market in 1953 when the Army Signal Corps offered it a contract to construct a new laboratory for missile countermeasures. The Signal Corps had been considering some kind of facility for "quick reaction capability" (QRC) in electronic warfare since 1949,[40] and, forced into action by the Korean emergency, offered Stanford a $5 million contract in 1952 to develop "engineering test models" of guided missile countermeasures. (All of the missiles in the U.S. and Soviet inventories in those days used radio guidance.) Concerned that any new contract might overwhelm its already taxed resources, Stanford begged off.[41] So the next year, following a formal competition, the Signal Corps awarded Sylvania a $3 million initial contract for studying and designing prototype electronic countermeasures against surface-to-target missiles and proximity fuses, two-thirds of the money for R&D and the rest for quick reaction tasks. The army would equip the laboratory and fund the research, while Sylvania would provide the land and the building and recruit the staff. For the company, the contract represented a quick, and very inexpensive, entry into the military electronics business. For the army, the laboratory represented an important step toward parity with the air force and navy in the missile race.

Although Stanford would not manage the laboratory directly, it nonetheless played a significant role in determining the laboratory's eventual location and research priorities. Sylvania's central research laboratory was then in Bayside, Long Island, New York. The army, however, insisted on a site that would not present such an obvious target. Sylvania knew all about Stanford's expertise in electronic countermeasures. Moreover, the company already had a small tube plant in nearby Mountain View. So Sylvania built its new Electronics Defense Laboratory (EDL) there, close to prospective Stanford faculty consultants and newly graduated engineers. The Signal Corps similarly recognized the advantages of putting the laboratory within Stanford's orbit, where subcontracts for search receivers, converters, special tubes, and other electronic warfare equipment developed by university researchers could more easily be arranged.[42]

Over its first decade, EDL grew into one of the largest electronics enterprises in the valley, with some 1300 employees (including more than 500 scientists and engineers) and annual contracts of $18 million.[43] (It currently has 3500 employees.) From a "captive" Signal Corps laboratory dedicated to missile countermeasures, EDL branched out into tactical countermeasures (against surface-to-air missiles and artillary fuses), and into electronic intelligence (intercepting and interpreting missile telemetry and guidance signals) for all the defense agencies.[44] By 1964 electronic intelligence accounted for two-thirds of the laboratory's revenues. EDL also earned a reputation for its QRC work, notably the spread-spectrum communications gear built, on a month's notice, for the Berlin crisis.[45]

As anticipated, EDL drew extensively on its Stanford connections. It recruited heavily among both research associates and recent graduates. It hired several top faculty members as consultants, including Terman himself. And it became the first participant in the honors cooperative program, Stanford's pioneering effort to encourage more formal collaboration between high-technology enterprise and the university.

Local companies, starting with EDL and Hewlett-Packard, sent their best young engineers back to school part-time for advanced degrees. EDL got better-trained people, plus a direct pipeline to Stanford ideas. By the early 1960s EDL was sending 92 people a year to the program.

Along the way, EDL spun off several laboratories devoted to specific technologies. In 1956 Sylvania set up an independent Microwave Physics Laboratory for advanced research on ferrites and plasma.[46] The next year it established the Reconnaissance Systems Laboratories, specializing in satellite detection and other air force priorities, first in a converted supermarket in downtown Mountain View and later in its own facilities next to EDL.[47] Four EDL engineers broke away in 1956 to form Microwave Engineering Laboratories, initially concentrating on solid-state microwave devices for the military market.[48] And in 1964 EDL director William Perry, frustrated with what he considered home office exploitation of the laboratory, defected, along with a half dozen senior managers, to found Electronic Systems Laboratories (ESL, Inc.) as a direct competitor in electronic intelligence.

General Electric moved west in 1954 looking for ways to enlarge its already considerable share of the defense electronics business by tapping Stanford expertise. GE's Electronics Division had recently established an advanced radar laboratory in Ithaca, New York (on Cornell University land) to assist its heavy military electronics group in Syracuse. At Stanford, it saw a similar opportunity to cash in on academic research in high-power klystrons, TWTs, and other exotic hardware.[49] In 1954 it opened what it called the General Electric Microwave Laboratory at Stanford in the Industrial Park. Like Sylvania, GE hired a number of recent graduates and research associates outright, including coupled-cavity TWT pioneer Erwin Nalos (a former Chodorow student), signed up several faculty consultants, and sent dozens of its most promising engineers to the honors cooperative program.[50] Sixteen of its forty top scientists and engineers had been at one time either graduate students or faculty members at Stanford.[51]

At first the laboratory concentrated almost entirely on elaborating concepts originally developed at the university. Gradually, however, it established its own reputation as a center for work on high-power klystrons and TWTs (for radar systems) and on low-noise TWTs, including the first metal ceramic designs (for electronic countermeasures systems). By 1956 it was bringing in two-thirds of its annual research budget in independent military contracts.[52] It supplied the TWTs for GE's Rainbow, the first frequency diversity radar, the klystrons for the Nike-Hercules radar, the mammoth klystrons for Westinghouse's missile defense system, and the small low-noise TWTs for Sylvania's countermeasures systems.[53] The laboratory doubled in size after its first two years, doubled again a few years later, and then doubled once more, to 336 employees and a $5 million annual budget, by 1958.[54]

Following Sylvania and GE's lead, other East Coast companies established outposts in the area. Sensing the shift in the market, Chicago-based television and radio giant Admiral, which had been supporting a small color television laboratory in Palo Alto since 1952, opened a new laboratory in the Stanford Industrial Park in 1955 for research on radar, guided missiles, and air navigation and communication systems.[55] It later won large air force and navy contracts for designing and manufacturing automatic decoders for identification, friend or foe (IFF) systems.[56] In 1956 Zenith set up a research laboratory nearby, under one of Terman's former group leaders at RRL.[57]

Lockheed Missiles and Space came to the valley in 1956 looking to break into the missiles and space market by breaking out of a corporate culture dominated by airplane enthusiasts. It opened a major manufacturing facility in Sunnyvale and a complementary laboratory complex in the Industrial Park. Significantly, in selecting the Stanford location Lockheed's president stressed the university's reputation in electronics rather than aeronautics. With the increasing complexity and sophistication of guidance and communications systems, Lockheed felt it could no longer rely on outside electronics expertise and would have to develop its own. "To handle these big defense systems involving billions not millions of dollars and covering a multitude of sciences, we must broaden and deepen our competence into fields related to ours," Lockheed's president stressed. "The one I think of as most logical and natural is electronics."[58]

Lockheed's investment paid off immediately and spectacularly. Lockheed Missiles and Space won the Polaris submarine missile contract (initially worth $62 million), from the navy, and the first reconnaissance and surveillance satellite contracts from the CIA and the air force.[59] On the strength of those projects, Lockheed's employment soared from 200 in 1956 to 9000 in 1958 to 25,000 in 1964 (with 1200 in the research laboratories alone), making Lockheed, by an order of magnitude, the biggest employer in the valley.

Lockheed provided a crucial catalyst for further high-technology growth. Lured by the prospects of lucrative subcontracts for the ground support and tracking network for the air force satellite programs, Philco broke ground for its multimillion-dollar Western Development Laboratories (WDL) in Palo Alto in 1957. About 90 percent of its sales in the early years came from air force contracts for satellite tracking and command systems.[60] WDL later won a Signal Corps contract for Courier, the first active-repeater communications satellite, a $31 million army contract for a worldwide teletype and high-speed digital data communications system, and a $25 million contract for a Department of Defense (DOD) communications satellite network.[61] These and other contracts pushed WDL employment to 2500 by 1960. Ford, frankly looking for a toehold in the defense and space business, bought Philco the next year and made WDL the core of its new aerospace division.[62] Under Ford, WDL continued to be a major player in the satellite business, winning additional large contracts for communications satellites, antenna systems, and the NASA flight control center in Houston.

The aerospace industry offered opportunities for smaller companies as well. Four local scientists founded Vidya in 1959 to conduct supersonic wind tunnel tests on the Polaris nose cones. Itek, the Massachusetts-based antenna manufacturer, bought out Applied Technology to give it a West Coast presence. Link Aviation, the Binghamton-based flight simulator manufacturer, shifted its advanced engineering laboratory to Palo Alto in 1957, adding a line of simulators for guided missiles. Kaiser Aerospace relocated to the Industrial Park a few years later. Even local tape maker Ampex found a booming new market for its recording systems in reconnaissance satellites and guided missiles.

When Fairchild Semiconductor was still just Robert Noyce and two dozen bright young engineers, the Undersecretary of Commerce was calling Santa Clara County the "microwave capital" of the world.[63] Indeed, by 1960 it had already become the center of an aerospace complex rooted in microwave electronics technology for reconnaissance, communications, and countermeasures, with its main trunk at Lockheed Missiles and Space and the adjoining Air Force Satellite Control Facility (or the Blue Cube)[64] and its branches extending in all directions. Electronics Defense Laboratory director William Perry caught something of how the corporate components of this complex intertwined:

> We are continually demanding microwave tube performance beyond the state of the art. We were one of the companies pushing that industry to get more and more bandwidth, more and more power, more and more ease of tuning. So there were an amazing set of technical developments going on in tubes at that time and they were being driven by electronic countermeasures companies.[65]

Similarly, Watkins-Johnson bought low-noise tubes from GE's microwave laboratory, reverse-engineered them, and then brought out its own. Those tubes and others like them went into the systems Sylvania was building for Lockheed's satellites, and into the communications and tracking gear being designed by Philco's Western Development Laboratories. Microwave tubes provided the "linchpins" for virtually every contemporary military electronics system, from radar to electronic warfare. And not just anyone could build them. The biggest cost upwards of $200,000 each, and took such skill to manufacture properly that insiders liked to say that to get one right "you pray over it, you nurse it, you make love to it."[66]

Hard Times in the Valley

The aerospace complex prospered in the post-Sputnik defense boom, but at the cost of increased isolation from the commercial world outside. GE's Microwave Laboratory never really found a place for itself in the larger corporation. Other divisions, lacking experience in the microwave tube art, could never satisfactorily duplicate TWTs and other tubes based on the laboratory's designs. From the perspective of GE's power tube division, the laboratory's corporate parent, high-power microwave tubes offered limited commercial possibilities. So rather than using the laboratory to break into new high-technology markets, upper management turned it instead to "putting out fires for other manufacturing divisions."[67] Dissatisfied with that role, many of the best engineers left for more promising opportunities elsewhere, some of them right next door. By 1965 the GE Microwave Laboratory staff was down to 170, less than half its peak strength.

Sylvania similarly failed to capitalize on EDL. Although the division itself remained profitable, it developed only the most tenuous connections with the rest of the corporation. GTE bought out Sylvania in 1960, in part to acquire a central laboratory for its telephone business. Despite some attempts to spin off commercial technologies, including electronic security systems, testing devices for telephone headsets, industrial lasers, and even a Sociosystems Products division, GTE Government Systems (as it was renamed) remained too specialized and too expensive to compete in the civilian world. "The government doesn't train us to do things cheaply," one senior scientist explained.[68] While continuing to do 90 percent or more of its business with the military,[69] GTE also tried to set up a separate commercial laboratory in Palo Alto, a "miniature Bell Telephone Laboratories for serving the GT & E system, and financed at least in part from telephone revenues,"[70] and, surprisingly enough, hired the recently retired Chief Signal Officer to organize and run it. GTE's operating divisions, convinced that such an enterprise was unlikely to contribute much to their mission, immediately backed out, and put their money into the old Bayside laboratories instead.

One by one, the transplants to the valley shut down or sold out. Admiral closed its Palo Alto laboratory in 1964 and sent the 100 remaining researchers back to Chicago,[71] as did Zenith. Sylvania sold off its TWT division to Microwave Electronics and its ferrite components division to MELabs to concentrate on its core defense business. Varian, looking to make up lost ground in the TWT market, bought up what was left of the GE Microwave Laboratory in 1966 and merged it with its tube division.[72]

With the conspicuous exception of Hewlett-Packard, which had always concentrated on commercial technologies, the remaining microwave electronics companies never really cracked the civilian market. Varian diversified into analytical instruments and medical electronics, as did a few of its local competitors, but none of them managed to break their essential dependence on defense contracts, or on the culture of classified projects and security clearances that sustained those contracts. Like Lockheed itself, which virtually abandoned the civilian market altogether, they staked their futures on the procurement policies of the national security establishment.

Nor did the microwave electronics companies make the transition to the semiconductor business—again with the conspicuous exception of Hewlett-Packard—although their experiences served as the prototype for the integration of academic, corporate, and military R&D behind Silicon Valley's later takeoff. Some of these companies served as important customers for the emerging semiconductor industry, mostly for specialized military devices; others, recognizing the growing importance of solid-state devices for their own businesses, built up semiconductor expertise in-house. Most lost at least some of their best engineers to the semiconductor start-ups, since in those days no one knew more about electron physics than the tube specialists. But none of them cashed in on the chip bonanza that gave Silicon Valley its name and reputation.

The Silicon Valley Model?

Back in 1965, as Silicon Valley was just beginning to take off, Bell Laboratories president James Fisk cautioned against placing too much confidence on this model of industrial competitiveness. Thanks to "intense federal subsidy of electronics, space vehicle and guidance operations, communications and computer programs," places like Silicon Valley and Route 128 (Massachusetts) appeared to be seedbeds of innovation. But the innovations spawned there, however important for the national defense, would not necessarily translate into "the sort of enduring, economically productive high employment industries which are the backbone of this nation," he warned. "We believe it would be inaccurate and probably eventually dangerous to persist in the presumption that this is the way to start and maintain important industrial innovation."[73] What America really needed to compete were policies aimed at strengthening and revitalizing older industries as well as creating new ones. And that could not be done by following a model of industrial development that "depends so heavily on federal subsidy as do these classic spinoffs from the universities."

In the short run, Fisk was wrong. If few of the original electronics companies in the valley succeeded in breaking their dependence on federal subsidy, second- and third-generation companies often did, sometimes in spectacular fashion. But even they could not seem to master the "missing consumer connection" dividing the high-tech world of Silicon Valley from the larger world of consumer electronics,[74] no doubt in part because that connection had never been an integral part of Silicon Valley. Consequently, as Fish had foreseen, Silicon Valley could not by itself revitalize America's basic industries, or restore American competitiveness.

Notes

1. Dirk Hansen, *The New Alchemists: Silicon Valley and the Microelectronics Revolution* (Boston: Little, Brown, 1982).

2. Michael Malone, *The Big Score: The Billion Dollar Story of Silicon Valley* (New York: Doubleday, 1985).

3. Everett Rogers and Judith Larsen, *Silicon Valley Fever: Growth and High Technology Culture* (New York: Basic Books, 1982).

4. A. Markusen, P. Hall, S. Campbell, and S. Deitrick, *The Rise of the Gunbelt: The Military Remapping of Industrial America* (New York: Oxford University Press, 1991) makes a strong case for seeing cold war industrial policy as a deliberate strategy of the Pentagon and its corporate contractors. While I am not convinced of the intentions, I am convinced of the implications they describe.

5. Richard Florida and Martin Kenney, *The Breakthrough Illusion: Corporate America's Failure to Move from Innovation to Mass Production* (New York: Basic Books, 1990) challenge the appropriateness of the Silicon Valley model on the grounds of its present difficulties in exploiting innovation, without attention to either the character or pattern of that innovation.

6. Arthur L. Norberg, "The origins of the electronics industry on the Pacific coast," *Proc. IEEE*, Vol. 64, No. 9, September 1976, pp. 1314–1322, is the best account of the early West Coast radio industry.

7. See Hugh Aitken, *The Continuous Wave: Technology and American Radio, 1900–1932* (Princeton, N.J.: Princeton Univ. Press, 1985), pp. 233–246.

8. Norberg, *Proc. IEEE*, op. cit., pp. 1318–1319; ———, "Eitel-McCullough, Inc.," *Microwave J.*, August 1960, pp. 85–90.

9. The best sketch of Terman's early career is A. Michal McMahon, *The Making of a Profession: A Century of Electrical Engineering in America* (New York: IEEE Press, 1984), pp. 183–87.

10. Edward Ginzton, "The $100 idea," *IEEE Spectrum*, Vol. 10, February 1975, pp. 30–39, recounts the origins of the klystron.

11. Peter Galison, Bruce Hevly, and Rebecca Lowen, "Controlling the monster: Stanford and the growth of physics research, 1935–1962," in *Big Science: The Growth of Large Scale Research*, P. Galison and B. Hevly, eds.,(Palo Alto, Calif.: Stanford Univ. Press, 1991) pp. 46–77, offers the best account of this episode.

12. See John Bryant, "Microwave technology and careers in transition: The interests and activities of visitors to the Sperry Gyroscope Company's klystron plant in 1939–40," *IEEE Trans. Microwave Theory Tech.*, Vol. MTT-38, November 1990, pp. 1545–1558.

13. See Norberg, *Proc. IEEE*, op. cit., p. 1319, for details on Eitel-McCullough's production innovations.

14. Norberg, *Proc. IEEE*, ibid., p. 1321.

15. *The Microwave Journal*, "Hewlett-Packard Company," October 1959, pp. 56–57.

16. *The Microwave Journal*, "Eitel-McCullough, Inc.," August 1960, pp. 85–86.

17. F. Terman to H. Laun, December 17, 1953, Stanford University Archives, Frederick Terman Papers (hereafter cited as SAFT) series V, box 6, file 13.

18. F. Terman to H. Skilling, June 20, 1944, SAFT, Series I, box 1, file 11.

19. F. Terman, "Dean's Report, School of Engineering, 1946–47," Stanford University Archives, S.E. Wallace Sterling Papers, box 39, School of Engineering file.

20. *Stanford Engineering News*, "Stanford Electronics attracts national attention: The traveling wave tube," Vol. 6, May 1950.

21. On the technical contributions of the Stanford program, see S. E. Harris and J. S. Harris, "Stanford University Electronics Laboratory and Microwave-Ginzton Laboratory," in *Fortieth Anniversary of the Joint Services Electronics Program* (Arlington, VA: ANSER, 1986), pp. 104 *ff*.

22. For the early history of Varian Associates, see Dorothy Varian, *The Pilot and the Inventor*. Palo Alto, Calif.: Pacific Press, 1983.

23. James Clayton, "Defense spending: Key to California's growth," *West. Polit. Q.*, Vol. 15, 1962, pp. 280–293.

24. Clayton, *West. Polit. Q.*, ibid., p. 286.

25. *Varian: 25 Years, 1948–1973* (Palo Alto, Calif., 1973), p. 15.

26. Varian Associates Minute Books, June 3, 1951 and October 7, 1952.

27. Varian Minute Books, January 22, 1960; also, *Varian: 25 Years, 1948–1973*, p. 14.

28. Henry Lowood, "From steeples of excellence to Silicon Valley," *Stanford Campus Report* (March 9, 1988), pp. 11–13, provides the best history of the Industrial Park.

29. F. Terman to H. Laun, November 5, 1953, SAFT, Series V, box 6, file 13.

30. Litton Industries, Quarterly Fiscal Report, 1956–57, Bancroft Library, C. Litton Papers, box 75, file 7c.

31. *The Microwave Journal*, op. cit., pp. 86–87.

32. *The Microwave Journal*, "Huggins Laboratories, Inc.," February 1961, pp. 109–112.

33. Adelaide Paine, "Ray Stewart," *Microwave J.*, November 1962, pp. 35–39.

34. David Simon, "Dr. John Van Nuys Granger," *Microwave J.*, June 1960, pp. 25–29.

35. F. Terman to W. Cooley, April 24, 1959, SAFT, series V, box 7, file 7; also *The Microwave Journal*, "Applied Technology, Inc.," June 1961, pp. 122–24.

36. Adelaide Paine, "Stanley F. Kaisel," *Microwave J.*, December 1962, pp. 19–26; also *The Microwave Journal*, "MEC," August 1963, pp. 120–27.

37. F. Terman to W. Cooley, December 11, 1957, SAFT, series V, box 7, file 6.

38. Watkins-Johnson Company, Prospectus, June 18, 1964.

39. William B. Harris, "The electronics business," *Fortune*, April 1957, pp. 139–141.

40. "Briefing on Department of Army Quick Reaction Capability in Electronic Warfare," n.d., U.S. Army Communications-Electronics Command Archives, Fort Monmouth, N.J.

41. Donald Harris, "Countermeasures-guided missiles Signal Corps contract," June 2, 1952, SAFT, series V, box 17, file 11.

42. F. F. Urhane to Chief, Engineering and Technical Division, Office of the Chief Signal Officer, September 17, 1953, U.S. Army Communications-Electronics Command, Fort Monmouth, N.J.

43. S. J. Schulman, "EDL—Yesterday and Today," September 14, 1964, U.S. Army Communications-Electronics Command, Fort Monmoth, N.J.

44. Author interview with William Perry, August 21, 1991.

45. Robert A. Scholtz, "The origins of spread-spectrum communications," *IEEE Trans. Commun. Electron.*, Vol. 30, No. 5, May 1982, pp. 822–854.

46. Adelaide Paine, "Dr. Romayne Whitmet," *Microwave J.*, June 1962, pp. 37–42.

47. Author interview with Meyer Leifer and Walter Sernuik, May 21, 1991.

48. *The Microwave Journal*, "MELabs, Inc.," July 1959, pp. 44–47; also Adelaide Paine, "Microwave People—Dr. Wesley P. Ayres," *Microwave J.*, July 1963, pp. 30–34 + .

49. F. Terman to W. Cooley, May 2, 1955, SA SC 160 V 7/5.

50. Author interview with Erwin Nalos, August 1991.

51. Hugh Enochs, 1958, "The first fifty years of electronics research," *Tall Tree*, Vol. 1, No. 9, Palo Alto Chamber of Commerce, Palo Alto, Calif., May, p. 34.

52. General Electric Microwave Laboratory at Stanford, Proposed 1956 Project Budget, Erwin Nalos Papers.

53. Author interview with Chester Lob, August 22, 1991.

54. F. Terman to W. Cooley, April 9, 1958, SA SC 160 V 7/7.

55. Hugh Enochs, 1958, op. cit., p. 36.

56. F. Terman to J. Hawkinson, November 1, 1963, SA SC 160 V 7/9.

57. F. Terman to W. Cooley, March 1, 1956, SA SC 160 V 7/6.

58. A. W. Jessup, *Aviation Week*, "Lockheed attune to USAF warning, plans expansion in avionics," July 8, 1957, pp. 29–30.

59. Herbert York and G. Allen Greb, "Strategic reconnaissance," *Bull. At. Sci.*, April 1977, pp. 33–42.

60. Robert Lindsey, "Philco division completes reorientation," *Missiles Rockets*, June 15, 1964, p. 28.

61. Philip Siekman, "Henry Ford and his electronic can of worms," *Fortune*, February 1966, p. 119.

62. *Time*, "Marriage of the giants," September 22, 1961, p. 112.

63. Hugh Enochs, op. cit., p. 30.

64. James Schultz, "Inside the Blue Cube," *Defense Electron.*, April 1983, pp. 52–58.

65. Author interview with William Perry, August 21, 1991.

66. Author interview with Chester Lob, August 22, 1991.

67. F. Terman to J. Hawkinson, February 1, 1966, SAFT, Series V, box 7, file 12.

68. Author interview with Nelson Blachman, August 21, 1991.

69. Paul Voakes, "Sylvania one of the first in the valley—25 years ago," *Palo Alto Times*, July 18, 1978.

70. F. Terman to J. Hawkinson, November 30, 1962, SAFT, series V, box 7, file 9.

71. F. Terman to J. Hawkinson, February 3, 1964, SAFT, series V, box 7, file 9.

72. F. Terman to J. Hawkinson, February 1, 1966, SAFT, series V, box 7, file 12.

73. James Fisk, "The new role of graduate education in industrial innovation" Bell Laboratories, Murray Hill, NJ: W. O. Baker Papers, November 3, 1965.

74. Florida and Kenney, *The Breakthrough Illusion*, pp. 125–126, emphasize this missing link as a key element in America's recent failures in consumer electronics and other industries.

Big Science, Competitiveness, and the Great Chain of Being

Robert W. Smith

During the 1980s in the United States, issues of Big Science and national competitiveness became entwined as advocates of Big Science projects increasingly sought to justify them to patrons in the White House and Congress in terms of competitiveness. I shall examine this aspect of U.S. public policy and what it has to say about the discourses on Big Science and competitiveness, discourses in which to a large extent the role of technology has been treated as unproblematic and in certain ways as invisible. I shall therefore also touch upon changing ideas among policymakers and those who spend government money on the appropriate role of government in technological innovation.[1] In particular, I shall point to the continued exploitation of the "technology as applied science" model despite the fact that the underpinnings of the model have long been exploded by historians of technology.

Definitions

But to clear the ground for the later discussion, I turn first to the issue of definitions. Both of the terms in the title of the chapter have come to assume a wide, often muddied, and still shifting set of meanings. A recent report by the Office of Technology Assessment, for example, notes that Big Science "can mean large and expensive facilities. It can refer to large, multidisciplinary team efforts that entail cooperative planning and therefore require individual scientists to sacrifice some freedom in choosing goals and methods. Or it can refer to bureaucratic central management by government administrators."[2] The common equation of Big Science—that big bucks plus a big machine equals Big Science—is also flawed. Users of very expensive and big machines can certainly work in the spirit of small-scale science. For example, in

90

the case of the International Ultraviolet Explorer, an international astronomical satellite launched in 1977 that cost well over $100 million to build, the users have to a very large degree followed the methods of small-scale science. A definition of Big Science that centers on money *and* scientific and technical practice is therefore a much more useful historical tool.[3] Of course, not only has Big Science implied somewhat different things to different users of the term, but it has also taken on different meanings at different times. When a historical actor of the late 1960s refers to Big Science, he or she is not referring to the same historical phenomenon as a historical actor of the early 1990s.

With these warnings in mind and for the purposes of this chapter, I shall take Big Science to mean very expensive projects that are directed toward the production of scientific results and that involve large multidisciplinary teams, not only for the building of the technologies for Big Science but also their use. In Big Science, the design and construction of the technologies that make the science possible have been very largely the task of industrial contractors. Their resources and expertise have indeed generally been essential. The costs of Big Science are also so high that the federal government has almost invariably been the sponsor of such endeavors. Designing, building, and funding the tools of Big Science have thus engaged the horizontal association or cooperation of different sectors of society: government, industry, and academe.

As seen in other papers in this volume, the meaning and use of the word "competitiveness" has also shifted, as has its rhetorical power. National, or industrial, or technological competitiveness have taken on a variety of meanings in their employment by economists, public officials, and others. Competitiveness has thus proved an elusive concept that cannot be reduced to any one variable. There is, nevertheless, a growing agreement among economists that an industry or firm is competitive if it is capable of maintaining its share of existing markets or of conquering new ones.

At this point it is also worth emphasizing that it is only quite recently that technology has begun to find a place in economists' analyses of international trade. The previous dominant approach was that of those who dealt with competitiveness in terms of wage and price rates. Neoclassical theory claimed that technological differences could be understood by so-called production factors that were taken to be identical throughout the world, and so in this way technology, in effect, disappeared.[4] Some economists, however, have more recently taken a very different tack. François Chesnais, for example, stresses the role of the state in the constitution and maintenance of a national productive system: "This structure is based on the technical system (a concept developed by Bertrand Gille), a key factor in the determination of inter-industry relations. In this network of interdependencies, the manufacturing of industrial machinery determines the structural base of competitive national economies."[5]

The Great Chain of Being

The two terms, Big Science and competitiveness, have been widely and explicitly linked in the last decade. Those doing the linking have claimed or accepted that the pursuit of various Big Science projects increases competitiveness. For example, in the recent debates on whether or not the federal government should support the Superconducting Supercollider—a multibillion-dollar high-energy physics accelerator—the project has been portrayed by advocates in the executive branch, the congress, and the scientific community as an investment in industrial competitiveness. Such debates have now taken on a particular edge for two reasons. First, such Big Science projects have been slated to absorb large chunks of the new discretionary spending in the federal budget. Second, these machines and systems have become for many Americans *the* symbols of the cutting edge of American technology, surrogates for national technical prowess.[6] In 1989, during the House floor debate on the Superconducting Supercollider, one representative termed it an "investment in the new wealth of tomorrow." Another, anxious about Japanese gains in high technology, called the Supercollider "an opportunity to gain that technology back," while a colleague urged "Vote yes for America's future."[7] When the Mayor of Waxahachie, Texas—the site of the Superconducting Supercollider—tells us of mankind's need to find out whether or not an exotic subatomic particle such as the Higgs boson exists, we can legitimately question the sincerity of the claim.[8] But while some of these claims are paper-thin disguises for pork-barrel politics, surely the same cannot be said for all of them.

Such demands and pleas for major national investments in Big Science enterprises, when meant seriously, immediately engage the debate over the relationship between science and technology. Historians of technology have long dismissed the vision of technology as merely applied science, and have generally embraced the view of technology as knowledge instead. In his excellent 1985 review of the relationship between science and technology, George Wise made particular reference to a 1972 meeting at the Burndy Library, the proceedings of which were published four years later in *Technology and Culture*. This meeting, Wise argued, was an extended "funeral" for the old technology-as-applied-science view.[9]

But such a view has been a central justification for the federal support of science since World War II and it has proved extremely robust. One image it conjures up is of a pool of scientific knowledge from which those who thirst after technological innovations can drink. Adding new knowledge to the pool increases the chances of additional technological advances.[10] I am of course not denying that science can be immensely important for new technologies. As, for example, Braun and McDonald argued in *Revolution in Miniature*, "the technology of semiconductor electronics is distinguished by its very great dependence on science. Perhaps more than any other innovation, modern electronics owes its existence to science; it is truly an innovation based on science."[11] What historians of technology do dispute is the notion that basic science runs naturally and in an orderly way to applied science and thence to development and commercial applications, and that the process is somehow inevitable. George Wise characterized this vision of the relationship between basic science and technology as the assembly line model. It is also the argument that Derek deSolla Price derisively referred to as the great chain of being. Later in the chapter I shall draw together some of the criticisms made of this argument.

The Promotion of Technology

In order to provide a context for the later discussion, I shall first sketch briefly the changing ideas on the federal government's role in the promotion of novel technology. In the late 1940s, the major figures and framers of federal postwar science and technology policy felt little need to push innovation and commercialization. Neither the Bush Report nor the Truman administration's 1947 Steelman Report paid much attention to industrial innovation. The Steelman Report was nevertheless closer to New Deal political thinking than the more famous Bush Report. Even so it envisaged only a limited role for government.[12] As Bruce Smith has argued, it called for constant innovation so that American industry could keep ahead of growing foreign competition. How was this to be accomplished? The answer was "by making sure the United States maintained overall scientific and technological leadership through a strong effort in basic and applied research and the education of high-quality scientists and engineers. Market forces would ensure that research resulted in products, economic growth, and jobs. Entrepreneurs rather than government planners should guide investment."[13] America's industrial history, it was argued, showed that the economy would generate innovations fast enough without the need for explicit policies. For policymakers in the late 1940s, as Harvey Brooks has expressed it, "technology was essentially the application of leading-edge science and that, if the country created and sustained a first-class science establishment based primarily in the universities, new technology for national security, economic growth, job creation, and social welfare would be generated almost automatically without explicit policy attention to all the other complementary aspects of innovation."[14]

Although there were various special cases before the early 1960s, the first really broad efforts to foster the commercialization of civilian technology as a matter of public policy started in the early 1960s in the Kennedy administration. Disturbed by a sluggish economy, in the summer of 1962 Kennedy established a Cabinet Committee on Growth. At the time, the president's science advisers were examining the same issues. The major conclusions of the two groups were very similar. In their opinion, the mechanism of the marketplace had successfully fostered innovation, but flaws in the market were becoming apparent. As Smith has noted:

> Some firms were portrayed as short-sighted and lacking the expertise to estimate the benefits of investing in new technologies. Others could make accurate, short-run benefit-cost calculations but could not take into account industry wide or society wide effects that would come from the adoption of new processes or products. This problem was exacerbated because the federal government, by monopolizing many of the nation's best scientists and engineers in the defense and space programs, diminished the pool of talent available to civil technology. Committing resources to research and development in defense and space science was appropriate but contributed little directly to economic growth. More efforts were therefore needed to stimulate civilian technology and expand the pool of talent so that the government's own programs would not be a brake on economic expansion.[15]

(As an aside, it is worth noting that while the reports differed a little, they did agree that the needs of defense and civil technology were in conflict.)

To address these perceived problems, the administration formed the Civilian Industrial Technology program, the first of many government initiatives to stimulate innovation in the civilian economy. The program, however, was defeated in the Congress by the very industries it was supposed to help. But it was, after modifications, reborn in the Johnson administration as the State Technical Services Act, in which guise it emphasized the exchange of technical information and consultation among industry, the universities, and state governments.[16]

There were other, related efforts during the Kennedy and Johnson Administrations. As Michal McMahon has shown, one came in the form of NASA's attempt to reshape the space agency's university program, a reshaping that sought to merge organizational and technological systems so as to achieve, in the words of an M.I.T. engineer, "inventions on schedule."[17] For NASA administrator James Webb, the goal was multidisciplinary research, to be brought about by gathering different disciplines to work in parallel within a center so as to stimulate cross-fertilization. The research was also to be interdisciplinary. It would involve researchers from different disciplines working together toward a common goal. "Webb," McMahon argued, "also wanted to use NASA to stimulate the universities to more actively transfer their knowledge to industry and to local governments working with community and social problems. This was an aspect of NASA's fervent desire to see more technological spin-offs from the space program."[18] But Webb and NASA ended up disappointed. By the standards set out in agreements between NASA and the universities, the program was a failure. It was axed by the Bureau of the Budget in 1970.

Justifying Big Science

During the rest of the 1960s, the 1970s, and the 1980s, in all administrations, there were other moves by the federal government to stimulate technological innovation. But of central concern for this chapter is that at roughly the same time as the national policy on technology and innovation shifted in the early 1960s, there was also a shift in the way advocates talked about Big Science projects.

In the early 1960s physical scientists usually had not felt driven to make direct claims to Congress about the technological spin-offs of Big Science research. Arguing for increased funding for the multi-hundred-million-dollar Stanford Linear Accelerator in 1964, its director stated that: "I am not of the school who tries to defend this kind of work through its byproducts. I believe if you want the byproduct, you should develop the byproduct. I think you would do it more economically and do it more effectively. If you want to push high powered radio tubes, then the best way to do so is to push high powered radio tubes and not to build accelerators which require high powered radio tubes."[19]

Big science for the sake of Big Science was hardly enough to sell really large-scale scientific projects in the late 1960s or during the 1970s. In the mid-1970s, for example, the scientific promise of the Space Telescope was simply not sufficient to win federal funding. While NASA was ostensibly selling in its public testimonies a scientific instrument of potentially prodigious power, Congress and the executive branch were buying much more, and the telescope advocates (among NASA, astronomers, and industry) had shaped the arguments Congress was buying.[20]

In seeking to justify the Telescope in 1975, for instance, NASA administrator James Fletcher told a congressional hearing that

> . . . the benefits of astronomy are generally longer term than some of the others we talked about. On the other hand, they are far-reaching in their impact. The benefit from Galileo's experiments was literally the industrial revolution. How can you put a figure on that? . . . There could be brand new energy sources downstream, just as nuclear energy came out of Einstein's investigations. By the way, that was astronomy too. The whole idea of relativity came out of astronomy."

When his congressional questioners pressed him to quantify the possible benefits, Fletcher responded that "Even though you try to put probabilities on realizing benefits, even if it is only 5 to 10 per cent, we are not talking about billions or trillions of dollars, we are talking about the salvation of the world."[21]

A Lockheed Missiles and Space Company document from 1975 that was used by advocates to sell the Space Telescope argued:

> Important as the direct benefits of the [Space Telescope's] investigations are apt to be, the program will also provide several more immediate but less apparent economic benefits. Many economists agree that advances in technology constitute a prime source of economic growth and increased productivity . . . It is also generally recognized that today this nation's ability to maintain a favorable balance of trade depends to a significant degree upon the pace of our technological developments. Today's science is tomorrow's technology, and advanced technology may well be the only unique product the U.S. has to export. The National Science Foundation has pointed out that high-technology products represent the only category of exports in recent years that have maintained a favorable trade balance.
>
> The technological demands of a program such as [Space Telescope] will thus contribute to economic growth by providing a basis for increasing productivity and the maintenance of trade balances.[22]

If we move forward to the 1980s, the arrival of Ronald Reagan in the White House caused some alarm among advocates of federally supported basic research. Milton Friedman, for example, proposed major cuts in the National Science Foundation budget as a step toward the Foundation's abolition.[23] He was also supposed to have the ear of the incoming administration. But Reagan's rhetoric about the evils of big government did not mesh with the actions of his administration in the field of science policy. A more reliable guide to the administration's science policy would turn out to be a Heritage Institute study that stressed how central basic scientific research was to the nation's future.[24] As David Dickson has pointed out, this study was delivered to the incoming Reagan administration shortly after the 1980 election. It provided economic and cultural reasons to support science, and argued that "in a study filled with accounts of federal program failures it is refreshing to find an area filled with spectacular success—space and general science."[25]

In the last year of the Reagan administration the explicit linking of science and competitiveness, most strikingly Big Science and competitiveness, had become national policy. "The administration," Smith notes, "having backed off from its earlier plans for a more selective pattern of research support, now embraced scientific advance as the answer to the lagging productivity rate and the nation's problems of economic competitiveness. It invoked the unexpected synergies of research, along with the need to have patience and to avoid excessive 'targeting' so that long term benefits and spillover effects from research could be realized."[26] We thus see again the great chain of being argument, with Big Science portrayed as Big Business by another route. (Of course, there are many similarities between the two: scale, organizational complexity, costs, and technologies.) But at the same time, government-funded Big Science had become a very powerful symbol of national technical prowess, a point that I think helps to explain the outpouring of anger and confusion over the Space Telescope's flawed mirror discovered shortly after it was launched into space in 1990.

In recent years, then, the economic arguments deployed to justify Big Science projects have intensified. But as Michael Reagan and others have long pointed out, the kind of arguments used to link basic science and technology are similar to arguments made in classic economics. For classic economists, there was a hidden hand at work that translated the pursuit of individual self-interest into the pursuit of the general good. The hidden hand was identified with the mechanism of the marketplace. The Big Science/Competitiveness arguments have followed the same sort of structure. If scientists remain free to pursue their calling as they see fit, to satisfy their intellectual curiosity about nature, their efforts would inevitably—and without need for conscious intent on their part—contribute to the general good. Whereas classic economists had pointed to the marketplace as the hidden hand, the scientists and their advocates point to no such mechanism.[27] The impression given is that

> if one scatters a handful of basic research findings out among several industries and an assortment of engineers, and adds to that some open ended funding, one can guarantee technological success. On the contrary, there are a myriad of other issues and influences that can float or sink the technological boat. To mention just a few we know that tax policy, patent policy, availability of venture capital, antitrust laws, technological literacy in the workforce, industrial productivity, and innovation, are all factors of significant influence.[28]

Rather than attempt to break down the "Big Science equals increased competitiveness" arguments further, let me just focus on one version of this, that increasing national competitiveness arises from the novel technologies constructed to make the Big Science possible. A crucial point here is that Big Science projects cost so much that their advocates have generally been driven to be conservative in their choices of technology. One of the standard arguments made in favor of Big Science projects is in fact that they will rely on proven technology. In effect, existing technology has to be deployed to sell the project to the White House and Congress in the first place.

Hence the emphasis in building the technologies for Big Science has been on engineering ingenuity in devising new arrangements for existing technologies, not on making radical innovations. This is certainly not to say that such problems are straightforward, but it was not, for example, the experts in superconducting magnets at the national accelerator labs who made the recent breakthroughs in high-temperature superconductors.[29] The Hubble Space Telescope is also a combination of very well-established technologies.

One exception to this rule are the small electronic devices for detecting light known as charge-coupled devices (CCDs) carried in one of the Telescope's scientific instruments. But the development of CCDs for astronomy has been piggybacked onto commercial and military needs, not the other way around. The story of the CCDs is a very interesting one, but here I will say only that the concept that underlies them and its practical demonstration were achieved at Bell Labs in 1969. Three main U.S. companies developed the capacity to manufacture the CCDs: Texas Instruments, RCA, and Fairchild. The early development was driven by (1) the military and (2) the companies themselves, since they were interested in the potential of CCDs, in particular, for the home market. By the early 1980s, the only CCDs being manufactured in the United States were on a small scale for specialist scientific markets, while the manufacture of chips for commercial use had become dominated by Japan.[30]

Conclusion

In 1985, George Wise argued that the refutation of the assembly line model stands as a major contribution of historians to the discussion of the relation between science and technology in modern America. He nevertheless conceded that the evidence of the thinking of policymakers on the model was ambiguous. I think it is clearer now. For historians the message is not encouraging. In the realm of Big Science, the assembly line model, while it does not have complete sway, has in fact prospered on Capitol Hill and at the White House. In the face of such claims by advocates of Big Science, the arguments advanced by historians have often failed to be heard or have been brushed aside.

American policymakers have thus chosen to pin so much faith on huge government-sponsored projects; but none of the recently established projects for Big Science facilities seem to have much to do with industrial innovation or productivity, whatever the advocates might insist.[31] To analyze this situation, a French observer of the American scene, Jean-Claude Derian, has made use of the simile of technology as a mirage. "To Derian the mirage is something promising that becomes increasingly inaccessible—the brass ring that always remains just out of reach. But Americans have grasped that ring and flung it around the moon. We built the industries that set the target for others to challenge."[32] The American problem, long-time observer and analyst of American science and technology, Lewis Branscomb, has suggested, is not that the technology remains out of reach: "The problem is that the government's technology strategies and the management of the program have lacked precision, integrity, and discipline."[33] Justifying Big Science on the basis of the assembly line model of technology is, at best, one part of that lack of precision, and, at worst, integrity.

Acknowledgments

I would like to thank Paul Ceruzzi and Stuart W. Leslie for their helpful comments on an earlier version of this paper.

Notes

1. In what follows, I shall also restrict my comments to Big Science associated with the physical sciences; for example, with the burgeoning of biotechnology industries, the situation for the biological sciences is different.

2. Office of Technology Assessment, *Mapping our Genes. The Genome Projects: How Big, How Fast* (Washington, D.C.: U.S. Government Printing Office, 1988), p. 125.

3. See Robert W. Smith, "The biggest kind of big science: astronomers and the Space Telescope," in *Big Science*, P. Galison and B. Hevly, eds., (Palo Alto, Calif.: Stanford University Press, 1992), 184–211.

4. See Jorge Niosi, Introduction, pp. xv–xix, and François Chesnais, "Technological competitiveness considered as a form of structural competitiveness," pp. 142–176, in *Technology and National Competitiveness, Oligopoly, Technological Innovation, and International Competition*, J. Niosi, ed., (Montreal and Kingston: 1991).

5. See Niosi, *Technology and National Competitiveness, ibid.*, p. xvii. Gille's concept of technical system seems similar in certain respects to Thomas Hughes's ideas of heterogeneous engineering: see, for example, Thomas P. Hughes, "The seamless web: technology, science, etcetera, etcetera," *Soc. Studies Sci.*, Vol. 16, 1986, pp. 281–292; also, ———, 1983, *Networks of Power: Electrification in Western Society, 1880–1930* (Baltimore, Md.: The Johns Hopkins University Press, 1983).

6. This point is made by Lewis Branscomb in his Foreward to Jean-Claude Derian's *America's Struggle for Leadership in Technology* (Cambridge, Mass.: 1990), pp. vii–x, vii.

7. *Washington Post*, "Supercosts of the supercollider," July 10, 1989, p. A10.

8. *Los Angeles Times*, "Atom smasher proposal weds science and politics," December 6, 1987, p. 10.

9. George Wise, "Science and technology," *Osiris*, Vol. 1, 1985, pp. 229–246, 236.

10. Vannevar Bush, for example, exploited this argument in his famous *Science, The Endless Frontier: A Report to the President* (Washington, D.C.: U. S. Government Printing Office, 1945).

11. Ernest Braun and Stuart MacDonald, *Revolution in Miniature* (Cambridge: Cambridge University Press, 1978), p. 1.

12. John R. Steelman, *Science and Public Policy: A Report to the President, Volume 1: A Program for the Nation* (Washington, D.C.: U. S. Government Printing Office, 1947).

13. Bruce L. R. Smith, *American Science Policy Since World War II* (Washington, D.C.: Brookings Institution, 1990), p. 85.

14. Harvey Brooks, "What's the national agenda for science and how did it come about?" *Amer. Sci.*, Vol. 75, 1987, p. 512.

15. Smith, *American Science Policy*, op. cit., p. 87.

16. Smith, *American Science Policy*, ibid., pp. 87–88.

17. Quoted in A. Michal McMahon, "Shaping a 'space-oriented complex': NASA and the universities in the 1960s," paper presented to the "'Science, Technology, and the Military'" workshop at The Johns Hopkins University, Baltimore, Md., 1986, p. 4.

18. McMahon, "Shaping a 'space-oriented complex,' " ibid., p. 16.

19. House Committee, "Testimony of W. Panofsky on the Stanford Accelerator Power Supply: Hearing Before the Joint Committee," 88th Congress, 2nd session, January 29, 1964, pp. 24–25.

20. Robert W. Smith (with contributions by Paul Hanle, Robert Kargon, and Joseph N. Tatarewicz), *The Space Telescope: A Study of NASA, Science, Technology, and Politics*, Chaps. 4 and 5, New York: Cambridge University Press, 1989).

21. House Committee on Appropriations, "Department of Housing and Urban Development-Independent Agencies Appropriations for 1976: Hearings Before the Subcommittee on HUD-Independent Agencies, pt. 2, NASA," 94th Congress, 1st session, March 4, 1975, p. 427.

22. Lockheed document, "Potential benefits of the Large Space Telescope," January 27, 1975, copy in Space Telescope History Project Files, Smithsonian Institution, Washington, D.C.

23. Milton Friedman, "An open letter on grants," *Newsweek*, May 18, 1981, p. 99.

24. This was pointed out in Smith, *American Science Policy*, op. cit., pp. 109–110.

25. Quoted in David Dickson, *The New Politics of Science* (New York: Pantheon, 1984), p. 39.

26. Smith, *American Science Policy*, op cit., p. 157.

27. Michael Reagan, *Science and the Federal Patron* (New York: Oxford University Press, 1969), pp. 40–41.

28. Chairman's Report to the Committee on Science and Technology, House of Representatives, "American science and policy issues," 99th Congress, 2nd session, December 1986, p. 120.

29. J. L. Heilbron and D. J. Kevles, "Mapping and sequencing the human genome: Considerations from the history of particle accelerators," in *Mapping our Genes. Federal Genome Projects. How Vast, How Fast*, Vol. 1 (Washington, D.C.: U. S. Government Printing Office, 1988), pp. 160–179.

30. On the CCDs, see Robert W. Smith and Joseph N. Tatarewicz, "Counting on invention: Devices, telescopes, and black boxes," *Osiris*, in press.

31. Branscomb, *America's Struggle*, op. cit., p. vii.

32. Branscomb, *America's Struggle*, op. cit., p. viii.

33. Ibid.

PART III

Computing

Part III turns from electronics to the closely allied topic of electronic computers. The first chapter is written by Martin Campbell-Kelly, a historian and computer scientist at the University of Warwick who has written the definitive study of the leading British computer manufacturer (ICL). Drawing from that study, Campbell-Kelly investigates British government policies for promoting and defending the indigenous U.K. computer industry against foreign, especially American, competitors between 1949 and 1985. He describes British military sponsorship of three computer centers that spun off their prototype computer systems to the commercial sector, efforts to guarantee markets for British computer firms, government intervention to rationalize the computer industry through forced consolidation, and actions to protect the remaining firm (ICL) from market forces so that it could undertake research and implement other long-term strategies.

Boelie Elzen, a historian of technology at the University of Nijmegen in the Netherlands, and Donald MacKenzie, a sociologist of science and technology at the University of Edinburgh in Scotland, prepared the other chapter of this part. They explore the interplay between technical development and social relations in the historical development of the U.S. supercomputer industry, and use their analysis to argue against two widely held beliefs: This industry is on the brink of collapse and American competitiveness is being compromised by the insufficient supercomputing resources for the nation's scientists and engineers. Elzen and MacKenzie show how the nature of competitiveness in the supercomputing field changed over a period of 30 years from delivery of the fastest hardware to total solutions to problems confronting their customers. One of the authors' major findings is that the social networks established between manufacturers of supercomputers and their customers created a mutual dependency, which imposed a barrier on new entrants to the supercomputer

industry and which affected the design of subsequent generations of supercomputers, e.g., giving diminished value to computing speed.

Campbell-Kelly's chapter suggests at least three lines of inquiry. The British
government's intervention in the computer industry can be seen largely as a failure.
Not only could it not keep the original wolf (IBM) at bay, the entire British computer
industry—as consolidated by the British government in the form of ICL—was eventually sold out to the Japanese. The outcomes of British and Japanese government
programs to set national computing policies and protect their native computer industries from foreign competition could not have been more different. A comparative historical study of these two cases is warranted. Comparisons of the British
computer industry with other British industries, in particular automobiles, in which
the British government took similar protectionist measures might also be instructive.

Campbell-Kelly alludes to the particular difficulties ICL and its predecessors
faced in consolidating companies, especially by forcible means, to work as a single,
unified, viable, competitive firm. Have consolidations been good or bad for competitiveness? Have companies had problems managing the workforce effectively after
consolidation, and have they been able to rationalize staff and plants, blend product
lines and service operations, and mesh corporate goals and cultures? Unisys's formation from Sperry and Burroughs, and the previous mergers that formed Sperry,
present another good case for study within the computer industry. But these types of
mergers undoubtedly also took place in other industries, such as the British automobile and British aircraft industries. Additional historical studies might indicate if
the nature of the industry bears upon the effectiveness of consolidations.

Campbell-Kelly cites various protectionist activities adopted by the British government. How have quotas, tariffs, import licensing, and other measures worked for
other countries in protecting home high-tech industries? The French, Brazilian, and
Japanese governments, for example, have tried to protect their computer industries
in this way. The United States and many European governments have tried to protect
their automobile industries. Few of these efforts seem at first glance to have been
extremely successful. Further study is needed to confirm these appearances and explain them.

Elzen and MacKenzie's chapter suggests a method for application to other
questions of technological competitiveness. It has become fashionable for historians
and sociologists to investigate how culture (as opposed to the internal dynamics of a
technology itself) has shaped technological artifacts. This movement toward a social
construction of technology has seldom, if ever, been applied directly to issues of
technological competitiveness. The social dynamics of a closed community creating a
barrier to entry of new players (and perhaps new technologies), which Elzen and
MacKenzie describe for the supercomputer field, is likely at work in other industries. For example, while the small community of academic superstars created by
DARPA's Information Processing Techniques Office made some important contributions to networking, graphics, and artificial intelligence, overall their hegemony may
have retarded the advance of computer science in the United States in the 1970s. The
social organization and values established in the DARPA computing community dis-
enfranchised all but a few leading institutions from the cutting edge of computer science research, and most educational training programs languished. The DARPA

computing program is now being explored in a study by Arthur Norberg and Judy O'Neill of the Charles Babbage Institute, although they have not adopted the methods of social construction as foremost.

There are no doubt many other communities in which high-end or leading-edge technologies are shaped significantly by social forces. For example, MacKenzie himself has investigated the social forces that made the German scientists and engineers working for the U.S. Army, the academic scientists at MIT's Draper Laboratory, and industrial scientists, such as those at Autonetics, forge different approaches to guidance systems for missiles.[1] In another example, the social ideals of European and American city planners have led them to build transportation systems that differ, for example, in their use of trolleys or electric locomotives, or concern for fuel consumption in automobiles.

Notes

1. Donald MacKenzie, *Inventing Accuracy: A Historical Sociology of Inertial Missile Guidance* (Cambridge, MA: MIT Press, 1990).

ICL and the American Challenge

British Government Policies
for the Computer Industry, 1949–1985

Martin Campbell-Kelly

Introduction

Over the last 40 years, the policies of successive U.K. governments toward the computer industry have had two broad aims:

- Defense of the balance of payments
- Maintenance of a strategic information-technology industry

These aims have not always been explicitly stated, and over time and different governments the relative balance between them has shifted.

By the late 1940s it was becoming clear that computers and electronic data processing would become significant economic activities, perhaps of a similar magnitude to pharmaceuticals, aerospace, electronics, or office machinery. While the United Kingdom had maintained a reasonable position in the first three of these industries, it had always been a net importer of advanced office machinery. It was recognized by some that special measures would therefore be needed to ensure a successful computer industry, and this was to be the principal task of the National Research Development Corporation (NRDC), which was established in 1949.

While the existence of a national information-technology industry had significant economic benefits for the balance of payments, there was also a political objective in ensuring that the United Kingdom had a world-class indigenous computer industry. The reasons for this have never been quantified, but they relate to feelings of national pride, arguments about spin-off, and the need for self-sufficiency in defense procurement. To quote a Ministry of Technology memorandum:

> To fail to produce an indigenous industry would expose the country to the possibilities that industrial, commercial, strategic or political decisions made in America could heavily influence our ability to manufacture, to trade, to govern or to defend.[1]

For Labour governments, in particular, there has been a strong emotional commitment to ICL as a "national champion" computer manufacturer.

The NRDC: An Early Policy Failure, 1949–1963

The Postwar Scene

The early history of British computers has been well documented.[2] Among the major European countries, the United Kingdom was the least damaged physically and economically by World War II. This, and the electronics leadership established during the war, enabled Britain to make the most rapid progress of any European country in developing the newly invented stored-program computer.

From the close of World War II, the British defense ministry (the Ministry of Supply) and the Department of Scientific and Industrial Research (DSIR) were keen to establish a national computer project so that universities and government research organizations could have the benefit of this powerful new tool. In the event no less than three major computer centers were established by 1946: at Cambridge University, Manchester University, and the National Physical Laboratory. Each of these centers had a prototype computer working, or on the verge of working, during 1949.

In the mid-1940s, it had never been envisaged that there would be a demand for more than two or three large scientific machines in the United Kingdom, but by about 1950 it was evident that there would be a significant market for electronic computers. As a result three firms tentatively entered the computer market by manufacturing one of the three British research computers, in a classic example of technology transfer. Thus the electrical engineering and electronics firm Ferranti started to manufacture and market the Manchester University computer, and English Electric began to produce the National Physical Laboratory's machine. The bakery firm of Lyons—a leader in modern management techniques—also began a partnership with Cambridge University to make the LEO computer. Leo Computers Limited was formed in 1955 to produce LEO II, based on the successful LEO. By this time several other firms had come into the computer market, some of them as a direct result of the stimulus of the NRDC.

Two firms that had *not* entered the computer field, however, were the punched-card machine manufacturers—the British Tabulating Machine Company (BTM), the licensee of IBM in Britain and the Commonwealth, and Powers-Samas, a one-time licensee of Remington Rand. The reason for their not entering the computer market in the early 1950s was both understandable and rational. At this time, the market for computers was perceived as being a small one—selling "mathematical instruments" to a largely technical market. The punched-card machine manufacturers, long used to selling or renting a high volume of relatively low-cost machines, did not see electronic computers as being an appropriate business into which to make a major entry. In addition, in October 1949, BTM and IBM had decided by mutual consent to break their long-standing agreement and to go into open competition worldwide. BTM was thus burdened with a massive research and development (R&D) program in conventional punched-card machinery merely to keep abreast of IBM. Powers-Samas, also exposed to competition from IBM for the first time, was in much the same position.[3]

The NRDC

The National Research Development Corporation (NRDC) was established in May 1949 under the Development of Inventions Act of 1948, with the stated aim of fostering the patenting and commercial exploitation of British inventions.[4] The first managing director of the NRDC was Lord Halsbury, a research administrator of great experience. On its formation, the NRDC acquired the Manchester University patents for the Williams Tube memory, and one of Halsbury's first tasks was to negotiate a license for IBM in New York, which needed the memory for its Defense Calculator (later sold as the IBM 701). Halsbury came away from IBM convinced that it was only a matter of time before they produced a commercial data-processing computer.

So that Britain should not be left behind in developing a data-processing computer industry, in December 1949 Halsbury brought the punched-card machine manufacturers and the electronics companies together at a roundtable conference to try to persuade them to work together to develop a data-processing machine. Unfortunately, Halsbury was unable to convince the punched-card machine manufacturers that they lacked electronics expertise; nor could he convince the electronic companies that they lacked marketing know-how. All the manufacturers preferred to go their own separate ways. Halsbury[5] recalls being told at the time by the managing director of the British Tabulating Machine Company: "You haven't got what you wanted, but you may have started something that will bear fruit." "Sixteen years later," Halsbury notes, "the fruit dropped off the tree. Too little, too late." That the transformation came too late is borne out by the contrast with U.S. office-machine firms, such as Remington Rand, Burroughs, and NCR, which all acquired fledgling computer companies in the early 1950s in order to bring in electronics and computer expertise. These firms later became major players in the mainframe computer business.

Failing in the initial attempt to create a major data-processing computer initiative, Halsbury spent the remainder of the 1950s on piecemeal efforts to bring what strength he could to the industry with his very limited resources of £5 million. For example, the NRDC helped Ferranti cope with the early commercial risk of entering the computer business by guaranteeing the sales of its Mark I* computer. A development contract was made with Elliott Brothers to develop packaged circuit technology. This technology was subsequently used in the Ferranti Pegasus computer, whose design was specified, and whose sales were guaranteed, by the NRDC.

In most respects Halsbury was unique in the higher echelons of government science policy in his unwavering vision of computing as the growth industry of the future. However, he did make a major error of policy implementation by focusing on large prestige computer projects at the expense of bread-and-butter data-processing computers and peripherals. One failed project, for example, was a large tape-based data-processing computer, the EMI 2400, which the NRDC intended to be competitive with the IBM 7000 series. Only three, rather unreliable, computers were ever delivered. The NRDC also diverted its limited resources into sponsoring not one but *two* giant computer projects, the EMI 3400 and the Ferranti Atlas. These sponsorships took place against a backdrop of growing political concern about the prestigious U.S. giant computer projects, the IBM Stretch and the Univac LARC in 1956–1958. In the event, the EMI 3400 never saw the light of day, and although the Atlas was a superb technical success, it came to the market too late in 1964 to be a commercial success.[4]

A second major policy error was the failure to recognize the magnitude of the challenge that the switch to transistor electronics represented. While Britain had been a leader in thermionic-tube electronics in the 1950s, transistor electronics was a completely new area in which experience in the old technology counted for very little. Leadership in transistor electronics called for the same order of commitment to R&D that had produced Britain's preeminence in pulse electronics during World War II. This commitment was never given, nor was it even within the financial scope of the NRDC.

The First Merger Wave, 1959–1963

Another major policy shortcoming of the NRDC was its inability to "pick a winner" into which it could pour, undiluted, its limited resources. The barriers to entry into the computer business in the mid-1950s were already sufficiently low so that there was no shortage of electronics and control companies, such as Elliott Brothers, STC, Decca, GEC, and Plessey, that were willing to enter the field. In this respect, the NRDC in sponsoring several other firms just made the oversupply situation worse. By 1959 there were in the region of ten British computer manufacturers competing for a very small domestic market and an even smaller export market. Probably none of the British firms was making money from computers, and several firms had already left the computer business of their own volition.[6]

The watershed for the British computer industry really came with the announcement of the IBM 1401 computer in October 1959. The 1401 captured the U.S. data-processing computer market to an extent that took IBM by surprise, and exceeded all forecasts: a thousand orders were taken in the first few weeks following the announcement, and the machine went on to sell a total far in excess of 10,000 installations.[7] The success of the 1401 has often been attributed to the model 1403 chain printer that accompanied it; printing at 600 lines per minute, it enabled a single

1401 to replace four conventional punched-card accounting machines. But at least as much of the 1401's success was due to the fact that it was an integrated system, whereas other manufacturers, in the United States as much as in Britain, had yet to offer computers that were an integrated system of processor, peripherals, and software.

Another effect of the IBM 1401 launch was that it transformed the computer industry from one that had been based on the sale of high-cost capital electronic goods in low volumes, to one selling relatively low-cost machines in a much higher volume. The selling organizations of the traditional business-machine manufacturers were well adapted to this new market environment; whereas the electronics and control manufacturers who had prospered in the earlier conditions now found themselves in a market in which it was much more difficult to compete.

Each firm in the British computer industry was thus faced with the same decision: whether to stay in the industry for the long haul, or to get out while the going was good. The overall result of these individual decisions was the first merger wave of 1959–1964 (see Fig. 1). In 1959 the two punched-card machine manufacturers, BTM and Powers-Samas, merged to form International Computers and Tabulators (ICT) in order to compete more effectively against IBM. ICT lacked electronics expertise, however, so it bought out the computer interests successively of GEC, EMI, and Ferranti. In a parallel merger move, English Electric decided to complement and enhance its electronics expertise by buying up the data-processing computer manufacturer Leo Computers in 1963, and by incorporating the microelectronics know-how of Marconi the following year. By 1964 there were just three companies remaining: ICT, English Electric-Leo-Marconi (EELM), and Elliott Automation.

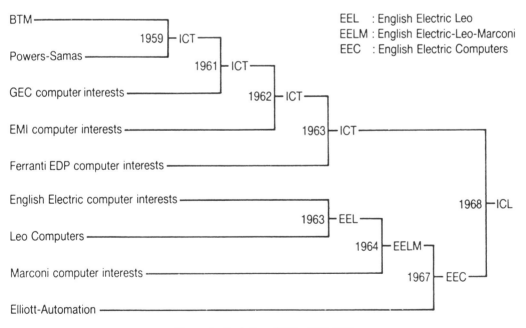

Figure 1. Evolution of ICL, 1959–1968.

The Formation of ICL, 1964–1970

System/360: The American Challenge

The IBM System/360, announced on April 7, 1964, was a compatible family of third-generation computers. The line consisted of six distinct processors and 40 peripherals, which were intended to replace all of IBM's current computers, except the smallest and the largest. The R&D cost of System/360 was reported to be $500 million, a figure that was nearly twice the annual revenue of the entire British computer industry. The scale of the announcement was entirely unprecedented, and all the evidence is that it took the rest of the industry largely by surprise.[8]

System/360 completely changed the computer market, and there were essentially three responses that a manufacturer could make: to develop an IBM-compatible line of computers; to develop a non-IBM-compatible line; or to move into a "niche" area, such as very large or small computers. ICT never seriously considered going into a niche market, as this was incompatible with being Britain's leading mainframe manufacturer. Likewise, IBM-compatibility was seen to be a poor competitive strategy for ICT. The only logical argument for a user buying an IBM-compatible computer in preference to a machine manufactured by IBM, it was felt, was because it had a better price/performance ratio, or technical superiority. ICT doubted if it could achieve this superiority, but in any case there was a deep cultural resistance toward slavishly following the IBM line.

ICT thus decided to develop its own compatible range of computers, the 1900 series, which was based on an existing Canadian design, the Ferranti-Packard 6000. An important advantage of using an existing design was that it allowed you to reduce the development lead time very considerably. The 1900 series was launched in September 1964, based on a line of seven distinct processors and a total of 27 different peripherals. The first production model was delivered in January 1965, only four months after the 1900 series announcement. The short lead time of the 1900 series proved to be a major competitive advantage over System/360, for which U.K. deliveries did not take place until spring 1966.

Turning to Britain's other major EDP-computer manufacturer, English Electric, planning activity began on a line of third-generation machines soon after the merger with Leo Computers had taken place in April 1963. These plans were initially focused on an entirely new range that was known internally as "Project KLX." With the announcement of System/360 and the 1900 series during the course of 1964, however, the pace and scale of innovation increased, and it was clear within English Electric that there was a need to contain development costs within realistic bounds. As it happened, English Electric had a long-standing technology-sharing agreement with RCA, so it decided to abandon the KLX project and take up the option of manufacturing RCA's IBM-compatible Spectra 70 series under license.

The Labour Government and Industrial Policy

The decisions of ICT and English Electric to independently embark on their own third-generation computer lines took place against a backdrop of growing political concern at the increasing dominance of the high-technology industries by multinational companies with headquarters in the United States. This mood was captured admirably by J.-J. Servan-Schreiber's popular book *The American Challenge*,[9] which was a best-seller in both France and England.

When Harold Wilson's Labour Government came to power with a slim majority in October 1964, one of its first acts was to establish a Ministry of Technology (Mintech), which was envisaged as an organization to "guide and stimulate a major national effort to bring advanced technology and new processes into British industry."[10] Wilson placed the British computer industry at the very top of Mintech's agenda:

> My frequent meetings with leading scientists, technologists and industrialists in the last two or three years of Opposition had convinced me that, if action was not taken quickly, the British computer industry would rapidly cease to exist, facing as was the case in other European countries, the most formidable competition from the American giants. When, on the evening we took office, I asked Frank Cousins to become the first Minister of Technology, I told him that he had, in my view, about a month to save the British computer industry and that this must be his first priority.[11]

Accordingly, in November 1964, the newly appointed Minister of Technology held talks with both ICT and English Electric, in what was to be the first of many attempts to persuade the companies to bring together their computer interests. But these talks came to nothing, mainly because the development of their third-generation lines had passed the point of no return, and their incompatibility meant it would not be possible to gain any significant economies of scale from a merger.

In March 1966 the Wilson Government was reelected, more determined than ever to revitalize Britain's industrial base. The role of the Ministry of Technology was expanded, and a new organization, the Industrial Reorganization Corporation (IRC), was given the mission of "promoting industrial efficiency and profitability and assisting the economy of the UK".[12] Working with the IRC, the Ministry of Technology commissioned an independent report into the possibility of a merger between ICT and English Electric-Leo-Marconi. But the report confirmed the companies' view that a merger was not a practical possibility while they were developing their third-generation lines, and that a union would not become practical until the time came to produce a new line in the 1970s.

The Ministry therefore decided to deal with the rationalization of the British computer industry in two stages: first the rationalization of the process-control computer industry, and second that of the EDP-computer industry. The former proved relatively straightforward and English Electric absorbed Elliott Automation in June 1967. The new English Electric subsidiary was named English Electric Computers Limited.

The ICL New Line

It now remained to rationalize the EDP sector of the industry. In April 1967, the minister and his technical advisors once again called a meeting with the top management of ICT and English Electric to persuade them to merge their EDP computer interests. Mintech accepted that the main impediment to a merger was the incompatibility of the current lines, and therefore offered *inter alia* a nonrepayable grant in the region of £25 million toward the development of a new line of computers for delivery in the early 1970s.

If ICT and English Electric had moved decisively, an early merger would no doubt have been achieved, but the terms of the merger were not agreed upon until early 1968, and the delay—each company hoping for marginally better terms—was to prove disastrous. During the autumn of 1967, the U.K. economic climate had worsened dramatically, culminating in the devaluation of the pound in November 1967 and the public expenditure cuts of January 1968. A government subvention of the order of £25 million was now seen as politically unacceptable, and the Treasury was thinking in terms of about half that amount—in fact, £13.5 million was eventually provided. But the merger plans were now so far advanced that there was no going back. On March 21, 1968 the Minister of Technology presented a white paper on the computer merger to the House of Commons, and ICL was vested on July 9, 1968. ICL was the largest non-American computer manufacturer, with a workforce of 34,000.

The New Range development created a mild euphoria in the newly formed ICL: it was regarded as a once-in-a-lifetime opportunity that was eagerly grasped. The project was very much in the spirit of the 1960s, and captured the national mood in a manner similar to, though milder than, the one the Concorde had. However, the reduced R&D subvention meant that the New Range development was underfunded from the start, which led to a financial crisis in the 1970s. Moreover, the logistical and financial implications of developing a complete new line *ab initio* had not really been thought through, so that a project that was intended to take 3 years eventually took well over 5 years, and it was not until 1974–1976 that the complete line was available. Serious as the delays were from a marketing viewpoint, the biggest difficulty was in keeping the project viable through the various policy shifts during the 1970s.

The 1970s and 1980s: Shifting Policies

The Political Dimension

To understand British information-technology policy in the last 20 years, it is necessary to appreciate the economic and political outlooks of successive U.K. governments, that is, under Edward Heath, Harold Wilson, and Margaret Thatcher:

- Conservative Government (Edward Heath), June 1970–October 1974
- Labour Government (Harold Wilson, James Callaghan), October 1974–May 1979
- Conservative Government (Margaret Thatcher), May 1979–November 1990

The Heath Government started off in a strong noninterventionist style, which was partly a reaction to the policy failures of the Wilson Government of 1964–1970. This noninterventionist resolve, however, was strongly undermined during the economic recession of 1971–1972. The Labour Government of Harold Wilson, which was returned to office in 1974, continued the strong interventionist policy of the 1960s, but also turned increasingly to demand-side measures to stimulate the use of information technology. Finally, the Conservative Government of Margaret Thatcher, which came into office in 1979, was far more robustly noninterventionist than any previous government, and was neutral or even negative to the computer industry. It did, however, have a strong demand-side orientation.

By the early 1970s, computers and the computer industry had become controversial political issues, and the subject of much open discussion. The major political forum for debate was the Select Committee of Science and Technology, a nonparty parliamentary body that met to conduct inquiries into the government's science and industrial policy in various fields. Two inquiries into the computer industry were held, one in 1969–1971 and one in 1972–1973. These inquiries generated several thousand pages of evidence that are a superb source for the history of the computer industry and government information-technology policy.[13] Unfortunately, political concern over information technology was not sustained at the level of the early 1970s, and there were no further select committee inquiries until 1988, a period of 15 years.[14] This will make the analysis of policy between 1975 and 1985 somewhat daunting until State papers become available under the 30-year rule.

Policies Toward ICL and the Computer Industry

As already noted, the Heath Government, elected in June 1970, was doctrinarily noninterventionist toward industry, and one of its first acts was to disband the Industrial Reorganization Corporation and to narrow the scope of the Ministry of Technology and rename it the Department of Industry. The nonparty select committee on the computer industry was highly critical of the government's attitude, however, arguing that more rather than less support should be given to the computer industry. This is important, because it indicates that in 1970–1971 there was a consensus in favor of state intervention in the computer industry, notwithstanding the government's noninterventionist policies.

The British computer industry was soon caught up in the 1970–1971 computer recession. This was the same recession that saw the withdrawal of the U.S. industrial giants RCA and General Electric from the data-processing computer field. By summer 1971, ICL was in crisis and forced to lay off workers and review its R&D program for the New Range. Initially, the government refused assistance, and obliged the company to consider a merger with a U.S. company, such as Univac or Burroughs. When the government was forced to rescue Rolls Royce from financial collapse in 1972, however, its "lame-duck" policy was weakened.[15] The government eventually agreed to a loan of £27 million to ICL which was to be repaid out of profits. This enabled the New Range development to continue.

The reelection of Wilson's Labour Government in October 1974 coincided with ICL's best-ever years, and it needed no direct help to successfully launch the

New Range. Much criticism had been leveled at the Labour Government, however, because its computer industry policies were almost exclusively focused on ICL as the national champion mainframe manufacturer. It was argued that this fixation on ICL caused the government to neglect the minicomputer industry, so that British companies such as CTL and Arcturus had foundered. This criticism was partly redressed by the formation of the National Enterprise Board (NEB) in 1975, which enabled the government to attempt to "pick winners" and to invest in them directly, somewhat in the manner of a state bank. Besides investing in several fledgling and small information-technology companies, the NEB took a 25 percent share holding in ICL, and had a director on its main board. The NEB also financed the launch of two major companies, Inmos and Nexos. Inmos was formed in 1978 with the intention of restoring the United Kingdom's position in semiconductor manufacturing, initially producing memory chips. Some £115 million was provided between 1978 and 1980. The office automation company Nexos was formed in 1979, with initial funds of £40 million.[16]

With the election of the Thatcher Government in May 1979, the political pendulum once more swung toward nonintervention in industry. The NEB's shareholding in ICL was sold, and the NEB was itself heavily curtailed and merged with the NRDC to form the British Technology Group (BTG) in February 1981. Although funds were provided for the survival of Inmos and Nexos during the 1980–1981 recession, the government sold both companies as soon as was practical, Nexos in 1982 and Inmos to Thorn-EMI in 1984.

The noninterventionist policy of the Thatcher Government had its severest test in 1981 when ICL ran into a financial crisis. The government was caught in the dilemma of either making a policy U-turn, or allowing ICL to fall into U.S. hands. Eventually a brilliantly face-saving solution was found by which the government guaranteed bank loans of £200 million. This enabled ICL to survive without any direct financial assistance from the government (although it can be argued that the government underwrote some hefty insurance).

Competition, Protection, and Procurement

So far, I have only considered the positive aspects of industrial policy that were aimed at helping ICL to become competitive by enabling it to undertake long-term R&D, and to adopt a longer term view of the industry than would have been possible under ordinary commercial conditions. A second, and much more controversial, policy, however, was that of protecting ICL through procurement policies aimed at maintaining its dominance of the U.K. market.

Up to the late 1950s a procurement policy had been largely unnecessary, because British computers had generally been price-competitive with American machines, and the postwar "Buy British" attitude made a home-produced article generally preferable, all other things being equal. In the 1960s, however, with the arrival of second-generation computer systems, British machines became far less competitive. While private industry frequently bought superior U.S. machines, the public sector—that is, national and local government, defense, quasi-government organizations, education, and nationalized industries—were pressured to buy British. Even so, between 1962 and 1967, the sales of British-produced computer systems fell from 80 percent to 45 percent of the domestic market.[17]

During the 1960s, the government's procurement policy had never been formally documented, and its unofficial status was "shrouded in mystery."[18] The 1970 Select Committee on Science and Technology, however, succeeded in prizing out of the Civil Service Department its unpublished guidelines for computer purchase:

1. To acquire large computers (those more powerful than Atlas) by single tender action from I.C.L., subject to satisfactory price, performance and delivery dates.

2. To acquire smaller computers by single tender action (normally from I.C.L.) when they are intended to lead-in to the use of a large computer of the same family or where there are other reasons for seeking compatibility or flexibility by the use of machines of the same family, subject to the same proviso about price, performance and delivery.

3. In all other cases, including large computers where I.C.L. are unable to meet all the conditions specified in (1) above, to seek competitive tenders from not less than 3 firms, . . . allowing preference in favour of any British machine provided that there is no undue price differential as compared with overseas supplies, that the British machine is technically suitable and that no undue delay is involved.[19]

Clearly, rule 1 was designed to protect the large, prestige computer market; this would help ensure the survival of ICL's top-end machines, which were considered an essential marketing requirement of a compatible range. Rule 2 was intended to ensure that small and first-time users became locked into an ICL range rather than a U.S. one. And, finally, rule 3 ensured that even when ICL could not supply a suitable machine, a U.S. alternative could not be chosen without considerable bureaucratic obstacle. The effect of the procurement policy was that between 1969 and 1971, ICL's share of government orders rose from 69 percent to 90 percent.

Not surprisingly, U.S. manufacturers complained about the preference given to ICL. Honeywell, in particular, pointed out that its machines used more British components than ICL's, and it had a factory in Scotland that it had set up in the expectation of receiving orders from the public sector, in accordance with Mintech's stated policy that "machines made in Britain by subsidiaries of foreign firms are regarded in this context as British."[20] On the other hand, as further evidence presented to the subcommittee revealed, U.S. manufacturers were well protected by the Buy America Act, and the French, German, and Japanese governments were each protecting their own computer industries. In fact, ICL's view was that the procurement policy was something of a distraction, since the government accounted for a mere 15 percent of national computer orders. In the United States, government orders accounted for perhaps one-third of the overall market. If the British Government merely increased its demand in proportion, it would be of more value to ICL than the procurement policy.

There was also a view from economic commentators outside the industry that the competitiveness of British industry generally was being damaged by having unsuitable computers foisted on it. In the light of the hostile attitude to the procurement policy, which in any case damaged ICL's image, the procurement guidelines were generally relaxed from the mid-1970s. And following the privatization programs of the Thatcher government, and a move away from mainframe-based computing, its importance diminished further.

Conclusion. Policy Analysis: Success or Failure?

It was stated at the beginning of this chapter that British policies toward the computer industry had two broad aims: the defense of the balance of payments, and the maintenance of a strategic information-technology industry.

The balance of trade is the easiest policy aim to quantify. Table 1 shows the import–export performance of the U.K. information-technology industry over the period 1965–1985, in 5-year intervals. There was a persistent trade deficit in information-technology goods throughout this period, although as a proportion of the total market the deficit has shown an improving trend. What is not clear, however, is the extent to which intervention in the British computer industry has affected these figures. For example, it is well known that IBM tends to maintain a net input–output trade balance in whatever country it operates. Consequently, if ICL had not existed, its products would have been largely substituted for by those of IBM, and the effect on the balance of trade would have been small, and possibly even favorable. Indeed, the policy emphasis on the balance of payments was probably misplaced. A program directed primarily at increasing the per capita consumption of computers in Britain, instead of merely improving the balance of payments, might have been a blunter yet far more effective policy instrument.

So far as maintaining a strategic national computer industry is concerned, there were both policy successes and failures. A national mainframe industry was successfully maintained, and at an astonishingly low direct cost of £40 million. (And if one takes into account the profit realized in the sale of the government's share holding in ICL in 1979, there was no cost at all.) But there were unquantifiable indirect costs due to the procurement policy that obliged the public sector to use sub-state-of-the-art computers. The industrial policy was much less successful in fostering the mini- and microcomputer industries: the former because it was overshadowed by ICL in the mid-1970s, and the latter because investment went into the semiconductor industry (i.e., Inmos), instead of supporting a personal-computer industry.

TABLE I.   U.K. Balance of Trade in Information Technology, 1965–1985

	1965	1970[a]	1975	1980	1985
Imports (£ millions)	18.6	111	383	1080	3919
Exports (£ millions)	7.2	52	242	936	3314
Balance (£ millions)	−11.4	−59	−141	−144	−605

[a]Nine months.

Sources: Select Committee on Science and Technology, 1971 and 1973,[15,16] and the Trade and Industry Committee, 1988.[14]

Probably the main failure of the computer policy, however, was tactical rather than strategic, that is, it was the failure to realize that there could never be a once-and-for-all solution to the ICL problem. If it had been understood in 1968 that ICL would always need a drip-feed of cash for R&D, and financial support to get it through cyclical recessions in the computer industry, then the policy might have been more decisive: either giving no support at all, and allowing the industry to fall into U.S. hands, or supporting ICL handsomely so that it could compete much more strongly in terms of technology.

Since 1982 there has been no direct government investment in the computer industry, and a diminishing concern over its sovereignty. During the last 3 years, ICL has been sold to Fujitsu; Inmos has been sold to Italian and French interests; and several major players in the U.K. software and services industry have been allowed to fall into French and U.S. ownership. The importance of having a strategic information-technology industry has become a smaller political concern in recent years, for it is now understood that no nation's computer industry can be independent of Japan or the United States for its supply of semiconductor chips and software. While a substantial information-technology R&D activity remains in Britain, strategic control has unquestionably been lost. It is far from clear whether this actually matters or not.

Acknowledgments

I am most grateful to Emerson Pugh of IBM for his valuable critique on a preliminary draft of the manuscript.

Notes

1. Stuart Hodges, *Multinational Corporations and Government: A Case Study of the United Kingdom's Experience, 1964–1970* (Farnborough, England: Saxon, 1974), p. 227.

2. Mary Croarken, *Early Scientific Computing in Britain* (Oxford: Oxford Univ. Press, 1990); and S. H. L. Lavington, *Early British Computers* (Manchester, England: Manchester Univ. Press, 1980).

3. M. Campbell-Kelly, *ICL: A Business and Technical History* (Oxford: Oxford Univ. Press, 1989).

4. John Hendry, *Innovating for Failure: Government Policy and the Early British Computer Industry* (Cambridge, Mass.: M.I.T. Press, 1989).

5. Halsbury, 3d Earl of, "Innovation for failure—Some reflections on the work of the NRDC relevant to the early history of the computer industry in the UK," *Comput. J.*, Vol. 34, 1991, pp. 272–279.

6. C. Freeman, C. J. E. Harlow, J. K. Fuller, and R. C. Curnow, "Research and development in electronic capital goods," *Nat. Inst. Econ. Rev.*, Vol. 34, November 1965, pp. 40–91.

7. C. J. Bashe, L. R. Johnson, and J. H. Palmer, *IBM's Early Computers* (Cambridge, Mass.: M.I.T. Press, 1985).

8. E. W. Pugh, L. R. Johnson, and J. H. Palmer, *IBM's 360 and Early 370 Systems* (Cambridge Mass.: M.I.T. Press, 1991).

9. J.-J. Servan-Schreiber, *The American Challenge* (London: Hamilton, 1968).

10. R. Clarke, "Mintech in retrospect," *Omega*, Vol. 1, 1973, pp. 26–38, 137–163.

11. H. Wilson, *The Labour Government 1964–1970* (London: Weidenfeld and Nicolson and Micheal Joseph, 1971), p. 8.

12. D. Hague and G. Wilkinson, *The IRC—An Experiment in Industrial Intervention* (London: George Allen & Unwin, 1983).

13. Select Committee on Science and Technology (Sub-Committee D), Session 1969–70, *Minutes of Evidence* (London: Her Majesty's Stationery Office, 1971); Select Committee on Science and Technology (Sub-Committee A), Session 1970–71, *The Prospects for the United Kingdom Computer Industry in the 1970's* (London: Her Majesty's Stationery Office, 1971); Select Committee on Science and Technology (Sub-Committee A), Session 1972–73, *Second Report on the U.K. Computer Industry* (London: Her Majesty's Stationery Office, 1973).

14. Trade and Industry Committee, Session 1988–89, *Information Technology* (London: Her Majesty's Stationery Office, 1988).

15. P. Mottershead, "Industrial Policy," in *British Economic Policy, 1960–74*, ed. F. T. Blackaby (London: Duckworth, 1978).

16. John Redwood, *Going for Broke . . . Gambling with Taxpayers' Money* (Oxford: Blackwell, 1984); Tessa Blackstone and William Plowden, *Inside the Think Tank: Advising the Cabinet 1971–83* (London: Heineman, 1988).

17. Organization for Economic Cooperation and Development, *Gaps in Technology: Electronic Computers* (Paris, 1969).

18. Eric Moonman, ed., *British Computers and Industrial Innovation* (London: Allen & Unwin, 1971), p. 4.

19. Select Committee on Science and Technology, *Minutes of Evidence*, op. cit., pp. 455–456.

20. Judith Hills, *Information Technology and Industrial Policy* (London: Croom Helm, 1984), p. 23.

From Megaflops
to Total Solutions

The Changing Dynamics of Competitiveness
in Supercomputing

Boelie Elzen   Donald MacKenzie

Introduction

In the latter part of the 1980s, headlines in U.S. newspapers suggested that the American supercomputer industry was on the brink of collapse. United States science and technology was losing its competitive advantage because American scientists and engineers did not have sufficient access to supercomputer power.

In this chapter[1] we will examine the validity of these claims and conclude that they are unfounded. To this end, we will first give an historical sketch of the development of supercomputers over the past three decades. We will describe the development of the machines in conjunction with the development of the network of social relationships connected to them. We will trace both how technological development affected social relations and how social relations affected subsequent technological development, creating a coherent "sociotechnical network"[2] which is difficult for outside competitors to break into. In a concluding section we argue that reports on the "bad shape" of the American supercomputer industry are unduly pessimistic because they neglect the coherency of this network and are based on too narrow a view of what is and has been going on.

Supercomputers can be defined pragmatically as the fastest computers at any given time.[3] This definition suggests that the development of supercomputers is primarily driven by a quest for higher speeds. Indeed, the early history of supercomputing shows that certain factors that were of prime importance in the development of commercial mainframe computers were subservient to speed considerations in the development of supercomputers. This led to the emergence of a class of machines that, despite their high cost (of the order of $10 million or more), found their way to quite a number of users. The coming into being of a network of relationships between supercomputer manufacturers and these users created a mutual dependency that affected the design of subsequent generations of machine. Paradoxically, one of the effects of the development of this network is that speed has become a less dominant factor in the development of supercomputers.

Control Data Corporation

Around 1960 the performance and reliability of computers leapt forward as the result of the introduction of a new component technology: the transistor. Early commercial transistorized computers were delivered by IBM and the Control Data Corporation (CDC), notably the IBM 7090 and the CDC 1604.[4] IBM, of course, was already a well-established company, while CDC was incorporated only in 1957. The 1604 was CDC's first product, designed in three years by a team directed by Seymour R. Cray.[5]

Seymour Cray had studied electrical engineering and applied mathematics at the University of Minnesota. In 1950 he was recruited by Engineering Research Associates (ERA) of St. Paul, Minnesota.[6] With its origins in wartime cryptanalytic work, ERA was one of the pioneers of digital computing in the United States, though the secrecy of the code-breaking task (its continuing primary market) meant that the firm's work was much less well known than that of J. Presper Eckert and John W. Mauchly in Philadelphia. In May 1952, however, ERA was sold to Remington Rand, which already owned Eckert-Mauchly, and in June 1955 Remington Rand merged with the Sperry Corporation to form Sperry Rand.

There are few known details of Cray's work for ERA and Sperry Rand, though the young Cray quickly won considerable responsibility, notably for Sperry Rand's Naval Tactical Data System (NTDS) computer. He was thus already a figure of some importance to his first start-up company, the Control Data Corporation, formed when Cray and eight others, most famously William C. Norris, left Sperry Rand in 1957. Cray was the chief designer of Control Data's first computer, the CDC 1604, announced in October 1959. Built from transistors, rather than the previously pervasive vacuum tubes, the highly successful 1604 moved Control Data into profit and launched it on a path that was to enable it briefly to challenge IBM's dominance of the computer industry, a dominance that was already hardening by 1957.

The NDTS, and especially the 1604, were considerable achievements, and secured Cray's growing reputation as a computer designer. Yet neither was the stuff of legend, nor—beyond the beginnings of anecdotes concerning his preference for simple designs and intolerance of those he considered fools[7]—is there much evidence of a distinctive "Cray style" in their development.

The origins of both legend and style, and the first clear manifestation of what was to become Cray's distinctive sociotechnical strategy, can first be seen unequivocally in discussions within Control Data on what to do to follow the company's success with the 1604. The obvious step was to build directly on that success, offering an improved machine, but one compatible with the 1604 (so users of the latter could run their programs unaltered). While the 1604 had been oriented to the demands of "scientific" users, such as defense contractors and universities, there was a growing sense within Control Data of the need to orient at least equally to business data processing, where arithmetic speed was of less concern than the capacity to manipulate large data sets. Compatibility and business orientation were not necessarily at odds. By adding new instructions, specially tailored for commercial usage, to the instruction set of the 1604, business demands could be catered to without sacrificing compatibility with the previous machine.

This emerging strategy was perfectly sensible. It was indeed similar to, if less ambitious than, that to be announced in 1964 by IBM, with its famous System 360. This was a series of compatible machines, some oriented to the business and some to the scientific market, but all sharing the same basic architecture, and with an instruction set rich enough to cater to both sorts of demand. Cray, however, disagreed with all elements of the strategy—compatibility with the existing machine, orientation to the commercial as well as scientific market, a complex instruction set.

His alternative strategy prioritized speed: in particular, speed at the "floating-point" arithmetic operations that were the dominant concern of defense and scientific users. In that prioritization, Cray did not wish to be constrained by choices made in the development of the 1604. Compatibility was to be sacrificed to speed. As one of his famous maxims has it, he likes to start the design of a new-generation machine with "a clean sheet of paper." He had no interest in business data processing, and abhorred the complexity that arose from trying to satisfy both scientific and business users.

The 1604 was making a lot of money for Control Data, and so it seemed possible to pursue both strategies simultaneously. One group of designers went on to develop a series of complex-instruction-set computers compatible with the 1604 (the Control Data 3600 series), with a primary orientation to the commercial market. A second group, led by Cray, set out to develop the fastest machine they could conceive of, which became the CDC 6600.

Cray's status as the chief designer of the corporation's first and most successful computer, and the threat (possibly explicit) that he would leave,[8] enabled him to negotiate in 1961/1962 a remarkable arrangement with Control Data chairman Norris. He was allowed to move, with the small team working on the 6600, a hundred miles away from Control Data's headquarters in Minneapolis-St. Paul, to a newly built laboratory on a plot of country land, owned by Cray personally and close to his house, in woods overlooking the Chippewa River. Cray thus won a remarkable degree of autonomy from corporate control. Even Norris had to seek Cray's permission to come to the Chippewa laboratory, and Cray visited Control Data headquarters only every few months.

The technical and social aspects of Cray's strategy were closely related. Chippewa-style isolation would have been incompatible with successfully building a series of compatible, general-purpose computers, which required determining the needs of different kinds of users; balancing one technical characteristic against another; giving attention to software as well as hardware; keeping different projects connected together; harnessing all the different parts of a growing corporation to a common, but diffuse, set of tasks; "committee design."[9] By the move to Chippewa, Cray created a geographical and social barrier between his team and all this negotiation and compromise.

The instruction set for the computer designed at Chippewa, the Control Data 6600, is emblematic of Cray's sociotechnical strategy. It contained only 64 instructions, at a time when a hundred or more were common. When the attempt is being made to satisfy a variety of different user concerns, the easiest means of harmonization is to satisfy vested interests by adding instructions. The IBM Stretch computer, designed in the late 1950s, is an extreme example. An intensely ambitious project, intended to combine extreme speed with an attempt to straddle the scientific, cryptanalyst, and business markets, Stretch had an instruction set of no fewer than 735 instructions.[10]

A simple instruction set for the 6600 permitted most of those instructions to have their own hardware support, tailor-made for speed. Ten independent processing units separately handled logical operations, multiplication, division, and so on. Input/output operations were hived off to ten independent peripheral processing units (PPU) (see Fig. 1).

Striking though its overall design is, the 6600 by no means emerged, Athena-like, simply from the brain of Seymour Cray. The instruction-set simplicity of the 6600 became architectural complexity, for example, as a sophisticated "scoreboard" unit had to be designed to keep the different independent processors working harmoniously. Even Cray could not on his own master all the details, so even within his small team an internal division of labor was needed. James Thornton, in particular, took responsibility for much of the detailed design.

The combination of Cray's intense personal involvement and the laboratory's isolation lent coherence to the project: "A team spirit developed and carried over into sporting and recreational events in the community."[11] Developing the 6600,

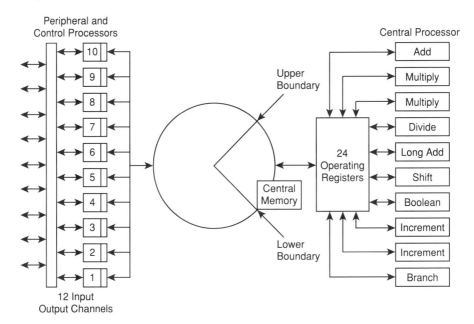

Figure 1. Block diagram of the Control Data 6600. (*Source:* James E. Thornton, "The CDC 6600 Project," *Ann. His. Comput.*, Vol. 2, no. 4, October 1980, pp. 338–348, 346)

however, involved far more than the sociotechnical work of leading the team at Chippewa. Cray did not attempt to develop the basic components for the machine: developing an innovative configuration or "architecture" for them was work enough. This placed his team on the horns of a dilemma. A conservative choice of components would reduce risks, but might not give the speed that was necessary. The other Control Data teams were no slouches, despite the range of needs they were seeking to satisfy, and to justify itself within Control Data, much less find a place on the market, the 6600 project had to be a lot faster than the 3600 series. Components at the state of the art, or just beyond it, would give the edge in speed, but would place the fate of Cray's project in the hands of their developers, over whom he had no control.

Cray's preferred approach was conservative—"keep a decade behind" is one of his sayings on display at Boston's Computer Museum—and his team began by trying to wring a 15- to 20-fold speed increase over the 1604 without a radical change in components. They found this impossible to achieve. Fortunately, a new silicon transistor, manufactured by Fairchild Semiconductor, appeared on the market in time to salvage the project, and design was begun again with that as its basis, though the speed goal of the delayed project had to be increased relative to the 3600 to make up for the lost time.

The problematic relationship between computer designer and component supplier is a theme that was to recur in the history of supercomputing. So is another issue that came to the fore during the development of the 6600. Like almost all other computers, the 6600's operations were synchronized by pulses in the control circuitry; the intervals between those pulses were its "clock cycle." The target clock cycle for the 6600 was 100 nanoseconds, one ten-millionth of a second. In such a tiny interval of time, the finite speed of electrical signals became a constraint. If the wires were too long, a signal would not arrive at its destination within one cycle of the clock. So the circuitry of the 6600 had to be packaged very densely. With the silicon transistors they got a 10-fold density improvement, but dense packaging meant intense heat generation.

This heat had to be removed. Cray grasped the centrality of what others might have considered a menial aspect of computer design, and superintended the design of a special cooling system, with Freon refrigerant circulating though pipes in the machine's structure to remove the heat.

To produce a machine of the 6600's daunting complexity was no easy task. The wider computer industry had already started applying its own products in more and more automated design and production systems. Cray took a step in the opposite direction. The most sophisticated computer of its day was, in effect, handcrafted. Cray was even reluctant to turn it over to the Control Data production facilities in the Minneapolis suburb of Arden Hills, so the first few 6600s were built at Chippewa. Finally, the transition was successfully made, but it was no simple matter of handing over blueprints. The production process, and integrating the large network of suppliers whose parts went into the 6600, required the most careful attention, though not from Cray himself. His habit was to delegate the task to others in his team, but he was always fortunate in the people to whom he delegated it. Les Davis, who was Cray's chief engineer for almost three decades, played a particularly crucial role in making Seymour Cray's ideas work.

This connection to the outside world was not the only way the boundary around Chippewa had to be made permeable. Potential customers also had to have access, so while users in general were kept at arm's length, a few select people passed relatively freely between Chippewa and sites where the 6600 might be used. The most crucial such site was the nuclear weapons laboratory at Livermore, California. As it turned out, the Livermore Director of Computing, Sidney Fernbach, had easier access to Cray's laboratory than Norris did, and close liaison developed between the two sites. Cray, widely considered a "technical dictator," was prepared to listen to Fernbach's advice about how to shape the 6600 to make sure it met Livermore's unique needs for computer power.[12]

As a result, the 6600 provided a quantum leap in the computing power available to Livermore and its competitor nuclear laboratory at Los Alamos. It even gave the United States a temporary lever in its attempt to control French nuclear weapons policy, the American government in 1966 blocking the export of a Control Data 6600 destined for the French bomb program (though the requisite calculations were performed surreptitiously on an apparently civil 6600).[13] Although the term was not yet used, the 6600 was indeed a supercomputer, enjoying a significant advantage in arithmetic speed over all other machines of its day, worldwide.

Even Control Data, which had had to proceed much more on faith than had Fernbach—Cray's reports to his employers were delightfully succinct and uninformative[14]—was repaid. The largest sales achieved by any previous supercomputer, IBM's Stretch, was eight. Soon after its introduction in 1964, the 6600 became a big success and, before the decade was out, had orders exceeding 100, at around $8 million a machine. IBM was rattled, the 6600 prompting a famous acerbic memo from chairman Thomas J. Watson, Jr., to his staff, enquiring why Cray's team of "34 people—including the janitor" had outperformed the computing industry's mightiest corporation.[15]

"Big Blue," as the rest of the industry called IBM, bent its efforts to developing, out of the basic multipurpose Series 360 architecture, "top-end" machines, to compete with Cray. Although IBM controlled vastly more resources, and had at its call considerable talent (including Gene Amdahl, a computer designer of great skill who was to become almost as famous as Cray), it failed. Ultimately, IBM was not prepared to sacrifice compatibility for speed; nor, perhaps, were the "social" aspects of Cray's strategy replicable within a giant organization with a notoriously conformist corporate culture. The 1967 IBM 360/91 surpassed the 6600, but Cray was a moving target, and had his successor machine, the 7600, ready by 1969. It was 1971 when IBM, with the 360/195, caught up. IBM sought to compensate for its lag by announcing these machines well in advance of their readiness. Control Data responded with the computer industry's most famous law suit, using the U.S.'s antitrust laws to charge IBM with illegal monopolistic practices.

Yet all was not entirely well with Cray's strategy, and IBM's countermoves were only part of the problem. The 7600 was built very much according to the same priorities as the 6600, but while the 6600 offered a speed advantage of as much as 20 over previous-generation computers, the 7600 was only four times faster than the 6600. Was it worth spending a further $10 million and significant amounts of time modifying programs, to obtain that degree of speed-up? Some 6600 users, notably the nuclear weapons laboratories, answered in the affirmative. But many others said "no." Sales of the 7600, while still healthy, were only half those of the 6600. In particular, universities, a large sector of the 6600's market, failed to upgrade.

Initially, Cray seemed unperturbed. He and his team began designing a further machine, the 8600. This involved a bigger break from the 7600 than that between the 7600 and 6600. Despairing of achieving large enough speed increases by new components and incremental changes to architecture, Cray moved to embrace the much discussed, but as yet little practiced, principle of parallelism. The 8600 was to have four central processing units working simultaneously, while all previous Cray machines (and nearly all previous computers of whatever kind) had but one. Again, an idea that seems simple in principle turned out complex in practice. Ensuring adequate communication between the processors, and preventing them from contending for access to the computer's one memory, were formidable problems.[16]

While Seymour Cray and his team were working on the 8600, another team within Control Data, led initially by Cray's former deputy James Thornton, was working on a rival machine: the STAR-100. Central to the STAR-100 was an idea at least as novel as multiple central processors: vector processing. In a vector processor one instruction can be used to perform a certain operation, not just on one or two pieces of data (as in a conventional "scalar" computer), but on large ordered sets ("strings" or vectors). An example would be an instruction to add two strings each of 100 figures to give one string of 100 figures as a result. If the data could be organized in this way (and many of the problems of interest to the weapons designers at Livermore appeared, at least at first sight, to have this kind of regularity), considerable gains in speed could be achieved without the complexity of multiple central processors.

With the backing of Fernbach and Livermore, Control Data began work on the STAR-100 (a STring ARray processor with the goal of 100 million results per second), but at the Arden Hills site, not Chippewa. The strategy differed from Cray's. Speed was indeed a priority, but users of different kinds had to be catered to. The cryptanalysts of the National Security Agency persuaded the STAR's developers to add hardware support for what those developers referred to as "spook instructions": data manipulations of particular interest to cryptanalysis. Control Data management (which had much greater access to the design process of the STAR than to that of the Cray machines) saw the STAR as the centerpiece of an integrated, compatible set of computers analogous to, but more advanced than, the IBM 360 Series. The result was a very large instruction set of over 200 instructions. For a long period, too, leadership of the project was ambiguous, the machine becoming an "engineers' paradise" in which everybody could have some novel ideas incorporated, but in which communication and coordination was poor. Only determined action by Neil Lincoln, who eventually replaced Thornton as project leader (Thornton left Control Data to set up his own firm, Network Systems Corporation) finally achieved delivery of the STAR to Livermore in 1974, four years late.[17]

The STAR was—indeed still is—a controversial machine. Its adherents point out that it did achieve, indeed, surpassed, its impressive goal of 100 million results per second, and note that the vector processing pioneered on the STAR was to dominate at least the next two decades of supercomputing. Its detractors point out that it only approached its top speed on special programs that allowed extensive use of its vector capabilities. In scalar mode, in which one instruction produces one result, the machine was slower than the CDC 7600 of five years previous. The judgment of the market at the time was with the detractors: only three STARS were sold.

The very existence of the STAR project in the late 1960s and early 1970s, however, added further to the internal troubles of the 8600 project. Both factors were compounded by a change in direction at the top level of Control Data. Diagnosing "a great change" taking place in the supercomputer market, William C. Norris, CDC's President and Chairman of the Board, said that Control Data's high-speed scientific computers had developed to a point where customers now needed little more in the way of increased speed and power. Instead, said Norris, supercomputer users were demanding service and software to help them get more effective use of the speed they already had. "In other words," he concluded, "the emphasis today shifts to applying very large computers as opposed to development of more power." Although Control Data would continue to build and market large-scale scientific computers, investment in their research and development would be curtailed.[18]

Control Data's new corporate plan allowed for supercomputer development, but not at the pace Cray wanted—a completely fresh, significantly faster machine, every five years. The increasingly tenuous ties between Cray and Control Data were severed in 1972: "Since building large computers is my hobby, I decided that with this shift in emphasis, it was time for me to make a change," Cray said. He left to start his own company, taking four colleagues with him.[19]

Cray Research

It says a lot about the respect in which Cray was held that the split was surprisingly amicable. Control Data's Commercial Credit Company even invested $500,000 in the new Cray Research, Inc. (CRI), adding to $500,000 of Cray's own money and a total of $1,500,000 from 14 other investors: the computer business had been sufficiently profitable that Cray had several personal friends within it who were able to put in as much as $250,000 each. Cray was both president and chief executive officer. Finally, he could give full expression to his sociotechnical strategy, without even the residual encumberances of a large corporation.

The strategy was of breathtaking simplicity, but it also made sense. Cray Research would build and sell one machine at a time, and each machine would be a supercomputer. There would be no diversified product range, no attempt to make money (as Control Data very successfully did) primarily from the sale of peripherals like disk drives and printers, no dilution of the commitment to build the fastest possible machine. By delimiting the goal, and keeping to a single development team of perhaps 20 people under the undistracted command of Seymour Cray himself, costs could be kept small. A selling price sufficiently above cost would be set to cover research and development expenditures.[19]

That the customer base for the world's fastest computer was small—Cray estimated it at 50—did not disturb him. Indeed, it was to his advantage that he already knew who his potential customers were—those purchasers of the 6600 and 7600, such as the nuclear weapons laboratories, whose demand for speed was still unsatisfied and was perhaps insatiable. They would be prepared to pay the by now traditional supercomputer price of around $8 million to $10 million per machine. The economics of his enterprise was, indeed, clear. If he could achieve the high-performance computer industry's traditional margin of a selling price of three times manufacturing cost, the proceeds of a single sale would recoup the entire initial capital investment.

Cray could not afford to take any risks with component technology, and certainly could not afford to develop it within Cray Research. He chose a very simple, but reliable, integrated circuit. It was, however, by no means fast enough on its own to give anything like the increase in speed needed to establish his new machine, to be called simply the CRAY-1.

It was in the choice of the Cray-1's architecture that Cray displayed a flexibility often absent in single-minded, dominant technical entrepreneurs.[20] He abandoned the multiple processor approach that had failed on the CDC 8600, and adopted that of its rival, the STAR-100—vector processing.[21] However, he had the advantage over the STAR's designers that he had the failings of a real machine (or at least, an advanced development project) to learn from. Like others, he concluded that the STAR had two interrelated flaws.

First, the STAR's scalar performance was far slower than its vector speed, so if even a small part of a program could not be made suitable for vector processing, the overall speed of running that program would be drastically reduced. Cray therefore decided to place great emphasis on giving the CRAY-1 the fastest possible scalar processor. Second, the full vector speed of the STAR was achieved only if data could be packaged into regular vectors of considerable size. This was partly attributed to the fact that the STAR processed the vectors directly from memory and then sent the results back to memory, in effect using a "pipeline" that was very fast when full, but which took a relatively long time to fill. Cray decided instead to introduce a small intermediate storage level ("vector registers"), built from very fast, but extremely expensive, memory chips.

Other differences between the CRAY-1 and the STAR were predictable consequences of their very different circumstances of development. Cray did not worry about compatibility with any other machine, whether designed by him or anyone else. Once again, he had his "clean sheet of paper." The CRAY-1's instruction set is in fact more complex than the 6600's—it may be that Cray's old links to cryptanalysis came into play—but the great elaboration of the STAR was avoided. The old issues of physical size and cooling were once again central. The STAR's "memory-to-memory" pipeline, and relatively slow scalar unit, permitted a physically large machine. Cray's fast scalar unit, and vector register design, did not.

His goal was a clock cycle of 12.5 nanoseconds, well below the 40 nanoseconds of the STAR. In the former time interval, even light in free space travels no more than 4 meters, and an electric signal in a wire is slower. This goal influenced several technical decisions. Along with the continuing fear of placing himself in the hands of others whom he could not control, it persuaded even Cray to override, as far as memory design was concerned, his motto about keeping "a decade behind." In previous machines he had always used magnetic core memories. Under the impact of competition from the new semiconductor memories, however, the manufacturers of core memories were concentrating on the cheap, low-performance end of the market. Cray therefore decided to opt for slower, but physically smaller and reliably available, semiconductor memory chips.[22]

Shrinking the machine also intensified the familiar problem of heat. The CRAY-1 generated about four times as much heat per cubic centimeter as the 7600. Cray's team therefore developed a new cooling scheme for the CRAY-1. Its integrated circuits were mounted on boards back-to-back with copper plates built onto vertical columns of "cold bars"—aluminum blocks containing stainless steel tubes through which Freon coolant flowed. The complete machine consisted of twelve columns arranged in a 270-degree arc, thus giving the machine its now famously elegant C-shaped horizontal cross-section[23] (see Fig. 2).

The CRAY-1 was as much a *tour de force* as the 6600. All but a few adherents of the STAR accepted that the CRAY-1 was, by a large margin, the world's fastest machine when it appeared in 1976. It is interesting to note, however, that it was a triumph of Cray's general sociotechnical strategy and insight into the weak points of previous designs, rather than of specific invention. Among the few parts of the original design that were patented were the cooling system and the vector registers.

It was nevertheless a technical triumph. This time around, IBM did not even try to compete: corporate pride was outweighed by the memory of past failures and by a sense that supercomputing was merely a market niche of limited size, rather than the flagship of all computing. Control Data tried, with a reengineered, improved version of the STAR, the 1981 Cyber 205. It was a strong technical rival to the CRAY-1—faster on long vectors, though still not as fast on short ones—but it was too late. By 1985, around 30 Cyber 205s had been sold—not bad by the standards of the 1960s, but as we shall see, not good enough by the new standards of the 1980s, standards set by Cray Research.

The Transformation of the Cray Strategy

What made the chase ultimately fruitless was not any entrenched speed advantage of the CRAY-1 and successor Cray Research machines. The Cyber 205, and its successor, the ETA[10], were indeed faster on some measures than the Cray machines. Similarly, the Japanese industry's entry into supercomputing during the 1980s led to machines that were faster than Cray Research's on some criteria, and the American suppliers of "massively parallel" computers regularly quote performance figures far higher than those of Cray Research's modestly parallel vector processors. Rather, Seymour Cray's sociotechnical strategy was quietly transformed. The resulting "sociotechnical network," consisting of designers, users, and machines, ultimately had no place for Cray himself. Still, it has to date proved remarkably durable.

The transformation began with the second CRAY-1 to be sold. The first sale was the classic CRAY linkage of raw speed with the needs and resources of a nuclear weapons laboratory (Los Alamos, this time, not Livermore, since Fernbach had committed that laboratory to a second STAR 100), together with the classic Cray confidence. Los Alamos had not budgeted for a new supercomputer before 1977, and by

Figure 2. The CRAY-1 computer. (*Source:* David E. Lundstrom, *A Few Good Men from Univac,* M.I.T. Press, Cambridge, Mass., 1987).

the mid-1970s the weapons laboratory's computer acquisition process had become much more bureaucratized than in the 1950s and 1960s. Cray Research, without any sales four years after it had been set up, had to establish itself, and few customers other than Los Alamos would have the interest and the resources to accept a new machine that was almost devoid of software and was incompatible with its existing computers. Cray gambled and offered Los Alamos CRAY-1 Serial 1 on loan. "If the machine hadn't performed, Cray Research wouldn't have continued as a company."[24]

The customer identified for the next CRAY-1, Serial 3,[25] was not a nuclear weapons laboratory, but the National Center for Atmospheric Research. Although attracted by the CRAY-1's speed, the Boulder, Colorado, meteorological bureau refused to buy the machine unless Cray Research supplied the systems software as well.

Cray's strategy of building "the fastest computer in the world" and letting the users worry about software was put to the test. By 1976, the management of Cray Research was no longer solely in Seymour Cray's hands. Cray could raise money from friends, but he was not the man to negotiate details with Wall Street. Another mid-westerner, also an electrical engineer, but with a Harvard MBA, had been hired in 1975 as chief financial officer: 34-year-old John Rollwagen, who organized the successful 1976 public flotation of Cray Research. Rollwagen and others concluded that a more accommodating approach to users had to be taken, and committed the company to supplying the National Center for Atmospheric Research with systems software—an operating system and a Fortran compiler—as well as hardware, thereby initiating a major software development effort (located, significantly, in Minneapolis, not Chippewa) to parallel Cray's hardware development. In July 1977 CRAY-1, Serial 3 was shipped to Boulder, and by the end of the year three more computers had been sold. The company made its first net profit—$2 million—and John Rollwagen became president and chief executive officer.[26]

Although the sales of the CRAY-1 were just beginning, thoughts within Cray Research had already begun to turn to what to do next. There was discussion in the company about whether or not to move into the "low end," that is, to make smaller machines (what in the 1980s would come to be called minisupercomputers), derived from the CRAY-1, that would be cheaper and aim at a larger market. Seymour Cray disagreed, explicitly turning his back on the lure of growth. In the 1978 Annual Report he wrote:

> I would rather use the corporate resources to explore and develop newer and more unique computing equipment. Such a course will keep the Company in a position of providing advanced equipment to a small customer base in an area where no other manufacturer offers competitive products. This course also tends to limit the rate of growth of the company by moving out of market areas when competitive equipments begin to impact our sales. I think it is in the long-term best interests of the stockholders to limit growth in this manner and maintain a good profit margin on a smaller sales base.[27]

As always, Cray put his technological effort where his mouth was, starting work in 1978 on the CRAY-2, with the goal of a sixfold increase in speed over the CRAY-1—nearing the tantalizing target of the gigaflop, a thousand million floating-point arithmetic operations per second.

No one defied the founder by beginning work on a minisupercomputer. Nevertheless, Cray Research's development effort was not restricted to the CRAY-2, and extensive efforts were made to make the existing CRAY-1 attractive for a broader range of customers. The CRAY 1S, announced in 1979, kept to the founder's intention by offering improved performance: an input–output subsystem to remove bottlenecks that slowed the original CRAY-1, and a larger memory. In 1982, however, it was followed by the CRAY-1M, which offered the same performance as the 1S, but, through the use of a different, less expensive component technology, at a significantly lower price—$4 to $7 million, rather than the $8.5 to $13.3 million of the machines in the 1S series. The CRAY-1M was no "mini," but it could be seen as a step in that direction.

Changing the hardware on offer was only one aspect of the new, different strategy that began to develop at Cray Research. Systematically, different categories of users (not just weapons laboratories and weather bureaus, important though those remained) were cultivated. Their needs were explored and, where necessary, technology altered or developed to meet them. The oil industry was first, with four years of cultivation between first contacts and the first sale, in 1980. That industry's most relevant computational need was for the processing of seismic data, in quantities far exceeding even the weapons laboratories or weather bureaus. A specially developed additional memory—the Solid-State Device (SSD)—helped, but a crucial (and symbolically significant) step was Cray Research's investment in the development of a link between IBM magnetic tape equipment and a Cray supercomputer, together with software to handle tapes that had suffered physically from the rigors of oil exploration.[28]

Aerospace, the automotive industry, and chemicals were further targets for successive waves of focused cultivation and "network building." Although physical devices had sometimes to be developed to cement links, software development was far more important. It was no longer sufficient, as it had been at the sale of Serial 3, to supply an operating system and a Fortran compiler. Compilers for other programming languages were developed, and particular attention was devoted to "vectorizing" compilers, which would enable the users of Cray supercomputers to take advantage of their machines' vector speed without having to invest large amounts of time in rewriting programs (as the Livermore users of the STAR-100 had had to do). Cray Research even took upon itself the conversion for use on its machines of specific computer packages that were important in areas being targeted for sales, such as the PAMCRASH automobile crash simulation program. By 1985, 200 major applications packages had been converted to run on Cray machines.[29]

The result of all this effort was that during the 1980s Cray Research's expenditure on software development came to equal that of hardware development. Seymour Cray should not be thought of as opposed to this. Ever flexible about the means to achieve the goal of speed, if not about the goal itself, he could even be seen to be in the lead of this effort, abandoning, for the CRAY-2, Cray Research's own Cray Operating System (COS), and moving instead to UNIX, which was rapidly becoming a standard operating system, and which was much better at handling time-sharing and interactive computing than Cray Research's original system. Cray's flavor of UNIX was christened UNICOS.

But his readiness to make the shift also indicated a widening chasm. The change was in part sensible because the CRAY-2 differed so radically in architecture from the CRAY-1 that converting the Cray Operating System was scarcely any easier than shifting to UNIX. Once again, Seymour Cray had started with a clean sheet of paper in his search for speed. But with the company paying closer attention to the priorities of users disinclined to invest in rewriting programs, and with the growing Cray Research investment in software, the clean sheet of paper was beginning to seem a problem, not an advantage, to others in the company.[30]

Here, furthermore, the unpredictability of trying to implement a strategy in an only partially tractable world, rather than rational choice between strategies, played a decisive role, and added to the centrifugal forces already pushing Seymour Cray away from the center of the company he had founded. To gain his desired speed increase, Cray was pursuing an ambitious design that combined new, faster chips (developed by Motorola and Fairchild in cooperation with Cray), multiple central processing, and a processor architecture significantly different from that of the CRAY-1. Despite their respect for Cray, others in the firm questioned whether he could succeed in all these innovations simultaneously, and difficulties and delays in the CRAY-2 project reinforced their fears.

Les Davis, Cray's chief engineer, began the process by which an alternative to the CRAY-2 emerged. He suggested that these new chips be used in a multiprocessor design, but one in which the basic processor was essentially the same as in the CRAY-1. Such a machine would enjoy greater software compatibility with the CRAY-1, and even if no product emerged, it would allow the increasingly important software developers to experiment with parallel processing in advance of the CRAY-2. On Davis's instigation a second design team was formed, headed by a young Taiwan-born engineer, Steve Chen, to pursue a low-level, cheap effort along these lines.

The effort greatly surpassed the hopes of its instigator. John Rollwagen, concerned that Cray Research's future was being staked too exclusively on the CRAY-2, decided to sell the Davis–Chen machine as a product. The CRAY X-MP, announced in 1982, offered up to five times the performance of the CRAY-1S, nearly as much as the CRAY-2's as yet unmet goal, but with the advantage of substantial software compatibility with the CRAY-1.[31] The X-MP fitted its niche beautifully, in both a physical sense (the use of more advanced chips meant that multiple processors could be fitted into a cabinet very similar to that of the CRAY-1) and a commercial sense, given the importance of software to Cray Research and its users. It became more popular than any previous supercomputer, with almost 160 sales of different versions by the end of 1989.[32]

Seymour Cray managed to snatch partial success for the CRAY-2 from what was rapidly beginning to look like a path to oblivion: an advanced design route to a new computer offering little, if any, speed increase on the X-MP, which was fast becoming an established product. He managed to differentiate the CRAY-2 from the X-MP by using slow but relatively inexpensive chips to offer a massive memory of up to 256 megawords, two orders of magnitude more than existing machines at the time. He compensated for this slowness of this massive memory by attaching small, fast memories to each of the CRAY-2's four processors. This tactic worked only partially: very careful management of memory resources by users of the CRAY-2 is needed to prevent the slow main memory from becoming a bottleneck. But a sufficient number of users wanted a massive memory (by the end of 1989 twenty-four CRAY-2s had been sold)[32] for there to be reasons other than sentiment for Cray Research to market its founder's design.

The most immediate reason for the CRAY-2's dangerous delay (it came on the market only in 1985, three years after the X-MP) was problems with cooling, and the various approaches that were taken to solve these problems are a further interesting indicator of the specificity of Cray's preferred sociotechnical style. The CRAY-2's components were packaged even more closely than in previous machines, and Cray, despite repeated efforts, could not make his existing approach to cooling, based on circulating Freon refrigerant, work well enough:

> You don't know you are going down the wrong road on a design until you have invested six months or a year in it. I had about three of those false starts on the CRAY-2. The cooling mechanism in those designs didn't work.[33]

In a "last desperate attempt" Cray tried a completely new cooling approach in which the whole machine would be immersed in a cooling liquid that, by its forced circulation, would remove the heat produced. When he proposed the scheme nobody took it seriously. "[E]veryone on the project laughed, in fact they rolled in the aisles. Because everybody knew the boards would swell up and it just wouldn't work."[34] Indeed, liquid immersion cooling had been tried before, and a variety of known coolants had been investigated, all of which in a short time damaged the printed circuit boards. But Seymour Cray took a different approach, selecting liquids not primarily because of their cooling properties, but on the basis of their known inertness. One of the liquids he subsequently tried was a substance that was used in artificial blood. This finally worked, and allowed Cray to build a machine that was very densely packed but that could still be cooled[35] (see Fig. 3).

An Amicable Parting

The great success of the X-MP, and partial success of the CRAY-2, contributed to Cray Research's continuing growth. Despite its specific market, the company's sales began to nudge it into the ranks of the dozen or so leading computer suppliers in the world, albeit still far behind the giant IBM. That success, however, masked the deepening of the divide between its founder and the bulk of the company he had founded. In 1989, four years after the CRAY-2 went on the market, Seymour Cray left Cray Research.

During the latter part of the 1980s, Seymour Cray's strategy, and that dominant in Cray Research, had continued to diverge. The Cray Research strategy was to build on the success of the X-MP and the growing user base that made that success possible, seeking systematically to develop new fields of application and strengthening relations with existing customers. The purchaser of an X-MP (or the improved, but compatible, Y-MP) is now buying not raw speed, but access to extensive software resources and services. Cray Research will help customers new to supercomputing to plan their installations, and provide on-site support for the life of the installation. The firm guarantees that should a Cray Research supercomputer fail anywhere in the world, a Cray engineer will be on site within two hours to solve the problem.

Far from keeping users at arm's length, Cray Research seeks to bind them ever more tightly to the company. A Cray User Group has been set up, which holds meetings for all users of Cray supercomputers every year. These meetings are attended by

Figure 3. The CRAY-2 computer. (Photograph by Paul Shambroom; reprinted with permission from Cray Research, Inc.)

Cray representatives, enabling the company to respond quickly to any problems or desires that may emerge from these meetings. Cray Research is also paying increasing attention to links with other suppliers, as well as to users. The announcement in 1990 of a "network supercomputing" strategy for Cray Research made this explicit: the supercomputer is no longer to be seen as an artifact standing on its own, but as a central part of complex companywide networks, many parts of which will be supplied by companies other than Cray.[36]

If this strategy begins to sound a little like the statements by Norris that were instrumental in Cray leaving Control Data, one crucial difference should be emphasized: Cray Research is still very concerned with speed. The CRAY Y-MP, which came onto the market in 1988, is about two to three times faster than the X-MP, though comparison is difficult because both machines have been made available in many different processor numbers and memory sizes to suit different kinds of customers. The successor to the Y-MP, generally referred to as the C-90, will be a further expression of this technological approach: it will be compatible with its predecessors, and of broadly similar design, but will be significantly faster, embodying improved component technologies, more central processors (16 rather than the 8 of the top-of-the-range Y-MP), and a larger memory.[37]

Simultaneously, however, the heretical step "down" toward the minisupercomputer has also been made. In 1990, Cray Research announced an air-cooled version of the Y-MP series: slower, but, at $2.2 million and up, significantly cheaper, though still more expensive than most minisupers. Cray Research launched the Y-MP/EL late in 1991, configured with up to four CPUs, with each CPU costing $300,000. Each CPU costs about 1.5 percent of the price, in real terms, of the original CRAY-1, launched in 1976, but with the same performance.[38]

Seymour Cray's commitment to speed, on the other hand, remained much more obvious. His goal for the CRAY-3 is a twelvefold increase in speed over the CRAY-2, to sixteen thousand million floating-point arithmetic operations per second.[39] The machine will be compatible with the CRAY-2, but it will not be compatible with the X-MP, Y-MP, or C-90.

In one crucial respect, however, the CRAY-3 is a departure from Cray's previous strategy. A fourfold improvement in speed over the CRAY-2 is expected to come from using 16 processors compared to four on the CRAY-2, but that leaves a factor of at least 3 to come from faster components. As we have seen, Cray's preference in all previous machines was to remain well within the state of the art in component technology—to avoid both risk and also a complex division of labor. But, for the CRAY-3, he concluded that the state of the art would not sustain the sought-for increase in component speed, and so for the CRAY-3 he has taken the "high-technology approach" that he eschewed for the CRAY-2.

Nor is the form taken by this approach the silicon very large-scale integration (VLSI) path, which, though new to Cray, had many analogues in the wider computer industry. Instead, Seymour Cray became the first computer designer to commit himself to using processor chips made out of gallium arsenide rather than silicon. Gallium arsenide had long been discussed as a faster substitute for silicon (Cray himself had investigated but rejected it for the CRAY-2), but there were known to be daunting difficulties: in the number of circuits that could be implemented on a gallium arsenide chip, in manufacturing the chips, and in their reliability. Around the computer industry, the prevalent jibe was that "gallium arsenide is the technology of the future, always has been, always will be."[40]

With the CRAY-3, Seymour Cray gambled that the future was about to arrive, and that he could manage a more complex process of technological development, involving not just his own design team but also groups outside the company developing gallium arsenide components for the project. Reports suggest that he has been successful. The CRAY-3 project has, however, met with serious delays. The problems have arisen, it seems, not from the gallium arsenide, but from the continuing miniaturization needed to sustain ever-increasing speed. The CRAY-3 is planned to operate with a 2-nanosecond clock period, handling one scalar instruction every clock period. For this to be possible, given the finite speed of electrical signals, the maximum allowable wire length is 16 inches. So the CRAY-3 modules are unprecedentedly small for a supercomputer. Seymour Cray's design calls for cramming 1,024 chips into a module measuring just 4 by 4 by 1/4 inches—so delicate a job that special robots will be needed. Such a module has nine functional layers that are interconnected vertically with up to 15,000 twist pin jumpers that are inserted through holes in each layer. The whole CRAY-3, meaning 16 processors and 512 Mwords of memory, will use 336 of those modules and will be packed in a box less than a cubic foot in size.[41]

Sustaining both the CRAY-3 and C-90 projects, together with the growing range of other development activities (especially in software) that Cray Research was becoming committed to, began to place strains on the company. During the first quarter of 1989, research and development expenses were about 35 percent higher than in the first quarter of the preceding year, even after the cancellation of another ambitious project, the MP project led by Steve Chen. At the same time, Cray Research's annual growth of revenues had slowed from about 50 percent in the early 1980s to about 10 percent in 1988.[42] The share price of Cray Research, long the darling of Wall Street, was beginning to slump drastically. Either the CRAY-3 or C-90 had to go.

Which was it to be? With the delays in the CRAY-3, it and the C-90 were expected to appear at roughly the same time, 1990/1991, and were going to be similar in speed and memory sizes. The main difference was in compatibility. The CRAY-3 would be compatible with the CRAY-2, of which about 25 machines had been sold. The C-90 would be compatible with the X-MP and Y-MP line, with an installed base of around two hundred. The logic was clear. The C-90 had to be preserved and the CRAY-3 canceled.

Yet it could not be as simple as that. John Rollwagen knew that "not choosing Seymour's machine would have torn the company apart." "After six months mulling over alternatives," Rollwagen proposed to Cray yet another "amicable divorce."[43] A new company would be incorporated to undertake the further development of the CRAY-3. The new company would at first be a wholly owned subsidiary of Cray Research, with Cray Research transferring to it $50 million worth of facilities and up to $100 million in operating funds over two years. For Cray Research, with a revenue of $750 million a year, this was a lot of money. However, Cray Research's shareholders would be rewarded by receiving shares in the new company on a tax-free basis, Cray

Research would now be able to concentrate its efforts and resources on the one project, and failure of the CRAY-3 would not endanger Cray Research's existence.

While making it clear that the split was not his idea, Seymour Cray agreed to it: "I don't mind this role. I kind of like starting over."[44] Once again, he was working for a small start-up company, this time called the Cray Computer Corporation. This time, however, it was not in Chippewa. Prior to the split, the CRAY-3 team had moved to Colorado Springs, in the foothills of the Rocky Mountains. Nor is the world the same as in 1957, or in 1972. In 1972, in particular, Cray Research's commitment to building the world's fastest computer was unique. It had no direct competitor, the less than wholehearted effort at Control Data aside. At the start of the 1990s, Cray Research, the Japanese supercomputer companies, and Steve Chen (who left Cray Research when his MP project was canceled, to form a new firm backed by IBM) are all pursuing speed, as are a number of other companies that have developed or are developing machines of a quite different structure to those characteristic of "mainstream supercomputing."

Growing Networks Limit Room to Move

In this newly competitive marketplace, Cray Research still enjoys a dominant position, not through speed alone, but more through the diverse, entrenched links it has built with users. Over the years a network of relationships has evolved in which the technology under development binds users and manufacturers together. For both, this network limits their room to move, unless they are prepared to put at stake what has been built up. In the 1960s and early 1970s relationships between users and manufacturers of supercomputers were close only in the period of the actual sales. Subsequently, to put it baldly, the two parted with a "see you around in five years" (when a new supercomputer would be ready for sale). Especially during the early 1980s, with the broadening of the customer base, relationships intensified considerably. As noted earlier, Cray Research opened new markets by having extensive talks with new customers, trying to understand their problems, and subsequently trying to solve these problems by undertaking the development of specific hardware and software. Once a deal was made, Cray Research provided its customers with a variety of support services, from preinstallation site planning to on-site support for the life of the installation.

Concerning software, Cray Research established applications groups within the company that deal with the various fields of applications, keep in touch with the people in the field, try to develop new applications, or to develop solutions to emerging problems. Taking on software development implied not only a shift in its activities, but also an extension of the network of relationships surrounding supercomputers. Rather than starting software applications development from scratch, Cray Research developed relationships with a variety of third-party software vendors in order to optimize the existing codes for Cray machines, thus creating a triangular relationship with these vendors and (potential) users of Cray supercomputers. As a result of such efforts, over 200 major application packages were available on Cray systems by 1985.[45]

In order not to alienate the existing customer base, Cray Research is compelled to continue building on the existing technology, that is, both hardware and software. This clearly limits its freedom to maneuver; only Seymour Cray himself, by virtue of his high prestige, can afford to "start with a clean sheet of paper," and even his sheet is no longer as clean as it used to be. But while the sociotechnical network surrounding supercomputing limits innovation, it is also a formidable barrier to competition from outsiders.

Network Relations as a Shield against Competitors

Cray Research currently enjoys a near monopoly in terms of actual sales of supercomputers. This is not because there is no competition, but, as we just said, because it has built a network of relationships with a substantial range of customers that is based on more than just a fast computer. This network encompasses advanced software as well as advanced hardware, and includes Cray Research as the manufacturer of supercomputers, a wide variety of users, and a large number of software vendors.

In the early 1980s the only serious competitor to Cray Research was CDC. For certain applications the performance of CDC's CYBER-205 compared favorably to that of the CRAY-1, which enabled CDC to seize about 20 percent of the supercomputer market. But after Cray Research offered the X-MP and the CRAY-2, not many 205s were sold. In September 1983, CDC founded a separate company, ETA Systems Inc., to develop CDC's next-generation supercomputer. ETA announced the target of 10 gigaflops for their ETA[10] machine, that is, an order of magnitude faster than the CRAY-2 and X-MP, then the fastest machines. The architecture of the 205 was taken as a point of departure. Since this, in its turn, was based on that of the STAR-100, program compatibility would be maintained with the software developed for the STAR and CYBER-205.

The increase in speed of the ETA[10] over the CYBER-205 was to come from using faster circuits and incorporating eight processors. This goal was achieved by using complementary metal oxide semiconductor (CMOS) chip technology rather than the bipolar technology traditional in supercomputing. The gap in speed between CMOS and the faster bipolar technology had been narrowing and it also appeared that CMOS could be speeded up by a factor of about 2 by cooling it down to the temperature of liquid nitrogen, or about $-200°C$. The ETA[10] thus became the first supercomputer to use cryogenic cooling.

In a technological sense, the ETA[10] was a considerable success. Late in 1986, just over three years after the incorporation of ETA Systems, the first machine was sold, albeit in the rawest of states, to Florida State University. Independent analysts expected that "(w)ith this interesting development one can be assured that the CYBER 205 architecture will . . . be of lasting interest."[46] They were wrong. The immediate problem was the financial difficulties of ETA's parent company, CDC. CDC therefore started to sell or liquidate divisions or subsidiaries that were losing money, one of which was ETA. In April 1989 ETA was closed brutally and painfully with total losses of $490 million.[47]

As a result, Cray Research had lost one potential competitor. During the 1980s, however, a number of other competitors had appeared on the scene. First was Japan. In October 1981, at a conference in Tokyo, the Japanese Ministry of Trade and Industry presented a plan to leapfrog current technology and secure the world lead in advanced computing by the late 1990s. One part of the plan, the National Superspeed Computer Project, involved spending an estimated $200 million over eight years to develop a supercomputer capable of executing 10 gigaflops, or 65 times faster than the CRAY-1, the fastest machine at the time.[48] In 1985, the Nippon Electric Company (NEC) introduced the SX-2, with an announced peak speed of 1.3 gigaflops, which took direct aim at the CRAY-2, which also appeared that year. In 1985, NEC became the first foreign supercomputer maker to install a machine on U.S. soil. The SX-2's buyer was the Houston Area Research Centre (HARC), a consortium of four Texas universities. But further sales of NEC, Hitachi, and Fujitsu supercomputers outside Japan remained very limited. Although there has been strong political resistance in the United States to the purchase of Japanese supercomputers, the Japanese companies also have not been able to supply the range of software that is available for the Cray machines. Gigaflops were no longer all that counted. As Cray president John Rollwagen put it: "(A) supercomputer's peak speed is comparable to the speed of the spinning wheels of a car on blocks: The motion is meaningless unless useful work is being done."[49] Japanese companies are trying to fill the software gap and also continue developing faster machines. In April 1990, NEC announced that it would shortly introduce a computer with a top speed of 22 gigaflops.[50]

A second source of new competition has been IBM. The growth of the supercomputing market (a growth, as we have seen, largely stimulated by deliberate actions of Cray Research) persuaded IBM to reconsider its strategy of leaving this "niche" to Cray Research. Like Hitachi and Fujitsu, IBM achieved supercomputer performance by adding vector processors to a basic mainframe design, the IBM 3090. The IBM philosophy is, however, somewhat different. The Japanese manufacturers achieve high theoretical performance by emphasizing very high levels of vectorization, while IBM has focused upon more modest levels of vectorization, accompanied by high scalar speed. Cycle time for the initial 3090 was 18.5 nanoseconds.[51]

This means that, in scalar mode, this IBM machine is a factor of 2 to 3 slower than the Cray supercomputers, and therefore IBM cannot compete with Cray Research for customers that want the greatest performance per se. But there is a gray area of customers that are interested in "almost the fastest computer in the world" with all the advantages of IBM compatibility. For them, the 0.5-gigaflop performance of a six-processor IBM-3090 with vector facilities[52] may be very attractive. Like Cray Research, IBM has not concentrated on hardware alone. It, too, has looked at specific groups of users, analyzed their problems, and subsequently developed software dedicated to their applications. As a result, in terms of sheer numbers, IBM has probably sold the most vector computers.[53] This policy, together with the fast growth of much cheaper "minisupercomputers" from a variety of vendors, may well limit Cray Research's possibilities for growth into the "near supercomputer" market.

At the same time, by teaming up with Steve Chen after he left Cray Research and formed Supercomputer Systems, Inc., IBM has also left itself the option of trying to get a stake in the market for the fastest machines. IBM partly funds development at Chen's firm in exchange for access to its technology. Little has been disclosed about the machine Chen is working on, but it is believed to be a radically parallel (but probably not massively parallel) design. The performance goal is set very aggressively at the teraflops range (1000 gigaflops), but the machine is not expected to be available until 1995. There are reports that Chen's machine will be significantly more expensive than today's most costly supercomputers, costing perhaps as much as $60 million.[54]

It is striking how most attempts to attack Cray Research's position are not all-out attempts to develop the fastest machine in the world (like Seymour Cray attempted with the 6600, the CRAY-1, and the CRAY-2), but are built on previous work and an established customer base. CDC took the 205 as a point of departure, IBM built further on its 3090, and the Japanese companies generally sought compatibility with IBM. Even Seymour Cray will now make the CRAY-3 compatible with the CRAY-2. Only Steve Chen is reportedly working on a "revolutionary" design. Consequently, no user can simply migrate from a Cray machine to one of the competitors without investing a considerable amount of time and money in problems of conversion.

As a result, Cray Research still dominates the high end of the market. ETA was dead before it had a chance to establish itself; IBM has basically only succeeded in "stretching" its existing market; and the Japanese companies have sold only in modest numbers outside Japan, and then mainly to scientific institutions to which they sell at a large discount. By contrast, Cray has gained a strong foothold in the Japanese private sector, with sales to automotive, electronics, chemical, and aerospace firms.

Aside from the entry of Japan, the most discussed form of competition to the Cray machines is "massively parallel processing." Instead of using a small number of very fast processors, as in a "classic supercomputer," massive parallelism uses a very large number (up to tens of thousands) of relatively slow microprocessors. The difficulty, of course, is that to make such numbers of processors work harmoniously together on a single job poses a tremendous software problem. Some massively parallel computers have achieved top speeds on particular problems in excess of the speed of classic supercomputers, but parallelizing compilers to permit ready generalization of this performance are still far from being realized. Some people therefore believe that the future of massive parallelism lies not in "general-purpose" computing, but rather as dedicated "add-ons" to more general-purpose machines. Certainly, massive parallelism shows that sheer speed is now far from sufficient for supercomputing success.

The worldwide market for massively parallel machines is estimated to be about $200 million in 1990, and is still heavily subsidized by government bodies. This is, however, about one-fourth of Cray Research's annual turnover. Cray Research has its own massive parallelism project, but rather than aiming to supplant mainstream supercomputing, Cray Research sees massive parallelism as an enhancement of general-purpose supercomputing and pursues integration of the two different architectural approaches. The firm hopes that users will do their general-purpose super-computing as they always have, while improving the performance of their highly parallel, specialized jobs on a massively parallel system designed and manufactured by Cray Research.[55]

National Interests

Competition in the supercomputer arena is not only an intercompany issue, it also has international dimensions. In the 1980s, the use and production of super-computers became a national issue in the United States. Supercomputer use was portrayed as being of vital importance to the country's national security and to the economic competition with Europe and Japan. It was argued that U.S. scientists and engineers had insufficient access to supercomputing facilities. Successive panels, composed of scientists from many fields as well as computer specialists, examined the situation and issued reports deploring it. One theme was stressed repeatedly: the United States could lose its leadership in technology because its scientists lacked adequate access to this fundamental tool of advanced research. Admonitory fingers were pointed toward Japan and Europe, where super-computers were being installed and used at a growing rate. The picture was sketched of an imminent and perhaps irreversible loss of America's international competitiveness.

Petitioners from universities looked primarily to Congress and a variety of sources of federal funds for academic research. Requests for support were directed to the National Institutes of Health, the National Science Foundation (NSF), the National Aeronautics and Space Administration (NASA), the Department of Energy, the Defense Advanced Research Projects Agency (DARPA), other parts of the Department of Defense, and smaller federal agencies. During the mid-1980s, an increasing number of these projects found favor in Congress and among the budget makers of these agencies. Ears that did not heed earlier appeals emphasizing scientific need became responsive to arguments about preserving America's prestige, American jobs, and American technological leadership. Legislators and administrators frustrated by the difficulty of finding solutions to problems of industrial policy, protectionism, exchange rates, and the cultural differences between Japanese and American factories discovered a talisman. It wasn't easy to fix all those other things, but it was possible to do something about the supercomputer shortage.[56]

The NSF decided to devote $200 million for the support of the supercomputing initiative over a five-year period, beginning in fiscal year 1985. It started by buying time at existing facilities and moved swiftly to select and fund five new supercomputer centers. All over North America, states and universities that did not secure formal federal support—or preferred to go their own way—also launched supercomputer programs. Around 1987 more than one hundred North American institutions participated in supercomputing.[57]

Another initiative was taken by the Office of Science and Technology (OSTP) when it launched the High-Performance Computing Initiative. This was intended to maintain the U.S. edge by focusing the research advantage in high-performance computing toward applications with high value to the economy and national security. The OSTP identified a wide range of scientific and engineering problems that it called "Grand Challenges." A Grand Challenge would be a fundamental problem with potentially broad economic, political, or scientific impact, that could be solved by applying supercomputer resources. While Grand Challenges usually were already being addressed by existing resources, it was argued that progress was limited because of the state of both hardware and software technology.[58]

Training in supercomputing also expanded rapidly during the period. The NSF-supported centers and many other facilities offered one-day introductory workshops for potential users, more thorough seminars, summer institutes for graduate students and other researchers, and additional opportunities. The Department of Energy offered summer institutes in supercomputing for promising high school students; other courses and summer internships were available at supercomputing centers in the national laboratories. Supercomputing facilities at universities offered similar opportunities.[59]

Besides access to supercomputers by scientists and engineers, another national issue was the competitiveness of the U.S. supercomputer industry. First to cause alarm was the Japanese government-funded program to leapfrog state-of-the-art technology. These fears were aggravated when Japanese companies started to offer supercomputers on the U.S. market in the mid-1980s. Articles in the *New York Times* and the *Washington Post* suggested that the U.S. supercomputer industry was on the brink of decline.

IEEE's Scientific Supercomputer Committee, chaired by Sidney Fernbach, former head of Livermore's computing division, recommended in a 1983 report that the government should commit itself to buying by 1987 a dozen supercomputers specified to have significantly increased performance. George Michael of Los Alamos National Laboratory doubted that this would help U.S. industry, since "Cray and CDC aren't positioned well for hotshot competition because they're not vertically integrated like the Japanese companies."[60]

The supercomputer was only one of several commercial products on which the United States felt it was losing ground to the Japanese. The U.S. government and various industry groups claimed that Japan was using unfair trade practices in a number of areas, ranging from semiconductors to construction contracts. These allegations spread to include supercomputing when NEC sold an SX-2 to the Houston Consortium. This U.S.–Japanese "trade war" cumulated in 1987 in the imposition of (now lifted) trade sanctions on Japan.

Interestingly, Cray Research did not welcome these sanctions. It had to compete with the Japanese companies everywhere in the world, not just in Japan and the United States. In that competition U.S. export licensing procedures were a handicap to Cray Research. Furthermore, Cray Research bought components from Japan and also sold computers to Japan (considerably more than the Japanese sold in the United States). The paradox is that it was not until Fujitsu and Hitachi entered the supercomputer market that Cray Research started to sell supercomputers in Japan. The firm was convinced that it could create additional business by having more alternatives, more competitors, more activity.[61]

From Megaflops to Total Solutions

In summarizing the historical sketch presented in this chapter we can identify three important changes in the dynamics of the supercomputer world. These are:

- It is no longer sheer performance that encourages the development of next machines, but rather performance combined with compatibility.
- Software has become increasingly important, also leading to the involvement of third-party vendors.
- The user base has expanded considerably and, moreover, has changed in character, with users from a larger variety of sectors and different levels of in-house computing expertise.

J. Neil Weintraut, a computer industry analyst, characterized the situation of the supercomputer market in the late 1980s as follows: "Cray Research will be facing increasing competition in the 1990s from Japanese firms, IBM, and Cray Computer at a time when the supercomputer market's annual growth has slowed from about 50 percent [in the early 1980s] to about 10 percent [in 1988]."[62] Other analyses doubted whether there would be any place for the United States in the world market in the 1990s because of the bad state that U.S. supercomputing was in. ETA had died in 1988 and Cray Research's revenues were leveling off. The spinning off of Cray Computer was not seen as a good sign either.

To assess these arguments, let us take a closer look at what happened. We have already described a number of attempts to build supercomputers faster than those of Cray Research. The end products of several of those attempts have claimed success over the past decade, but in the early 1990s Cray Research still dominates the supercomputing market. In the 1980s, too, U.S. supercomputing was perceived to be at the brink of collapse, which everyone feared would be caused by Japanese competition. Yet the 1990s see the Japanese companies being far from dominant, and the trade sanctions against Japan (never welcomed by Cray Research) have been dropped. Finally, in the 1980s it was widely predicted that massive parallelism would rapidly replace conventional supercomputing. This, too, has not happened.

All these failed predictions underestimated the sources of stability in high performance. They focused on either "the social" (e.g., Japanese competition) or "the technical" (the theoretical advantages of massive parallelism), without grasping the interrelations of the social and the technical, interrelations that give the field its stability.

One source of stability is that companies with an established customer base first of all seek not to alienate their current users and to build follow-on machines that are compatible with their predecessors. Cray Research, for example, has developed an evolutionary product line starting with the CRAY-1 that, via the 1S, 1M, X-MP, X-MP EA, and Y-MP, was continued up till its most recent undertaking, the C-90. The commitment of the company to this line became most evident when, in the second half of the 1980s, strains increased on research and development funds. As a result, Chen's MP project was killed and, when that did not solve the problem, Seymour Cray's CRAY-3 was spun off.

The CYBER-205 and ETA engineers did not change the basic architecture of their machines either. When they argued, in connection with the ETA, that a new operating system would be needed, CDC management forced them to port the old CYBER operating system to the ETA[10]. They were allowed, however, to start a low-level effort to port UNIX to the new machine.[63] The designers of the vector box at IBM could get no architectural relief from the 3090's basic architecture, while the Japanese took their existing mainframes as a starting point. Even Seymour Cray modified his "clean sheet of paper" approach and has designed the CRAY-3 to be compatible with the CRAY-2.

This implies that when users change vendors they have to modify their programs while, when they buy follow-ons from the same vendor, they can run them again immediately (although some conversion effort may lead to additional speed-up by making use of novel features on the new machine). Therefore, when performance and price of different machines are comparable, users are not likely to turn to a different vendor.

The quoted performance figures for supercomputers currently available (or near availability) are all in the same ball park. Although quoted peak performances may vary, such values have limited meaning in practice. Performance often depends on the type of code run and how well the code is optimized to the various architectures. So users, when they initially buy a supercomputer, choose the vendor and architecture that offers the best solution to the user's specific requirements. With vendors offering compatible follow-on machines, and no vendor offering a completely decisive general speed advantage, users have few incentives to change vendors.

The phrase "user specific requirements" is key in the preceding paragraph, since its meaning has changed considerably over time. Initially, with only a small number of highly sophisticated users (particularly nuclear weapons laboratories), it predominantly meant more megaflops. Through the 1980s, however, with the increase in commercial customers, it came to refer to "total solutions," to imply fast hardware, software, and support. Concerning hardware, it not only referred to the number of megaflops, but also to input/output devices, high-speed channels, and high-speed graphics. Concerning software, users expected connectivity, interactivity, ease of use, upgrades, and so forth. In both hard- and software they wanted reliability and support.

In the 1970s Cray Research was able to take over CDC's leading position in the supercomputer arena. This seems to contradict the argument made earlier about the lack of incentives for users to change vendors. That argument is, however, valid only if all major vendors play in the same ball park as regards performance, which they do now, but did not in, say, 1976. Then, looking only at the megaflops, Cray Research and (belatedly) CDC were the only players in the top of the league. What Cray Research then did was to go after "hero-problems" in industry; that is, offering solutions to problems that could not be solved before. When the users got interested, Cray Research worked closely with them and third parties to develop the total solution these users sought. In this respect, Cray Research had the advantage that its products, especially the combination of its architecture and compiler, were more general-purpose than those of CDC and the Japanese supercomputers that came to the market in the 1980s.

When the name of the game was "more megaflops," users were prepared to change vendors on the basis of who offered most of those and had the sophistication and resources to overcome the accompanying problems. That was the basis of Seymour Cray's great successes, the CDC-6600 and CRAY-1. What Cray Research has subsequently done, however, is to change the rules of the game from more megaflops to "total solutions." So catching up with Cray Research in megaflops, or even surpassing it, is no longer enough. IBM and the Japanese companies know this, and offer "total solutions" of their own. But without a decisive speed advantage, there is little reason for users to migrate from one "total solution" to another. For individual companies, the growth will mainly have to come from finding new customers that are not tied too much to one of the competitors. This is a key rationale for Cray Research offering "low-end" products compatible with its top-of-the-line models.

Thus there is little reason to expect sudden dramatic realignments within mainstream supercomputing. But what about change from outside, such as from massive parallelism?

In creating a machine with a parallel architecture, designers must address several critical questions. First, how many processors are necessary? Depending on the type of problem a machine is intended to solve, the number may vary from a few dozen powerful units (the so-called large-grain approach) to thousands or millions of less powerful units (the small-grain approach). For instance, the small-grain approach may be well-suited to problems that are easily broken into many parts, such as artificial intelligence programs requiring the machine to retrieve information quickly from enormous data bases. The second question concerns the fact that the more processors the machine contains, the more critical is the scheme by which they are linked to each other, and the way they are synchronized. Therefore, should each processor be able to communicate with every other one, or only with its nearest neighbors? Similar questions arise with respect to memory: Should each processor be connected to a small amount of distributed memory, or should all the processors share a single large memory? Then there is the issue of memory bandwidth, especially when memory is shared among many processors. Finally, designers and software engineers must decide who should be responsible for dividing a problem into parts to run on the parallel machine. Programming is simplified if the computer is equipped with software that can perform this chore automatically, but chances are the resulting program will be inefficient. Leaving the job to the human programmer might make for greater efficiency, but requires programs to be expensively rewritten for parallel machines.[64]

There is thus a dilemma to be faced, which is well spelt out by former ETA chief Carl Ledbetter: "Parallelism is an extremely difficult technology, the software and management, the overhead management systems, the operating systems and management systems are very complex. Bandwidth issues for instance, where to put the memory in and how to move data; very complex. Nevertheless it is all there is left to hope for [if we want to achieve] another factor of [a] thousand or ten thousand in performance."[65]

This latter claim provides the key to much of the activity in massive parallelism. Until the 1970s, supercomputer developers could simply ride the bandwagon of the semiconductor industry that offered faster and denser chips "for free." The increased strain on packaging and the divergence between the demands of supercomputing and the hugely expanding microprocessor business meant that supercomputer manufacturers started to have to try to drive technological development rather than sit back and wait. This was true, for instance, for ETA, Cray Research, and the Cray Computer Corporation.

The increased strain on packaging was a result of design choices in which, for all of the individual supercomputer vendors, the basic architecture of the processor had become relatively fixed. This implied that further speed-up had to come from using faster technology and using more processors per system. Because of signal propagation delays, using faster clocks implied that the machine had to be shrunk physically. The same was true for the requirement that to increase speed the number of processors needed to be increased. Thus, to a certain extent, on the technological level the name of the game has become "packaging and cooling." Many people, however, see that game reaching its limits. To put it euphemistically, even Seymour Cray has had some trouble incorporating a 2-nanosecond clock and 16 processors into a Cray-3. Many people therefore believe that large increases in speed can only come from massive parallelism.

As a result, although there is now widespread awareness of the difficulties of massive parallelism, most supercomputer centers are experimenting with such architectures, and there has been very considerable state support for their development, particularly from DARPA. Several firms—Thinking Machines, Intel, NCube, and Meiko, for example—have begun to enjoy commercial success with their massively parallel machines (although, as noted before, their combined sales are still dwarfed by those of Cray Research).

It may well be wrong to see an "either/or" future in which either conventional supercomputing or massive parallelism must triumph. Various forms of hybrid systems are likely to develop. The first signs of such systems have already appeared, with a classic supercomputer and a Connection Machine becoming part of the same network and being looked at as a "total system." The specific architecture of the massively parallel component of such a system might make a specific "metacomputer" more suited to some jobs rather than others, and might lead to the development of different "classes of architectures" optimized for different "classes of codes." On the basis of their own requirements, users would then have the options of choosing which parallel architecture(s) to incorporate in the system. There might even be some problems that make it worthwhile to develop a wholly dedicated machine. Some commercial applications might also be so economically valuable that it makes sense to consider spending tens of million of dollars to develop a machine that does nothing but those jobs.

Does this mean that general-purpose supercomputing, to quote Carl Ledbetter, has become an oxymoron? In many ways it does, particularly in connection with production codes that have stabilized. Architectures that are (partly) dedicated may then provide a much more cost-effective way to solve the problems at hand. However, when the user is doing new research and does not know what the applications really are or what they look like, a special-purpose machine is of no use. In that environment, the most appropriate solution is to have the fastest general-purpose machine possible, that is, a computer that does everything "reasonably well." Unless massively parallel machines become much more general-purpose, there will thus be a major role for large vector machines and for moderately parallel machines, that is, a place for the CRAY Y-MP and its successor, for the IBM 3090/VF and its successors, etc. They may not be the fastest machines in the world, but could be expected to be very important machines when used for generic research.[65]

Indeed, the way the supercomputer world has developed implies that the concept of "fastest computer in the world" has lost much of its meaning. Perhaps classic supercomputers will become faster by one, two, or even more orders of magnitude, but here too the bulk of the speed-up is expected to come from increasing the number of processors. Therefore, software development for these machines will increasingly have to address multiprocessing issues akin to those of massive parallelism. Faster hardware for them now seems increasingly to mean exotic technologies, and that means increased cost. The gallium arsenide, ultradensely packed CRAY-3 is quoted as likely to cost on the order of $30 million, while Steve Chen's S-1 might even cost double that. A combination of a less powerful classic design with a massively parallel architecture may then provide a much more cost-effective solution to many problems. In that case, the question of the fastest machine in the world becomes the matter of the *fastest code in the world*, and loses much of the prestige that is now often attributed to it.

Don't Judge Tools by Their Gloss

Nevertheless, the megaflops figure especially prominently in the public debates. In an earlier epoch, IBM's Thomas Watson refused to be second best. In the 1980s, the Japanese were seen as threatening "our number one position." CDC entered the 205 in the *Guinness Book of World Records*.[66] Glitter and glamour also play an important role, and even the physical appearance of supercomputers matters. The CRAY-1's "love seat design" appealed to many. The same is also true for the CRAY-2's very visible liquid immersion cooling system[67] and the ETA[10]'s not so visible cryogenic cooling system. There has been much attention paid to the use of gallium arsenide for the CRAY-3, which has attracted much more publicity than the C-90, although both aim for similar speeds.

Thus, supercomputers appeal to the general public as well as to policymakers. It is easy to talk about supercomputers in a rhetorical way and to connect them to national security and economic competitiveness, and that rhetoric certainly played a key role in the United States during the 1980s. Yet it is difficult to gauge just how important supercomputer development really is for security and competitiveness. An increase in speed of three- or fourfold, as is typical for Cray Research's products, implies that in three-dimensional models (the type of codes most frequently run) the linear dimensions of cells in a model can be reduced by a factor of 1.5. Helpful, yes, but surely not decisive.

In any case, the direction in which supercomputing is developing implies that narrow nationalism will be self-defeating. Future supercomputing environments can be expected to be much more heterogeneous than current ones, with a variety of hard- and software all linked together. In this context, it is surely advantageous for users to be able to choose from a variety of products coming from different vendors. A combination of U.S., European, and Japanese products may often appear to be called for, and any country taking a protectionist line would harm its own industry and research institutes by outlawing any one of them.

Supercomputers started being developed in an esoteric world, for computer élites at Los Alamos, Livermore, the National Security Agency, and some other key users. Over time, however, they have become embedded in a wider environment, where they are used as tools to solve practical problems—no more, no less. In public debates, however, they are still considered to be the highly prestigious flagship of high-tech, the yardstick of "where we stand in the world." It makes more sense, however, to see them in the context of all of their interrelationships in the current world. Such a view could prevent panic reactions on the basis of hurt pride that only have counterproductive effects.

Acknowledgments

The research reported on here is partly based on interviews with a large number of people who are or have been engaged in the development or use of supercomputers. We appreciate the time they spent with us and the information they provided. Organizing these interviews was greatly facilitated by the hospitality and resources of the Charles Babbage Institute at the University of Minnesota. The research was supported by the U.K. Economic and Social Research Council, under the Programme on Information and Communication Technologies (PICT). Some sections of this article were published earlier in the Dutch *Yearbook for Corporate History and History of Technology*. We thank the editors of the Yearbook for their permission to reprint those sections here.

Notes

1. A previous article by one of the authors examined the influence of one particular category of user—the nuclear weapons laboratories—on supercomputing: Donald MacKenzie, "The influence of the Los Alamos and Livermore National Laboratories on the development of supercomputing," *Ann. Hist. Comput.*, Vol. 13, 1991, pp. 179–201. In another article we focused on Seymour Cray's role in the development of supercomputing: Boelie Elzen and Donald MacKenzie, "The charismatic engineer—Seymour Cray and the development of supercomputing," in *Jaarboek voor de Geschiedenis van Bedriff en Techniek (Yearbook for Corporate History and History of Technology)*, Vol. 8 (Amsterdam: NEHA, 1991), pp. 248–277.

2. We use the term "network" in the sense that the term has been used in recent sociology of science and technology. See, for example, Boelie Elzen, Bert Enserink, and Wim A. Smit, "Weapon innovation—Networks and guiding principles," *Sci. Public Policy*, June

1990, pp. 171–193; or Bruno Latour, *Science in Action*, ed. Milton Keynes (London: Open Univ. Press, 1987). In these approaches, a network does not consist of artifacts alone (as in more technical uses of the word), nor of human beings alone (as in traditional sociology), but of both. There are important issues in the newer sociological usage concerning whether artifacts are to be considered as agents equivalent to human actors, but these are not central to our discussion here.

3. There is ambiguity in this definition as there is no universally accepted way of establishing the speed of a computer. Due to differences in architecture and software a computer that is the fastest on a specific code need not be the fastest on another code. The pragmatic definition given here, however, suits our needs because everybody in the computer world would agree that the machines we discuss should be classified as supercomputers.

4. The following discussion of the 1604 and 6600 is based on James E. Thornton, "The CDC 6600 Project," *Ann. Hist. Comput.*, Vol. 2, No. 4, October 1980, pp. 338–348; and on an interview with James E. Thornton, Minneapolis, Minn., April 3, 1990. Thornton helped design these computers.

5. Biographical notes on Cray can be found in Chapter 18 of Robert Slater, *Portraits in Silicon* (Cambridge, Mass.: M.I.T. Press, 1987).

6. For the history of Engineering Research Associates, see Erwin Tomash and Arnold A. Cohen, "The birth of an ERA: Engineering Research Associates, Inc., 1946–1955," *Ann. Hist. Comput.*, Vol. 1, No. 2, October 1979, pp. 83–97.

7. David E. Lundstrom, *A Few Good Men from Univac* (Cambridge, Mass.: M.I.T. Press, 1987), p. 136.

8. Slater, *Portraits*, op. cit., suggests that Cray told Norris he was leaving.

9. On "committee design," see Lundstrom, *Univac*, op. cit.

10. Charles J. Bashe et al., *IBM's Early Computers* (Cambridge, Mass.: M.I.T. Press, 1986), p. 446.

11. Thornton, *Ann. Hist. Comput.*, op. cit., p. 343.

12. Lundstrom, *Univac*, op. cit., p. 214; MacKenzie, *Ann. Hist. Comput.*, op. cit.

13. Kenneth Flamm, *Creating the Computer: Government, Industry and High Technology* (Washington, D.C.: Brookings, 1988), pp. 152–155. See Jacques Jublin and Jean-Michel Quatrepoint, *French Ordinateurs—de l'Affair Bull à l'Assassinat du Plan Calcul* (Paris: Alain Moreau, 1976).

14. Lundstrom, *Univac*, op. cit., p. 138, quotes the entirety of one report: "Activity is progressing satisfactorily as outlined under the June plan. There have been no significant changes or deviations from the outlined June plan." This contrasted with 20- or 30-page reports from the leaders of comparable parts of the corporation.

15. Quoted in, for example, Russ Mitchell, "The genius—Meet Seymour Cray, father of the supercomputer," *Bus. Week*, April 30, 1990, pp. 81–88.

16. Interview with Les Davis, Chippewa Falls, Wis., May 3, 1990.

17. Interviews with Neil Lincoln, April 3, 1990; Chuck Purcell, April 4, 1990; and James Thornton, op. cit., all in Minneapolis, Minn. Purcell worked as a salesman of the STAR and also took part in its design.

18. *Chippewa Falls Herald-Telegram*, March 15, 1972, quoted in *Speed and Power—Understanding Computers* (Alexandria, Va.: Time-Life Books, 1987), p. 32.

19. John M. Lavine, "New firm here blueprinting most powerful computer in the world— Cray Research Inc. putting together 'think tank', production facilities," *Chippewa Herald–Telegram*, May 17, 1972, pp. 1, 4.

20. See, for example, the discussion of the work of guidance engineer Charles Stark Draper in D. MacKenzie, *Inventing Accuracy: A Historical Sociology of Nuclear Missile Guidance* (Cambridge, Mass.: M.I.T. Press, 1990).

21. Cray acknowledged the debt of the CRAY-1 to the STAR-100 in a lecture at the annual supercomputing meeting in Florida on November 15, 1988. This lecture has been recorded on video: Seymour Cray, "What's all this about gallium arsenide?"

22. Interview with Les Davis, op. cit.

23. A more thorough technical description of the CRAY-1 can be found Richard M. Russell, "The CRAY-1 computer system," *Commun. ACM*, Vol. 21, No. 1, January 1978, pp. 63–72.

24. John Rollwagen, quoted in "Gambling on the new frontier," *Interface*, Vol. 9, No. 8, September 1986, pp. 6–7.

25. Construction of Serial 2 was halted when Serial 1 displayed a high level of memory errors when installed at Los Alamos, perhaps because of the high incidence of cosmic rays at the nuclear laboratory, high in the mountains above the New Mexico desert. Error detection and correction facilities were added to later models, starting with Serial 3.

26. Bradford W. Ketchum, "From Start-up to $60 million in Nanoseconds," *INC.*, November 1980, p. 56.

27. Cray Research, Inc., *Annual Report 1978*, Minneapolis, Minn., 1979, p. 2.

28. "The seismic processing problem: Cray Research's response," *Cray Channels*, Vol. 5, No. 2, 1983, pp. 6–9; also interview with Dave Sadler, Minneapolis, Minn., May 2, 1990. Sadler worked on the software for handlng the tapes.

29. Cray Research, Inc., *Annual Report 1984*, Minneapolis, Minn., 1985, p. 2.

30. Interview with Margaret Loftus, Minneapolis, Minn., May 4, 1990. Loftus was Cray Research's vice-president of software at the time.

31. Cray Research, Inc., *Annual Report 1982*, Minneapolis, Minn., 1983; also interviews with Les Davis, op. cit., and John Rollwagen, Minneapolis, Minn., April 2, 1990.

32. "Cray Research Fact Sheet" giving marketing data as of December 31, 1989.

33. Steve Gross, "Quicker computer? Cray leads the way," *Minneapolis Star*, December 22, 1981.

34. Cray video, op. cit.

35. Interview with Les Davis, op. cit.

36. Interview with John Rollwagen, op. cit.

37. "What comes after Y?" *Interface*, Vol. 12, No. 6, Summer 1989, p. 8.

38. "Cray lures users with entry-level price supermini," *Computing*, October 31, 1991, p. 8.

39. The following description of the CRAY-3 is largely based on the Cray video, op. cit.

40. Marc H. Brodsky, "Progress in gallium arsenide semiconductors," *Sci. Am.*, February 1990, pp. 56–63.

41. Letter from Neil Davenport, president of Cray Computer Corporation, to the authors, December 27, 1990.

42. Video tape "Cray Private," May 15, 1989, on which John Rollwagen explains the reasons for splitting off Cray Computer Corporation from Cray Research. See also Steve Gross, "Will Cray suffer without its founder?" *Star Tribune*, May 21, 1989.

43. Rollwagen quoted in Carla Lazzarechi, "Cray left his company to prevent internal conflict," *Los Angeles Times*, June 4, 1989, part IV, p. 4, and in Russell Mitchell, "Now Cray faces life without Cray," *Bus. Week*, May 29, 1989, p. 27.

44. Cray, quoted in Mitchell, ibid.

45. Cray Research, Inc., *1984 Annual Report*, Minneapolis, Minn., 1985, p. 2.

46. R. W. Hockney and C. R. Jesshope, *Parallel Computers 2—Architecture, Programming and Algorithms* (Bristol/Philadelphia: Adam Hilger, 1988), p. 117.

47. Interviews with Neil Lincoln, op. cit.; Tony Vacca, Chippewa Falls, Wis., May 3, 1990; and Carl Ledbetter, St. Paul, Minn., May 17, 1990. Lincoln and Vacca worked on various CDC and ETA machines, while Ledbetter was president of ETA.

48. *Speed and Power*, op. cit., p. 89.

49. Ibid, 91.

50. Thomas Levenson, "Wetenschap op topsnelheid" ("Science at topspeed"), *Intermediair*, Vol. 26, No. 20A, May 18, 1990, p. 29.

51. Sidney Karin and Norris Parker Smith, *The Supercomputer Era* (Boston/New York: Harcourt Brace Jovanovich, 1987), p. 252.

52. Argonne National Laboratory; quoted in John Markoff, "A computer star's new advance," *New York Times*, February 17, 1990, pp. 2 and 21.

53. This is a rough estimate because, as a matter of policy, IBM does not release figures about numbers of machines installed; Karin and Smith, *Supercomputer Era*, op. cit., p. 291.

54. Markoff, *New York Times*, op. cit., p. 21; Amanda Mitchell, "Renegade supercomputer maker pushing frontiers of technology," *Parallellogram*, October 1990, p. 9; Mitchell, *Bus. Week*, op. cit., p. 85.

55. Jerry Sanders and Amanda Mitchell, "Dateline 1995!" *Parallellogram*, October 1990, pp. 8–9.

56. Karin and Smith, *Supercomputer Era*, op. cit., pp. 105–106.

57. Ibid., pp. 107–108, 110–114.

58. The Superperformance Computing Service, *Superperformance End-User Requirements and Expectations*, Mountain View, Calif., 1990, p. II-3.

59. Karin and Smith, *Supercomputer Era*, op. cit. pp. 109–110.

60. Willie Schatz, "A call to arms," *Datamation*, April 1, 1984, p. 34.

61. Cray Research, Inc., "Keeping up with current events—An interview with John Rollwagen," *Interface*, Vol. 10, No. 5, May 1987, pp. 6–7.

62. Quoted in Gross, *Star Tribune*, op. cit.

63. Interviews with Carl Ledbetter and Neil Lincoln, op. cit.

64. *Speed and Power*, op. cit., p. 97.

65. Interview with Carl Ledbetter, op. cit.

66. Davis Stamps, "The Cray style—John Rollwagen has a company to run and a reclusive genius to satisfy. The trick is to do both at the same time," *Corp. Rep.*, December 1982, pp. 68–72.

67. The CRAY-2 is sometimes referred to as "the world's most expensive aquarium."

PART IV

Telecommunications

Part IV considers competitiveness in the telecommunications field. In the first chapter, Kenneth Lipartito, a business historian at the Harvard Business School, notes that the term "technological competitiveness" is usually applied to companies that compete with one another for customers, profits, markets, or survival—or more recently to nations or other geopolitical units that compete to ensure wealth for their region through the success of their technological businesses. It is difficult to understand, he maintains, how this concept applies to industries that are monopolistic or publicly owned. In order to discuss competitiveness in the telephone industry, Lipartito extends the notion to include the rivalry between different groups for the determination of how a technology should be employed, to what aims, and for what benefits. He explores this broader concept of competitiveness through a case study of telecommunications in the American South between 1880 and 1920. He recounts the struggle between American Bell Telephone officials in Boston, who regarded the telephone as a business tool, and managers of Southern Bell and independent local telephone companies in the south, who regarded the telephone as property for social purposes.

Pascal Griset, a historian of technology at the *Centre national de la recherche scientifique* in Paris, considers competitiveness in the French telephone industry since 1945. At the beginning of this period, the French telephone system was antiquated and French telephone companies were subsidiaries of foreign companies. A modern national telephone system was deemed necessary to improve the competitiveness of France's commerce and industry. It would have been easier to employ the resources of those established foreign companies to build a new telephone system for France, but the French government wanted an indigenous telephone industry to develop the new telephone system so as to reduce the nation's dependence on foreign technology and to improve its national balance of payments. The tension between these two different ways in which France wanted to become competitive, by building a strong national telephone company and by building a good national telephone system, is the main subject of the chapter.

Amos Joel, a retired Bell Laboratories engineer and a leading authority on telephone switching, provides commentary on the Lipartito and Griset chapters. Building on the themes in these chapters and in a conference presentation by Frank Thomas (not published here), Joel discusses changes in the 1980s caused by competition in interexchange toll service. He speculates on additional competition that he believes is likely to occur in the near future through the introduction of new technologies.

The type of competitiveness explored in Lipartito's chapter also occurs in industries that are neither monopolistic nor under public ownership. A later chapter in this volume, by Susan Douglas, for example, explores a competition between hi-fi enthusiasts and large, established manufacturers of home entertainment systems over what the directions and uses of high fidelity audio technology should be. A similar dynamic has been played out between computer hackers and corporate America over the "proper" use and direction of computers, especially personal computers. These types of battles do not always line up hobbyists against corporate institutions, however. For example, the struggle between the educational community (as represented by Educom) and the military (as represented by DARPA) over the proper use of and access to computer networking technology shows many parallels to the cases of hi-fi and personal computing. It may be that this type of competition to define the aims and "proper" uses of technology is more widespread than the historical literature suggests, especially in the case of technology-driven products.

Many countries are faced with the choice between using foreign agents to modernize technological systems and cultivating the country's own technological expertise. It is a question that virtually all developing countries must face in their quest for independent standing. Sometimes industry rather than government addresses the question, e.g., as Geoffrey Tweedale details in his study of American and British steelmaking in the nineteenth and early twentieth centuries.[1] More often, especially in the twentieth century, governments have felt the need to take direct action, such as the French government with its computer and telephone industries.[2] Today, eastern European countries must decide whether to apply protectionist measures and develop from within or try to catch up more rapidly through the introduction of western Europe's technological might. General Electric has recently acquired Hungary's leading electrical manufacturer, which was independent and innovative for a century; and Siemens is rapidly expanding into markets across eastern Europe.

One might also consider Griset's question from the other side, by examining the obstacles confronting a major multinational technology company, such as Siemens, Philips, General Electric, or IBM, as it tries to expand its markets into developing countries; and consider its effect on the development of these countries. Different countries have taken very different attitudes about foreign companies in their marketplaces. The French government outspokenly worried in the 1970s about the evils of IBM and the cultural imperialism of the United States and tried with only limited success to resist them. On the other hand, many countries, recognizing that they could not develop their own hydroelectric power resources, have welcomed the presence of Siemens, AEG, Westinghouse, General Electric, and other transnational companies.

Notes

1. Geoffrey Tweedale, *Sheffield Steel and America: A Century of Commercial and Technological Interdependence, 1830–1930* (New York: Cambridge University Press, 1987).
2. Simon Nora and Alain Minc, *The Computerization of Society* (Cambridge, Mass.: MIT Press, 1980).

The Strategy of System-Building

Telecommunications and the American South, 1885–1920

Kenneth Lipartito

Competitiveness has been used extensively to describe rivalry between firms for customers, profits, markets, and even survival. More recently, it has been applied to nation-states, as well as larger and smaller geopolitical units such as regions and cities. Thus the United States is said to compete with Japan for the worldwide semiconductor market and with members of the European Economic Community to supply their citizens with agricultural commodities. Places as diverse as Detroit, Brazil, and South Korea may compete with each other for the location of automobile plants.[1] In this sort of competition, technology is one of the chief weapons that firms and nations employ to achieve competitive ends. Businesses engage in research and development (R&D) to gain market share by differentiating their products or achieving scale economies in production. Companies seek through technological innovation new products and services to sell. Technological competitiveness understood in this way is a part of the broader competition between business firms in market economies.

Although this definition of technological competitiveness is a useful and accurate one, there are also other links between technology and competition. Certain industries, for example, are not characterized by market competition. Yet even under monopoly or public ownership, technological competitiveness may arise. In this case, the fight is not between firms or nations but between and among user groups, engineers, and managers. The object of this sort of struggle is not greater market share, higher profits, or sustainable advantages over rival producers, but something more fundamental: the nature, meaning, and purpose of a specific technology.[2] Different groups, whether they be the users or makers of a technology, often have different ideas about how that technology should be employed, what its social purpose should be, and who should benefit from it. Where these goals cannot be expressed in market competition, they may still come out in the political system, in internal struggles within professional associations, or inside of large, monopolistic firms.

These two types of technological competitiveness are not mutually exclusive. Both often appear in industries characterized by large numbers of firms, as well as those dominated by just a few players. Conflicts between profit-minded managers and technically oriented engineers and scientists are a problem in many organizations.[3] By the same token, few ironclad monopolies exist for long, and even publicly owned firms may be pulled and tugged by demands from both market and nonmarket venues. Perhaps there is no better example of how these two types of technological competitiveness interact than AT&T during its recent transition from monopoly to competition. Political pressures, emerging marketplace exigencies, organized customer protests, sharp-toothed rival firms, and explosive technological changes all buffeted the Bell System between the late 1950s and its breakup in 1984. This combination of market and nonmarket forces helped to redefine telecommunications services and products in the United States.

In this case study of the American South between 1880 and 1920, I hope to show how both of these types of competition affected the technology of telecommunications in that region, and how AT&T responded to these challenges by forging a new national competitive strategy. The implications of this study are, I shall argue, that the definition of technological competitiveness should be broadened to include not only rivalry between firms for markets but conflicts and struggles between many actors involved in the creation of technology. Often what is at stake in such competition is not just a more or less transitory market advantage, but the power to shape and define important technologies for society. Firms and nations that recognize these aspects of technological competitiveness will have to be prepared to enter into market and nonmarket arenas where are found the conflicting interests, values, and passions of many different groups. Strategy formed on this basis can significantly reinforce the strength of a particular technology and enable firms to emerge from competitive struggles with a dominant market position.

The American South in 1880 might seem an inauspicious place to begin a study of either technology or competitiveness. It was the least economically developed part of the United States at that time, with a regional income only 51 percent the national average.[4] Largely rural and agrarian with few universities or technical colleges, it was hardly a likely source of technological innovation. Certainly not in a new industry like telephony, which would soon provide some of the leading examples of the use of science-based knowledge in corporate research and development. Nonetheless, with the help of resources from outside the region, telephone technology was transferred to the South in these early years. Entrepreneurs found that demand for telephones existed in the South, though it was not nearly as large a demand as that of the more economically advanced Northeast. It was sufficient, however, to permit the Bell licensee in the region, Southern Bell Telephone and Telegraph Company, to earn a gross income of over $300,000 and provide telephone service to over five thousand customers by 1885.[5]

Between 1880 and 1894 the telephone industry in the United States was a monopoly firmly under the control of the American Bell Telephone Company (ABT), which held the key patents on the basic telephone instrument and closely related apparatus.[6] Yet even under these conditions and from the otherwise undynamic South issued examples of technological competition from nonmarket sources. The nature of this competition was intrafirm, between managers at Southern Bell and executives and engineers at American Bell in Boston. At stake in these conflicts were questions of where telephone service should be extended, how it should be developed, and, most fundamentally, what the technology should do.

These conflicts emerged from the different perceptions of the market held by top ABT executives in Boston, and regional managers in the South. The Boston group saw in the South limited potential for the system of technology they had fostered under their patent monopoly. Seeking the choicest markets, they had concentrated on large urban areas and spent few resources on the rural hinterland or smaller towns and cities.[7] In the mid-1880s, the company began building its first intercity toll lines. Though initially expensive and of poor quality, they opened up a new market among businesses in need of rapid, long-distance communications in what was becoming a truly national economy.

Large cities had the commercial customers who would pay top dollar for this telephone service. Cities also presented some of the most challenging technical problems in telecommunications. For a monopolist seeking monopoly rents, consumers whose demand curves enabled them to pay the highest prices were favored customers indeed. For a strategically minded firm, attacking the technical problems of big city markets—high-capacity switching, efficient underground cables, and effective long-distance lines—also made sense. The monopoly would not last forever, and it was best to be strong in the largest markets when the patents finally expired.

Standardization was another aspect of this early strategy. After the formation of AT&T in 1885 as the Bell long-distance subsidiary, the company saw a great need to standardize service and equipment across markets. Before technological breakthroughs in the early twentieth century, such as the loading coil, repeater, and vacuum tube, substantially lowered the cost and increased the range of long-distance communications, the effectiveness of this premium service was closely tied to the quality of plant, equipment, and maintenance at local exchanges.[8] For these reasons, it made sense to the executives of AT&T and American Bell to set high technical standards across markets; the company was relying on its strength in large urban areas and in interexchange service to keep it on top of the telephone industry.

Bell's early strategic vision of an interlinked system of urban telephone exchanges joined by long-distance lines offered little to customers who neither needed nor could afford this type and quality of service. Many such customers resided in the largely agrarian and underdeveloped South. Under competitive conditions, one might expect rival firms offering different types of products and services to spring up and meet those needs Bell was not meeting. Something along these lines happened after the end of Bell's patent monopoly in 1894, but even earlier demands from those not satisfied with the Bell strategy made their way through the seemingly impervious monopoly. Like hot gasses escaping a volcano, they found their way to the surface, if not by the most direct route as they would in a competitive environment, then through side vents and fissures.

One startling example of this sort of nonmarket conflict can be found in disputes between Southern Bell and ABT over the Law Telephone Switchboard.

Invented in 1878, this device was one of several adopted in the early years of telephony for connecting customers with each other. Early on it was the switchboard of choice for several Bell licensees, who appreciated its speed, low cost, and ease of use and maintenance.[9] The limits of this technology, however, became apparent as telephone demand increased; it could not provide the necessary capacity to serve large, densely populated markets, and so was soon surpassed by the "multiple" switchboard.[10]

In the South, and in regions whose economic conditions resembled the South, the Law Board survived into the 1890s. The reasons for its survival were several: customers in such places were very price sensitive, population density and telephone demand remained low, maintenance of complicated equipment was difficult, and trained technicians were rare. All of these conditions argued that simple, inexpensive, familiar equipment might well be economically more rational than newer, more sophisticated equipment. It was not clear to managers of Southern Bell that the Law equipment was in any sense inferior, particularly since most of the company's exchanges did not face the capacity constraint that limited employment of the Law board elsewhere. Expected to earn a profit in their territory, Southern Bell managers responded through their choice of equipment to demands for telephone service not met by the technology and business strategy developed at Bell headquarters.

Perhaps it is not surprising that one division of a corporation would seek to use technology that fit the markets it had to serve. What is striking is how the parent company reacted to this "technological independence." Letter after letter flowed between executives of American Bell and those of Southern Bell over this issue. The parent firm implored its southern licensee to adopt "standard" switchboard technology. ABT's Thomas Lockwood, who through the 1880s and 1890s had the ear of top Bell executives on matters of technology, and Chief Engineer Hammond Hayes went to great lengths to convince operating companies to abandon the Law board.[11] Deviations from company policy on technology apparently so threatened ABT's strategic vision that it was willing to sacrifice immediate customer satisfaction in places such as the South for the longer-term goal of building an interconnected system that provided local and long-distance service in major urban markets.

Gradually, stronger top-down management, systemwide conferences on technology, and the creation of substantial R&D capabilities within American Bell allowed the company to take greater control of technology. ABT was forced by internal competitive pressures over technology and its own plans for standardization to abandon its original decentralized structure and become more of a managerial firm.[12] Even stronger pressures on the company would arise in the competitive period that followed 1894, forcing ABT to rethink its whole strategy. In many ways, these market pressures were the continuation of the conflicts over technology that had developed within the company earlier.

Much has been written about the competitive period of the early twentieth century, but little of this literature has focused on the technological differences between competing firms. Some writers have portrayed the so-called independent telephone companies that arose between 1894 and 1920 as small "Bell Systems," seeking to match their larger rival with their own integrated local and long-distance systems.[13] It is true that some of the larger independents built extensive regional systems, often controlling both local and long-distance service over wide areas. Others tried with mixed results to enter the crucial big-city markets dominated by Bell. Still others formed associations to coordinate activities and achieve vertical integration between manufacturing and sales and service. Such activity was, however, confined to a few midwestern independents and did not engage the thousands of other non-Bell companies that sprang up in this era. Even among the more ambitious new members of the telephone industry, moreover, there was dissention and division. Many firms were content to cultivate their own markets and eschew the more grandiose (and expensive) scheme of forming an integrated long-distance system in competition with AT&T.[14] In doing so, they developed a different system of telecommunications technology.

Beneath the top layer of the independent companies were numerous small and local firms that filled market niches long ignored by Bell.[15] Such companies were particularly common in the South, which has often been inaccurately characterized as competitively sluggish in this period. In fact, southern independents, though small in absolute numbers, were second only to the aggressive midwestern firms in taking market share from ABT. (Table I) They did so, however, by developing alternative business strategies and using different systems of technology to serve different groups of customers than their rival. In effect, these firms competed by redefining the uses of and market for telephone service.

The organizations serving farmers were an important segment of the independent telephone industry. Operating in the South's vast rural market, they were often organized, capitalized, and run by farmers themselves, sometimes as mutual companies. Using the most rudimentary technology and setting entry level prices extremely low (at or below $1.00 per month), they met a type of demand that Bell had found extremely difficult to serve. The cost of extending a line to remote farms and then into the nearest urban exchange, Bell found, was often prohibitively high.[16] Farmers' systems, however, began by providing inexpensive local service. Rather than radiating outward from urban centers, they gradually moved in from the farm. Many eventually gained sufficient customers to bargain for connection with either the Bell or independent companies serving nearby towns and cities.[17]

Many of the next level independents—urban commercial firms—also concentrated on different markets than had Bell. In the South, a few challenged the company in the region's largest cities, such as Atlanta, but like their counterparts elsewhere they enjoyed mixed success in such head-to-head struggles with their larger, wealthier competitor. In the smaller towns and cities that made up much of the South, however, they did significantly better. Since these places contained a preponderance of the region's population, the independents were able to quickly take market share from Bell.

Some of the most successful of these firms arose in North Carolina, a state of many small towns, emerging midsize cities, and modest farms, but no large metropolis. Here local businessmen, dissatisfied with Bell service, founded telephone companies such as North Carolina Interstate. Despite its name, this firm operated on a regional not national level, providing connections between Durham, Raleigh, Goldsboro, Winston-Salem, and Charlottesville, Virginia.[18] Customers in such places were unwilling to pay for Bell's more extensive and integrated service, but were attracted

TABLE I

Region	% Bell 1907	% Independent 1907
New England		
Maine	69.8	30.2
N.H.	77.6	22.4
Vt.	54.9	45.1
Mass.	97.5	2.5
Conn. & R.I.	97.7	2.3
Mid-Atlantic		
N.Y.	73.6	26.4
N.J.	83.6	16.4
Pa.	61.2	38.8
Midwest		
Ohio	37	63
Ind.	25	75
Ill.	48.9	51.1
Mich.	49.5	50.5
Iowa	30.7	84.1
South		
Va.	56.6	43.3
N.C.	44.5	55.5
S.C.	62.4	37.6
Ga.	57.9	42.1
Fla.	36.3	63.7
Ala.	63	37
United States	51.2	48.8

Source: U.S. Bureau of the Census, *Telephones and Telegraphs 1912*, table 24.

by North Carolina Interstate's cheap local service and lines to nearby cities. As Bell's own studies soon showed, this was a strategy it could not match and still earn the profits independents were earning.[19]

The success of southern independent companies hinged on their ability to differentiate their service from that of their chief competitor's. In part, this strategy was grounded in the use of different technology. Farmers' companies deployed multiparty-line service to keep rates down and did not construct their lines to the exacting requirements of long-distance communications. Other non-Bell firms quickly adopted the automatic switching equipment invented by Almon Strowger. Fearful that this new technology would inhibit technical standardization and slow network expansion by limiting capacity and interfering with long-distance service, AT&T refused at first to employ it.[20] But many customers saw distinct advantages in automatic switching. It did not require a full-time human operator, so it offered both greater privacy and lower labor costs. This advantage was especially valued in small towns, where residents recognized that human operators could not only learn everyone's business, but often commanded wages that added substantially to rates in markets where demand for telephones was still small.

Even more significant than the technology that went into independent telephone operations was the business–technological strategy developed by these companies. Since most of them did not seek to compete with Bell head-on, they could concentrate on their local markets without incurring the expenses and technical difficulties of building an integrated local and long-distance system. Most of their patrons had little use for a line between Atlanta and Washington, for example. First and foremost they wanted low-priced local service, and then perhaps a few regional toll connections to the nearest towns and villages.[21] Building from the ground up rather than the top down, independents were able to provide extremely inexpensive ("cut-rate") local service at rates below those that Bell could offer.[22]

Cultivating their local markets enabled independents to understand the distinctive needs of their customers. Among farmers and small town residents, the telephone was not just the business device that Bell managers had conceived it to be, but was an instrument of cultural and social interchange among isolated men and women in America's vast hinterland. The independents discovered before Bell did the "sociability" of the telephone.[23] Unlike their larger rival, the independents recognized that ordinary men and women using the telephone for social conversation were as important a group to serve as were businessmen who used it for commercial purposes. Operating outside of the Bell System, these entrepreneurs and their customers stretched the notion of what a telephone was and what it could do to new limits.[24]

The success of independent entrepreneurs also rested on their effective use of the political system. Southern town and city governments were keenly interested in having telephone technology serve what were seen as crucial local needs. In the early twentieth century, Atlanta, for example, used political power to control and shape telephone service in line with larger community objectives. Noted for its progressive, active elite and strong booster tradition, the city enacted a comprehensive regulatory policy on key urban services designed to enhance its economic position. In a 1906 agreement, North Georgia Electric, a power company, cooperated with the locally owned Southern Power and Light Company and the independent Atlanta Telephone and Telegraph Company to bring inexpensive electricity and telephone service to Atlanta by sharing facilities, construction costs, and net profits. The city government participated in and supported this venture, providing the necessary right-of-way franchise for use of municipal thoroughfares. Through this arrangement, Atlanta's local independent telephone company was able to compete against Southern Bell in what was one of the largest and most strategically important markets in the South.[25]

Other municipalities used their political power in equally effective ways to extract from telephone companies concessions that served local interests. Ashville, North Carolina, and Richmond, Virginia, granted Bell a needed right-of-way franchise only after Bell agreed to set limits on rates. Tampa, Florida, demanded steep discounts on city-owned telephones. Still other places made technology and service their prime concerns, requiring that companies install specific types of equipment and provide valued connections to nearby towns and cities.[26]

Municipal regulation of this sort was the political expression of the same demands that came out of the market after the rise of competition in 1894. In both cases, groups strove to shape telephone service in line with what were seen as vital local exigencies at a time when AT&T was committed to building a national interconnected system of telecommunications. Resistance to Bell's policy in the form of local independent companies and municipal telephone regulations spoke to the demands of many sections of society not yet a part of the growing national culture and economy. For them, local interests still took precedence over interregional or national ones. They wanted the technology of telephony to serve those interests, and their political and market-based resistance to the Bell System expressed an abiding faith that even as economic growth, technological innovation, and new institutions altered the shape of society, communities could ride the crest of change and emerge not only intact but better off than before.[27]

This localistic vision went well beyond the South, finding expression in the telephone wars of midwestern states such as Iowa, Illinois, Wisconsin, and Michigan.[28] There too numerous small independents penetrated market after market on the fringes of urban America. There too municipal interests vied with AT&T for greater local control of telecommunications. As in the South, competition and localistic strategies dramatically increased telephone distribution among the very customers Bell managers had believed could not be widely served—farmers and other rural residents. Even as AT&T was building longer toll lines and mapping out a national system of communications, the humble efforts of non-Bell firms in Iowa gave that state the highest number of telephones per population by 1912 (see Table II).

TABLE II Comparative Telephone Use and Distribution, 1902, 1912, All Systems[a]

Region	Telephones/1000
New England	
1912	27
1902	9
Mid-Atlantic	
1912	90
1902	29
Midwest	
1912	135
1902	50
South	
1912	32
1902	11
U.S.	
1912	91
1902	30

[a]Regional totals are simple average for 1902, weighted average for 1912

Source: U.S. Bureau of the Census, *Telephones and Telegraphs 1912*, table 5, table 20.

It was hardly clear at this time which vision of telecommunications would triumph in America. Since only 3 percent of all calls were toll calls, a significant percentage of the U.S. population likely saw the telephone as a local service, rather than as part of a vast interregional system of communications. But localism interfered with the plans of the architects of the Bell System. In their view, local service had to comport with the requirements of long-distance service. The prime telephone customers were businessmen, professionals, and the wealthy of large cities, who would pay for such a system, not the local merchants, farmers, and ordinary consumers of small towns. It was a vision that initially provided little room for those who would not accept these values. As many communities eventually learned, the company was dedicated to its vision of telephony, and possessed substantial resources to bring it to fruition. As AT&T learned, however, it would have to modify its original strategy to accommodate some of those other groups.

As AT&T joined the competitive fray in earnest, it made good use of its strengths. These included a substantial head start, size, organizational capability, and, what seemed to many informed observers, the most logical and rational approach to telephone service. Certainly, it could be argued, a universal interconnected network in which any user could communicate with any other user was superior to several smaller regional or local networks. Although this idea had great appeal to members of the urban and industrial Northeast, it was, as we have seen, much less warmly received in other places. Convincing the public that universal, interconnected service was inherently the best means of using telephone technology was the key to AT&T's success. Once it sold a majority of telephone patrons and key politicians on this idea, it gained the capacity to determine the path of telephone development in America, a prerogative in other nations enjoyed only by governments.

The reasons for AT&T's success lay in four areas: control of capital, a shift in regulatory policy, compromise with independent companies and state authorities, and, most importantly, a revised national strategy for telephony.[29] As critics of AT&T have often lamented, size and wealth gave the company formidable economic and political power. Its enormous cash flow and access to capital enabled it to buy outright many of its struggling competitors, or else surreptitiously gain control of them through loans and stock purchases.[30] The large number of acquisitions made by Southern Bell certainly helped it regain top position in the telephone industry in the South.

AT&T also benefited from a sudden change in public policy, which brought state and federal authorities into telephone regulation after 1910. These officials were much less sympathetic to local needs than were municipal governments. They regarded competition as inefficient and viewed locally based communications systems as inherently inferior to a single national system. Many states began to prohibit or discourage competition; others made it difficult for municipal governments to favor local telephone firms over AT&T.[31]

While AT&T profited from both its market power and the new regulatory regime, it also made effective use of skillful compromises. In the South and similar areas still affected by the economics and politics of localism, astute Bell company managers came to realize that existing patterns of demand and traditional sentiment against large, outside corporations did not favor service predicated on an interconnected national network. Even if a nationwide network might eventually become attractive in these markets, the here and now often favored more modest, less expensive, indigenously owned operations. Theoretical efficiency and future benefits did not always win customers.

Southern Bell enacted several types of compromise to meet these conditions. The least dramatic involved little more than "selling" the concept of the system. Until recently, the idea of marketing telephone service may have seemed absurd, but since the reintroduction of competition, and with it the emergence of many new technologies of telecommunications, it has again become apparent that there are many different ways of using telephones and configuring telephone systems. Modern-day telephone company managers have had to relearn the value of marketing, something well understood by their predecessors.

In the early competitive era, marketing Bell service involved going into towns and cities, contacting members of the business class—who would most likely support Bell's long-distance network—and getting their assistance in fights with municipal officials and independent firms. At a time when the number of telephone subscribers was small, especially in the South, gaining just a few adherents to the system was often enough to capture the entire market. Many times, in fact, these negotiations took place with people who were simultaneously the economic elite, the political leadership, and the promoters of competing companies. In Ashville, North Carolina, for example, Southern Bell gave the owners of a competing exchange a windfall $85,000 in preferred stock for their interests, and then came to terms with the city government by agreeing to keep rates to a yearly maximum of $40.00 for businesses and $24.00 for individuals. In Richmond in the early 1890s, Southern Bell at first encountered a hostile city government and business elite determined to revoke the company's franchise. Yet through negotiation, Southern Bell obtained a new franchise—on more favorable terms for the city, of course—and in 1901 bought out the competing company.[32]

Many markets were secured through the policy of sublicensing competitors. Using this tactic, Bell let its opposition have certain markets that it believed it could not effectively serve, but it tied these firms into its system through sublicense contracts that offered capital and technical assistance in exchange for conformity with Bell System policy and technical requirements. The purposes of the contracts were clear: to limit competition—generally Bell withdrew from the independent's market with the understanding that the independent would not try to expand or to build its own toll lines—and they were designed "to control [the opposition] and have [it] operated to our benefit," by ensuring that AT&T retained final say over matters of policy, technological choice, and long-distance system configuration.[33] In the South between 1900 and 1911, the percentage of sublicensed stations increased from 5 to 43 percent.[34]

Over and above all of these important activities, however, was the new national strategy for AT&T articulated by Theodore Vail. Appointed president of AT&T in 1907, he designed a far-reaching set of policies that set the Bell System on its successful course for the next 70 years. Under Vail, AT&T embraced the concept of universal service, which he defined as the fullest possible extension of telephone service to the citizens of the United States. Universal service preserved what had been Bell's

TABLE III   Percentage
of Independent
Telephones Connected
with the Bell System

1900	3.8
1905	13.3
1910	52.6
1915	71

Source: Bell System Statistical Manual.

traditional strategy—an interconnected, national network based in the nation's largest cities—but added to it an even more ambitious plan: AT&T would assure that all customers had access to all parts of the network at all times. The company thereby committed itself to serving customer groups it had earlier been either unable or unwilling to reach.[35]

Vail's new order involved revolutions in both the strategy and structure of the Bell System. Structurally, the company balanced the advantages of central control with the flexibility of decentralized operations. Vail put into place a three-column functional management plan that gave top executives greater control over their sprawling organization.[36] Yet this centralization of authority was matched by an equally important devolution of control down the line, to regional operating companies, individual city exchanges, and sublicensed non-Bell companies. As AT&T vice president E. J. Hall, one of the most perceptive students of telephony, realized, centralization as a "method of organization could not be expanded indefinitely." Instead, AT&T had to "find an effective method of administration through subcompany organizations, controlled by a general staff."[37] Thus AT&T would perform research and development, engineering, and manufacturing using a vertically integrated structure and centralized management, but regional Bell companies would retain considerable latitude on more routine engineering, construction, and maintenance matters, as well as the day-to-day operations in their individual markets.

Decentralization also involved increased sublicensing, which grew rapidly under Vail (Table III). Rather than try to dominate every market with the same technology, Bell would concentrate on key urban areas and the interexchange business, leaving many of the numerous, differentiated local markets in the hands of non-Bell firms. Tied to the main part of the system by sublicense contracts, their service to their customers would increase the universality of the system. The link between the corporation and its constituent parts would be in large part technological; non-Bell firms and individual operating companies would accede to the engineering and research expertise of the central company in all matters that could affect overall system performance.

Over time Vail expanded on the strategic implications of universal service, implications both for his firm and for the industry as a whole. He realized that to succeed against independents he had to engage head-on the alternative concepts of telephone service that had arisen since the end of the Bell monopoly. He also saw that such a fight would of necessity take his company beyond the market into politics and into the shadowy realm of cultural values. Universal service was the conceptual means to attack all of these fronts.

As defined in Vail's exceptionally frank and detailed annual reports, as well as numerous published writings and speeches, universal service meant immediate, comprehensive, high-quality, interconnected local and long-distance service. The first part of the concept—the broad extension of telephone service to all who wanted it—in many ways was not a Bell but an independent innovation. They, after all, had been the ones to bring down prices and penetrate the numerous markets beyond urban and industrial America.[38] But in Vail's hands, this market-driven activity was modified by the second part of the concept, the one that stressed quality and interconnection of local and long-distance service. Universal service now meant not simply the extension of telephony to every place and market, but the ability of any customer to call any other customer anywhere in the United States at any time. And to call them quickly, with minimal delay and minimal effort on the customer's part. Gone were the alternative technologies embraced in farmers' lines, mutual companies, and regional systems. As Vail noted, "a national service, a comprehensive universal service requires that the plant and equipment of the system be of the very highest."[39] Multiparty lines, experimental technologies such as automatic switching, equipment, and construction designed to provide basic local service first and interexchange connections second would not find much favor in this system.

A system predicated on providing the "best" service to all the nation could not afford the inevitable price/quality trade-offs of competitive markets. Universal service implied, therefore, the end of competition; in Vail's own words, "one system, one policy." Competition not only encouraged deviations from standard technology, it resulted in fierce price wars for market share that starved companies of the capital they needed for expensive, long-term construction.[40] To some extent, therefore, the universal system served as a justification for the anticompetitive moves that Bell had been making: buying competitors, driving them from key markets, and sublicensing those that could not be brought to heel otherwise. It also permitted Vail to launch his boldest move—the embrace of government regulation.

Since the market could not be counted on to foster universal service, it was necessary for the government to step in and separate competitors. State regulatory agencies had been doing some of this since 1910. They reduced head-to-head competition, oversaw the quality of service, standardized technology, and limited the power of locally minded municipalities over telephony. But Vail wanted the government to go further and help set rates. It was clearly more expensive to engineer an interconnected than a local system.[41] Appealing to a public authority would shield AT&T from the inevitable customer complaints that would result as rates stabilized or even rose from their extremely low competitive levels. Strong faith in science and technology convinced Vail that once the universal system was secured, research and development would generate price-lowering improvements in efficiency and productivity. But it was crucial that the hand of the government stay crafty competitors from entering the business by what would later be called "creamskimming"—underpricing some part of the whole bundle of services offered by the Bell System.[42] Limiting destructive competition would encourage regular, orderly growth of the universal system. Market rivalry would give way to what Vail preferred to call "participation" among firms, which was conducted on the basis of "fair rates" to maintain high quality in the industry.[43]

Vail's canny proposals have to be understood more as a vision of what telephone service should be than a description of what it was. When he took the helm of AT&T in 1907 competitors still had half the market and the government was not looking to assist the company but to bring it to trial in an antitrust suit. The universal system, if it existed at all at this time, was confined to the largest urban markets. In the rest of the nation Bell's competitive tactics and sublicensing were bringing places in line. For the new order to last, however, a revolution in thought among the actors with the most power over telephony would be required—government officials, important customers, competing firms, and even members of the Bell System.[44]

A sophisticated interpretation of history enabled Vail to argue persuasively for his vision of the future of telephony. As he repeated over and over again, the advance of civilization depended on the progress of transportation and "intercommunication." "Intercommunication, of which the telephone is the latest exponent," he explained to the members of the National Geographic Society, "binds this world together."[45] Human progress followed as isolated groups came into contact with each other. An interconnected system of communication was clearly the most refined means yet for carrying the banner of civilization to remote parts of the world. Seen in this way, locally based communications systems were primitive, backward, and out of step with history. Extensive, comprehensive, interconnected systems, on the other hand, represented progress, enlightenment, and the future of mankind. Only the most audacious competitor could counter this rhetorical onslaught.

Although proposed as an inevitability, Vail's interpretation of human history was part of his vision of what society should be and how communications should help it get there. If, after all, intercommunication was inevitable, then why worry about rates, competition, and alternative technologies? All of those things should fade away with time. But experience had already shown they did not fade away; people clung to their local sentiments, ignored the import of universal service, and placed the immediate gratification of low prices over the value of a well-organized, interconnected network. As America's railroad experience also showed, the path to rationality could be long, arduous, and costly. Vail's experience with railroads throughout his career convinced him that small, isolated systems had to grow into larger, interconnected ones. But there were plenty of examples from the history of railroading of unscrupulous competitors, avaricious financiers, and misguided shippers wrecking railroad systems.[46] Indeed, for Vail and for like-minded businessmen and government regulators, railroads offered a cautionary tale as to what could go wrong if unchecked market forces had free rein with a system technology. For those afraid that telephony would recapitulate the railroad experience, Vail's beneficent vision likely struck a responsive chord.

Although Vail's interpretation of history did not by itself settle any of the pressing matters AT&T confronted, it did provide a rationale for the important steps he was taking. "Society has never allowed that which is crucial to existence to be entirely controlled by private interest," he noted.[47] Intercommunication, as he described it, was certainly crucial, so here was a justification for government intervention into the telephone industry. Here, too, was a strong argument for central control of telephone service by AT&T. Intercommunication brought with it specialization—an important force for progress in society—and in turn the need for coordination among numerous specialized activities. The hierarchical organization of the Bell System could provide that order. It coordinated the many parts of telephone service, furnished centralized R&D to advance the technology of communications, and carried out the planning required in such pivotal social technology.[48]

Vail's vision also suggested several new functions for AT&T to undertake. In a complex, specialized, interdependent society, few people could understand more than a fraction of the forces and institutions that impinged on their lives.[49] This situation, of course, necessitated control of telephony by expert engineers and managers, but it also warranted a role for education. Education overcame the ignorance that resulted from specialization, and reinforced cooperation among members of society. Vail himself was keenly interested and personally involved in public education, but his most important endeavor in this regard was the large investment he made in the new science of public relations. To Vail public relations was public education—explaining to the populace the value, indeed the inevitability, of universal service. AT&T became one of the pioneering companies in the field of corporate image making.[50] Under Vail public relations became a permanent department, a continuous function of the corporate hierarchy.[51]

The new strategy had two final implications, which completed the structure of the Bell System. One was the importance of political influence throughout the nation. Help from the government would not come through political appointees and "demagogues" in southern and western cities or from traditional party hacks. The company had to overstep these antiquated institutions and appeal to the new class of independent experts in charge of regulatory commissions. Even more important were direct appeals to the public. Once people were convinced of the superiority and rationality of the Bell System, the proper public policies would follow. Besides extensive public relations campaigns, the public could be reached through the many operating companies that made up the Bell System and the growing number of stockholders who held shares in AT&T.[52]

Broad distribution of stock ownership was Vail's final innovation. It comported with both his political and his competitive strategy. Politically, broad ownership gave a substantial portion of the most influential members of the public a stake in the Bell System. By 1920 this group included entrepreneurs who had founded competing companies as well as small town business and political leaders. They had to embrace universal service if it was to succeed. Broad ownership also permitted AT&T to undertake the long-term investments required of the universal system. If short-sighted investors controlled the company, they would have the same effect as marketplace rivals, forcing AT&T to place immediate profitability ahead of long-term development.

Vail's carefully conceived, interrelated steps for completing the Bell System were more than business tactics to defeat rival firms. They served that purpose too, of course, though the actual competitive policies evolved more from the day-to-day experiences of managers in regions like the South. Vail went one step further, however, and engaged the issues that lay behind marketplace competition. He sought to define the technology of telephony—what the telephone should do, who should have it, how it should be controlled—in a way that met the challenges posed by the independent firms' alternative systems. In doing so, he moved telephony away from the marketplace—where Bell was enjoying mixed results—into another space somewhere between the market and the public sector. This space was distinctly nonmarket, though it was still capitalist and private.[53] The competitive pressures that remained in the industry would not be market-based, but intraorganizational—between and among members of the extensive Bell System. In fighting these battles, AT&T had enjoyed much more success than it had in the marketplace, so there was every reason to expect it would succeed against what opposition remained to its strategy.

In less than a decade, AT&T experienced a dramatic turnaround, both in the market and in the political realm. It is tempting to see this change as Vail saw it—the inevitable results of human progress. After all, large integrated systems do offer more connections than small ones; centralized R&D was impressive at AT&T; natural monopolies can limit market competition in industries like telecommunications. Add to these forces the more traditional competitive tactics pursued by Bell—predatory pricing and the acquisition of rivals—and you may have most of the explanation of how the Bell System arose. But these forces are not enough.

The shift from localism to cosmopolitanism, although a theme in modern industrial societies, was not an inevitability. One of the forces that made this shift possible was the completion of an integrated national system of communications. The Bell System was as much a cause as an effect of the broad historical forces Vail identified. In 1907 customers in small southern towns and midwestern cities did not just wake up and change their preferences to comport with the requirements of universal service. In the day-to-day activities of individual Bell companies and in the policies and vision of Theodore Vail AT&T consciously sought to change customers' conception of telephony. Bell's victory was not secured by market share alone; as had happened before the competitive period, it was always possible for the intraorganizational consensus to break down and for alternative technological visions to seep up from individual parts of the Bell System. Sustaining victory on technological competitiveness required a strong conception of what the technology of telephony should be and why it should be that way.

Theodore Vail recognized that technological competitiveness extended beyond the search for profits and markets, and beyond the marketplace itself. In a telling early statement, he wrote, "public action is based on opinion which is often controlled by promises or misunderstanding."[54] He could have been referring to either the market or politics. Promises offered by both competitors and politicians seduced the public with false notions of telephony, and generated a misunderstanding of the complex, specialized, but vital technology of communications. By changing the structure of the industry, reorganizing his firm, appealing to new political institutions, and reasserting the Bell definition of technology, Vail was able to control these forces.

The willingness of AT&T's president to engage the basic issue of defining technology helped assure the success of the Bell System for the next 70 years. It did not, however, end technological competitiveness. The history of the Bell System that followed is one of more and less successful efforts to deal with demands from the political world, from consumers, from would-be rival firms, and from members of the organization itself to pursue different avenues and develop alternative technologies. Most of these pressures were contained, particularly the organizational ones. Vail and his successor were extremely successful at building an organization and a firm culture dedicated to a coherent vision of telephone technology. It took many years to replace the Bell System, but its demise was brought about in large part when these contained pressures and an alternate concept of technology worked their way to the surface.

Notes

1. Michael Porter, *Competitive Strategy* (New York: The Free Press, 1980); and *The Competitive Advantage of Nations* (New York: The Free Press, 1990).

2. The fight may be said to be over "core design concepts." See William Abernathy and James Utterbeck, "Innovation," *Technol. Rev.*, June/July 1978, pp. 41–47; also Rebecca Henderson and Kim Clark, "Architectural innovation: The reconfiguration of existing product technologies and the failure of established firms," *Adm. Sci. Q.*, Vol. 35, 1990, pp. 9–30.

3. Margaret Graham, "Corporate research and development: The latest transformation," *Technol. Soc.*, Vol. 7, 1985, pp. 179–195; also Robert Harris and David Mowrey, "Strategies for innovation: An overview," *Calif. Manag. Rev.*, Spring 1990, pp. 7–16.

4. Richard Easterlin, "Regional income trends, 1840–1950," in eds. Robert Fogel and Stanley Engerman, *The Reinterpretation of American Economic History* (New York: Harper & Row, 1971).

5. Southern Bell Telephone and Telegraph Company (SBT&T), Annual Reports.

6. Up to 1899, ABT was the parent organization of all the regional Bell companies; beginning in 1900 that role was taken over by AT&T. In this chapter, the name ABT will be used until that date, while AT&T will designate the Bell long-distance organization, the original function of AT&T.

7. Bell's early strategy is discussed in Gerald Brock, *The Telecommunications Industry: The Dynamics of Market Structure* (Cambridge, Mass.: Harvard Univ. Press, 1981), pp. 110–14; John Langdale, "The growth of long distance telephony in the Bell System, 1875–1907," *J. Hist. Geogr.*, Vol. 4, No. 2, 1978, pp. 150–52; and Richard Gabel, "The early competitive era in telephone communications, 1893–1920," *Law Contemp. Prob.*, Vol. 34, Spring 1969, p. 342.

8. Robert Garnet, *The Telephone Enterprise: The Evolution of the Bell System's Horizontal Structure* (Baltimore Md.: The Johns Hopkins Univ. Press, 1985), pp. 78–83, discusses the early realization of this problem at AT&T.

9. The advantages of this technology are described in American Telephone and Telegraph Company Archives (ATT), box 1236, Law System Advantages and Disadvantages. See also box 1236, Law System, Use by East Tennessee Telephone Company, and box 1236, Mann (Law) System.

10. ATT box 1055, Law System *v.* Multiple Board. The multiple was the answer to capacity limits in exchanges. Morton D. Fagen, ed., *A History of Engineering and Science in the Bell System, I: The Early Years, 1875–1925* (Bell Labs, 1975), pp. 484, 489–96.

11. ATT box 1236, Law System Advantages, op. cit. ATT box 1240, Southern Bell, Infringement of Western Electric Patents, Hayes-Davis, July 11, 1895; ———— , Hayes-French, June 14, 1895.

12. See John J. Carty, "The new era in telephony," ATT National Telephone Exchange Managers Meeting, 1889; also Garnet, *The Telephone Enterprise*, op. cit., pp. 90–108.

13. Robert Bornholz and David Evans, "The early history of competition in the telephone industry," in eds. R. Bornholz and D. Evans, *Breaking Up Bell: Essays on Industrial Organization and Regulation* (New York: North Holland, 1983), pp. 7–40; David Gabel, "What was the loser doing? A reappraisal of the role of the *Visible Hand* in the telephone industry," unpublished manuscript, 1989.

14. ATT box 1337, Interstate Independent Telephone Association Convention, 1902; box 1277, Inter-state Local Telephone Association, 1896; ATT box 177 10 01 01, Independent Telephony, Interstate, 1898–1902. ATT Archives, 46 02 02 27, Allen Report on Telephone Competition.

15. ATT box 1375, Effects of Competition on Development and Rates, 1909–1910. This study shows that independents were strongest in places of less than 25,000 people, and that only 15 percent of the public had to subscribe to the services of two different companies. This lack of overlap and duplication suggests that at this time the nation was composed of distinct, nonconnecting markets.

16. "To the farmer," Bell agent W. S. Allen noted, "the quality of service is distinctly subordinate to cheapness." ATT box 46 02 01 01, Allen-Fish, November 6, 1902. See also ATT box 46 02 01 02, Allen-Fish, February 16, 1903. On low rates, see ATT box 1337, Interstate Independent Telephone Association, 1902, Allen-Fish, December 30, 1902.

17. ATT box 46 02 01 02, Allen-Fish, April 6, 1903; April 9, 1903. Claude Fisher, "The revolution in rural telephony," *J. Soc. Hist.*, Vol. 12, No. 1, 1989, pp. 1–26.

18. ATT box 1163, North Carolina Interstate Telephone Company, 1900.

19. ATT box 1348, Sub-Licensing, Advantages to Operating Companies, 1903, Hall-Fish, July 31, 1903.

20. For more information on this episode, see Kenneth Lipartito, "Corporate strategy and technology choice: The early history of automatic switching in the American telephone industry, 1889–1925," paper presented at the Society for the History of Technology Meeting, Madison, Wis., 1991; also, M. D. Fagen, ed., *A History of Science and Engineering*, pp. 544–554; Milton Mueller, "The switchboard problem: Scale, signalling, and organization in manual telephone switching, 1877–1897," *Technol. Cult.*, Vol. 30, No. 3, 1989, pp. 544–545, 558–559.

21. See, for example, *Huntsville Mercury*, January 31, 1900.

22. On the rapid decline in telephone rates during competition, see Richard Gabel, "The early competitive era," pp. 345–346; and Gerald Brock, *The Telecommunications Industry*, op. cit. Bell managers began to realize that these firms and the farmers' companies responded to "actual needs of smaller communities," and met "a real need of modern life." ATT box 46 02 01 02, Allen-Fish, op. cit.

23. Claude Fisher, "Touch someone: The telephone discovers sociability," *Technol. Cult.*, Vol. 29, No. 1, 1988, pp. 32–61.

24. Carolyn Marvin, *When Old Technologies Were New: Thinking About Communications in the Late Nineteenth Century* (New York: Oxford Univ. Press, 1988).

25. ATT Box 1148, Atlanta, Georgia Franchise, Meany-Fish, September 6, 1902; also General Manager's Letterbooks (GMLB) 923, 1907, pp. 78–112.

26. See Kenneth Lipartito, *The Bell System and Regional Business: The Telephone in the South, 1877–1920* (Baltimore, Md.: The Johns Hopkins Univ. Press, 1989), pp. 175–207 for more examples.

27. John L. Larson, *Bonds of Enterprise: John Murray Forbes and Western Development in America's Railway Age* (Cambridge, Mass.: Harvard Univ. Press, 1984) discusses localism and the railroad.

28. In rural New England, upstate New York, and western Pennsylvania, independents found the same types of customers as did their southern counterparts—those whose main concerns were affordable local service and perhaps a few regional interexchange connections.

29. Noobar T. Danielian, *AT&T: The Story of Industrial Conquest* (New York: The Vanguard Press, 1939); Gabel, "The Early Competitive Era," op. cit.

30. ATT box 1263, Sub-License Contracts, 1898–99, Easterlin-Wilson, September 26, 1898. For more examples, see SBT&T Minutes of the Board of Directors, June 4, 1903; November 9, 1903; November 8, 1906; May 9, 1907; April 4, 1907; and January 10, 1907.

31. These episodes are recounted in greater detail in Lipartito, *The Bell System and Regional Business*, op. cit. 175–207.

32. ATT box 1340, Acquisition and Sale of Exchanges in North Carolina, 1903, Agreement with Asheville Telephone and Telegraph, June 5, 1903; also ATT box 1340, Acquisition of Independent Companies, 1897–1901, Hall-Hudson, February 21, 1898; November 10, 1899; May 29, 1899; also ATT box 1033, Richmond, Virginia, "The Telephone In Virginia," *Richmond News Leader*, December 31, 1925.

33. ATT box 1263, Interconnection with Southern States Telephone and Telegraph, Easterlin-Carson, April 5, 1897.

34. SBT&T, Annual Reports.

35. Louis Galambos, "Theodore N. Vail and the Role of Innovation in the Modern Bell System," *Bus. Hist. Rev.*, forthcoming, deals with Vail's impact on technological innovation in the Bell organization.

36. Garnet, *The Telephone Enterprise*, op. cit. 128–154; Lipartito, *The Bell System and Regional Business*, op. cit. 113–148.

37. ATT box 2029, Development of Functional Organization in the Bell System, Hall-Vail, September 27, 1909.

38. Milton Mueller, "Universal service as a product of competitive struggle," paper presented at the International Communications Association Meeting, Chicago, Ill., 1991.

39. ATT box 49, Bell System, Policy, Organization, Functions, T. N. Vail, "The Policy of the Bell System," 1919.

40. ATT box 1081, T. N. Vail Articles, 1909–1919, "Public Utilities and Public Policy," 1913.

41. ATT box 49, Bell System, Policy, Organization, Functions, T. N. Vail, 1919.

42. ATT box 1081, T. N. Vail Articles, 1909–1919, "Mutual Relations and Interests of the Bell System and the Public," 1913; also, ATT box 5, Toll Line Connections with Independent Companies, memorandum of February 5, 1915.

43. ATT box 1081, T. N. Vail Articles, 1909–1919, 1913.

44. ATT box 49, Bell System, Policy, Organization, Functions, T. N. Vail, "Lest we Forget," 1919.

45. ATT box 1081, T. N. Vail Articles, 1909–1919, "Intercommunication, Commerce, and Civilization," 1917; also Box 1080, T. N. Vail Speeches, 1913–1919, Address at Annual Banquet of the National Geographic Society, 1916.

46. ATT box 1081, T. N. Vail Articles, 1909–1919, "Vermont, An Address by Theodore Vail before the Greater Vermont Association," 1915.

47. ATT box 1081, T. N. Vail Articles, 1909–1919, "Some Observations on Modern Tendencies," 1915.

48. ATT box 49, Bell System, Policy, Organization, Functions, T. N. Vail, "The Policy of the Bell System," 1919.

49. ATT box 1080, T. N. Vail Speeches, 1913–1919, "Some Truths and Some Conclusions,"

50. Richard Tedlow, *Keeping the Corporate Image: Public Relations and Business, 1900–50* (Greenwich, Conn.: JAI Press, 1979), pp. 11–13.

51. ATT box 2027, Vail, Public Relations Policy, 1919.

52. ATT box 49, Bell System, Policy, Organization, Functions, T. N. Vail, "Lest we Forget," 1919.

53. ATT box 1081, T. N. Vail Articles, 1909–1919, "Mutual Relations and Interests of the Bell System and the Public." Vail carefully distinguished between government participation and government control and ownership, which would have been in Vail's mind disastrous. See ATT box 1081, T. N. Vail Articles, 1909–1919, "Some Observations on Modern Tendencies," 1913.

54. ATT box 1080, T. N. Vail Speeches, 1913–1919, Address at President's Dinner, Metropolitan Club, 1916.

The Centre National d'Etude des Télécommunications and the Competitiveness of French Telephone Industry, 1945–1980

Pascal Griset

Introduction

The control of telecommunications is a central stake that largely determines the balance of power among nations.[1] In 1950, France was completely dependent on foreign companies to equip its telephone network. French companies were mainly subsidiaries of ITT[2] and, through lack of funds, the network was old and inefficient. Thus, the problem of competitiveness was twofold. Firstly, the French telephone industry was not able to compete with foreign industries. The national market was therefore totally open to foreign technology, which for a strategic industry had tragic consequences from the point of view of independence and commercial balance. Secondly, the telephone network was not able to perform efficiently, which handicapped the economic development of the country. The solution to this last problem was not in fact really complex—all Postes, Télégraphes, Téléphone (PTT) needed was money to build new lines and provide service to its customers. ITT's subsidiaries were ready to supply new and efficient equipment. However, this solution would make the problem of dependence on foreign technology considerably worse as well as hurt the balance of payments.[3] In order to resolve the two problems simultaneously, France had first to create an independent telephone industry.[4] Competitiveness was the key to achieving this goal. Beyond the "symbolic significance" of this word, "the critical determinants of competitiveness are productivity, improvements, and technological innovation."[5] After the drama of World War II, and starting at a very low level, this multidimensional project constituted a real challenge. This quest for competitiveness has to be analyzed as a fundamental chapter of the history of French industry, but it also constitutes part of a wider ev-

176

olution included in the context presented by Stanley Hoffmann as ". . . the eternal drama of the relations between the French and their government."[6]

The Technological Bet

According to two leading economic historians, David Mowery and Nathan Rosenberg, "the process of technical innovation has to be conceived of as an ongoing search activity that is shaped and structured not only by economic forces that reflect cost considerations and resource endowments but also by the present state of technological knowledge, and by consumer demand for different categories of products and services." A study of French industrial policy demonstrates that there is another basic element: the pursuit of national independence.

The French Telephone Industry after World War II

A dramatic situation

Compare to other European countries or to the United States, the French telephone network was underdeveloped in 1945. During the first years of telephony, the government had been unable to develop an efficient network. After a brief period of private concession,[8] a completely state-owned monopoly was reestablished in 1889.[9] This nationalization did not result in an improvement in equipment, mostly because of political disinterest, the lack of dynamism on the part of PTT, and budget problems. In 1910 there were only 230,000 telephone sets in France compared with 650,000 in Great Britain, 1,060,000 in Germany, and 7,600,000 in the United States. All efforts to increase financing made during the early 1920s were ended by the Depression. As a result, in 1938, France had only 1.6 million telephone sets, Great Britain 3.4 million, Germany 4.2 million, and the United States 20.8 million. The war blocked any further development and destroyed many understructures.

In this context no strong national industry could emerge, so when the war ended in 1945, the industry was unable to meet the needs of an industrialized nation. At the same time, the French market was completely controlled by foreign technology: The Compagnie Générale de Construction Téléphonique (CGCT)[10] and Le Matériel Téléphonique (LMT)[11] were ITT subsidiaries;[12] the Société Française des Téléphones Ericsson (STE) was a subsidiary of the Swedish group LM Ericsson. These three companies controlled 65 percent of the market. The technology came from foreign laboratories, and even la Compagnie Industrielle des Téléphones (CIT), the only significant French manufacturer, had to produce switching equipment under license from the foreign-based companies.[13] Thus, in order to create an independent industry, France first needed to end its reliance on foreign technology.

Seeds of hope

Established in May 1944,[14] and confirmed by the Provisional Government,[15] the Centre National d'Etude des Télécommunications (CNET) was the end result of a process begun in the interwar period.[16] Its role was to develop research in order to satisfy the needs of the administration. The text defining the mission of the new institution included a modern definition of the word "telecommunications." "CNET is entrusted with scientific research and general studies of national application in the domain of telecommunications (telephone, telegraph, broadcasting, teleconferencing, beacons, security systems, etc. . . ."[17] Its first responsibility was to the research groups scattered among several institutions: ". . . The essential idea was to create a kind of pool of state laboratories working in the sphere of telecommunications whose activities until then had been separated by watertight barriers."[18]

CNET also had to coordinate the development of the industry. This was a radically new responsibility for it. In a 1945 memorandum the director of CNET wrote: "The telecommunications industry and CNET will grow in parallel; the force of the one will develop the force of the others. Trust and understanding will necessarily be born from the work and the common effort." This optimistic point of view soon came face to face with administrative realities. Between 1945 and 1954, CNET's development depended on the decisions of a long series of succeeding governments—too many to allow harmonious collaboration. At last, in 1954 a reform initiated by the PTT allowed the Center to find a real homogeneity under the exclusive leadership of the telecommunication administration. Pierre Marzin, the head of this "CNET Mark II," decided to increase public research and tried to coordinate the development of private companies.

An Ambitious Research Policy

Organization and first explorations

In the early 1950s telephone switching was still accomplished electromechanically. Then, in 1957, three engineers returning from a symposium organized by AT&T told Pierre Marzin about the recent evolution of electronic telephone switching in the United States. Convinced that electronics was the way to go in developing the next generation of exchanges, Marzin created a new division in CNET, called Recherche sur les Machines Electroniques (RME). Its mission was to create an electronic switching system. Louis Joseph Libois was in charge of this new division. In creating this new division, Marzin went against the company's organization chart, according to which the "telephone switching division" should have been given the task of developing the new switching system. Instead, Marzin gave the responsibility of the program to new men assembled from different divisions.[19]

The RME team started with basic research in order to explore, without preconception, a wide variety of directions. Its first achievement was the building of two prototypes, ANTINEA (1958–1960) and ANTARES (1961–1963), which allowed the team to evaluate the problem in two main directions:

- The right use of electronic components
- The methods to conceive software

At the same time, the team studied the technologies developed in the English-speaking world. At the end of the 1950s, despite the development of transistors, the electronics industry still relied on tubes. In this context, the British decided to build a fully electronic exchange using tubes. Their prototype, nicknamed the "gas plant," was extremely bulky, needed an air-cooling system, and functioned below expectations. As a result, its sad career ended in 1963. After this expensive failure, the British stayed out of the electronic switching field for the next twenty years.

The Americans were less ambitious, deciding to first explore "space division technology." Bell Labs succeeded and chose Morris, Illinois, as the location of the first central system of this type, which it completed in November 1960.[20] AT&T created components especially designed for use in this kind of system. This part of the project was one of the most expensive. But neither the American plan, which was too expensive, nor the British plan, which had failed, could be adopted by CNET. Thanks to these different experiences, the RME engineers decided to adopt what they felt was a more realistic process: "The policy adopted at this time was to try to use the components that were supposed to become very widely used in the future. That meant they had to follow, as closely as possible, the evolution of computer technology, taking into account that this market would quickly become the main outlet for electronic components."[21]

At the same time, a specific effort was made to develop new software. In this area, the researchers were surprised by the complexity of the problems they had to solve, and their evaluation took a long time. When they occurred, these delays were caused by an underestimation of the time it would take to write and test the software.[22]

The first successes

Since the number of people involved in the project increased continuously, the first results seemed to be encouraging. Even though time-division switching was the primary long-term objective, it was impossible to neglect space-division technology completely. Thus these two branches were worked on simultaneously during the 1960s, with the first results occurring in space-division technology. The results were in the form of two prototypes that allowed CNET scientists to explore different ways of development and test many different solutions.

ARISTOTE[23] was to be used in setting up a high-capacity system organized around one central processor and a number of peripheral secondary processors. ARISTOTE was purely electronic, the switching network consisting of matrices of transistors. Its central processor (RAMSES) had been developed from ANTINEA.[24]

SOCRATE[25] was much more traditional and was essentially based on crossbar components.[26] Its main purpose was to develop new software for the control system.[27] ARISTOTE and SOCRATE were both connected to the network in Lannion in the mid-1960s. The main decisions reached by CNET as a result of these experiences decisively influenced the development of electronic switching.[28]

Based on these results, a new period in CNET's research began in 1965, and two new prototypes were developed. The first one, PERICLES (space-division switching) was created in association with the manufacturers; the second one, PLATON[29] (fully electronic) was undertaken exclusively by CNET.

PERICLES led to the installation in 1970 of the first telephone exchange in Clamart.[30] This system formed the basis of the Metaconta developed later by LMT.

It was the prototype of a system that was intended to provide 30,000 subscriber lines. The design adopted was conventional, in line with the principles considered at that time most appropriate for space-division switching exchange.[31]

PLATON was completely different. Designed by Louis Joseph Libois, it was based on the principles of time-division digital switching. In order to create a system suitable for commercial manufacture, PLATON was conceived of as a low-capacity system, based on the simplest possible architecture, using a minimum of new types of equipment. Nevertheless, its architecture was revolutionary.

> The principles behind Platon's design may be seen by an expert eye to foreshadow two major trends that were to become increasingly important from the late 1970s onwards: decentralization of the control units and the use of microcomputers for that purpose. It will be noted that in the early 1970s when Platon was in the process of being developed, microprocessors were just beginning to appear and the very term "microprocessor" had yet to be coined.[32]

In January 1970 PLATON was connected to the networks at Perros-Guirec, where it initially serviced 700 subscribers. A few months later the system was enlarged to connect 2000 subscribers. This was a world premiere. Pierre Marzin liked to jokingly say that his butcher's complaints about the problems of connection informed him about the development problems a few days before his engineers' reports.[33]

From these two prototypes, CNET was able to develop both space-division and time-division technologies. Even though the first prototype was shared with the manufacturers (and specifically the ITT subsidiaries), the second was controlled exclusively by CNET. Nevertheless, CNET, which was part of the PTT, was not in a position to manufacture this new equipment. In order to equip the French network with the new technology many problems had yet to be solved, among them choosing and training the right manufacturers and finding the funding.

From Research to Industry

In order to allow France to take an international industrial lead, CNET decided to bypass the space-division step and to develop directly time-division technology. But, even if PLATON and time-division technology proved its feasibility, there was still the time gap between the prototype and production to be covered.[34]

A French Company for a French Technology

Transfer of technology

CNET decided to lead French industry to independence by the development of the time-division technology. To this end, the center asked CIT to produce the new system. The managers of this relatively small company were at first reluctant to take on the project, which involved a completely new field. But the offer was so nice, it was impossible to refuse. As a subsidiary of the Compagnie Générale d'Electricité (CGE), CIT also had to consider Ambroise Roux's opinion. Roux, who was chairman of CGE, was very much in favor of the project, first because of the profits that would be generated, and second because the "gaullist" nature of the industrial ambition coincided with his political beliefs. A subsidiary of CIT, La Société Lannionnaise d'Electronique (SLE), created in Lannion at the end of the 1960s, was the perfect organization to assume the most difficult part of the plan: the transfer of the technology from a state laboratory to a private company. For one thing, none of the engineers working for CIT had the knowledge or skills necessary to work effectively with the new technology. Therefore, SLE, which was a small company, was able to act as an interface between CNET and CIT. During the period that PLATON was being developed, SLE's engineers were closely involved in CNET's work.

The industrialization

In the last phase of development, the CNET engineers in charge of the project, with the blessing of CNET's director, "deserted" and joined SLE. This last part of the project consisted of the adaptation of the technical specifications to market standards. The choice of new electronic components[35] and new developments in software led to the E10A system. A factory specifically designed to produce the system was set up in Lannion in 1972. By 1975 its annual production capacity had reached 200,000 lines.

The product was ready. All that remained was for PTT to buy it.

However, to go back in time a bit, during the 1960s and 1970s the developmental level of the French telephone network progressed from being a problem to being a scandal. The humorist Fernand Reynaud wrote a successful sketch titled "Le 22 à Asnières" that pointed up the unfortunate situation of the French subscribers. People used to say: "In France half of the population wait to get the telephone; the other half wait to get the tone." As a result, President Pompidou decided to put an end to the situation. The determination of Bernard Esambert, the president's adviser, and the action of Yves Guéna, minister of PTT, were instrumental in initiating a powerful plan. At the same time the promotion of Pierre Marzin from the direction of CNET (where he was replaced by Louis Joseph Libois) to the direction of the administration of telecommunication showed that the future of the national network would be based on French technology. According to the plan, the reorganization would be both structural and financial, but the financial effort was so huge that the budget was not able to support it. The government therefore had to take out a loan in order to continue the financing. The main decision was made in 1969, and four companies were created to arrange for these loans:

FINEXTEL (February 1970)
CODETEL (January 1971)
AGRITEL (June 1972)
CREDITEL (October 1972)

To give the plan a fair chance of success the old and conservative PTT administration also had to be overhauled. A separate presentation to the Parliament of the Post Office's and Telecommunications' budgets in 1970 and the suppression of the Secrétariat Général aux PTT in 1971 signaled the liberation of the telecommunications branch.

Development of the Network and Industrial Policy

A change of course

In 1974 everything necessary to accomplish the great project initiated in 1957 was ready: an independent French technology existed; a French company was prepared to use this technology to build operational telephone switching equipment; and the financial problems were resolved. The next step would be simple. PTT would call for time-division equipment, but only one company, CIT, which had a jump of several years to its competitors, would be able to answer. Unable to propose any system of this quality, ITT's subsidiaries would be "naturally" supplanted. With American imperialism neutralized, the victory would not only be total but elegant. Unfortunately, the death of President Pompidou destroyed these hopes.

After the election of Valery Giscard d'Estaing a completely different approach prevailed. National independence no longer had priority. The goal of the new administration was to quickly equip the country and to obtain lower prices from the manufacturers. On October 16, 1974, Gérard Théry was nominated to replace Louis Joseph Libois as head of the Direction Générale des Télécommunications. The entire policy of CNET for the past twenty years was criticized, and the center was accused of abuse of power. In essence the new executives said that CNET's role was to do research, not to decide industrial policy. A few months later a reform reduced the power of the center. "All of the organization which allowed CNET to manage the innovation process was called into question. This was pretty serious when you know the time necessary to constitute [a] high level research team."[36]

To make a complex history short, the new Administration decided to create a competitive market in France.[37] Time-division technology was abandoned by the new administration, because this technology, for so long nurtured to compete with ITT's subsidiaries, was suddenly considered to be too risky and too expensive. Instead, space-division technology was chosen because it was considered to be more cost-efficient. PTT therefore invited bids in order to equip the network with space-division switching, but CIT, prepared for many years to develop time-division switching equipment, was unable to respond. Instead, ITT's subsidiaries were able to offer space-division switching equipment that was based on American patents. "The public authorities made internationalization their key word. But isn't the better the enemy of the good? There are moments, especially in the latest technologies, when it is necessary to stop a policy and consider it. Competition is a good thing if it does not turn into anarchy." The planned defeat of ITT was transformed into a victory. . . .[38]

But this doctrinal liberalism proved to be intolerable in a political context. Therefore, putting liberalism aside for a while, Giscard's men decided to reorganize the telephone industry in order to avoid a new era of American domination. Pressure applied to ITT convinced the American company to sell one of its subsidiaries to a French group. The plan was intended to reduce ITT's market share while creating competition between two French companies. The company entering the telephone market was Thomson. This initiative postponed the agreement signed in 1969 between CGE and Thomson.[39] According to this "Yalta de l'électronique," the telephone industry was reserved for CGE. Thomson's comeback was strongly supported by the new government, but for some commentators the liberal doctrine was not the only explanation: "In its principal activities, CGE has just lost in some cases its hopes, in some cases its leadership. Industrial setback or political cabal? . . . In this country where everything begins and everything ends by political tunes, there are those who sing in more than one key; the government, VGE leading, intends to eliminate whoever was the friend of Pompidou." (Ambroise. Roux)[40] The industrial consequences of these changes were catastrophic: "Some considerable investments were dedicated to the putting in the place of the products of intermediary technology . . . Some factories had been totally disrupted, training programs had been put in place for thousands of workers, laboratories had been entirely dedicated to the development of space-division technology."[41] As a matter of fact, two years later, the choice of space-division technology was criticized and time-division technology was finally adopted. Thus, a huge investment was lost: "On the very day that the new factory intended for these products was inaugurated, the administration of PTT announced that it would not order more of those materials and that its purchases henceforth would focus on the products of the new electronic generation."[41] This strategy was a major failure and delayed the international development of the French industry. This new change in technology meant that Thomson had to develop its own time-division system. Since this meant competing with Alcatel, which owned CNET's technology free of charge, Thomson was forced to give up for financial reasons, and in 1983, it sold its telephone department to Alcatel. Many years and billions of francs had been lost in this Franco–French competition.

A worldwide manufacturer and a modern network

Despite the incorrect analysis of the Giscard d'Estaing administration, the results of CNET's action seem to be positive. The double goals of equipping the country and developing an independent industry were accomplished.

The competitiveness of the French economy was enhanced by the most modern telephone network in the world. The first step in achieving this was the elimination of the antiquated system that handicapped the country, an effort that began vigorously in the mid-1970s. From the Côtes du Nord, modernization of the network progressed quickly until, in 1990, with 28 million main telephone lines, the density of the French network was one of the most impressive in the world. Seventy-five percent of the switching and 80 percent of the transmission were digital. This evolution allowed the opening of the first ISDN network in the world in 1987 in Britanny. Then in 1990 the entire national network was upgraded to its present quality. As a result, it became possible for any subscriber to be connected to this service, commercially called "Numeris." The E10B and E10MT equipment, manufactured by

Alcatel, enhanced the network to a high level of quality. On average, one line is in trouble once every seven years. During the same period, the price of intercity communications decreased from 3.80 francs in 1985 to 2.60 in 1990. With its new status, the telephone administration is currently much more independent. In 1990 its activities exceeded 100 billion francs.

At the same time the small, dependent industry of the 1960s was transformed into a world leader with a high level technology. After 1983 CIT-Alcatel became the only French manufacturer of telephone switching equipment. "It is that, with nearly ten years' delay, which the men of Georges Pompidou wished to do."[42] All the equipment in the country was based on nationally owned patents and exportation was increasing. In order to expand its activities to the international level, Alcatel had to find allies. Its first break came from its old enemy, ITT. In February 1986, ITT withdrew the 1240 system from the U.S. market, because the company had neglected to adapt the system, originally created in Europe, to American specifications.[43] In June 1986, ITT transferred about 70 percent of its vast array of telecommunication industries to Compagnie Générale d'Electricité. These interests amounted to a veritable empire that operated in almost 100 countries, with those engaged in switching equipment manufacture accounting for 10 percent of the world market. The agreement took effect on December 30, 1986, creating the world's second largest supplier in telecommunications after AT&T. Registered in Amsterdam as Alcatel NV, the group's activities are mainly based on the technology developed over many years by CIT-Alcatel. Thus, the 1957 goal had not only been achieved, but largely surpassed. However, in order to preserve competitiveness in the French market, Alcatel does not enjoy a monopoly. In 1987 CGCT, nationalized since 1982, was sold by the government. As a result of heavy competition from AT&T and Siemens, a third contender, LM Ericsson, was selected to join with the French company Matra.[44]

Conclusion

"The force of all advice yields to the times the opportunities and the methods roll along and change without cease."[45] The controlled experiment of the 1960s and 1970s does not constitute a "model" for today, nor is it a countermodel to be destroyed on the bonfire of liberalism. The action of the French telecommunication administration cause the competitiveness within the national telephone industry to increase dramatically, while at the same time, the country was able to build the telephone network that had been needed for many decades. Considering the weakness of the French industry at the beginning of the 1950s, an interventionist strategy was the only one possible. Certainly, its success is partial, but like an efficient medicine, interventionism has some side effects. The link between political evolution and industrial strategy is certainly the worst of them. When the industrial policy changes each time the political majority changes, it is impossible to succeed.

At the edge of the twenty-first century, with Japanese industry challenging European and American technology everywhere, the existence of a group like Alcatel is certainly a trump card for the future of French industry. Similarly, the development of France Telecom proves that a state-owned monopoly is not condemned to failure. If France Telecom has to change in the near future, its base is strong.

From a technological point of view, time-division switching technology is a major event. As of now, computers and telecommunications are evolving separately, but they will converge sooner or later.

To compete means to have a will to succeed. Competitiveness is the main goal for a company or, more and more often, for a country. This convergence of national and private interest is not new and is not specifically French. The path followed by France to reach competitiveness in the telecommunication industry could be analyzed through the framework proposed by Kilmann, Shelleman, and Uzzi.[46] The second quadrant, where the role of technology and the influence of government are crucial, would surely parallel the French telephone switching experiment.

The convergent efforts of a state-owned laboratory, of an old administration deeply renewed, and of a private company seem to be a good example of the "holistic, integrated and collective approach not only desirable but also imperative . . . in the face of unprecedented global competition."[47]

In the case of countries facing a long delay, this will to succeed means that the challenger is entitled to adopt its own rules and to accept the challenge only when it is ready. To fight on the field and at the time chosen by the enemy is surely not the best way to compete. Neither interventionism nor liberalism is a pragmatic panacea. Adaptation of an industrial policy to a nation's needs and abilities, and adjustment to international context are certainly two elements leading to competitiveness.

Notes

1. P. Hall, *The Carrier Wave: New Information Technology and the Geography of Innovation, 1846–2003* (London: Unwin Hayman, 1988). Concerning telecommunications and geostrategy: D. Headrick, *The Invisible Weapon; Telecommunications and International Politics, 1851–1945.* (Oxford: Oxford Univ. Press, 1991). P. Griset, *Les révolutions de la communication, XIX°–XX° siècles* (Paris: Hachette, 1991). A. Smith, *The Geopolitics of Information* (London: 1980). T. MacPhail, *Electronic Colonialism* (Los Angeles: SAGE, 1987).

2. P. Griset, "Fondation et empire: l'hégémonie américaine dans les télécommunications internationales: 1919–1980," *Réseaux*, No. 49, Septembre–Octobre 1991, pp. 73–89.

3. Usually, the equipment sold to the French administration had to be built in France, but the royalties and profits collected by ITT's subsidiaries were not nationally controlled.

4. D. Mowery and N. Rosenberg, *Technology and the Pursuit of Economic Growth* (Cambridge, England: Cambridge Univ. Press, 1989).

5. L. D'andrea Tyson, "Competitiveness; An analysis of the problem and a perspective on future policy," in *Global Competitiveness: Getting the U.S. Back on Track*, ed. M. Starr (New York: Norton), pp. 95–121. See also: *The Competitive Edge: Research Priorities for U.S. Manufacturing: Report of the Committee on Analysis of Research Directions and Needs in U.S. Manufacturing*, Manufacturing Studies Board, Commission on Engineering and Technical Systems, National Research Council, National Academy Press, 1991.

6. S. Hoffman, *Sur la France* (Paris: Seuil, 1976).

7. Mowery and Rosenberg, *Technology*, op. cit., p. 8.

8. The State monopoly on telecommunications was proclaimed in May 1837. The text was extremely clear: "Quiconque transmettra sans autorisation des signaux d'un lieu à un autre, soit à l'aide de machines télégraphiques, soit par tout autre moyen, sera puni d'un emprisonnement d'un mois à un an et d'une amende de 1000 à 10 000 francs . . . le tribunal ordonnera la destruction des postes, des machines et des moyens de transmission."

9. In 1879, two companies, La Compagnie des télélphones (Bell patents) and Berthon et Compagnie (Edison patents) were allowed to develop a privately owned and operated telephone network. They merged in December 1880 to form La Société Générale des Téléphones. In 1889 the slowly growing network was nationalized.

10. The CGCT mostly equipped small cities.

11. LMT mostly equipped large towns and very large cities.

12. R. Sobel, *ITT: The Management of Opportunity* (New York: 1982). ITT's "real politic" is still a subject of controversy. Concerning the "Pro-Nazi" tactic in Germany see: A. Sampson, *The Sovereign State of ITT* (New York: Stein & Day, 1973).

13. The ITT European research laboratories were based in Bruxelles. Ericsson's central laboratories in Midsommarkransen in Stockholm provided a very high level of technology.

14. *Loi*, No. 102, May 4, 1944.

15. Ordonnance de validation du 29 janvier 1945.

16. The main steps of this evolution, which created a centralized research structure in the field of telecommunications, correspond to the creation of different instituions: in 1916, the Service d'Etudes et de Recherches Techniques (SERT); in 1941, the Direction des Recherches et du Contrôle Technique (DRCT).

17. Article 2.

18. P. Tucoulat, Director of CNET, Note, September 1947.

19. Concerning this kind of problem in France, see P. Bernoux, *La sociologie des organisations* (Paris: Seuil, 1985) and M. Crozier, *Le phénomène bureaucratique* (Paris: Seuil, 1963).

20. About Bell Labs see M. Fagen, *A History of Science and Engineering in the Bell System* (Murray Hill, N.J.: Bell Laboratories, 1975 and 1978).

21. P. Lucas, "Les progrès de la commutation électronique dans le monde," *Commutation Electron.*, Vol. 44, January 1974.

22. The Morris, central's software, had already 50,000 lines.

23. Appareillage Réalisant Intégralement et Systématiquement Toute Opération de Téléphonie Electronique.

24. See P. Lucas, A. Profit, J. Pouliquen, and M. Rouzier, "Aristote electronic telephone exchange in Lannion," *Proceedings of the 1966 Paris International Switching Symposium*, pp. 1105–1145.

25. Systeme Original de Commutation Rapide Automatique à Traitement Electronique.

26. CP 400.

27. P. Lucas, J. Duquesne, J. Pouliquen, and J. P. Berger, "Semi-electronic switching system of Lannion (project Socrate)," Proceedings of the 1966 Paris International Switching Symposium, pp. 116–127.

28. That is (1) for the switching network, to abandon electronic crosspoints in favor of matrices of reed relays in a sealed tube; (2) to adopt the principle of load sharing between the processors of the control unit; to have the central processor handle all the functions of signal registration, signal translation, and call recording for billing subscribers.

29. Prototype Lanionnais d'Autocommutateur Téléphonique à Organisation Numérique. Lannion is a town in the north of Brittany. The politics of decentralization led to the transfer of part of the CNET staff from Issy les Moulineux (a suburb of Paris) to Lannion. This small city became the most important research center in the field of electronic switching. The fact that Lannion was the birthplace of the director of CNET had, of course, nothing to do with this choice of place.

30. Serving 800 subscribers.

31. See L. J. Libois, P. Lucas, J. Dondoux, and J. Duquesne, "Basic principles of the Pericles system," *Commutation Electron.* October 1967, pp. 5–21.

32. R. Chapuis and J. Amos, *Electronics, Computers and Telephone Switching* (Amsterdam/ New York/Oxford: North-Holland, 1990), p. 223.

33. This jest underlined the decisive importance of in situ development. When it comes from the laboratory, the switching system is far from ready.

34. See C. Freeman, *The Economics of Industrial Innovation* (London: Frances Pinter, 1982); N. Rosenberg, *Inside the Black Box: Technology and Economics* (Cambridge, England: Cambridge Univ. Press, 1982); and F. Caron, *Le résistible déclin des sociétés industrielles* (Paris: Perrin, 1985).

35. The evolution of electronic components was decisive in order to prove the profitability of electronic switching; cf. E. Braun and S. Macdonald, *Revolution in Miniature: The History and Impact of Semiconductors Electronics* (Cambridge, England: Cambridge Univ. Press, 1982); A. Beltran and P. Griset, *Histoire des techniques XIX°–XX° siècles* (Paris: Colin, 1990).

36. M. Nouvion, *L'automatisation des télécommunications* (Lyon: PUL, 1982), p. 303.

37. For more details see P. Griset, "Le développement du téléphone en France depuis les années 1950. Politique de recherche et recherche d'une politique," *Vingtième siècle revue d'histoire*, October–December 1989, pp. 41–53.

38. J. M. Quatrepoint, *Le Monde*, July 30, 1976.

39. Thomson entered the telephone field in 1904 with the acquisition of Postel-Vinay. In 1927, Thomson left this company, renamed Compagnie des téléphones Thomson Houston, to ITT.

40. *Le Point*, May 17, 1976.

41. J. Darmon, *Le grande dérangement* (Paris: J. C. Lattès, 1985), p. 168.

42. *Le Matin*, September 9, 1983.

43. One hundred and fifty million dollars in research were lost.

44. This was a reintroduction of the AXE exchange, but in a digital version. Before the transaction, the administration guaranteed a 16 percent market share for the company.

45. M. Montaigne, *Essais*, Vol. 3 (Paris: Gallimard, 1965), p. 55.

46. R. Kilmann, J. Shellemann, and B. Uzzi. "Integrating different approaches for achieving competitiveness," in *Making Organizations Competitive*, ed. R. Kilmann (San Francisco: Bass, 1991), p. 110.

47. Ibid., p. 122.

Comments
on Technological Competitiveness
in Telecommunications

with Emphasis on Switching

Amos E. Joel, Jr.

Introduction

The chapters in this section represent various areas of the world where, at different times, competition has aided public utilities in bringing new technology to the consumer. Today, depending on your point of view, unfortunately or fortunately the United States is leading the way in the application of competition to telecommunications.

As illustrated in Professor Lipartito's article, which concentrates on the southern part of the United States during the early part of this century, competition declined as a result of the vigorous enforcement of the Bell patent monopoly. The nascent independent telephone industry was therefore destined to be absorbed into the Bell System until the Kingsbury agreement in 1915 halted further acquisitions.

Like many human and economic endeavors cycles are discernible. In the United States we are about to complete the cycle of competition in the telecommunications service and manufacturing industries with the government mandating competition in the delivery of local service.

As a youth I remember local telephone service competition in Philadelphia, the last large city in the United States to maintain this practice. Franchises were held by two companies, Bell and Postal (unrelated to the mail service). The two systems were not interconnected. To have full telephone access one had to subscribe to the services of both companies.

With today's technology it is, as we have seen with interexchange (IX) (toll) service, possible to select the carrier of your choice and still, for the most part, have complete access to all subscribers in the public network. This is due in large measure to retaining universal use of the North American (telephone) numbering plan.

Change Wrought by Competition in IX

The consent decree agreement the U.S. Justice Department made terminating its antitrust suit against AT&T in 1982 made the United States the first country to break the telephone monopoly. The agreement divided the former Bell System into seven regional companies, each with a virtual local-service monopoly in its respective territory and with AT&T providing nationwide IX telecommunication services.

There were already competitors in the IX service. Part of the agreement required the local companies to provide subscribers "equal access" to all IXs that wished to serve an exchange. This provision could not have been possible if it were not for the technology known as "stored program control" (SPC) made possible during the previous two decades by the development and wide deployment in the United States of switches using electronic technology. Only modern SPC electronic offices were required to provide equal access.

After the initial subsidization of the other IXs, the long-distance telephone services provided users with more choices. Typical competitive forces have been evident. The average cost of long-distance service has decreased. At the same time the cost of local service has increased, since it has to be supported with a smaller contribution from the toll portion of the business.

Service quality is difficult to measure, but examination of the press during the past seven years indicates that in general competition has brought with it poorer service. Billing as well as technical service outages have plagued the industry. IXs have even resorted to business practices that have resulted in complaints of purloining customers from one another.

To compete, technologies that once concentrated resources and operations have been deployed in a way that makes the service more vulnerable to massive outages, which in turn attract more public attention than before divestiture. The effects of service outages have increased because the many different carriers are unable to pool their resources. Under monopoly these resources would have continued to grow as part of a single coordinated service.

Service is provided more rapidly. In general, one can obtain service, particularly from IXs, more quickly that one could prior to divestiture. Furthermore, a greater variety of service tariffs are now available to subscribers. These different charging plans are the principal differences among the IXs.

Another interesting aspect of competition is that technological information is exchanged less freely. Furthermore, the lack of uniformity results in greater complexity. More carriers are involved in providing the most basic of services.

The breakup of the Bell System took place on January 1, 1984. It freed the Bell local service companies to purchase equipment from sources other than the former sole provider, the Western Electric Co.

Divestiture brought changes in the deployment of new technologies that had been planned earlier. At about the same time as divestiture, manufacturers of equipment for the independent telephone industry were introducing a new generation of switching systems, known as *time-division digital switching*. The opportunity of selling equipment in this large U.S. market encouraged several foreign manufacturers to establish development and manufacturing operations in the United States.

The regional Bell operating companies (RBOCs) now saw an opportunity to use competition to reduce the price of their most costly expenditure, the introduction of new switching systems into their networks. With system equipment from many manufacturers being mixed together in their networks, the training, servicing, engineering, and administration resulted in an increasing and expensive complexity, which made it more difficult to render a uniform quality of service.

The introduction of new technology has been impeded by the introduction of competition. No longer can one body by itself decide what is to be used in the public network. Standards are established by consensus in committees comprising representatives from industry and the carriers. This process can take considerable time, during which vendors introducing new products must take the risk that the technologies they employ in these products are not likely to become the standard.

At the same time, many different products and services that accomplish the same functions may be introduced into the network. Also each local and IX carrier has its own plans for when new services will be introduced and how they will function. This lack of uniformity makes it difficult for subscribers to plan for and utilize network-wide services.

Plans already underway to introduce new services more rapidly using the so-called "intelligent networks" will further compound this difficulty for nationwide, and eventually worldwide, users.

The Future Technology Portends More Competition

What has happened over the past seven years is only the beginning of the effects of competition. Other service providers are requesting that telecommunication networks be "opened" so that they can offer their own versions of telecommunication services. To attain equality of opportunity, noncarriers and outside enhanced-service providers have demanded and received "equal access" to basic service elements. This has even resulted in competitors placing their own equipment in telecommunication wire centers belonging to the RBOCs.

Competitors employing new technologies are now threatening the monopolies of the local service providers. Using fiber, microwave, and cellular technologies, they offer new and broader band services to more users. In some cases, they bypass the local central offices.

Conversely, the RBOCs have found opportunities to move from regulated service obligations to competing in other geographical areas. They invest in foreign operating entities, and own cellular mobile radio franchises and nonregulated enterprises.

While the preceding has described briefly the results of using competing technologies in the telecommunications industry in the United States, it also represents the trend worldwide. Telecommunications is international, and many users make heavy use of international networks and services. These users are demanding the same services wherever they do business, so it is only a matter of time before the dilution of what was once deemed a "natural monopoly" occurs throughout the world in one form or another.

PART V

Electrical Technology for the Home Market

This section considers electrical technology for the home. In the first paper, Arne Kaijser, a historian of technology in the Royal Institute of Technology in Stockholm, analyzes the fierce competition among three technologies (gas, oil, and electricity) for the domestic lighting and cooking markets in Sweden between 1880 and 1960. Two aspects of his analysis have wide applicability beyond his case study. The first is his analysis of technical performance, pricing, propaganda (advertising), and political pressure as factors in technological competitiveness. The second is his analysis of the competitive differences between grid-based energy systems (e.g., electricity, gas, and district heating), in which energy is delivered to users through a special physical network constructed for this purpose, and nongrid-based systems (e.g., oil, coal, and biomass fuels), in which energy is delivered to users through existing transport systems (such as highways and railroads).

Susan Douglas, a historian of technology at Hampshire College, prepared the other paper of this section. She uses the examples of ham radio operators, hi-fi enthusiasts, and FM programmers to exemplify "oppositional" uses of commercially developed technologies by subcultures of American tinkerers, and explains how these oppositional uses helped to identify underdeveloped or completely neglected technologies. Douglas uses the word "oppositional" to connote a set of activities she believes were consciously undertaken to oppose establishment forces, such as the government and large, established industrial firms, in the shaping, implementation, and distribution of new technologies.

In Kaijser's study, competition occurs among different technologies intended for the same application. This kind of competition is commonplace: radio vs. phonograph, television vs. cable television vs. movies, steam engines vs. gasoline vs. electric motors in manufacturing, electric vs. diesel railway trains, nuclear vs. hydro power, etc. Kaijser's analysis might be extended by considering the degree to which technological applications are either technology- or market-driven. Sometimes, a need becomes clear and various alternative technologies are proposed in response; other times, two or more technologies develop autonomously and only eventually come to vie for a particular application; more often, the situation lies between these two extremes. How, for example, do technology- and market-driven application areas map onto solutions that are grid- or nongrid-based? One might also ask where standardization fits in. It can be seen as an important part of the process of choosing a technology for an application.

Kaijser provides a matrix of factors (his "four P's") that affect the outcome of competition among different heating and cooking technologies. Rarely is one factor determinative in a competition among technologies, among firms, or among nations. A company must juggle many different parameters, which often are in conflict with one another, with the recognition that neglect of one of them might leave the company vulnerable. A company might develop a product that exceeds all competing products on technical grounds, for example, but the product still might not succeed because it is not marketed well, does not meet some legislated environmental criteria, or costs too much. Historians of technology have frequently discounted these non-technical factors in their discussions of the reception of technological products; and frequently when such factors are considered, the historian focuses on one to the exclusion of others. There is clearly a need for further investigation of the reception of technologies or technological products in the face of a matrix of business, technological, social, institutional, and economic factors.

Kaijser's discussion of the differences between grid- and nongrid-based energy systems has an interesting parallel in computing: software shared by means of punched cards, magnetic tapes, or standard telephone lines is nongrid, while that shared through specialized computer networks is grid-based. This similarity was noted by early computer network designers, who explicitly stated their intention to develop computer utilities resembling electric power utilities. Kaijser's analysis can also be seen as part of the larger movement in the history of technology to consider technological systems, which include technological devices, individual people, institutions, and other infrastructure. Thomas Hughes has given us a model of scholarship of how this applies to the electric power system,[1] but historians of technology are now just beginning to realize the full explanatory value of the systems concept.

Douglas's paper reminds us that the individuals and groups who develop technologies belong to cultures, which give meaning and shape to the technologies with which they work. In the introduction to Part IV, we suggested some of the other groups that compete over the development of new or neglected technologies, and we shall not pursue this matter further here. However, it should be noted that cultural analysis may be very helpful in understanding competition among nations. It is clear that technologies have a different place in third-world societies than they do in the United States or Europe. And although we in the west tend to Westernize in our minds our competition from the far east, the Japanese and Korean societies have very different relations to their technology than we do in the United States. Some of the first studies of the differences of eastern and western cultures on the development of technology are now beginning to appear.[2] Until we understand the various cultural meanings of technology across countries, it is nearly impossible to appreciate issues of competitiveness in these cultures—or even to know if technological competitiveness is a meaningful concept.

Notes

1. Thomas P. Hughes, *Networks of Power*, Baltimore and London: Johns Hopkins University Press, 1983.
2. Brian Pfaffenberger of the University of Virginia has been studying the reception of the personal computer in Sri Lanka; David Allison of the Smithsonian Institute is just beginning a comparative study of cultural differences on computing in Japan and the United States.

Fighting for Lighting and Cooking

Competing Energy Systems in Sweden, 1880–1960

Arne Kaijser

Introduction

The nineteenth century saw the successive introduction of three energy systems: gas, oil, and electricity. These were all high-value energy carriers that could be used for purposes from lighting to domestic heating. Their first applications were within the field of lighting, simply because this was the application that offered the greatest potential for charging the most for each kilowatt-hour. These energy systems then subsequently found their way to other energy markets—mechanical power, process heating, cooking, and space heating—where prices and quality requirements were lower.[1]

The introduction of new, high-value energy carriers into an energy market has generally given rise to a phase of intensive competition between traditional and new energy systems. In this chapter I will focus on two such competitions in Sweden: for the lighting and cooking markets. I will argue that the competitiveness of an energy system is dependent on one or several of the following means of competition ("the four p's"): *technical performance*, *pricing*, *propaganda*, and *political pressure*. In addition, I will discuss the fundamental difference between two kinds of energy systems: grid-based and non-grid-based systems.

I use the term *energy system* to signify a sociotechnical system, consisting not only of technical components but also of the people and organizations that build, operate, and use these plants, as well as the legal and economic framework of the system.

The purpose of an energy system is to provide a link between a raw material and particular energy needs. This link requires various forms of processing or conversion, as well as transportation. In terms of transportation requirements, energy systems can be divided into two main types:

- Grid-based energy systems (e.g., electricity, gas, district heating), in which final transportation to users is by means of a special physical network constructed solely for this purpose.
- Non-grid-based systems (e.g., oil products, coal, biomass fuels), where the final transportation to users is through existing transport systems.

These two types of energy systems differ in a number of respects. First, they differ in their *initial conditions*. A grid system requires a major initial investment before it can be put into operation: specifically, each new user must be connected to it by a separate pipe or wire. In contrast, a non-grid system can be built gradually, using existing roads, railways, and harbors.

The second difference relates to the *dependency factor*. A grid system creates a strong interdependency of suppliers and users. Users that employ the system for vital purposes depend on a supply without major interruptions, while suppliers depend on their users staying with the system, since the physical network cannot be moved or used for other purposes. A non-grid system is considerably more flexible, and thus the mutual interdependence of suppliers and users is weaker.

Third, the *operating conditions* differ. A grid system should attempt to achieve a reasonably high load factor, both for economic and technical reasons. Usually, the final users lack storage facilities, which means that grid systems must meet high-reliability requirements, since the rate of production must closely follow the rate of consumption. Each customer of a non-grid system, on the other hand, has its own buffer store, which helps to make the system more robust and insensitive to external disturbances.

The final difference lies in the *degree of public involvement*. A grid system is part of the physical infrastructure of a society. The pipelines or wires must be run above or below privately owned or publicly owned ground, requiring special permission or concessions from the state or community. Further, the monopoly position generally enjoyed by such a system requires society to apply some measure of control to ensure that the monopoly is not misused.[2]

The Struggle for the Lighting Market

Until the mid-1800s, a fire in an open fireplace was the main source of light for most Swedish households, both in urban and in rural areas. The middle of the century saw the establishment of factories producing tallow and stearin candles, which met a rapidly growing demand. Gasworks were also established in larger and medium-sized towns, to supply gas for street lighting and for lighting in workplaces and the homes of the wealthy. Sweden had no coal deposits; therefore, gas production depended on coal imports.[1]

At the end of the 1860s, the kerosene lamp appeared as a new competitor on the lighting market. The development of oil drilling technology allowed kerosene to be supplied at quite a low cost compared to gas. Kerosene lamps were also simple and relatively inexpensive, and required no pipes. Compared to grid-based gas lighting, available only in major towns with gasworks, kerosene lighting spread very quickly, even to remote villages in the countryside.

At the beginning of the 1880s, a further competitor appeared on the scene: the incandescent electric lamp. Even at that early stage, it offered several important technical advantages. It was described as follows, in a lecture given in 1883 to the Swedish Engineers' Association:

> The light produced is delightful, burning steadily without the least flickering or change, and having the warm, comfortable colour to which we are accustomed from earlier times. It releases little heat and no products of combustion. All the lamps in a circuit light instantly without having to be touched, and can be surrounded by the most flammable of items without risk of conflagration. With these lamps, it is possible to provide lighting equivalent to 6, 12, 16 or even up to 20 standard candles. In a word, they possess most of the attributes that can be required of an artificial light.[3]

The author of this somewhat lyrical description was not any representative of the Edison Company, as the reader might suspect. On the contrary, it was one of the senior members of the Swedish gas industry, the chief engineer of the Stockholm gasworks, Adolf Ahlsell.

Ahlsell praised all the purely technical characteristics of the incandescent lamp, but was also careful to point out that its costs were so high that "the electric light (will not) in any way replace gas lighting. . . . It is likely to find its first more general application as luxury lighting, where cost is of no consideration."[3]

Around the turn of the century an intense struggle for the lighting market developed not only in Sweden but also internationally. Lighting was the first major market for oil, gas, and electricity, and so the outcome of this struggle was of considerable importance for the continued development of these energy systems.

Performance and political pressure became important means of competition in this battle.

Performance

The major cost element of all three types of lighting was that of energy itself, and so their efficiency (i.e., the amount of light produced in relation to the amount of energy used) was a factor of vital importance. During the decades around the turn of the century, international technical development in the lighting area was impressive.

The first major advance was made within the field of gas lighting, with the introduction of the incandescent mantle. In traditional gas lamps, the burning gas itself constituted the source of light, while in the incandescent gas lamp, the burning gases heated a mantle with special metal oxides. It was this mantle that created the light. The efficiency of the new lamps was eight times higher than that of traditional gas lamps. However, the light was perhaps not as aesthetically attractive; not, at any rate, if we are to believe this description by the Swedish novelist Hjalmar Söderberg in 1907:

> It is still dark. A single gas flame flickers lazily through the frosty haze, and I trudge to school. Oh, I still remember the reddish-orange gas lamps of my childhood: how warmly and welcomingly they shone over the snow! Then came the deathly green Auer light.[4]

The incandescent gas mantle achieved rapid acceptance during the 1890s, and contributed greatly to augmenting the competitiveness of gas lighting, making it even cheaper than kerosene lighting. This development fostered great optimism in the gas industry, as is illustrated by Figure 1.

The development of the incandescent mantle exemplifies a general tendency pointed out by the economic historian Nathan Rosenberg: an established technology threatened by a new technology often undergoes considerable improvement in a last effort to survive. This is often forgotten later when the new technology has pushed the old technology out of the market.[5,6]

The manufacturers of electric lamps also tried to improve efficiency. By the end of the 1800s, they had succeeded in developing a new type of carbon filament with a light output that was twice as high as that of the first carbon filaments. The major advance occurred, however, when manufacturers succeeded in producing metal-filament lamps shortly after the turn of the century. In 1910, a tungsten-filament lamp was three times as efficient as the best carbon-filament lamp, with a corresponding cost reduction, as shown in Figure 2. The new lamps were quickly accepted during the 1910s.[7]

The most spectacular technical development during the struggle for the lighting market therefore occurred with the lamps themselves: the efficiency of both gas and electric lighting increased by nearly ten times over a period of 30 years! However, important advances in production and distribution also occurred.

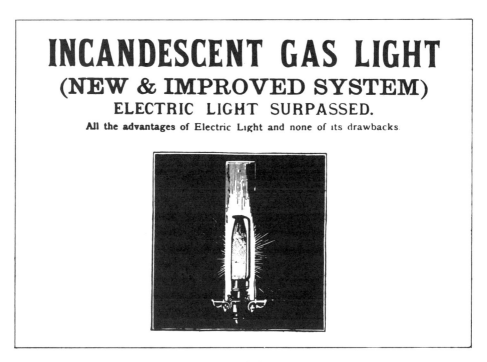

Figure 1. Advertisement in *Journal of Gas Lighting*, December 1890.

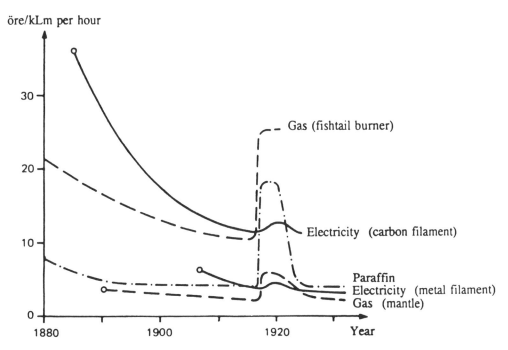

 öre/kLm per hour

Figure 2. Cost per unit of light for different types of lighting in Sweden, 1880–1930.

In the gas industry, considerable improvement took place in the performance of ovens through application of the regenerative principle, thus reducing their tendency to leak gas and increasing their size. As a result, overall efficiency of gas production (gas and coke production versus coal consumption) rose from 30 percent to 65 percent during the last decades of the nineteenth century. Further, the necessary labor force was reduced to about one-tenth. These advances allowed the price of gas in many towns to be halved between 1880 and the end of the century.[1]

In the electricity industry the most important development was in transmission. During the 1890s, alternating-current (ac) technology was developed, which made it possible to exploit waterfalls located at great distances from towns and industry. The proportion of hydropower in Sweden's electricity production increased from 18 percent in 1885 to 60 percent at the turn of the century, with resulting significant reductions in production costs.[8]

Political Pressure

In technical and economic terms, gas lighting was more or less comparable with electric lighting until the introduction of the metal-filament lamp. Until then, the poorer quality of gas lighting was made up for by its lower price. This equilibrium meant that institutional conditions played an important part in the struggle between the two systems.

At the end of the century, gas lighting was backed by powerful and influential interests. Almost all the largest towns in Sweden had gasworks that were owned and operated either by the town council or by a private company mostly owned by the town's wealthier citizens. In many towns with gasworks, the decision to build a power station was therefore preceded by a long, hard struggle. The town of Linköping is a typical example.

Linköping had a publicly owned gasworks built in 1861. The battle started in 1886, when the board of the gasworks applied to the town council for permission to rebuild the gasworks. However, the council decided first to investigate the feasibility of switching to electric lighting. Since the director of the gasworks was a powerful advocate of the scheme to enlarge the gasworks, while three council members had recently purchased a number of waterfalls close to the town, this decision triggered a battle that lasted for 10 years. The struggle surged back and forth, and dominated the political debate in the town.

In the end, the proposal of the gasworks board to build a new gasworks and to shelve the plans for an electrical power station was accepted in 1896. Then in 1902 an enterprising local businessman managed to obtain a concession to supply Linköping with electricity. He started supplying electricity to the town in the autumn of 1903— 17 years after the first proposal to investigate electric lighting had been put forward.[9]

In many other towns having gasworks, the establishment of electricity was delayed in the same way as in Linköping. This can be seen by comparing the introduction patterns of gas and electricity. As grid-based systems, both required major initial investments in production and distribution systems, which meant that the best markets for both existed in larger towns, where many potential customers lived close together and maximum economies of scale could be achieved. The pattern of events associated with the introduction of gas was also precisely as expected. The four first gasworks were built in the four largest towns, after which it took only 13 years before all but two of the other 20 largest towns had built gasworks.

The pattern for the introduction of electricity is completely different, due to the resistance from gas interests. Of the four largest towns at the time, Malmö was the third town in the country to have an electrical plant, Stockholm the twelfth, Gothenburg the seventeenth, and Norrköping the forty-eighth. In 1905, 20 years after the country's first electrical plant opened, seven of the twenty largest towns in the country still had no electricity.[10]

The Outcome

In the long run electrification could not be stopped. The introduction of efficient metal-filament incandescent lamps in the 1910s was one decisive reason electricity beat its competitors. Another important factor was the huge increases in the prices of imported coal (and thus gas) and kerosene that occurred during World War I (see Fig. 2). The price of electricity increased only marginally because it was produced mainly by domestic hydropower. This, of course, made electric lighting even more economically competitive.

By 1920 almost all urban households had adopted electric lighting. In the countryside, however, kerosene lighting had a significant market share until the 1940s. This was because, since rural electrification was much more costly and took much longer to accomplish than urban electrification,[11] many households were not yet connected to an electric network.

The Struggle for the Cooking Market

Long before the struggle for lighting ended, the gas industry became interested in two new markets: stoves and engines. In the middle of the 1880s, many Swedish gasworks actively encouraged these new applications through propaganda and new, differentiated gas tariffs. The gasworks were motivated by two main reasons. First, they wanted to ensure their continued existence in the face of the threat offered by the incandescent electric lamp, and second, engine gas and cooking gas (which were the terms used) were used mainly during the day, with consumption being more or less independent of the time of year. Any increase in these applications would therefore help to even out the load on the gasworks, thus making better use of capital.

Gas engines had only a brief popularity. Between 1895 and 1910, engine gas accounted for about 10 percent of total gas consumption, but during the 1920s gas engines quickly lost out to better and less expensive electric motors.

Conditions were much more favorable for cooking gas. By about 1910, it held the largest sector of the gas market. Existing wood stoves, however, were used not only for cooking but also for heating the kitchen during the winter. Therefore early gas cookers could not replace the wood stoves, but merely complement them, as illustrated by Figure 3. They were simple items, having one or two burners, and were mainly used during the summer. Gas stoves with an oven were very uncommon prior to 1910.

The competitiveness of gas stoves improved greatly around this time as a result of two external factors. One was the rising price of wood, caused by increasing

Figure 3. Gas cooker on top of a traditional wood stove. (Photo from the turn of the century)

demand from the pulp and paper industry. In the mid-1920s the cost of fuel for a wood stove, used only for cooking, was about three times higher than that of a gas stove. Furthermore, a gas stove was quicker, easier to control, and easier to use.[12]

Another important factor behind the growth in the use of cooking gas was the introduction of central heating. From 1910 onward, most new apartment buildings incorporated central heating systems, and by 1945 about 75 percent of the apartments in the larger towns had them. The introduction of central heating meant that wood stoves were no longer needed to warm the kitchen, thus eliminating its final competitive edge over the gas stove.

During the interwar years, the wood stove was (at least quantitatively) the main competitor of the gas stove. However, by the 1920s a competitor that the gasworks feared much more than the wood stove was already making its appearance—the electric stove. In order to understand why the electric stove was introduced at this time, we need to start with a brief background sketch.

By 1910, industry had become the major user of electricity, consuming about 90 percent of all electricity. However, domestic consumers were a much greater financial influence on the power and electric companies than their consumption might indicate, because they paid ten times more for their low-voltage electricity than industry did for its high-voltage electricity.[13] The importance of domestic subscribers became particularly apparent during the severe depression after World War I, when the use of electricity in industry fell by 30 percent over a period of a few years, while domestic use continued to increase.

It is against this background that we should view the strong interest of the electric industry in increased domestic use of electricity. In the 1920s, domestic apparatus, and stoves in particular, were felt to be of major importance.[13] Thus, from 1920 to 1960 an intensive competition for the cooking market took place. Three means of competition were employed in this struggle: performance, propaganda, and pricing.

Performance

The efficiency of stoves (expressed by the ratio of heat supplied to energy consumed) was an important cost factor, exactly as it had been for lamps. Ovens, in particular, wasted energy, since they were poorly sealed and lacked thermal insulation. Electric stoves suffered most from this drawback, because electric energy was more expensive. Spurred by this deficiency, manufacturers of electric stoves developed new, efficient ovens by the beginning of the 1930s. These manufacturers were also the first to realize the importance of the external appearance of their product. As a result, they started to manufacture stoves with white enamel surfaces and bright chrome fittings. It was not long before the competing gas and wood stove manufacturers followed their example.

A serious hurdle for electric cooking was that the majority of domestic consumers were connected to direct-current (dc) systems, which were designed for lighting, but not for the higher voltages required for cooking. Therefore, at the end of the 1920s, the electric companies started a changeover from dc to ac. This conversion required a massive capital investment and was not completed until the 1960s.

Another important factor in the competitiveness between gas and electric stoves was the improvement in the production and distribution systems. The conversion from dc to ac supplies in urban areas was carried out at the same time as major changes in the national electrical system. Progressive integration and standardization, together with the development of massive hydropower resources in the north of the country, resulted in significant reductions in the cost of electricity.[14] Compared to this, advances in the gas sector were considerably more modest. However, the efficiency of the actual process of producing gas continued to improve, with overall efficiency of the gas industry reaching more than 80 percent in 1950, as against about 65 percent at the beginning of the century.[15]

Propaganda

The second point of competition for the two energy systems was propaganda. As early as the 1880s the gas companies were publicizing gas for cooking. During the 1910s, it was common for gas companies to open permanent displays, where stoves and other gas apparatus could be demonstrated and sold. In some cities home consultants were employed as demonstrators to hold courses and give lectures on cooking on gas stoves. They also visited new subscribers in their homes and instructed them on how to use their new stoves. After World War I, many electric companies followed the example of the gas companies, opening permanent exhibitions and distributing brochures.[16]

On the national level, both the electric and gas industries developed internal cooperation and exchange of experience through the Association of Swedish Electric Utilities, which was founded in 1903, and the Swedish Gasworks' Association, founded in 1916. Both associations produced advertising material, which was available to their individual member companies. In 1927 the Association for the Rational Use of Electricity (FERA) was founded by power companies and local distributors as well as manufacturing firms such as ASEA. FERA's main objective was the dissemination of information on all the uses of electricity. It also produced brochures and other informational and advertising material aimed at different categories of users (see Fig. 4). The association also employed two home consultants who traveled around the country arranging courses in "electric cooking" for housewives. No association equivalent to FERA was formed by the gas industry, mainly because there was no national manufacturing company of gas equipment of any great importance.[17]

Pricing

The third competitive element was pricing. We have described how and why the gas companies introduced differentiated gas tariffs in the 1880s to encourage the use of both cooking and engine gas. These tariffs disappeared after World War I, simply because there was nothing left to differentiate between, since two of the three previous divisions, lighting and gas engines, no longer existed. However, the electric industry, having learned from the gas industry, began using pricing as an important means of competition, especially when entering new markets. The principles of such

Figure 4. Poster for promoting electric cooking, produced by FERA in 1941.

pricing were formulated clearly by Carl Rossander, a professor of electrical engineering at the Royal Institute of Technology in Stockholm, in a lecture given to the Association of Swedish Electric Utilities in 1925:

> Apart from the abnormal conditions during the war, the price of electric current for lighting in Sweden during recent years has generally been of the order of 30–40 öre/kWh, at which price the electric lamps (and particularly, of course, after the invention of the metal filament lamp) are economically superior to virtually all other light sources, while the price of this electricity is fully satisfactory to the electric companies. The price of electricity for small motors is generally one-half to two-thirds of this, which price is sufficiently low to allow electric motors to compete successfully with other forms of small motors and engines such as gas and kerosene engines, while experience has shown that the electricity companies can generally supply motor current at this price.
>
> If, on the other hand, electric energy for boiling and other food preparation is to be able to compete seriously with wood, gas, etc., then it would be necessary for the price of current not to exceed about 10 öre/kWh or thereabouts, even after making allowance for the advantages of electric cooking in terms of convenience, cleanliness, etc. Conditions will be even more unfavourable if electric energy is to be used for space heating, for which the price in general should be of the order of 2–3 öre/kWh. It is easy to understand if the majority of electric companies do not feel able to supply energy at such low prices.[18]

In other words, Rossander claimed that the necessary level of competitiveness of electricity in different markets determined its price. This was a controversial idea. The electric companies had a monopoly, but claimed that their tariffs reflected the cost of supplying electricity to their customers. The high price of electricity for lighting, for example, was justified by the unfavorable loading. However, it seems obvious that the electric companies exaggerated this factor and made a considerable profit from the lighting market.[13] These substantial profits then allowed them to subsidize the introduction of electric stoves during the 1930s with extremely low prices.

Encouraging households to adopt electric stoves was difficult. Including the necessary new saucepans (with flat bottoms) and installation, an electric stove represented a sizable investment. Therefore, operating costs had to be kept low in order to encourage consumers to lay out the money. Several of the more aggressive electric companies introduced new tariffs, supplying electricity for stoves at about 8 öre/kWh. They justified this (e.g., to their lighting subscribers, who were being charged 35 öre/kWh) by claiming that electric stoves resulted in much more uniform loading on the system than lighting did.

However, this was simply not true. A study of electric cooking carried out by the State Power Board in 1928 includes a load diagram from a Stockholm suburb for a winter day in 1926 that shows a very marked peak in demand by stoves immediately after 5 P.M., at which time the lighting load was at 90 percent of its maximum value.[19] In other words, the stove load was not at all favorable. The fact that lighting subscribers subsidized the introduction of electric stoves in this way was never openly admitted by the electric utilities.

The Outcome

In the 1950s electric stoves made considerable gains in urban areas. One of the reasons for this was that a lot had happened in terms of stove development. For example, hotplates had considerably higher ratings, and therefore cooked faster than before. Ovens now incorporated thermostats and good thermal insulation, so that they were quite economical. Prices, too, had been reduced as a result of long production runs. A second important factor was that the old dc networks in the larger town centers had by now been replaced by ac networks capable of supplying stove loads. Finally, while the average price of electricity had been halved in real terms between 1925 and 1950, the price of gas remained the same. As a result, many owners of gas stoves switched to electric stoves during the 1950s. For many gasworks this loss of cooking customers was a fatal financial blow, forcing them to go out of business. Of the 37 Swedish gasworks operating in 1950, only 8 remained in 1980.[1]

As in the case of lighting it took a long time for electric stoves to capture the rural stove market, the rate of adoption depending largely on how quickly the rural electrical networks were upgraded from dc to ac. By the end of the 1960s, however, the majority of rural households were using electric stoves.[11]

Conclusion

The struggle for the lighting and stove markets clearly illustrate how competition can encourage technical development and in particular the development of more energy-efficient designs. Sometimes, however, the competitive advantage of energy-efficient appliances was not fully understood by the energy suppliers. For example, many directors of electric companies regarded the metal-filament lamp as a serious threat when it first appeared because, for the same light output, it used less than half as much electricity as a carbon-filament lamp. As subscribers changed to the new lamps their use of electricity therefore decreased considerably.

Between 1905 and 1910 a substantial slowdown occurred in the previously rapidly growing use of electricity. In 1910 there was a lively debate among managers of electric companies, many of them expressing great concern about the metal-filament lamp. Others, however, were more farsighted and reassured their colleagues that "the time will come . . . when the electric works will owe a debt of gratitude to the current-saving lamps for a considerable increase in the use of electricity."[20] Today, a similar kind of ambiguity vis-à-vis energy-efficient technology can frequently be seen among energy suppliers.

The outcome of these struggles has depended not only on technical development but also on the political and economic strengths of the parties concerned. During the struggle for the lighting market, gas interests had the most political influence, and in many places were able to prevent the formation of electric companies for a long time. On the other hand, during the struggle for the stove market, the strong financial status of the electric companies played an important part in deciding the outcome.

The importance of financial strength is related to the advantage that established energy systems always have over new energy systems. From the consumer's point of view, a change of energy system represents a considerable investment in new equipment and, if it is a grid-based system, in new service connections. Good examples of this can be seen in the conversion from gas to electric lighting and from a wood to a gas stove.

In such conversions, the new energy system must be offered with favorable introductory terms so the change is attractive to the consumer. In the Swedish case, the electric companies, with their large financial resources, could offer significant tariff reductions at the time when they wanted to enter the stove market.

Once the consumers have made the necessary investment in new equipment and connections, there is little chance that they will give up the new system. Prices will have to rise significantly before they will even consider changing again.[2] We can find many contemporary analogies to the events and ideas given in this chapter.

Notes

1. A. Kaijser, "*Stadens ljus—Etableringen av de första svenska gasverken,*" in Linköping Studies in Arts and Science No. 4, Chap. 9, 1986.

2. A. Kaijser, A. Mogren, and P. Steen, *Att ändra riktning—Villkor för ny energiteknik* (Stockholm: Allmänna Förlaget, 1988). English Transl. 1991: *Changing Direction— Energy Policy and New Technology* (Stockholm: National Energy Administration, 1991), p. R5.

3. A. Ahlsell, "Om förhållandet mellan elektrisk belysning och gasbelysning," in *Ingeniörs-Föreningens Förhandlingar 1883* (Stockholm: 1883), pp. 47–50.

4. H. Söderberg, *Sekelskiftet*, ed. D. Hjorth (Stockholm: 1964), p. 39.

5. N. Rosenberg, *Perspectives on Technology* (Cambridge, England: Cambridge Univ. Press, 1976), p. 205ff.

6. H.-J. Braun, "Gas oder Elektrizität? Zur Konkurrenz zweier Beleuchtungssysteme, 1880– 1914," *Technikgeschichte*, Vol. 47, No. 1, 1980, pp. 1–19.

7. A. Bright, *The Electric Lamp Industry* (New York: MacMillan Co., 1949), Chap. 6.

8. F. Hjulström, *Sveriges elektrifiering* (Uppsala, Sweden: 1940).

9. O. Holmqvist, *Linköpings gasverk 1861–1936* (Linköping: 1936).

10. H. Lindblom and G. Bergqvist, *Kommunal affärsverksamhet i de svenska städerna* (Stockholm: 1924), p. 22ff.

11. J.-E. Hagberg, *Tekniken i kvinnornas händer. Hushållsarbete och hushållsteknik under tjugo-och trettiotalen*, Linköping Studies in Arts and Science, No. 7, 1986.

12. *Stockholm's gasverk 1853–1928* (Stockholm: 1928), p. 85.

13. J. Körner, *Sveriges elektricitetsverksindustri* (Stockholm: 1928).

14. Statens Vattenfallsverk, *Vattenfall under 75 år* (Stockholm: 1984).

15. *Gasverksföreningens årsbok 1951* (Stockholm: 1951).

16. *ERA*, No. 4, 1937, p. 56.

17. *ERA*, No. 23, 1952, p. 139.

18. C. Rossander, "Om tariffer för elektrisk energi," *Svenska Elverksföreningens Handlingar 1926*, No. 3 (Stockholm: 1926).

19. *Elektrisk kokning*, Tekniska Meedelanden från Kungl. Vattenfallsstyrelsen, Series E, No. 12, (Stockholm, 1928), p. 54.

20. *Teknisk Tidskrift*, Elektroteknik, Häfte 2, 1910, p. 28.

Oppositional Uses of Technology and Corporate Competition

The Case of Radio Broadcasting

Susan J. Douglas

Introduction

The study of technological competitiveness, especially in the United States in the twentieth century, usually focuses on competition within or between corporations, both large and small. Such studies also highlight the struggles between independent inventors and established industries. But as we consider how competition serves to stimulate or retard technological change, we also need to examine an area many corporations have sought to eliminate or suppress—the oppositional, often renegade applications of their devices or systems by subcultures of American tinkerers. This requires that we take a more bottom-up approach to competition.

This chapter focuses on the oppositional uses of audio technology, specifically radio and the hi-fi phonograph, and the key role these applications play in identifying underdeveloped or completely neglected areas of commercial development.[1] These appropriations of audio technology were pioneered by two often overlapping groups—the youth subculture and the engineering, tinkering subculture—in a way that often linked technical rebellion with cultural rebellion. This rebellion, which has been most recently dramatized by the controversies surrounding computer hackers, stems from a host of intersecting attitudes, which include a resistance to or rejection of technical hierarchies that seem too authoritarian and arbitrary, an antipathy toward corporations and corporate applications of technologies, and a sense of technical contempt or one-upmanship vis-à-vis devices made available to a mass market. Yet this corporate antipathy is often mixed with a need and desire to succeed in the corporate world, so these oppositional uses of technology are often the site of major cultural contradictions surrounding the corporate ethos in the United States.

This chapter considers three examples: the amateur wireless operators,[2] or "hams," who pioneered in radio broadcasting at the very earliest stages of the commercial exploitation of radio in the United States; the hi-fi enthusiasts of the late 1940s and early 1950s,[3] who challenged the corporate complacency surrounding phonograph equipment; and FM programmers of the late 1960s and early 1970s, who used this previously neglected technology to develop new broadcasting formats and to cultivate new audiences.[4]

What all these technical subcultures had in common was that their use of audio technology deviated significantly from the expectations of the originators and producers of these inventions, and from the business interests that took them over. The degree of conscious defiance animating members of these groups varied, however. While a subgroup of the hams challenged the government's automatic appropriation of portions of the electromagnetic spectrum for military uses, and the hi-fi enthusiasts repudiated what they saw as technological complacency in the phonograph industry, the underground FM programmers attacked the entire political and cultural establishment as they saw it. These technologies allowed for—even invited—oppositional, antiestablishment uses primarily by white middle-class men and boys, who were expected, and eventually compelled, to integrate into institutional bureaucracies, yet who yearned to postpone such integration. Their use of these technologies allowed them to rebel. But it also provided them with critical technical expertise that would subsequently become valuable in the job market.

In all of these cases—wireless, hi-fi, and FM—men with their own technical and social agendas appropriated still underdeveloped audio technology and pushed it to new levels of performance and new realms of application. Their oppositional activities exposed areas of corporate and technological myopia. The corporations managing these technologies had to respond to the innovations of these hobbyists, and did so by co-opting and taming outlaw practices to create huge new businesses.

A Brief History of the Radio Amateurs

On a Sunday in 1907, the *New York Times Magazine* featured as its lead story an article starring Walter J. Willenborg, a previously unknown wireless experimenter and a student at Stevens Institute of Technology in Hoboken, New Jersey.[5] A large oval portrait of Willenborg in the center of the page was surrounded by photographs of his homebuilt wireless station, which included transmitting and receiving equipment. The reporter described in excited detail all the messages he was privy to by listening in to "the ether" on Willenborg's headphones. Willenborg made such good copy that he was also featured in a 1908 issue of *St. Nicholas*, "An Illustrated Magazine for Young Folks."[6]

Willenborg was one of the young men the press chose to represent the burgeoning number of nameless amateur operators in the country. Since 1899, when Guglielmo Marconi (1874–1937) had first introduced his wireless telegraph to the United States during the America's Cup races, the prospect of sending telegraph messages through "the air" without wires had generated enormous excitement in newspapers, magazines, and the technical press. This excitement helped spark a new fad, and from 1906 onward, thousands of primarily white, middle-class boys and men began to construct their own wireless stations in their bedrooms, attics, or garages. Although they were to be found throughout the country, these amateur operators were most prevalent in urban areas, especially those with seaports. They hoped to listen in on messages sent by the navy, commercial ships, and shore stations, as well as to send Morse code messages back and forth to each other. They earned no money as operators, and had no particular corporate or professional affiliation. For them, wireless was a hobby, one that required technical knowledge and skill. The technical fraternity these amateurs formed was exclusive. Working-class boys with neither the time nor the money to tinker with wireless could not participate as easily. Neither could girls or young women, for whom technical tinkering was considered a distinctly inappropriate pastime and technical mastery a distinctly unacceptable goal.

The amateurs' ingenuity in converting a motley assortment of electrical and metal castoffs into working radio sets was quite impressive. With performance analogous to that of an expensive receiver now made available to them in the form of the inexpensive crystal detectors that had been introduced in 1906, the amateurs were prepared to improvise the rest of the set. Before 1908, they lacked this option, for very few companies sold equipment appropriate for home use. As the boom continued, however, children's books, wireless manuals, magazines, and even the Boy Scout manual offered diagrams and advice on radio construction.

In the hands of amateurs like Willenborg, all sorts of technical recycling took place. Discarded photography plates wrapped with foil served as condensers; cylindrical Quaker Oats containers wrapped with wires became tuning coils. One amateur recalled that he improvised a loudspeaker by rolling a newspaper into a tapered cone. Another inventor's apparatus was constructed ingeniously out of old cans, umbrella ribs, discarded bottles, and various other articles. The one component that was too complicated for most amateurs to duplicate, and too expensive to buy, was the headphone set. Consequently, telephones began to vanish from public booths across America as the amateurs took them for their own stations.

By 1910, amateurs surpassed the U.S. Navy (the major governmental user of wireless) and the private wireless companies in numbers and, often, in the quality of the apparatus they owned. In 1911, *Electrical World* reported:

> The number of wireless plants erected purely for amusement and without even the intention of serious experimenting is very large. One can scarcely go through a village without seeing evidence of this kind of activity, and around any of our large cities meddlesome antennae can be counted by the score.[7]

The *New York Times* estimated in 1912 that America had several hundred thousand active amateur operators.[8] Even after passage of the Radio Act of 1912, which sought to regulate and stifle amateur activity in the air, the number of enthusiasts continued to grow. Between 1915 and 1916, the Commerce Department licensed 8489 amateur stations, compared to fewer than 200 commercial shore stations. Estimates placed the number of unlicensed receiving stations at 150,000.

One characteristic seemed especially prevalent among these amateurs: their disdain for authority and their delight in using this new technology to flout it. While most amateurs used their equipment to gossip, trade technical information, share football or baseball scores, or compare homework, some were considerably more mischievous. The increased presence of amateurs on the airwaves, at a time when tuning was crude and interference was common, led to a struggle for control of the ether. This struggle especially pitted the more defiant amateurs against the U.S. Navy. Pretending to be military officials or commercial operators, they would dispatch naval vessels on all sorts of fabricated missions. Navy operators would receive emergency messages about a ship that was sinking off the coast. After hours of futile searching, the navy would hear the truth: the "foundering" ship had just arrived safely in port. For some, this was simple pranksterism, the sort of delinquency that is irresistible when the target is distant and detection virtually impossible. But other amateurs had a more thoroughgoing critique of what they saw as an arbitrary usurpation of the airwaves by the state, and expressed their indignation by sending obscene messages to naval stations, and arguing extensively with naval operators over ownership of the ether. Military officials complained bitterly to Congress about what they regarded as etheric outlaws, and the more politically conscious amateurs responded by sending their own representatives to Washington to testify against military domination of the spectrum. The navy was hardly helped in this skirmish by the often romanticized portrayals of wireless operators in the popular press.

Increasingly, magazines, newspapers, and popular fiction celebrated the wireless dabbling of these young men. Fictitious Tom Swift, boy inventor, used radio to rescue people in distress, and by the 1920s there was an entire series of adventure books called *The Radio Boys*. Stories like the ones written about Willenborg captured the many attractions that wireless experimentation might hold for a young man. On a practical level, a successful wireless dabbler could make extra money from his pastime. He would have technical knowledge and skills few others possessed. He learned a code and he became an explorer. Through wireless, he entered an invisible, mysterious realm, somewhere above and beyond everyday life, where the rules for behavior couldn't be enforced—in fact, were not yet even established. He could participate in contests of strength, power, and territory, by interfering with or interrupting other stations' messages, and win them without any risk or physical danger. In this realm, by mastering a new technology while letting his antisocial inclinations run loose, he could be, simultaneously, a boy and a man, a child and an adult.

A revolutionary social phenomenon was emerging. A large radio audience, whose attitude and involvement were unlike those of other, traditionally passive audiences, was taking shape. This was an active, committed, and participatory audience. Out of the camaraderies of the amateurs emerged more formal fraternities, the wireless clubs, which were organized all over America. One of the largest, formed in 1914 by the inventor Hiram Percy Maxim (1896–1936), was the American Radio Relay League (ARRL), which organized a national amateur network of stations across the country through which amateurs could relay messages to and for each other. Thus, by the mid-teens there existed in the United States a grass-roots, coast-to-coast communications network, and an incipient radio audience. When ARRL was formed, *Popular Mechanics* proclaimed "the beginning of a new epoch in the interchange of information and the transmission of messages."[9] The way these amateurs used the invention, trying to reach as many people and to be as inclusive as possible was the opposite of the more closed, exclusive policies of the private companies and the navy. Through their activities, the amateurs raised the question: "Why restrict this invention to a few select corporate and military senders and receivers when so many everyday people could benefit from and enjoy this device?"

Amateur activity increased dramatically during the second decade of the century, and some of the more powerful stations transmitted voice and music. As early as 1909, the radio inventor Lee De Forest (1873–1961) had begun using more sophisticated transmitting equipment to broadcast music and the human voice, and the amateurs' crystal detectors were capable of receiving such broadcasts. By 1914, De Forest was broadcasting voice and music fairly regularly from his station in Highbridge, New York, and other amateurs with similarly powerful equipment followed suit. By contrast, the wireless companies and the military stuck to sending the Morse code, and ignored this new use of radio. Amateur stations were temporarily shut down during World War I, but when they returned to the air in 1919, the amateurs with access to transmitting tubes began broadcasting voice and music on a more regular basis. Other amateurs listened in, and got their families and friends hooked on the hobby. It is important to emphasize that this way of using radio was completely at odds with how Marconi, the device's inventor, had envisioned its applications. He had seen radio as helping the military, shipping firms, and the press expedite the transmission of coded messages between specific senders and receivers. The broadcasting of voice and music was simply not part of his agenda: this was an innovation of the amateurs.

By 1920, there were 15 times as many amateur stations in America as all other types of stations combined. Yet the executives of the Radio Corporation of America (RCA), which was formed in 1919 to buy out the British-owned Marconi Company of America and to consolidate the U.S. radio industry, regarded its main business as the transmission of long-distance Morse code messages. By late 1920, however, with the amateurs leading a huge radio boom in the United States, RCA had to redefine its mission. The amateurs and their converts had constructed the beginnings of a broadcasting network and audience. They had embedded radio in a set of practices and meanings vastly different from those dominating the offices at RCA. Consequently, the radio trust had to reorient its manufacturing priorities, its corporate strategies, and, indeed, its entire way of thinking about the technology under its control.

By the 1930s, it was the major corporations, not the amateurs, who dominated America's airwaves. But a robust subculture of hams continued to transmit and to listen, especially with shortwave, and to tinker. One device they began tinkering with was the phonograph. By the early 1950s, this tinkering would revolutionize the recording industry in the United States.

Audiophilia

"A new neurosis has been discovered," *Time* sarcastically exclaimed in January of 1957, "audiophilia, or the excessive passion for hi-fi sound and equipment."[10] Sufferers were usually "middle-aged, male and intelligent, drawn largely from professions requiring highly conscientious performance."[10] Six years earlier, *The New Yorker* had described the hi-fi craze as the fastest growing hobby in America.[11] As early as 1952, the sales of hi-fi equipment to audiophiles had climbed to $70 million a year,[12] and sales figures were still soaring. And this was before corporations began to manufacture and market sets for the general, nontinkering public. By the mid-1950s, the phonograph industry, which had, according to a September 1957 article in *Business Week*, "once looked down on hi-fi fans as mere fanatics,"[13] was scrambling in to meet the new demand.

The hi-fi craze of the late 1940s and 1950s had been started by tinkerers dissatisfied with the sound quality available in commercially manufactured phonographs. They thus began assembling their own "rigs" out of separate components, paying special attention to and customizing the wiring that connected the parts into a whole. The proper matching and balancing of components was critical to success. The goal was to reproduce in one's living room the way classical music sounded in a concert hall. The most sensitive human ear can hear sounds ranging from 20 to 20,000 cycles per second (cps). Most old 78 rpm records could only play up to 7500 cps, and AM radio could reach a maximum of 10,000 but usually broadcast at 5000 cps. Audiophiles wanted to push beyond these restrictive ranges, which cut off the highs as well as the lows of most music.

This quest for fidelity gained impetus from several key developments during and just after World War II. The wartime shortage of shellac, the principal ingredient of records at that time, prompted research into other materials. The result was the introduction in 1946 of the vastly superior Vinylite. Columbia records used the material to introduce its new, 33⅓ rpm long-playing (LP) record in the spring of 1948. Using considerably finer grooves than the 78 rpm, the LP provided three to four times the playing time with considerably reduced surface noise, and with additional range and clarity. The LP could record up to 12,000 cps, twice the range of the shellac 78 record. In addition, the shift to magnetic tape in the late 1940s dramatically enriched the quality of recording. Yet most existing phonographs failed to do justice to the new LPs.

During the war, many service personnel and civilians were trained in the fundamentals of electronics in order to participate in the manufacture, installation, and operation of radar and other communication equipment. Those stationed in Europe, especially in England, became acquainted with the striking superiority of sound engineering abroad, and the significantly higher quality of music reproduction and phonograph equipment. After the war, when these men and women resumed civilian life, some brought imported audio components home, while others bought surplus amplifiers and other kinds of electronic gear from the government. Small electronics companies also began to improve amplifiers, speakers, and other components. Armed with their recent training, soldering irons, miles of wire, and a host of experimental circuit designs, these people formed the initial core of the hi-fi enthusiasts who sparked the skyrocketing component parts trade of the late 1940s and early 1950s. The custom-built sets they assembled often provided twice the fidelity of reproduction that one could get from the most expensive commercial system, and for one-half to one-third the price. Magazines from *Popular Mechanics* to *The Saturday Review* began to run regular features on hi-fi construction, musical developments, and the intense technical debates that raged among hobbyists. In 1951, a new quarterly called *High-Fidelity* began publication, and in one year its circulation leapt from zero to 20,000.[14]

The hobby's rate of growth was breathtaking, producing enormous sales for the small companies willing to cater to audiophiles by selling high-quality components. By 1953, approximately one million Americans had invested in custom-built sets. Firms such as Fisher Radio Corporation and Altec-Lansing reported that sales had increased by twenty times between 1947 and 1952.[15] The quality of sound on these sets often produced instant converts: once someone heard a record on a custom-built hi-fi, the listener had to have a set of his or her own. For those incapable of building their own sets, small firms such as Electronic Workshop would install a customized set. One repeatedly noted characteristic of audiophiles was that they were never satisfied; they were constantly striving for greater fidelity, and spent endless hours and hundreds of dollars a year trying to approximate perfection. They were also completely disdainful of corporate America's audio offerings.

Another characteristic many of these enthusiasts shared was a deep aversion to the other new electronic invention sweeping the United States, the television. Their devotion to musical authenticity, and their antipathy to the passive, physically idle consumption of popular culture, made many of these audiophiles the first dedicated listeners to FM radio. The quest for fidelity, in other words, was not only a technical quest driving the improvements in hi-fi equipment and then in FM transmitting and receiving, but also a cultural and political quest for an alternative medium marked by fidelity to musical creativity and cultural authenticity. The quest for fidelity meant the reduction of noise, not just from static, but also from the hucksterism of America's consumer culture. This mindset, which was adopted and reshaped by the next generation of rebellious young people, helped spawn a new group of audio outlaws, the underground FM programmers of the late 1960s and 1970s.

FM: The Industry Outcast

From the earliest beginnings of its technical, business, and regulatory history, FM was an industry outcast, an antiestablishment technology marginalized by vested corporate interests. Invented by Edwin Howard Armstrong (1890–1954) in the early 1930s, FM was immediately perceived by David Sarnoff (1891–1971), the head of RCA, as a major threat to the already established AM industry. Sarnoff reacted by doing all he could to try to thwart the invention. He blocked financial support for experimentation, and he worked from behind the scenes at the Federal Communications Commission (FCC) to block allocation of spectrum for FM use. It is not surprising, then, that FM's renaissance would be pioneered by those very much outside of—even at odds with—the media culture those corporations had created.

Despite efforts to suppress his invention, Armstrong had by the early 1940s developed a small FM network in the Northeast, and a small group of fans had acquired FM receivers. The FCC's decision in 1945 to reallocate FM's slot on the spectrum made those sets obsolete, and with FM's prospects seeming so uncertain, the number of stations actually declined in the early 1950s.[16] Beginning in 1958, however, FM began to experience a resurgence. The number of stations began to increase, and so did the audience. The AM spectrum had become so crowded, especially in major cities, that by the late 1950s there were few or no slots left. The only way to start a new station was to use FM. Hi-fi enthusiasts began to tinker with FM, and others bought the newly available sets, especially imported ones. Between 1960 and 1966, the annual sales of FM radio receivers increased more than fivefold, and by 1967 over one-third of all radio sets sold were equipped with FM reception.[17] In 1960, there were approximately 6.5 million households with FM; by 1966, that number had soared to 40 million.[18]

These early listeners to FM stations were usually more educated than the average American, and tended to have "high culture" tastes, preferring FM's music, intellectual fare, and lack of commercialism to the usual AM programming. The households that accounted for the bulk of FM listening were also the ones that watched the least amount of TV and, in fact, listened to FM rather than watching TV during the prime time evening hours.[19] FM audiences were concentrated in major metropolitan areas like New York, Chicago, Los Angeles, Washington, and Boston, and in the 1950s and early 1960s urban FM stations catered to their listeners' devotion to classical music. By the mid-1960s, however, 61 percent of FM stations played "middle of the road" music, which ranged from Frank Sinatra and Mantovani to Dave Brubeck.[20]

The immediate catalyst for the FM explosion in the late 1960s came from the FCC. Since the late 1940s, most of the FM outlets owned by AM stations had simply broadcast exactly the same programming as its AM parent. But by the early 1960s, FCC Commissioners Robert E. Lee and Kenneth Cox argued that frequencies had become so scarce that in the face of increasing demand, duplication was "a luxury we can't afford."[21] In May 1964, the FCC issued its nonduplication ruling, which was to take effect in January 1967. In cities with populations of more than 100,000, radio stations with both AM and FM could not duplicate more than 50 percent of their programming on both bands simultaneously. This ruling helped promote much more enterprising exploitation of the medium: between 1964 and 1967, 500 new commercial FM stations and 60 educational stations took to the air.

A handful of figures suffice to convey the magnitude of the FM revolution. In 1964, total net FM revenues were $19.7 million. Ten years later, that figure had increased thirteenfold to $248.2 million.[22] In 1962, according to the FCC, there were 983 commercial FM stations on the air;[23] in 1972, their number stood at 2328.[24] Four years later, there were nearly 3700 FM stations on the air.[25] By 1972, in cities such as Chicago and Boston, it was estimated that 95 percent of households had FM sets.[26] A few years later, that figure held for much of the country.[27]

While technical refinements, overcrowding in the AM band, and regulatory changes were obviously critical factors in the FM explosion, it was also the emergence of a profoundly anticommercial, anticorporate ethos in the 1960s that caused FM to flower. This ethos was marked especially by a contempt for what had come to be called "mass culture": a disdain for the "vast wasteland" of television and for the formulaic, overly commercialized offerings of radio. It also represented a scorn, first on the part of older intellectuals and, later, on the part of the counterculture, for the predictability and mindlessness of mainstream popular music. The rise of 1960s youth culture especially transformed FM's content and appeal. Bound together by rock and folk music, contemptuous of the commercialization that seemed to infuse and debase every aspect of American culture, and hostile to bourgeois values and the profit motive, members of that loose yet cohesive group known as the "counter-culture" were revolutionizing almost every aspect of American culture, from its popular music to its language and clothing.

Particularly hateful to these young people was what they saw as the lockstep conformity of American life that made everything from work to popular music joyless, unspontaneous, and false. They wanted something different: they wanted their lives to be less programmed, less predictable. The music these young people were listening to, which was not broadcast on AM, gave expression to their critique of mainstream culture. At this time, AM radio was characterized by incessant commercials, songs lasting no longer than three minutes, and repeated promotional jingles. It is no surprise then that when some of these young people, primarily men, worked their way into FM radio stations, they deliberately used their positions to challenge every aspect of what people heard and how they heard it on the airwaves. That challenge led to the proliferation of "underground" or "progressive" rock stations around the country.

Some of the earliest of these stations, which went on the air between 1967 and 1969, were KMPX in San Francisco, KPPC in Pasadena, KMET in Los Angeles, WOR and WNEW in New York, and WBCN in Boston. The rebellious young people staffing these underground stations differed somewhat from the amateurs and hi-fi audiophiles. They were less interested in technical tinkering, in getting inside the "black box" of FM, than they were in using the invention for cultural tinkering, to defy the establishment. When they started their own FM stations, they threw all the conventional industry rules and responses out the window. They eliminated advertising jingles, the repeated announcing of call letters, and the loud, insistent, firecracker delivery of AM disc jockeys. They repudiated conventional market research that sought to identify the "lowest common denominator" and thus reinforced the predictable repetition of the Top 40 AM songs. College stations around the country, not surprisingly, pioneered and embraced the underground format.

Instead of being required to select songs only from a tight "play list" determined by a programming manager, disc jockeys on progressive rock stations were given wide latitude to play what they wanted. They also sought and responded to listener requests. They avoided most Top 40 music and the playing of singles. Instead, a low-key, at times somnolent male voice talked to the audience in what was called a laid-back and intimate fashion in between long segments of music that included album cuts of rock, blues, folk, jazz, international, and even, on occasion, classical music. Progressive FM stations especially delighted in playing the longer cuts of a song, some of them running as long as 12 or 20 minutes, for an audience that could hear such music nowhere else on the spectrum. In 1969, *Broadcasting* labeled underground radio "the first really new programming idea in 10 years."[28]

The majority of listeners to these stations were educated, affluent young men, and they were extremely loyal to such stations. Like their predecessors the hi-fi enthusiasts, these men were dedicated to a musical cult of authenticity that emphasized the essential interconnections between composing, mastery of an instrument, and performance. The music they championed was usually complex, the lyrics metaphorical, political, or both, and spotlighted male virtuosos, especially on guitar or drums. Thus, while underground FM represented an explicate rejection of establishment notions of masculinity, it was also a deeply masculine enterprise focused on male performers, DJs, and listeners, all grappling with the crises surrounding traditional gender roles in the late 1960s and early 1970s. Progressive rock stations also specialized in information on the antiwar movement and general countercultural activities, rejecting the overly competitive and often destructive masculinity promoted in corporate and military circles.

Although underground radio represented only a tiny portion of FM stations, its impact on programming formats and content was enormous, precisely because it was so fresh, new, and compelling to listeners. In the 1970s, following this proliferation of stations and upheavals in program formats, the owners of FM stations saw an opportunity to make a profit. By October 1974, FM accounted for one-third of all radio listening, but only 14 percent of all radio revenues. One reason that so much experimentation had been possible with FM was precisely that advertisers exerted very little influence over the medium. Prejudiced by the notion that FM listening was the province of "eggheads and hi-fi buffs," advertisers had eschewed FM until the early 1970s. But both advertisers and owners of FM stations recognized that in spite of considerable alienation, American youth nonetheless constituted a big market, and as a result more and more stations converted to some type of rock format.

To appeal to the younger market, the ABC-FM network developed a hybrid format with the predictability of the AM format as far as music was concerned, but the underground style of announcing. In 1971, CBS-FM followed suit, co-opting some of the stylistic innovations of the underground while purging it of left-wing politics and too much musical heterogeneity. Such initiatives by the networks exploited some of FM's iconoclasm in order to turn the anticorporate ethos to the industry's advantage.

In 1974, *Broadcasting* featured an article that noted that many progressive stations were adopting tighter playlists and starting to rely on market research.[29] Albums out of the mainstream, once the mainstay of early FM, were now no longer given a chance at many stations. The playlist was agreed upon by committee or determined by the program manager, as it had been in AM during the early 1960s. Accompanying this trend toward homogenization was the adoption by different stations of a very particular, tightly circumscribed format: oldies, soft rock, album-oriented rock, or country and western, with very little, if any, overlap. By the late 1970s, the assembly line techniques that the early FM outlaws had deplored were now informing much of FM programming. As *Advertising Age* noted in May 1978, "The day of the disc jockey who controls his individual program is quickly becoming a dinosaur."[30] As had been the case with the amateur operators and the hi-fi audiophiles, the defiance of early FM enthusiasts invigorated an entrenched and complacent industry; but this defiance was quickly domesticated in the quest for massive audiences and profits.

Conclusion

The tinkering of these audio outlaws set the stage for radio broadcasting in the 1920s, revolutionized the phonograph and recording industries in the 1950s, and pioneered the use of a whole new frequency band, FM, in the late 1960s and early 1970s. All three groups of enthusiasts were outsiders who regarded the corporate uses of audio technology as unimaginative, technically backward, and culturally stunted. Each group, in its own way, challenged how the profit motive had circumscribed the exploitation of and access to audio technology. The ham operators still constitute a robust subgroup that exchanges messages around the world, proudly circumventing more established communications systems, while the more defiant technical outlaws have adopted the computer as their vehicle for fraternal rebellion.

Oppositional reactions against the dominant culture by technological enthusiasts have burst forward at various moments during our history. They represent serious, often passionately held views about what culture should be, and questions about the extent to which the demands of the marketplace should shape cultural practices and products. They also represent the vision of subcultural groups of men with often utopian ideas about how machines can promote a sense of community and reproduce cultural excellence. But one of capitalism's greatest strengths is its ability to incorporate the voices and styles of the opposition into a larger framework, and to adapt such opposition to its own ends.

Historians of business and technology need to consider more fully this process of opposition, co-optation, and taming, a process that incorporates certain oppositional applications of technology while simultaneously marginalizing the more iconoclastic elements of opposition that spawned the new applications in the first place. The cultural benefits are, of course, that mainstream culture does change, is enriched, and does, at moments of technological uncertainty and cultural upheaval, provide brief periods when diversity can really flower. But in times of more complete and entrenched corporate control over technology, and increased barriers to entry, can such competition from the bottom up still emerge and provoke new competitiveness in American engineering? That is certainly one of the major questions we face today.

Notes

1. The best general histories of broadcasting in the United States are Christopher Sterling and John M. Kittross, *Stay Tuned: A Concise History of American Broadcasting* (Belmont, Calif.: Wadsworth, 1990), and Erik Barnouw, *A History of Broadcasting in the United States*, 3 vols. (London/New York: Oxford Univ. Press, 1966, 1968, 1970).

2. The most detailed information on the early amateur operators can be found in Susan J. Douglas, *Inventing American Broadcasting, 1899–1922* (Baltimore, Md.: Johns Hopkins Univ. Press, 1987). The recollections of amateur operators can be found at the Columbia Oral History Library in New York City.

3. General histories of the phonograph include Oliver Read and Walter Welch, *From Tin Foil to Stereo: Evolution of the Phonograph* (Indianapolis, Ind.: Sams, 1976), and Roland Gelatt, *The Fabulous Phonograph, 1877–1977* (New York: Macmillan, 1977). Contem-

porary accounts of the hi-fi craze exist in various issues of *Business Week*, *The Saturday Review*, *Time*, and *Newsweek* in the early 1950s.

4. The best accounts of the underground FM movement are in issues of *Broadcasting*. See also Jim Ladd, *Radio Waves: Life and Revolution on the FM Dial* (New York: St. Martin's Press, 1991).

5. "New Wonders With Wireless—And By a Boy!" *New York Times*, November 3, 1907, pt. 5, p. 1.

6. Charles Barnard, "A Young Expert in Wireless Telegraphy," *St. Nicholas*, 35, April 1, 1908, pp. 530–32.

7. *Electrical World*, 57, no. 13, 1911, p. 760.

8. *New York Times*, March 29, 1912, p. 12.

9. Cited in Clinton De Soto, *Two Hundred Meters and Down: The Story of Amateur Radio* (West Hartford, CT: American Radio Relay League, 1936), p. 40.

10. "Audiophilia," *Time*, January 14, 1957, p. 44.

11. *The New Yorker*, November 24, 1951, p. 31.

12. "High Fidelity: Next Year a $300,000,000 Industry," *Newsweek*, December 21, 1953, p. 64.

13. "Everybody Gets in Hi-Fi Chorus," *Business Week*, September 21, 1957, p. 62.

14. "Cashing in on Finicky Ears," *Business Week*, March 22, 1952, p. 54.

15. Op. cit., p. 66.

16. Lawrence Lessing, *Man of High Fidelity* (New York: Bantam Books, 1969), p. 212; Sterling and Kittross, op. cit., p. 323.

17. *Media/Scope*, May 1967, p. 12.

18. *Ibid.*

19. *Broadcasting*, April 12, 1965, pp. 36–37.

20. *Media/Scope*, May 1967, p. 12.

21. *Broadcasting*, March 29, 1965, p. 88.

22. *Broadcasting*, September 13, 1976, p. 50.

23. *Newsweek*, May 22, 1972, p. 57 and Sterling and Kittross, p. 379.

24. *Ibid.*

25. *Ibid.*

26. *Broadcasting*, September 24, 1973, p. 31.

27. Sterling and Kittross, op. cit., p. 465.

28. *Broadcasting*, August 11, 1969, p. 46B.

29. "FM Rockers Are Taming Their Free Formats," *Broadcasting*, November 25, 1974, pp. 47–49.

30. *Advertising Age*, May 29, 1978, p. R1, R26.

PART VI

Electrical Technology for Industry and Commerce

This section considers electrical technology for industry and commerce. The first paper is by Eric Schatzberg, a historian of technology employed by the IEEE-Rutgers Center at the time of the conference (now at the University of Wisconsin). He investigates the competition among three technologies (steam, cable, and electricity) used in the last quarter of the nineteenth century to mechanize urban transit in the United States. He argues that electrical technology, which, in the end, won the competition, was not initially known to be clearly superior on cost. He gives two nontechnical reasons that provided support for electricity in this initial period when costs were uncertain: American enthusiasm for the progressive new electrical technology, and the structure of the electrical equipment industry.

The second paper is by Anne Milbrooke, for many years a historian of technology at United Technologies, the maker of Otis elevators. She traces the competition within Otis between hydraulic and electric elevator systems in the late nineteenth and twentieth centuries. Both technologies were used in the nineteenth century, and both are used today. She explains how, over a long period of time, business, technical, and regulatory factors reversed the applications for which these two technologies were used in the elevator business.

The third paper is by Ulrich Wengenroth, a historian of technology at the Technical University of Munich. Wengenroth examines the competition by which electric motors came to replace steam engines in the period 1890 to 1925. Steam engines were better suited for many manufacturing applications, less expensive per unit of energy produced, and more frequently customized to specific applications. Wengenroth explains how electric motors were nonetheless able to win the competition because they had greater versatility and allowed industrial designers to take a new approach to production technology.

W. Bernard Carlson, a historian of technology at the University of Virginia, is the author of the section's final paper. By considering events in the American electrical industry that led to the formation of General Electric in 1892, he illuminates the interplay between competition and consolidation in technological industries. While competition can lead to better products and lower prices, Carlson shows it can also create inefficiency, duplicative effort, and waste. Carlson's study also provides insight into the influence of individuals in the level of competition and timing of mergers, the importance of competition among firms for sources of capital, and the value of having the right organizational structure beyond having good products, low prices, and low production costs.

Schatzberg shows one way in which technology has been disseminated on the basis of perception rather than reality, and how these perceptions were shaped by the attitudes and values held by the designers and purchasers of technology. In a forthcoming book, he argues analogously that an ideology of progressiveness was an important factor in the transition from wood to metal in the construction of airplanes.[1] The progressive image has had a powerful role in other technological settings as well. With hindsight, it appears that many of the companies that manufactured computers in the 1950s, as well as an even greater number of companies that acquired them for their businesses, did so more for reasons of prestige than for what they would immediately contribute to the bottom line. Schatzberg's notion of progressiveness has appeared in another guise recently in the push for digitalization, which is perceived as more progressive than analog technology in many applications. While there are certainly many beneficial uses for digital technology, digitalization can deteriorate functionality in some application areas, such as automobile instrumentation and stereo equipment, and some companies have returned to analog approaches.

Progressivism and other general attitudes about aesthetics frequently come into play in product design. Model years and planned obsolescence, together with heavy reliance upon advertising that equated the new with the progressive, were masterfully introduced by the American automobile industry between the world wars. We are all familiar with the use of these techniques in the automobile and home appliance markets, but a closer examination may show these techniques to be much more widespread, e.g., in the design and sale of farm equipment, manufacturing equipment, jet fighters, and many other technologies. The marketing of technologies and the effect this marketing exerts on the dissemination of technology has often been neglected by historians of technology; and this ought not to be, since it is unclear in what ways planned obsolescence hinders or advances technological development. There is a common view that products strong in terms of technical specifications will necessarily be strong in the marketplace, but this is clearly erroneous.

Sometimes the proponents of competing technical solutions to a problem are not different companies, but instead different groups within the same company. In some companies, such as within NCR in the 1980s, intrafirm competition has become a conscious corporate strategy, involving corporate restructuring into different subcompanies that develop their own products and business plans and compete with one another for the company's central resources. Even where intrafirm competition has not been made into company policy, senior administrators within large technological corporations have frequently supported rival projects, sometimes without informing the competitors of one another's existence. Technologies may lose particular competitions within the firm, but the plans are hard to eradicate without removing the engineers and managers who champion them. Companies often reinforce this pattern by reviving previously unchosen technologies; and it has become high art in many corporations for engineers to find ways to bootleg resources to keep their pet project alive.[2] The internal dynamics of product development are clearly socially constructed and need more analysis based upon an analysis of the interests of the engineers and managers who are responsible for their development.[3] We must abandon this notion that internal development is based solely, or even primarily, upon intrinsic technical merits.

Wengenroth's paper introduces the important topic of rationalization of the manufacturing process. By changes in designs, materials, and components, the production process can be rationalized so that products can be made with less cost, higher efficiency, and improved quality, and changes in production can be accomplished more rapidly. This is a lesson that has been put to great effect by the Japanese electronics and automobile manufacturers. The use of fewer and more standardized parts, which can be packaged in more ways, translates into more efficiency and more rapid introduction of new products. Standardized parts is not always successful, however, as can be seen in the software industry's relatively unsuccessful efforts to introduce these same production-line efficiencies into their work, through the use of structured programming, modular programming, reusable software, and other software engineering methodologies. Greater attention to manufacturing technologies in the success or failure of products in the marketplace is certainly appropriate in many historical treatments.

Campbell-Kelly's paper in Section III has already raised some of the problems nations experience with consolidations, especially forced consolidations. The opposite strategy to consolidation is competition, and Carlson points out some of the problems that it creates for nations. These are problems commonly faced by small nations that desire indigenous industries but which cannot sustain large markets. The problem is also faced by larger nations in situations where product development is capital-intensive, such as with commercial aircraft or semiconductor devices. Even the largest multinational firms face unsupportably escalating costs for research and development and product development and testing. These companies have not only formed partnerships but also established consortia, such as Sematech, to share development costs, which may run to billions of dollars. Consortia and partnerships also help to ensure that these development costs result in products that become industry standards.

Carlson has studied the importance of organizational structure in his own careful examination of the formation of General Electric.[4] Stuart Leslie has examined this same issue in the automobile industry. He has shown, for example, how the structure of General Motors, which placed product-line divisions in an adversarial relationship with the research labs run by Boss Kettering, retarded product innovation.[5] David Halberstam has shown how Ford products became less innovative than Nissan products partly because Ford promoted its senior managers from the financial side of the operation while Nissan chose its senior managers from the engineering ranks.[6] Many companies have looked with envy at the success of small electronics firms in Silicon

Valley and have tried to emulate them by changing the organizational structure within larger corporate organizations to provide small, engineer-driven teams with the authority to make their own decisions, control their own procurement, etc. This is the course IBM pursued, for example, when it tried to break from its mainframe traditions and build its first personal computer. These and many other questions about organizational structure and the ability it provides to act in the marketplace are worthy of additional historical scrutiny.

Notes

1. "Ideology and Technical Choice: Wood versus Metal in American Airplane Design between the World Wars," Ph.D. Dissertation, Univ. of Pennsylvania, 1990. The dissertation is under revision for publication by Princeton University Press.
2. See David Lundstrom, *A Few Good Men from UNIVAC*. Cambridge, MA: MIT Press, 1987.
3. See, for example, Tracy Kidder, *Soul of a New Machine*. Boston: Little, Brown, 1981.
4. Carlson, W. Bernard, *Innovation as a Social Process*. Cambridge University Press, 1991.
5. Stuart W. Leslie, *Boss Kettering*. New York: Columbia University Press, 1983.
6. David Halberstam, *The Reckoning*. New York: Avon, 1986.

The Mechanization
of Urban Transit
in the United States

Electricity and Its Competitors

Eric Schatzberg

Introduction

The industrial revolutions of the nineteenth century encouraged rapid urbanization and the widespread use of mechanical power. Central to these industrial revolutions was improved transportation between cities.[1] The application of steam power to land transportation in the form of the railroad helped accelerate urbanization and industrialization. For transportation within cities, however, horses remained the dominant motive power until the last decade of the nineteenth century. By encouraging urbanization, intercity steam railroads increased the demand for intracity transportation. This demand was met by a massive application of animal power, made more efficient by the use of streetcars drawn along iron rails laid flush to the street. Despite numerous attempts to introduce mechanical transportation in urban streets, horses remained the dominant motive power for urban transit until the adoption of the electric streetcar in the 1890s.[2]

During the last quarter of the nineteenth century, three principal technologies competed to mechanize urban street transit in the United States: steam, cable, and electricity. These technologies competed with each other, with the existing horse-drawn streetcars, and with a variety of less-developed alternatives. Electricity proved the ultimate victor, not just for street railroads but also for subways, elevateds, and many commuter railroads.

Although electricity ultimately proved cheaper than all alternatives in terms of costs per passenger mile, comparative costs do not provide a sufficient historical explanation for the success of electric traction. Reliable comparisons of the actual costs of competing systems were almost unknown, especially comparisons that accounted fully for capital costs and depreciation. Predictions of future costs of competing

225

technologies were even more uncertain. The advantages of electric traction were es-tablished only after the inventors and engineers had devoted substantial resources to its development, and after street-railroad companies had made substantial invest-ments in electrically powered systems.

Two factors help explain this substantial investment in electric traction despite the uncertainty in comparative costs. First was the substantial enthusiasm that Americans had for the new electrical technologies, an enthusiasm that gripped profit-minded street-railroad entrepreneurs as well as the general public. In addi-tion, electric traction also benefited from the structure of the emerging electrical equipment industry, which supported the development of the electric streetcar in part to improve the profitability of electric lighting systems by providing a day-time load.[3]

Costs and Technical Choice

Naive theories of technical change treat the choice among competing technologies as simply a matter of costs. Business firms in a capitalist economy supposedly select, from a set of functionally equivalent alternatives, the methods that give them the lowest total factor costs. The existing state of technical knowledge defines this set of methods. Few historians and economists still accept this analysis, because it treats technical knowledge as an exogenous factor rather than as an integral part of the economy. However, when one attempts to consider the effect of the market on the creation of technical knowledge, costs no longer appear to be so decisive.[4] The suc-cess of a particular technology depends substantially on the ability of its promoters to mobilize support at early stages of its development, when costs are still uncertain. For emerging technologies, expectations of costs may be as important in garnering support as actual costs.[5] Although these expectations are in part based on extrapo-lations from physical theory and past experience, they remain highly speculative, and depend upon unexamined assumptions grounded in contemporary technical culture. Thus in choosing among new technologies, a whole range of cultural fac-tors inevitably play a role, including professional ideologies, aesthetic values, and class prejudices.

Several factors conspire to make it difficult to predict costs in emerging tech-nologies. The first set of uncertainties emerge in development, the process that transforms an invention into a working prototype, making the inventive idea progres-sively more concrete in conditions gradually approaching those of actual use.[6] In the process, an originally elegant invention often becomes encumbered with auxiliary components that increase its cost and reduce its effectiveness.[7] Despite the attempts of corporate managers to make the inventive process routine, the cost and perfor-mance of a new technology remain difficult to predict, given the compromises be-tween price and performance that invariably occur during development.

Even after development is substantially complete, and the new technology is ready to be introduced into actual conditions of use, the cost of the technology re-mains uncertain. One set of factors tends to raise costs. In new technologies, the ac-tual conditions of use invariably differ from those envisioned by the inventor, preventing the technology from operating as predicted. Even when conditions of use accurately reflect the inventor's expectations, dozens of unanticipated problems emerge. Inventors simply cannot afford the extensive, large-scale testing necessary to eliminate the host of minor problems that prevent new technologies from working dependably. The early users of an emerging technology also serve as testers, helping the manufacturer refine the design as components fail or wear faster than expected. Software developers use "beta" tests to formalize the role of users as testers, but informal beta testing occurs with all complex technologies. Finally, the depreciation rate of a new technology remains shrouded in mystery. Depreciation rates are always somewhat arbitrary. Users of mechanical technologies face gradually rising maintenance costs as their equipment ages. Eventually, it becomes less expensive to purchase new equipment instead of continuing to repair the old. The period may last three years or thirty, but users have no reliable means for predicting the real depreciation rate until they have gained substantial experience with the new technology.

While unforeseen problems tend to raise the costs of an emerging technology, other factors invariably work to lower costs. These factors include learning curve effects, economies of scale, and the concentration of inventive effort. Learning curve effects are perhaps the most important. Stated simply, the learning curve refers to the observation that the longer one does something, the better one gets at it. Economists first quantified this effect in the late 1930s, when they noticed that the cost of building airframes declined with the number produced, even though there was little change in technology, capital investment, or rate of production. In mechanical devices like streetcars, not only does accumulated experience in production tend to reduce the manufacturer's cost, but accumulated experience in use tends to reduce operating costs, as users refine operating strategies and improve maintenance procedures.[8] Economies of scale provide the second factor tending to lower costs. Both technical and market factors tend to reduce the unit costs of most complex technologies as rate of production or scale of application increases. Finally, the problems that emerge in the early applications of a new technology serve to focus inventive activity on that problem. In the terminology of Thomas P. Hughes, such problems identify reverse salients, weak components holding back the growth of an expanding technical system. As the technical community becomes aware of a reverse salient, its members focus inventive effort on solving the problems that create it. This mobilization of inventive effort can produce substantial savings for subsequent users.

These various sources of uncertainty make the cost of a new technology an imperfect measure of its competitiveness. Predictions of costs made during the development stage are unreliable, if only because proponents of a new technology typically underestimate costs in order to garner the necessary resources for its development. When a new technology is put into use, one set of factors tends to raise costs while another lowers them. The decision to invest in an emerging technology must therefore depend on expectations of future costs, rather than on present costs. But the benefits of scale economies and the learning curve can only be realized when investment in a new technology continues despite initial problems. Thus expectations for the success of a particular technology tend to become self-fulfilling.[9]

In a capitalist economy, where entrepreneurs obsessively discuss, dispute, and debate costs, costs do not serve as an objective determinant of technical choice. But costs still remain central. Costs provide data, but these data require interpretation before they can serve as a basis for technical choice. How costs are interpreted depends on the broader culture, including popular prejudices, utopian expectations, and general enthusiasm regarding various technologies.

The mechanization of street railroads provides an excellent example of both the centrality and indeterminacy of costs. Historians agree on the broad outline of the story, which includes the attempts to implement steam and cable systems before the final success of electricity. When it comes to the role of costs, the story is less clear.

The Evolution of Motive Power on Street Railroads

Soon after street railroads became widespread in the United States, proponents of mechanization began to criticize animal traction as expensive and inefficient. Nevertheless, urban horse railroads proved surprisingly competitive against mechanical alternatives for three decades. A few street railroads began using steam-powered streetcars during the Civil War, but the vast majority remained with horses. In the 1880s, most large American cities adopted cable systems, in which streetcars were propelled by moving underground cables driven by stationary steam engines. The huge initial cost of cable systems made them suitable for only the most dense urban areas, and horse railroads continued to dominate route mileage and passenger volume. Beginning in 1884, some cities began installing electric streetcar systems. All of these early systems proved failures, and many were replaced by cable cars. About 1888, however, the tide turned decisively in favor of electric traction. Electricity became the technology of choice for new street railroads, and existing horse railroads began converting to electricity in rapidly increasing numbers. By 1900, electricity powered almost all travel within American cities, except for walking.[10]

The earliest horse-drawn railroads, originally known as tramways, originated in mining before the development of the steam locomotive. The combination of a wheel with a rigid rail substantially reduced friction, thus increasing the load that a horse could pull over level ground. Urban tramways in the United States emerged with the first steam railroads, which were almost invariably refused permission to run steam locomotives in built-up urban areas. Beginning in the 1830s, steam railroads often continued their lines into central cities along existing streets, using horses instead of locomotives to draw the cars.[11]

These horse-drawn extensions of steam railroads spread little before the 1850s, in part because the raised "T" rail interfered with other street traffic. This problem was reduced in the 1850s by the use of grooved rails that lay flush with the street. Horsecars proliferated in the 1850s, so that by the Civil War most major American cities had significant street-railway systems. The street railroads soon drove the competing horse-drawn omnibuses from city streets, since a streetcar horse could pull twice the weight of an omnibus horse. Europeans, who lagged behind the United States in adopting urban tramways, praised the comfort and convenience of American streetcars.[12] By 1880, there were over 2050 miles of horsedrawn street railroads in American cities.[13]

American street railroads had been widespread for barely a decade before proponents of mechanization began to criticize animal power as expensive, unreliable, and unsanitary. These criticisms mounted in the 1870s and 1880s, but failed to convince streetcar companies to abandon horses and mules. Critics perceived animal power as expensive because the maintenance of horses comprised from one-third to one-half the operating costs of a street railroad.[14] Proponents of mechanization also branded as cruel the heavy work required of streetcar horses, and criticized horse droppings as a menace to public health. Horses were subject to infectious diseases that spread quickly in densely populated stables, at times paralyzing entire cities. Supporters of mechanical traction argued that it would eliminate all the drawbacks of animal power. According to one authority on street railroads, "the employment of horses on tramways is a misfit and a barbarism; and when the inertia of prejudice has become exhausted, the civiliser—mechanical power—will duly replace the horse as a motor."[15]

Despite the arguments of the mechanizers, evidence suggests that horses were quite well adapted to the demands of urban transportation. Proponents of mechanization generally avoided the question of capital costs, which were always less with animal power. Although coal was substantially cheaper than hay and oats, even in the most inefficient mechanical system, this advantage diminished substantially when maintenance and depreciation were included. Despite their short working life, retired streetcar horses could perform serviceably in other occupations, and returned a substantial percentage of their original purchase price. Compared to early mechanical systems, horses were quite reliable, being little injured by the dust and mud of nineteenth-century urban streets. Horse droppings also posed less of a problem than might be supposed, since the average streetcar horse only spent four hours daily outside of the stables, and much of the droppings could be returned as fertilizer to the farms that supplied the stables with hay.[16]

Limitations in the supply of unmechanized transit probably provided a more important spur to mechanization than the cost of horse feed.[17] The densely packed, rapidly expanding industrial cities of the post–Civil War era experienced unprecedented levels of street congestion. Streetcars, goods wagons, hackney coaches, and omnibuses vied for space in narrow streets. Under these conditions, horsecars averaged about 5 miles per hour. Even with very short headways between cars, a single set of tracks quickly reached maximum capacity. Despite the use of parallel streets, congestion remained high. In Philadelphia, for example, streetcar lines occupied almost every through street in the central district.[18] Finally, horsecar speeds remained limited to little more than a brisk walk, while urban areas continued to expand, creating a demand for faster forms of transit.

Given the success of the steam engine in intercity rail transportation, early proponents of mechanization quite naturally sought to apply steam to street railroads in a manner acceptable to urban residents. Cities had originally banned steam engines from their streets due to the smoke, noise, steam, and burning cinders emitted by early locomotives, and because steam engines often frightened horses. Inventors tried to eliminate the objections of urban residents by muffling the steam exhaust and by burning anthracite coal or coke to avoid smoke. Steamcar builders enclosed the working parts of the engine to make it resemble a horsedrawn streetcar. These disguised steamcars became known as "dummy" engines. Some steamcar builders combined a small steam engine and a passenger compartment in a single car, while others developed separate dummy engines to pull one or two passenger cars. By most accounts, the steam dummies emitted little visible smoke or steam, except in damp weather, and produced no more noise than a horsedrawn streetcar. Most observers of steam dummies in operation agreed that horses, although disturbed at first, quickly became used to the new vehicles. Some observers thought that steamcars would frighten horses less if they made more noise, since horses were apparently startled by the relative silence of the dummy's approach.[19]

Advocates of the dummy insisted that steam power cost less than horses. An 1877 article in *Engineering News* provides a typical comparison of horsecar and dummy, estimating weekly horse costs of $24, in contrast to a weekly coal consumption of 1.75 tons of anthracite at $8.75.[20] This comparison was somewhat disingenuous, since the cost for horse power almost certainly included "maintenance" in addition to feed, that is, the wages of hostlers, blacksmiths, and perhaps veterinarians, and also the costs of maintaining the stable itself. But even more careful cost estimates indicated a considerable advantage for steam. One British engineer who compared horse and steam streetcars, including estimates for depreciation and maintenance, calculated an operating cost of 8.67d. for horses, compared with 5d. for steam, still a substantial savings. He cautioned, however, that his estimate probably erred in favor of steam due to the uncertainty in maintenance costs.[21] Nevertheless, in terms of the total cost of motive power, steam streetcars appeared to have a definite cost advantage over horses.

American street railroads first adopted steam streetcars during the Civil War. Early experience with these steam streetcars seemed to confirm claims of lower costs, but street railroad companies did not turn to steam power on a large scale after the war. Steam street railroads received little attention from the technical press after the late 1870s, even though their numbers grew gradually, peaking at 815 cars and 642 miles of line in 1891.[22] At least one steam dummy line, from Frankford to Kensington in Philadelphia, operated quite successfully with steamcars from about 1861 to 1893.[23]

Several factors explain the reluctance of the street railroads to adopt steam despite its apparent cost advantage. Most cities continued to forbid steam dummies in central districts, despite the fairly successful efforts of inventors to make these cars inoffensive. Steam streetcars were thus consigned to outlying districts. A typical steamcar could haul twice as many passengers as a horsecar, but this advantage was largely wasted on lightly traveled suburban routes, though passengers did appreciate the greater speed of the dummy.[24] Serious maintenance problems also hindered the spread of the steam dummy. Conditions of street railroads differed considerably from those of mainline steam roads, making irrelevant a good deal of the experience of steam locomotive engineering. In particular, the streetcar running at street level faced much more dust and mud than a mainline locomotive running on a well-ballasted T-rail. Street dirt quickly destroyed exposed parts of the engine that would have lasted for years in mainline service.[25] Finally, lower prices for horse feed reduced the advantages of mechanization. The end of the Civil War ushered in an era of falling produce prices, particularly in farm products, which lasted until the 1890s.

Between the periods 1866–1870 and 1886–1890, for example, the price of corn fell 42 percent, oats 40 percent, and hay 37 percent. Although prices for coal also fell, declining materials prices reduced the advantage to be gained by replacing feed, a variable cost, with machinery, a fixed capital cost.[26]

While public opposition to mobile steam engines remained strong, city dwellers readily accepted stationary steam engines. One logical means for mechanizing urban transit, therefore, was to keep the steam engine fixed and transmit power to the streetcars by means of a moving cable. In 1873 San Francisco became the site of the first successful cable streetcar system, built by Andrew Hallidie (1836–1900), who had previously developed cable haulage machinery for mines. The Hallidie system provided a moving cable in a subsurface conduit located between the streetcar rails. The cars were attached to the cable by means of a releasable grip inserted in a narrow slot in the conduit. The cable system took hold in San Francisco because of its ability to mount steep grades, grades that made horsecar lines impractical. San Francisco remained the only city in the United States with cable traction until 1882, when Charles B. Holmes opened a large cable system in Chicago. Holmes, who was president of one of the largest street-railway systems in the country, believed that cable traction could be profitable on level terrain and in colder climates. Holmes proved correct, and cable systems spread to most major American cities by the early 1890s, reaching a peak of 305 miles in 1893. Route mileage, however, understates the relative importance of cable traction, since cable lines carried far more passengers per mile than horsecar lines. In 1890 cable systems carried annually 1.3 million passengers per mile of line, four times more than horsecar lines. In that year, cable systems accounted for 18 percent of all street-railway passengers.[27]

Despite the success of cable roads on heavily traveled routes in major cities, cable traction appeared unlikely to eliminate animal power. Cable systems required immense investments compared to horsecars, largely due to the heavy construction needed for the conduit and other machinery required to move the cable. This large fixed investment made cable traction practical only on routes with high traffic densities. Where such high traffic densities existed, power from the cable cost half as much as horse power per car mile.[28] Census data from a selection of cable roads in 1890 showed the costs of cable power to be 3.5¢/car-mile, including maintenance on the cable system and steam engines. The same report showed the costs of horse traction to be 6.1¢/car-mile, including the renewal of horses and all stabling costs. There were a number of attempts to modify cable technology to reduce construction costs, and thus make it practical for lighter traffic, but none of these succeeded before the rapid spread of the electric streetcar brought construction of new cable lines to a halt in 1895.[29]

While cable systems were spreading rapidly to large American cities, another form of motive power emerged as a serious competitor—electricity. In the United States, serious attempts to develop commercially viable electric traction began in the early 1880s, made possible by the improvements in the generation of electricity for lighting. Thomas Edison experimented with an electric locomotive in 1880, but devoted little effort to its commercialization. At the time, Edison hoped to compete with mainline steam railroads, rather than horsedrawn street railroads. Other inventors soon recognized the potential market offered by street railroads, and by the mid-1880s a number of systems were in commercial operation. These systems relied on direct-current (dc) dynamos driven by stationary steam engines, with the power transmitted to the vehicle by third rail, underground conduit, or overhead wire. Inventors used a variety of methods to connect the motor to the driving wheels, including belts, chains, friction drives, and various types of gears.[30]

These early electric streetcar systems received much favorable attention in the technical press, but they failed to thrive before 1888. At the beginning of 1888, there were only 13 electric railroads in the United States, with just over 48 miles of track and 95 cars, mostly operating on suburban routes or in small cities.[31] A good number of the earlier systems either returned to horse power or converted to cable.[32] In 1888, however, the tide turned in favor of electric traction. Historians generally credit the Richmond (Virginia) Union Passenger Railway, equipped by Frank J. Sprague (1857–1934), with providing the turning point in electric traction. Sprague's system, which opened in February 1888, was by far the largest built to that date, with 40 cars and 12 miles of track running through most of the city, including the downtown. Sprague assembled and perfected the basic arrangement of components that remained standard throughout the entire electric streetcar era, including the use of a single overhead wire and the flexible mounting of the motor underneath the car. Sprague's Richmond system directly inspired other street railroads to adopt electric traction, including the West End Street Railway of Boston, the largest street railroad in the United States.[33]

The impact of the Richmond system should not be overemphasized, however. In the summer of 1887, before Sprague had even begun work on the Richmond contract, 12 additional cities had begun building or had contracted to build electric streetcar systems, enough to double the number of electric street railroads in the United States.[34] Independently of Sprague, the Thomson-Houston company developed its own system of electric traction based on the work of Charles Van Depoele, whose company Thomson-Houston purchased. The first major Thomson-Houston system opened in July 1888, and subsequently the Thomson-Houston and Sprague companies roughly split the electric railway business until their merger in 1892.[35]

Beginning in 1888, electric streetcar systems began opening at a rapid and accelerating pace. With a few exceptions, electricity became the motive power of choice for new street railroads, and existing horsecar systems increasingly converted to electricity. By July 1, 1890, electricity powered almost 16 percent of American street railway track, and street-railway companies had spent almost 36 million dollars on electric railroads. Between 1888 and July 1890, 136 electric railroads began operating.[36] Just one year later, in July 1891, the number of electric railroads and miles of track had more than doubled.[37] By the end of 1893 fully 60 percent of American street-railway track had been electrified, reaching 98 percent by the end of 1903.[38] By the mid-1890s, electricity had become the dominant motive power on American street railroads.

The Role of Costs

Some historians have argued that cost advantages explain the triumph of electric traction over competing technologies. According to this view, sometime between 1887 and 1889 electricity clearly became cheaper than horse, steam, and cable power.

George Hilton specifies the beginning of electricity's superiority quite precisely: February 2, 1888, when Sprague opened his Richmond system. Before Sprague's success in Richmond, claims Hilton, cable traction had been "the most economic form of urban street transportation" from January 28, 1882, the opening of the first Chicago cable system.[39]

Perhaps Hilton has greater insight into the costs of competing street-railway systems than did the entrepreneurs of the time. But for street railway-men in the late nineteenth century, the costs of alternative systems hardly appeared so clear. Although proponents of specific systems always marshaled data showing that their methods had the lowest costs, other entrepreneurs and engineers emphasized the difficulty of obtaining comparable cost data and the uncertainty inherent in cost estimates. This uncertainty continued well into the 1890s. For example, an 1897 editorial in the *Street Railway Journal,* titled "The Battle of the Motive Powers," admitted that "the difficulties of making true [cost] comparisons are almost insuperable."[40] When an 1890 comparison of steam and electric locomotives on the Manhattan Elevated suggested that electricity would cost four times more than steam, a stormy debate ensued in the technical press over how to interpret the results.[41] A similar debate occurred in 1894 when the eminent railroad engineer Hermann Haupt (1817–1907) criticized the proposed use of electricity for rapid-transit lines.[42] The annual conventions of the American Street Railway Association produced lively discussions on the costs of various systems, discussions that revealed the ambiguities of cost comparisons. During the 1889 convention, for example, the operator of a Sprague trolley system in East Cleveland declined to give any quantitative estimate of his cost savings over horses, insisting that five to six years of experience were needed before one could calculate the savings accurately.[43] If comparative costs had been as clear as Hilton claims, serious professionals would not have wasted their time debating such questions.

Comparing the costs of emerging technologies is always difficult, but several factors made such comparisons especially problematic on street railroads. In the first place, street railroads did not use uniform methods of cost accounting.[44] The cost of motive power, for example, did not always include real estate, depreciation, or interest: With horses, depreciation and maintenance could be accurately measured using historical data, but depreciation for mechanical systems remained speculative, especially during the first few years of operation. Even when two street railroads used the same motive power, costs varied considerably due to differences in operating conditions, most notably the number and steepness of grades. Costs were commonly given in cents per car-mile, which neglected differences in thecapacity of cars, or cents per passenger, which ignored differences in length of travel. Street railroads did not use the modern measure of costs per passenger-mile until after 1900.[45] Finally, street railroads had monopolies along their specific routes, so there was no threat of direct competition to correct systematic biases in cost accounting.

Street-railroad companies had particular problems handling capital costs because of the widespread practice of stock watering. A common fraud followed the pattern of the Credit Mobilier scheme, in which a street railroad paid inflated prices to construction firms in which the principals of the street railroad had an interest.

Even where there was no outright fraud, street railroads commonly used company stock to pay for construction, stock that the construction company accepted at a steep discount, but which the street railroad listed at par, thus substantially overstating construction costs.[46] In 1890 Census data, horse railroads with similar traffic densities reported total costs for road and equipment ranging from $30,000 to $144,000 per mile of track, clear evidence of questionable capital accounting.[47]

The difficulties posed in obtaining accurate cost comparisons should raise doubts about Hilton's certitude. Even if Hilton did have an objective method for measuring costs retrospectively, we would still need an explanation for why street-railway companies chose electricity, since the companies clearly lacked access to such information. The triumph of electric traction undoubtedly brought a great increase in the supply of urban transit and a significant reduction in cost, especially if measured in cost per passenger-mile. John P. McKay convincingly demonstrates these cost savings in his analysis of data for Britain and France between 1896 and 1910.[48] Nevertheless, evidence for lower costs after the conversion to electricity does not explain why street-railway companies chose electricity in the first place, especially in the period from late 1887 through 1890.

A good example of the ambiguity of cost data is provided by Frank Sprague's Richmond trolley system, now considered the turning point in the success of electric traction. One would have expected Sprague to use his Richmond installation to generate detailed cost information to convince doubters of its economy. In June 1888 Sprague did present some data on the cost of motive power in Richmond, but these figures were only estimates, although based on actual data. Sprague calculated the cost of motive power at 4.32¢/car-mile, which he said was 40 percent less than the cost to operate the same number of horse cars under similar conditions. Sprague included reasonable estimates for depreciation, though his estimates for repairs appear somewhat low.[49]

Sprague did not continue to present cost data on the Richmond system, however. He turned the operation of the Richmond road over to its owners after their formal acceptance of the system on May 15, 1888.[50] As soon as Sprague withdrew from direct supervision of the system, it began to fall apart. When Sprague appeared at the annual American Street Railway Association (ASRA) convention in October 1888, he provided no detailed cost data. Several delegates questioned him about maintenance problems they had observed on recent visits to Richmond. One delegate found only 12 of the normal 30 cars in operation, due, he was told, to burned out motors. Another delegate discovered 18 men employed in the repair shops to care for 40 cars. In response, Sprague claimed that the road's owners had engaged in "the grossest mismanagement," neglecting maintenance and overloading the motors. Within a year, the Richmond system was in the hands of receivers, and barely operating. The receivers found themselves unable to determine operating costs.[51]

The problems with the Richmond system did not appear to hurt the Sprague company's business. By October 1888, the company had 28 contracts to install trolley systems, including one line on Boston's West End Railway.[52] The management of the Richmond system had undoubtedly been incompetent and corrupt. Nevertheless, the owners had probably not intended to reduce their company to insolvency in little more than a year; the electric system apparently proved less profitable than they had expected.

Sources of Success: Enthusiasm and Structure

Costs clearly seem inadequate to explain the turn to electric traction after 1877. Installations made before 1888 were either failures or marginal, and even Sprague's Richmond system did not operate reliably. In the late 1880s, street railways made large-scale commitments to electricity, providing a crucial impetus to the electric traction industry, raising its scale, advancing it down the learning curve, and focusing inventive effort on the perfection of electric traction. This early commitment was central to the trolley's overwhelming success against competing technologies in the 1890s.

Although explanations for the trolley's early success must remain somewhat speculative, two factors appear central. First is the nearly universal enthusiasm for electrical technology, an enthusiasm that did not extend to cable or steam streetcars. This enthusiasm for electricity encouraged an optimistic interpretation of its costs, and helped convince street-railway companies to invest in electric systems. The second key factor was the place of electric traction in the electric lighting industry. The trolley provided an additional market for manufacturers of central station equipment, and it also promised to make the electric lighting business more profitable by providing a daytime load for central generating stations. Because of this relationship, central-station interests provided essential support to the development of electric traction.

David Nye has ably documented American enthusiasm for electrical technology in the late nineteenth century. Popular enthusiasm for electricity far outstripped fear of this invisible and potentially lethal power. Various forms of conspicuous consumption provided an important early market for electric lighting.[53] Some businessmen in the electric lighting industry recognized the importance of this enthusiasm for their business. "The novelty of the electric light has largely been its stock in trade," wrote Alexander Stuart, an executive in an Edison subsidiary, to Alexander Insull in 1884. Stuart noted that recently improved gas burners were as bright as the standard Edison lamp. Stuart warned Insull that the novelty of the electric light would soon fade, and Americans would then "pant for something else."[54] Improved electric lighting systems eventually met the challenge of gas. Popular enthusiasm played a crucial role in this success, propelling the electric light down the learning and innovation curve during the early period when its profitability remained questionable. A similar enthusiasm played a role in the development of the electric streetcar.

Street-railway owners and managers fully shared the public's enthusiasm for electrical technology. One would think that these businessmen, comfortable with the world of horses, iron rails, and cobblestone paving, would have approached electricity with considerable skepticism, demanding proof of its economy and reliability before risking an investment in the new technology. Such skepticism existed to some extent, especially before 1888, but skepticism was overshadowed by palpable excitement over the potential of electric traction, and a widespread belief in the certainty of its application to street railroads.

ASRA's annual conventions provide striking evidence of enthusiasm for electric traction among street-railway men. In a brief address at the 1883 convention, association president H. H. Littell labeled electric traction as "the last and greatest discovery of the century." According to Littell, the "crude experiments already made with electricity as a motive power . . . clearly foreshadow the inevitable application of the new motor to our immediate interests."[55]

Passionate rhetoric in support of electricity continued in subsequent conventions, often phrased in the language of evangelical religion.[56] No member of the association surpassed in eloquence Calvin A. Richards, manager of the Metropolitan Railroad of Boston. At the 1884 convention, Richards likened electric traction to an infant, conferred by the Creator "as a new blessing on the world." Richards protested his ignorance of matters electric, but such ignorance did nothing to blunt his enthusiasm. In fact, technical details mattered little to Richards. "I care not what one tells me of the crude developments of [electric traction] today," argued Richards. For Richards, the dramatic technical progress that he had personally witnessed, especially the telegraph and telephone, convinced him that electricity's success was certain: "The next step, . . . as sure as God reigns, is going to be electricity!" Although Richards was not urging his colleagues to convert immediately to electricity, his belief in its inevitability convinced him to forgo other forms of mechanization while awaiting the perfection of the electric streetcar.[57]

Delegates rarely challenged this enthusiastic rhetoric. At the 1886 convention, however, one delegate did take exception to the dominant rhetoric. This delegate recalled Richards's metaphor of electricity as infant in order to dispute it. "I think that electricity is a pretty tough old maiden by this time," he said, and called for a "thorough discussion" of the reasons why electricity "has not reached that giant strength that Mr. Richards has foretold."[58] These incompatible metaphors for electricity were not empty rhetoric, but had direct implications for the technical choices being made by street-railway companies. If electricity was a "pretty tough old maiden" rather than an infant, then there was no reason to postpone cable or steam systems in anticipation of electric traction.

Enthusiasm for electric traction played an important role in the interpretation of cost data. Given the uncertainty of cost estimates, it would have been reasonable to greet claims for the economy of electric traction with considerable skepticism. But electrical enthusiasm ensured that street-railway men would give such cost data an optimistic interpretation. No one demanded an accurate accounting of capital costs. Unrealistic estimates of depreciation and maintenance passed without comment. Probing questions were often treated as insults, unworthy of response.[59]

By the early 1890s, this optimism had proved justified, at least as far as competition with horses was concerned. Electricity appeared to be the most economical power for a wide range of traffic densities, though horses still seemed preferable on lightly traveled lines, and cable traction appeared superior for very heavy traffic.[60] The belief of street-railway men in the success of electric traction was partly self-fulfilling, due to their willingness to invest in electric traction before obtaining accurate cost data. Before 1888, however, street railroads invested little money in electric traction. These companies would have found no electric traction systems to buy if the manufacturers of electric lighting equipment had not supported the development of electric streetcars.

Frank Sprague's relationship with the Edison companies illustrates the key role of central station interests in the development of electric traction. Without an electric motor load, most electric lighting plants had very poor load factors, since there was often insufficient power to operate them during the day. Edison recognized as early as 1878 that the addition of a motor load would improve the load factor of central plants, and thus improve the profitability of the investment.[61] Before the adoption of electric traction in the late 1880s, however, there was little opportunity for central stations to share motor and lighting loads.

Throughout his work on electric traction, Sprague remained intimately involved with the companies controlled by Thomas Edison and his associates. This close involvement continued despite personal animosity between Sprague and Samuel Insull, the manager of Edison's business interests. Sprague had worked briefly for Edison from 1883 to 1884, when Sprague left to seek fame and fortune as an independent inventor, modeling himself explicitly on Edison. Sprague soon patented an improved electric motor, and he formed the Sprague Electric Railway and Motor Company to develop and market it. Sprague's chief source of capital was Edward H. Johnson, a close associate of Edison and later president of the Edison Illuminating Company. The Sprague company contracted with the Edison Machine Works to manufacture the motors, and the Edison interests urged their central stations to promote sales of the Sprague motor in order to obtain a daytime load. The Sprague motor constituted a sizable part of the business at the Edison Machine Works.[62]

While Sprague was making a handsome profit selling electric motors, he diverted as much cash as possible to his electric traction experiments. Despite frequent complaints from Insull, Sprague repeatedly paid his bills late and disputed charges. Insull tolerated Sprague's behavior because of the importance of Sprague's work to the Edison system. The Edison Machine Works in effect provided Sprague with considerable additional capital by permitting him to pay his bills late. When Sprague needed more funds to promote his business, Edison's associates purchased the stock. After the success of Sprague's system became assured by 1889, the newly formed Edison General Electric purchased Sprague's company and forced him out of its management.[63]

The Thomson-Houston Company, Edison's chief competitor, also actively entered the electric traction business in early 1888 by purchasing Charles Van Depoele's company. Van Depoele was undoubtedly the leading supplier of electric traction systems before Sprague's success in Richmond. After buying the Van Depoele system, Thomson-Houston supplied the necessary capital and manufacturing expertise to make the system suitable for application on a large scale. Once again, the manufacturers of electric lighting equipment proved crucial to the success of electric traction.[64] Neither the horses, steam dummies, nor cable cars found similar dynamic and powerful allies in the American industrial structure.

Conclusion

No prudent historian would seriously argue that technical choice can be reduced to a matter of costs. Nevertheless, it is surprising how unimportant actual cost data were in the early success of electric traction. American street-railway companies invested $36,000,000 in electric railroads by mid-1890, mainly on the basis of speculative cost estimates.[65] For most of these street railroads, faith in electricity proved justified. Costs declined rapidly in the 1890s as manufacturers progressed rapidly down the learning curve. The price of electric motors for a single streetcar fell from $4500 in 1889 to $750 in 1895.[66] With the spread of rotary converters, street railroads were able to share the lower costs of alternating current (ac) generated by steam turbines and water power.[67] The electric streetcar spread far and wide, providing urban residents with cheap and plentiful transportation, while opening up huge areas to residential settlement. However, the subsequent costs of electric traction cannot serve as an explanation for the initial choice of electricity, since the early investors did not have access to the future.

Notes

1. See George Rogers Taylor, *The Transportation Revolution, 1815–1860* (New York: Rinehart, 1951).

2. John P. McKay, *Tramways and Trolleys: The Rise of Urban Mass Transport in Europe* (Princeton, N.J.: Princeton Univ. Press, 1976), pp. 50–51, 68–73; Clay McShane, *Technology and Reform: Street Railways and the Growth of Milwaukee, 1887–1900* (Madison: State Historical Society of Wisconsin for the Department of History, University of Wisconsin, 1974), pp. 1–10; George Rogers Taylor, "The beginnings of mass transportation in urban America," *Smithsonian J. Hist.*, Vol. 1, Summer 1966, pp. 35–40; Autumn 1966, pp. 39–52.

3. For different explanations of this competition in Europe, see McKay, *Tramways and Trolleys*, op. cit., pp. 25–67, and Anthony Sutcliffe, "Street transport in the second half of the nineteenth century: Mechanization delayed?" in *Technology and the Rise of the Networked City in Europe and America*, eds. Joel A. Tarr and Gabriel Dupuy (Philadelphia: Temple Univ. Press, 1988), pp. 22–39.

4. On the neoclassical (i.e., naive) theory, see Jon Elster, *Explaining Technical Change* (Cambridge, England: Cambridge Univ. Press, 1983), pp. 96–111; for a trenchant critique of this approach, see Paul A. David, *Technical Choice, Innovation and Economic Growth* (Cambridge, England: Cambridge Univ. Press, 1975), pp. 4–16.

5. Paul A. David, "Clio and the economics of QWERTY," *Am. Econ. Rev.*, Vol. 75, May 1985, pp. 332–336.

6. Thomas P. Hughes, "The development phase of technological change," *Technol. Culture*, Vol. 17, 1976, pp. 429–430.

7. The classic example is the diesel engine. See Lynwood Bryant, "The development of the diesel engine," *Technol. Culture*, Vol. 17, 1976, pp. 432–446.

8. Nathan Rosenberg, "Learning by using," in *Inside the Black Box: Technology and Economics* (Cambridge, England: Cambridge Univ. Press, 1982), pp. 120–140.

9. David, "Clio and the economics of QWERTY," op. cit., pp. 332–336; Donald MacKenzie, *Inventing Accuracy: A Historical Sociology of Nuclear Missile Guidance* (Cambridge, Mass.: M.I.T. Press, 1990), p. 168.

10. The best brief summary of the mechanization of American street railroads is McShane, *Technology and Reform*, pp. 6–17. On conversion of early electric systems to cable, see George W. Hilton, *The Cable Car in America: A New Treatise upon Cable or Rope Traction as Applied to the Working of Street and Other Railways*, rev. ed. (San Diego: Howell-North, 1982), p. 17. On 1888 as the turning point for electricity, see Eugene Griffin, "Three years' development of electric railways," *National Electric Light Association, Proceedings*, Vol. 14, September 7, 1891, pp. 234–235.

11. McKay, *Tramways and Trolleys*, op. cit., pp. 13–15; Taylor, "The Beginnings of Mass Transportation in Urban America," Autumn 1966, op. cit. pp. 33–39.

12. McKay, *Tramways and Trolleys*, op. cit., p. 14; Daniel Kinnear Clark, *Tramways, Their Construction and Working*, 1st ed. (London: Lockwood, 1878), p. 6; "American street railroads," *All Year Round*, Vol. 5, April 6, 1861, pp. 40–44.

13. *Report on Transportation Business in the United States at the Eleventh Census, 1890*, Vol. 1 (Washington, D.C.: U.S. Government Printing Office, 1894), p. 681.

14. McKay, *Tramways and Trolleys*, op. cit., p. 26; Clark, *Tramways*, op. cit., p. 416.

15. Clark, ibid.

16. F. M. L. Thompson, "Horses and hay in Britain, 1830–1918," in *Horses in European Economic History: A Preliminary Canter*, ed. F. M. L. Thompson (Reading, England: British Agricultural History Society, 1983), p. 64; F. M. L. Thompson, "Nineteenth-century horse sense," *Econ. Hist. Rev.*, Vol. 29, 2nd ser., 1976, pp. 60–81.

17. See McKay, *Tramways and Trolleys*, op. cit., p. 52.

18. *Philadelphia City Passenger Railway Guide and Advertising Medium, Embracing the Routes of City Passenger Railways* (Philadelphia: F. I. Mitchell, 1874).

19. Massachusetts Street Railway Commission, *Evidence Before the Street Railway Commissioners Appointed by the Massachusetts Legislature, Session of 1863–4* (Boston: Wright & Potter, Printers, 1864), pp. 89–95, 99, 102–110, 116–126; Baldwin Locomotive Works, Philadelphia, *Noiseless Motors and Steam Street Cars for City and Suburban Railways*, 3rd ed. (Philadelphia: Lippincott, 1890), Historical Society of Pennsylvania Library; "Trial of a steam street car," *The Railroad Gazette*, Vol. 8, April 28, 1876, p. 183; Clark, *Tramways*, op. cit., pp. 312–414.

20. "Steam on street railways," *Eng. News*, Vol. 4, March 10, 1877, p. 59. See also "Steam on street railways," *J. Franklin Inst.*, Vol. 103, 1877, p. 384; "Steam traction for tramways," *Street Railway Gazette*, Vol. 1, September 1886, pp. 264–265.

21. Robinson Souttar, "Street tramways," *Minutes of the Proceedings of the Institution of Civil Engineers*, Vol. 50, Part 4, April 24, 1877, pp. 18–19; for a similar British estimate, see Clark, *Tramways*, op. cit., p. 416; Richard Clere Parsons, "The working of tramways by steam," *Minutes of the Proceedings of the Institution of Civil Engineers*, Vol. 79, 1885, pp. 113–119.

22. "Comparison of mileage and cars of street railways in the United States for the years 1890–91," *Street Railway J.*, Vol. 8, April 1892, p. 213.

23. John H. White, "Grice and Long: Steam-car builders," *Prospects: An Annual of American Cultural Studies*, Vol. 2, 1976, p. 30.

24. Derek H. Aldcroft, "Urban transport problems in historical perspective," in *Business, Banking and Urban History: Essays in Honour of S. G. Checkland*, eds. Anthony Slaven

and Derek H. Aldcroft (Edinburgh: John Donald, 1982), p. 224; Massachusetts Street Railway Commission, *Evidence*, op. cit., pp. 106, 110, 124; McShane, *Technology and Reform*, op. cit., p. 8.

25. *ASRA Proceedings*, Vol. 2, 1883, pp. 89–90; *ASRA Proceedings*, Vol. 6, 1887, pp. 68–69; McKay, *Tramways and Trolleys*, op. cit., p. 30; John H. White, "Steam in the streets: The Grice and Long dummy," *Technol. Culture*, Vol. 27, 1986, pp. 108–109; Clark, *Tramways*, op. cit., p. 419.

26. *Historical Statistics of the United States: Colonial Times to 1957* (Washington D.C.: U.S. Bureau of the Census, 1960), pp. 297–298, 302; Sutcliffe, "Street transport in the second half of the nineteenth century," op. cit., p. 29.

27. Hilton, *The Cable Car in America*, op. cit., pp. 13–14, 17–27, 44; *Report on Transportation Business in the United States at the Eleventh Census*, 1890, op. cit., p. 682.

28. "Report of the committee on the cable system of motive power," *ASRA Proceedings*, Vol. 3, 1884, p. 147.

29. Hilton, *The Cable Car in America*, op. cit., pp. 40, 103; Charles H. Cooley, *The Relative Economy of Cable, Electric, and Animal Motive Power for Street Railways*, Census Bulletin No. 55 (Washington, D.C.: U.S. Department of the Interior, Census Office, 1891).

30. The best scholarly account of early electric traction developments in the United States remains Harold C. Passer, *The Electrical Manufacturers, 1875–1900: A Study in Competition, Entrepreneurship, Technical Change, and Economic Growth* (Cambridge, Mass.: Harvard Univ. Press, 1953), pp. 211–236. For a more detailed but less scholarly discussion, see John R. Stevens, ed., *Pioneers of Electric Railroading: Their Story in Words and Pictures* (New York: Electric Railroaders' Association, 1991).

31. Griffin, "Three years' development of electric railways," op. cit., p. 235. Griffin's figures are substantially less than those given in William D. Middleton, *The Time of the Trolley: The Street Railway from Horsecar to Light Rail*, Vol. 1 (San Marino, Calif.: Golden West, 1987), p. 65.

32. Hilton, *Cable Car in America*, op. cit., p. 17.

33. Passer, *Electrical Manufacturers*, op. cit., pp. 242–248.

34. T. Commerford Martin, "A few comparative statistics of electric railways," *AIEE Transactions*, Vol. 4, 1887, pp. 183–187.

35. Passer, *Electrical Manufacturers*, op. cit., pp. 248–253. The Sprague Electric Railway and Motor Company was bought by Edison General Electric at the end of 1889. In 1892 Edison General Electric merged with Thomson-Houston to form General Electric.

36. *Report on Transportation Business in the United States at the Eleventh Census*, 1890, op. cit., pp. 681–682.

37. Griffin, "Three years' development of electric railways," op. cit., p. 235.

38. McKay, *Tramways and Trolleys*, op. cit., pp. 50–51.

39. Passer, *Electrical Manufacturers*, op. cit., pp. 253–254; Hilton, *The Cable Car in America*, op. cit., p. 149.

40. "The Battle of the Motive Powers," *Street Railway J.*, Vol. 13, October 1897, pp. 650–653.

41. Lincoln Moss, "Comparative tests of an electric motor and a steam locomotive on the Manhattan (Elevated) Railway," *The Railroad Gazette*, Vol. 22, July 11, 1890, pp. 488–489; "Efficiency of the locomotive and electric motor," *The Railroad Gazette*, Vol. 22, July 11, 1890, pp. 494–495; Lincoln Moss, "Efficiency of the locomotive and electric motor," *The Railroad Gazette*, Vol. 22, July 18, 1890, pp. 503–504. See also the discus-

sion following Moss, "Comparative Tests of an Electric Motor and Steam Locomotive on Manhattan (Elevated) Railway, New York," *ASCE Transactions*, Vol. 23, October 1890, pp. 193–216.

42. Some of these articles are collected in Hermann Haupt, *Rapid Transit in New York; Open Letter to A. S. Hewitt, on the Various Motive Power Systems Proposed for the Operation of Rapid Transit Lines in the City of New York* (Washington D.C.: Adams, 1894). See also Haupt, *Street Railway Motors: With Descriptions and Cost of Plants and Operation of the Various Systems in Use or Proposed for Motive Power on Street Railways* (Philadelphia: Henry Carey Baird, 1893). Both these sources are detailed arguments in support of compressed-air motors.

43. "Remarks of Dr. A. Everett," *ASRA Proceedings*, Vol. 8, 1890, p. 74.

44. "Report of the Committee on 'A Uniform System of Accounts'," *ASRA Proceedings*, Vol. 3, 1894, p. 153.

45. McShane, *Technology and Reform*, op. cit., pp. 34–35.

46. Massachusetts Street Railway Commission, *Report . . . to the General Court*, Massachusetts House Rep. No. 15 (Boston: Wright & Potter, 1865), pp. 30–34; Robert B. Carson, *What Ever Happened to the Trolley* (Washington, D.C.: Univ. Press of America, 1978), pp. 29–32, 51–52; McShane, *Tramways and Trolleys*, op. cit., p. 34.

47. Cooley, *The Relative Economy of Cable, Electric, and Animal Motive Power*, op. cit., pp. 5–6. Calculations based on horse railroads numbered 1 through 6, table I.C.1.

48. McKay, *Tramways and Trolleys*, op. cit., pp. 58–61.

49. Frank J. Sprague, "The solution of municipal rapid transit," *AIEE Transactions*, Vol. 5, August 1888, p. 387.

50. Richmond Union Passenger Railway Company to Edward H. Johnson, Sprague Electric Railway and Motor Company, May 15, 1888, Frank J. Sprague papers, New York Public Library, box 1, folder 1887–88.

51. "Remarks of Mr. F. J. Sprague on Electric Railways and Motors," *ASRA Proceedings*, Vol. 7, 1888, pp. 101–109; "Remarks of Mr. John S. Wise on the Richmond Electric Road," *ASRA Proceedings*, Vol. 8, 1889, pp. 68–73.

52. *ASRA Proceedings*, Vol. 7, op. cit., p. 103.

53. David E. Nye, *Electrifying America: Social Meanings of a New Technology, 1880–1940* (Cambridge, Mass.: M.I.T. Press, 1990), pp. 85–137.

54. A. Stuart to Alexander Insull, April 17, 1884, *Thomas A. Edison Papers: A Selective Microfilm Edition*, Part II (Frederick, Md.: Univ. Publications of America, 1987), Vol. 75, p. 125.

55. "Address of the President," *ASRA Proceedings*, Vol. 2, 1883, pp. 8–9.

56. For an example of this rhetoric in aviation, see Joseph J. Corn, *The Winged Gospel: America's Romance with Aviation, 1900–1950* (New York: Oxford Univ. Press, 1983).

57. Remarks of C. A. Richards, *ASRA Proceedings*, Vol. 3, 1884, pp. 138–140.

58. Remarks of C. B. Holmes, *ASRA Proceedings*, Vol. 5, 1886, p. 86.

59. See, for example, remarks of Mr. Wharton, *ASRA Proceedings*, Vol. 5, 1886, p. 88; remarks of C. A. Richards, ibid., p. 94; remarks of Mr. Wharton, *ASRA Proceedings*, Vol. 6, 1887, p. 44.

60. R. J. McCarty, "Special report concerning the relative cost of motive power for street-railways," *ASRA Proceedings*, Vol. 9, 1890, pp. 70–74.

61. Passer, *Electrical Manufacturers*, op. cit., p. 218.

62. Frank J. Sprague to Thomas Edison, April 24, 1884, *Edison Papers*, op. cit., Vol. 74, p. 754; C. H. Coster, "Report of the special committee on the use of sprague motors," May 25, 1885, *Edison Papers*, op. cit., Vol. 77, p. 747; F. S. Hastings to the owners of Central and Village Station Companies, May 25, 1885, *Edison Papers*, Vol. 74, p. 749; Contract between the Edison Electric Light Company and the Sprague Electric Railway and Motor Company, June 16, 1885, *Edison Papers*, Vol. 88, p. 954. See also Harold C. Passer, "Frank Julian Sprague: Father of electric traction, 1857–1934," in *Men in Business: Essays in the History of Entrepreneurship*, ed. William Miller (Cambridge, Mass.: Harvard College, 1952), pp. 212–237.

63. Samuel Insull to Edward H. Johnson, April 7, 1887, D8736ABC; Insull to A. O. Tate, February 21, 1887, D8736AAQ; Frank J. Sprague to Johnson, April 11, 1887, D8736ABI; Insull to Edison, November 5, 1887, D8736AEL; J. H. McClement, "Supplementary report on financial condition, earnings and business of the Sprague Electric Railway and Motor Company," January 31, 1889, D8944AAB, Thomas A. Edison Papers, Edison National Historical Site, West Orange, N.J.; [Frank J. Sprague] to W. W. Gooch, November 21; Sprague to President and Board of Directors, Edison General Electric Co., December 2, 1890, Frank J. Sprague papers, New York Public Library, box 1.

64. Passer, *Electric Manufacturers*, op. cit., pp. 233, 249–250.

65. *Report on Transportation Business in the United States at the Eleventh Census, 1890*, op. cit., p. 682.

66. Passer, *Electrical Manufacturers*, op. cit., p. 264.

67. Sydney W. Ashe, *Electric Railways Theoretically and Practically Considered*, Vol. 2, *Engineering Preliminaries and Direct-Current Sub-Stations* (New York: Van Nostrand, 1907); Thomas P. Hughes, *Networks of Power: Electrification in Western Society, 1880–1930* (Baltimore, Md.: Johns Hopkins Univ. Press, 1983), pp. 120–126, 208–212.

from water turbines, which ran more smoothly and gave better results in some areas, such as papermaking and the weaving of fine cloth. Reasons had to be found why electric drives could have been superior. One reason, of course, was the cost of energy; another was the spread of industry to areas that were rich in water power but poor in easily accessible sites for manufacturing plants. In Europe these sites were mostly located in the regions near the Alps. Other major potential markets, however, existed where steam was already established and electricity could hardly compete because of energy costs. Thus, in these areas electric drives only had a chance if they could bring about something that could not easily be done with steam. In the early years of electric drives, this was seen as less an economic than a social achievement— the overcoming of centralized industry and the renaissance of small businesses and craft shops.

To give just one example of this societal electroutopia of the late nineteenth century, I shall quote Werner Siemens, industrially the most successful of the inventors of the electrodynamic principle, from his lecture, "On the Age of Science," in 1886:

> Until today big machines still produce mechanical labor much more cheaply than small ones, and the erection of the latter in the workers' dwellings is still met with great difficulty. Technology, however, will undoubtedly succeed in overcoming the obstacles to the return to competitive hand-labor by supplying the small workshop and dwellings of the workers and artisans with cheap mechanical power—the basis of all industry. A large number of factories in the hands of rich capitalists, where slaves of labor eke out their existence, is not the final goal of the development of the age of science, but the return to individual labor![1]

These views placed Siemens in the center of a broad discussion on the sociopolitical merits of the electric motor and its future employment in trade and industry.[2] When Siemens gave his lecture, his engineer Hoffmann had just successfully finished work on the first "dc inner-pole generator," which could be coupled directly to a steam engine—a major breakthrough in generator technology.[3] Since this new generator was working only a few minutes away in the Mauerstrasse of Berlin, supplying electricity for Berlin's first commercially used electric motor, Siemens' lecture was also a good piece of marketing.

In analyzing the future market, however, he was still very much caught up in utopian designs of a noncentralized and therefore socially peaceful industrial society. The kind of industry he among so many others had built up had become a hotbed of socialism. Siemens, like many other industrialists of the time, was haunted by fears that he was some kind of sorcerer's apprentice.

In the end, of course, the conspicuous affection of the nascent electrotechnical industry for artisans and domestic industries and their—one could say post-Fordist— concepts of organizing production was not only an emanation from the widespread conservative and even restorative convictions among industrialists but very much a response to the kind of demand that was felt on the market for stationary motors. There the foremost task was to replace the all-dominating steam engine. This, however, was only likely to succeed in those fields where the mature and well-proven principle of steam power had its conceptional limitations. These limitations were, first, the large space required for raising steam and storing fuel, and, second, the drastically rising costs per unit of power when the machine was used only sporadically. (One cannot easily store steam.) Both these shortcomings had their greatest impact in small workshops with few machines.

When electricity entered the field in the 1880s quite a lively competition already existed among the various forms of drives and motors (hot air engines, hydraulic motors, and, especially, gas motors) for the remaining share of the market.[4] In order to win against steam power in the major industries, however, electric motors had to be more than just a miniature drive—they had to be less expensive. While this took some time, for most small workshops the possibility of any form of motor at all was already such a big step forward that the comparative quality and economy of this motor was not severely scrutinized.

Although early analysis in the electrical industry predicted little impact of decentralization upon the development of industrial society, decentralization proved to be productive and far-reaching. Research and development (R&D) strategies focused on the two weak points of steam power for small workshops: space and stop-and-go work. A third strategy, more directly aimed at rationalization in big industry, that is, the smooth regulation of motor speeds to always achieve optimum operating speeds for any machine and any process, failed almost completely. The few exceptions to this rule are discussed below.

The Shortcomings of Early Motors

While the basic engineering problems of connecting a single machine tool to an individual electric motor had been solved with the "artisans dc motor"—a small dc motor connected to the public electric light network with a short leather belt between motor pulley and machine pulley—this combination did not pass the test of industry. The weakest point was the dc motor, since it did *not* have two of the essential qualities mechanical transmissions had, and which had therefore for a long time been taken for granted in production planning and organization of labor: a fairly constant rotational speed once it was set, and a high degree of reliability even if treated carelessly.

Certainly, in both these respects the dc motor was still better than small steam engines of the same capacity, which was the reason that big industry *did* use them very early for special machines whose locations in the factory were isolated and that had to have some form of individual motor.[5] But these heavy machines were operated by highly qualified personnel, who were best equipped to cope with irregular speeds and delicate apparatus, since this was not so different from their experience with individual steam drives. Moreover, these specialists did appreciate and make intelligent use of the possibility of being able to continuously regulate the motor's speed.

At these specific points of production it was not so much the ratio between labor-plus-capital-cost per kilogram of output that was decisive, but instead the uniquely large variety of possible ways to shape a product. In these places it was already profitable, *if* one could do it; energy and labor costs were of secondary importance. This somewhat resembled the situation in the crafts, so it is not surprising that individual electric drives spread first in those departments that resembled craft production, that is, isolated, highly qualified, and producing small batches.

Mass production, however, was quite "uncraftsmenlike." The prime object was a high rate of standardized products per unit of time, which did not encourage the semiskilled piece-rate workers to be overly patient with their machinery, or least of all to be careful when correcting irregularities in machine operations. The problems of the steadiness of rotational speed and the proneness to breakdowns therefore multiplied in the big workshops.

On one hand, the machine tools, looms, etc. used in mass production were usually smaller and weighed less than the separate electrically driven special machines, which made it harder to keep them at a constant working speed. After all, it had been one of the prime virtues of central transmission that it compensated for sudden peak loads with the enormous inertia and the great number of elastic belts the machines used.

On the other hand, the well-proven belt drives were quite resistant to ruthless treatment. If overloaded, they simply started to slip, thus producing a squealing sound that warned the operator in time to save the machine and the product from serious damage. Electric motors, however, continued operating, producing a bit of extra warmth and a pungent smell that came too late to be effective warning signs.

In practice, the most dangerous moments for electric drives were—and still are—the first seconds after being turned on with a load. After that, the most dangerous times were short time peaks or overloads. As a result, many workers never voluntarily turned off their machines when mounting new tools or workpieces, but let them run permanently like a central transmission. This, of course, made all calculations of energy savings with individual electric drives worthless. It was particularly true of small motors, which had an efficiency of about 75 percent, a rating that did not compare favorably with a central transmission.[6] But even then there were still the many costly breakdowns of overloaded motors.

Similar problems existed in the textile industry. In 1894 in Mittweida, Saxony, the first cotton-weaving factory to be equipped with individual dc electric drives paid dearly for its pioneering spirit.[7] Only a year after installation the whole factory had to be converted back to central transmissions, since none of the early hopes and promises had materialized. First, the service costs for the 600 loom motors were much higher than they had been with steam and shafts. Since weaving looms have to start very quickly under full load to prevent visible shadings in the cloth, the 600 motors were necessarily and constantly ill-treated and failed accordingly. Shunt-wound motors, which had to be used since they have a relatively constant rotational speed, unfortunately produce a fraction of their torque only when started, and therefore require a careful starting procedure to prevent them from overloading. In weaving, however, as in many other industries, this is the very moment when maximum torque is required. Hence the temptation to abbreviate the starting procedure was irresistible to the workers. Second, fuel consumption for the power plant was greater than it had been for steam only—no one stopped the motors during breaks contrary to what had been assumed in the cost estimates. And, third, because the electric plant cost much more than a comparable steam plant, losses occurred in all three major accounting areas: output, operating costs, and capital costs.

Identifying the Problem

Almost until the turn of the century the electric motors offered by manufacturers were influenced more by what was possible to do "by electricity" than by industry's production needs and traditions. Since only electric motors were usually "employed," the search continued for new possible applications for a given electric motor technology. If treated carefully by trained personnel or a cottage worker or artisan who had put his own money into the motor, these early dc-driven machines—from the variable-speed turning lathe, with its huge headstock motor, to the cottage weavers' ribbon loom, which was connected to the local electric light company—worked properly and in some respects quite impressively.[8] But just as artisans and cottage laborers in general could not withstand the competition from mass production, these motors could not hold their own against steam, shafts, and belts. For both dc motors and artisans there were only niches left in the market.

The breakthrough, as is well known, was brought about by the development of the asynchronous polyphase motor after 1888/1889. This motor, especially the squirrel-cage type, was put on the market in greater numbers at the turn of the century. By no means, however, were all problems solved by this "ideal" motor.

The *small* polyphase motor also began to be used where it could be employed unmodified, which meant with high and constant rotational speed. The 2- to 4-pole types of between 1/10 to 3 hp could not run at less than 2800 or 1400 rpm (with full load) on a 50-cycle ac motor. Not surprisingly, from the early 1890s technical journals were full of advertisements for polyphase centrifuges (separators!) and ventilators.[9] The high number of rpms of the small polyphase motors were the very obstacle to their use with machine tools or looms, which were designed to run at 20 to 300 rpm.

While in principle one could overcome this problem with the help of a belt or toothed back gears, these machines did not last too long because of the lack of experience with fast rotational speeds. Leather belts posed another restriction in that even the best material could not undergo more than 12,000 bendings (180°) per hour before it gave out from fatigue.[10] A 2-pole motor with a 12-cm pulley attached to it would have required a belt 11 m long (5.5 m with a 4-pole motor). Synthetic cone belts, which today solve this problem very well, did not appear in central Europe until the late 1920s, when an Italian engineer began production under American licenses.[11] At the turn of the century the only recognized solution was the toothed gear. But here, too, experience in its use was scarce.

In transmission technology, late 19th-century engineers had had to make do with peripheral gear speeds of between 2 and 3 m/sec.[12] With a 2-pole polyphase motor and these slow perimeter speeds, the diameter of the first gear could not have been more than about 2 cm! (Fifty cps for a 3-m perimeter = a 6-cm perimeter per revolution = a 2-cm diameter.) Realistically, one had to come to grips with perimeter speeds that were three to five times faster before one could entertain the idea of directly coupling a small polyphase motor to a machine tool.

Since turn-of-the-century manufacturers of machine tools weren't much interested in the problems of individual electric drives, the electric manufacturers had themselves to take up the development of small and inexpensive high-speed gears.

The pioneering work in matching small fast-running polyphase motors to slow-working machine tools via toothed gears in Europe was done by Otto Lasche, head engineer of the Allgemeine Elektrizitäts Gesellschaft (AEG). Lasche commenced his thorough R&D program on fast-running gears only a few months after his company had converted large portions of its workshops to individual electric drives with polyphase motors of between 960 and 1440 rpm and belt drives.[13] It is of some importance here to mention that these motors were by no means the cheapest and simplest of their size, but were rather expensive multipole models, since they had to be slow enough for the belts! But obviously they weren't.

Having affirmed the robustness of his company's polyphase motors, and having complained about the many breakdowns in practice, which according to him were in most cases due to the failure of the connecting links between motors and machines, Lasche proclaimed the following as the future task of R&D:

> To do without separate links (between motor and machine, UW) is impossible; neither can an electric motor be produced at competitive prices with the slow speed required, nor is it feasible to increase the speed of the machine tool for the benefit of the motor. The demand of practitioners for slow running power shafts is quite irrefutable and points to the necessity of back gears, and in fact toothed-wheel back gears to be sure.[14]

Lasche's work was unique in that he was the first to deliberately turn away from his own field of electrical engineering to solve the problems of electric drives. He did not see the future of the electric motor to be its versatility, which called upon the imagination of so many electrical engineers, but in its inconspicuousness. To enter the big market one did not need to show factory management what one *could do* with electric drives, but rather show what *did not happen* with it. Or in other words, the motor had to be a troubleshooter, not a wizard.

Back Gears

Lasche's basic work on fast-running back gears had discovered the main trouble point of individual electric drives and had paved the way for the future development of gearbox technology. In overcoming the problems of the fastest speed and greatest transmission ratio first, he had created the best preconditions for a further division of gears, even if this potential was not fully exploited until the 1920s. Until then gears were largely used only to reduce the speed of the motor to the speed required by a normal belt-driven loom or lathe.

For those machines that only had one constant working speed, all the basic problems were now solved. This is true for many parts of the textile industry, where polyphase plants with individually driven weaving looms became the rule shortly after the turn of the century.[15] Here again it is important to stress that the spread of individual electric drives in general owed less to savings in power costs than to the increased productivity of a given machine. It was this increasing demand that made mass production of small induction motors possible and triggered off a massive slide in prices. One-horse-power motors, which cost 450 marks in 1900, were available in 1908 for 160 marks in Germany.[16]

TABLE I   Distribution of the Costs of Production in the Textile Industry

	English Textile Industry (1) (%)	Cotton Spinning (2) (%)	Cotton Weaving (2) (%)	Cotton Spinning (3)			Cotton Weaving (4)	
				No. 40, 1913 (%)	No. 36, 1925 (%)	No. 20, 1913 (%)	1905 (%)	1925 (%)
1. Power and fuel	1.3	1.5	1.5	3.5	3.5	2.1	4.0	2.8
2. Raw materials	57.0	68.1	64.9	64.0	54.0	72.5	60.0	72.0
3. Wages	19.7	11.2	15.2	8.0	5.8	7.3	10.0	4.8
4. Other charges and profit	22.0	19.2	18.2	24.5	36.7	18.1	26.0	20.4
Total Percentage	100	100	100	100	100	100	100	100

Weaving Looms

If one takes, for example, the distribution of the costs of production in the textile industry, one can see that the proportion of power and fuel costs was of the order of only 1.3–4.0 percent of the total production costs (see Table I[17]). From this it is clear that even a very considerable saving in power costs can have only an infinitesimal effect on the price of the goods and the profit. Even a power saving of 20 percent would, if it could be obtained free of cost, only increase a 10 percent profit to something between 10.26 and 10.80 percent of the original amount. If against this we consider the effect of an increase in the quantity of production on the net profit, we obtain a totally different picture. A 10 percent increase in production due to individual electric drives, again in the textile industry, could typically increase an existing profit of 5 percent to 7–9 percent, and an existing profit of 15 percent to 17–19 percent. These figures were found in cost assessments in textile mills in the United States, England, and Germany between 1910 and 1920.[18]

The higher turnout of a given loom due to individual drives resulted from reduced variation and fluctuation of the working speed.[19] Figure 1 shows what happened with a conventional line-shaft transmission. In order not to exceed the maximum speed of the looms (spinning or weaving), the whole transmission had to run almost 10 percent slower than optimum speed because of the speed variations in the last row. It was said that it was impossible to operate some automatic looms under these conditions, and visible shadings in the cloth from normal looms meant cloth of an inferior quality. The same is true with spinning, although to a lesser extent.[20]

The main point I want to make here is that the introduction of individual electric drives was not just another form of energy, but a new approach to production technology. Electricity won the day not because it was cheaper, but because it enabled engineers to make a more sophisticated and more flexible use of motive power.

Machine Tools

A somewhat different situation than in textiles, however, prevailed in metal cutting. Here there wasn't one well-defined optimum speed, but a large number of different speeds required for cutting steel of various diameters, etc. And as the tech-

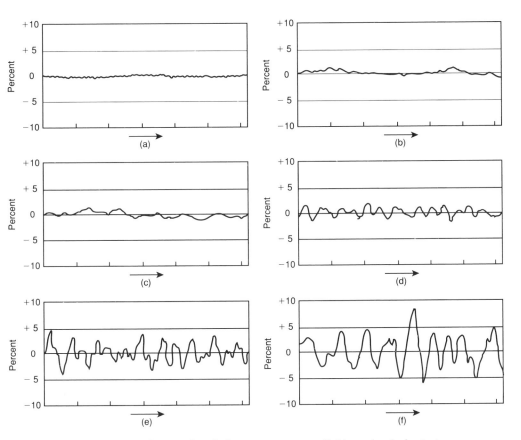

Figure 1. Speed tests on line shafting a jute weaving mill: (a) speed at the beginning of the main shaft; (b) speed in the center of the main shaft; (c) speed at the end of the main shaft; (d) speed at the beginning of the 13th group shaft; (e) speed in the centers of the 13th group shaft; (f) speed at the end of the 13th group shaft.

nology of cutting steel changed during the period from the late nineteenth century to the mid-1920s, the number of speeds required of a turning lathe, for example, also increased. At first glance, this seemed to make variable-speed dc-powered lathes more attractive at last, and a large number of designs for individually driven turning lathes with a dc headstock motor were advanced. With these motors it was, in fact, very easy to meet the demand of a narrow sequence of rotational speeds with steps based on $^{10}V10$ or $^{3}V2$, respectively ($= 1.26$).[21] Indeed, these machines would probably have been as successful as expected if it weren't for the small dc motor's speed variations under a changing load and semiskilled piece-rate work, neither of which the work force was experienced or patient enough to cope with.

In qualified hands, and without the pressure of time, these machines did their job admirably well and were the marvel of all engineering exhibitions. Still in 1926 the then most recent model of a dc headstock-driven turning lathe was presented by the manufacturer (Boehringer) to the *Deutsches Museum* as their most remarkable feat in machine tool design. And in a way it was, this model being a good example of the large disparity between engineering and industrial values. Industry did not buy these "marvels" in great numbers, however, but, until well after World War I, followed the more trouble-free path of electrification via group drives with big and medium polyphase motors (50–100 hp) or else stuck to steam engines.

Like Lasche before them, engineers in the electric industry or electrical engineers involved in machine building could only slowly overcome their belief that one should do "by electricity" what could be done "by electricity." It was obviously not easy for them *not* to use the inherent potential of electric drives—that is, adjustability—only because "uneducated" and impatient piece-rate workers continued to wreck their engineering marvels or were incapable of making intelligent use of the technologically elegant continuous-speed variation at their disposal.

The Motorized Machine Tool

Whether it was favorable circumstances (i.e., cutting-steel research simultaneously making enormous progress) or whether it was the eventual insight that production organization and the characteristics of shunt-wound dc motors were incompatible may be open to debate. Whatever the reason, developments in machine-tool design after the turn of the century focused more and more on the small polyphase squirrel-cage motor with a back gear.

The most important innovation at that time was, of course, the higher cutting speeds made possible by Taylor's high-speed steel and similar alloys. These developments not only meant an increase in turning speeds, but also an increase in the power transmitted to the headstock. Given the usual space constraints, the traditional belt drives now came under pressure from two sides: power and speed. A third severe limitation was caused by the demand that the universal turning lathe have at least 16 different speeds. While one could easily transmit more power with a belt by increasing its cross-sectional area—preferably its width—a thicker or wider belt made shifting gears more difficult. What should a leather-belt gear box for 16 speeds and 10 hp look like?

To cut a long story short, independent of the development of electric drives, engineers in machine-tool design shifted from few belt gears to a great number of toothed gears to achieve both the transmission of more power and a narrower ratio of speeds. The result of these efforts was the single-pulley turning lathe with an integrated gearbox.[22] Since the belt was no longer used to switch gears, it could now be made wide enough to transmit the necessary power from the line shaft to the one remaining pulley. It made little difference if this main pulley was driven by a belt or by an electric motor with back gears, as long as the back gear ran smoothly enough not to cause chatter marks on the workpiece.[23] It was no longer enough to have just any old back gear, as, for example, with weaving motors, but now a high-quality gear was required, especially if it were to be used for metal working.

After the mid-1920s all major manufacturers of machine tools equipped their lathes with an integrated gearbox that could be driven according to the specifications of the client, either by a belt or by a flanging motor. The machine tool remained the same whatever the power source. The move to standardize as many components of a machine tool as possible also helped make the polyphase motor more desirable than the dc drive.

Since in the 1920s the machine tool industry designed its gearboxes for the largest market, which was still line-shaft driving, it had to provide for the whole range of 16 to 18 gears. Once the problems of the 16-gear gearbox were solved, it was no longer financially viable to offer a simplified version for dc motors, where the adjustability of the motor would provide for, say, 12 of the 16 gears. To combine dc motors with these new gearboxes to achieve even finer steps between the 16 or 18 gears did not pay, since there was hardly any noticeable productivity gain with steps of less than $^{10}V10$. Moreover, mechanically shifting gears had the great advantage of being precise and reliable. Direct current motors remained what they always had been since the 1890s: expensive exceptions for use in the occasional unconventional machine.

First Conclusion

To state my first conclusion: It was progress in tooth construction and gearbox construction that, beginning with the critical point of fast-running back gears, eventually paved the way for the small polyphase motor to become the universal source of power for individual drives in industry. The electric industry's own contribution—apart from the motor itself—was pinpointing the motor's high speed as the weak spot and then designing a robust mechanical coupling link to reduce the rotational speed instead of insisting on adjusting the electrical current. These manufacturers were lucky, however, that their correct but incomplete engineering strategy coincided with a congenial strategy in machine-tool design that was based on progress in cutting technology. The electrification of the engineering industry was not just the adoption of electric motors, but resulted more from the shaping of a new synthesis of mechanical power and machine operations. In other words, it was only as a part of this new synthesis that the electric motor was universally adopted in industry.

But before electrification could succeed, the industry had to realize that what could be achieved through technology was relatively unimportant and that what was really essential was that these new motors accommodate the ways in which industrial production was organized. The exception to this insight was continuous-speed regulation through automation. This analysis is also supported by the important exceptions to the rule of the nonuse of continuous-speed regulation with electric drives. Apart from various forms of transport,[24] the most notable of these exceptions are to be found in the steel industry, paper making, and spinning.

Rolling Mills

Although among the first industries that built their own electric plants to make use of most waste heat and waste gases, the steel industry was particularly reluctant to adopt electric drives for use in rolling steel, the process that required the most motive power. In fact, so congenial was the steam engine to these erratic power demands that the rolling crews could barely conceive of using any other type of motor.

On the other hand, the general managers, who were interested to find ways to utilize, without extra cost, the huge quantities of gas and heat a steel plant produced as a by-product, were more open to other alternatives. Since heat is difficult to transport, their first attempt to get more out of these by-products was to use big gas motors in the rolling mills.[25] This experiment ended in complete failure, since the gas motors had no torque when they came close to a standstill, which resulted in many blocks being wasted or at the least needing to be reheated for a new try.

With the failure of gas engines, the managers turned to electric motors as their second choice, but even so, these motors often entered through the back door. Rather than starting them off at the huge roll stands of reversing mills, where the many-thousand-kilowatt Leonard drives (German: Ilgner-Umformer) were later employed,[26] electric motors were first widely used to drive the life rollers, which transported the steel blocks from one roll stand to the next. This was a simple task since, unlike their resistance to the forming operation under the rolls, the weight of the steel blocks could be easily measured. Electrically driven systems, unlike those powered by gas motors or steam engines, had the advantage that their rollers could be controlled from a good viewpoint, distant from the motor itself. Very often, slightly modified electric tramway motors were employed, and they soon became widely used throughout the steel plants to transport materials over roller tables, across tilting tables, through various manipulators, and vertically by cranes, which also used tramway motors.[27] These motors included a most important feature: an automatic contactor control that made it difficult to ruin them (see Fig. 2[28]). This

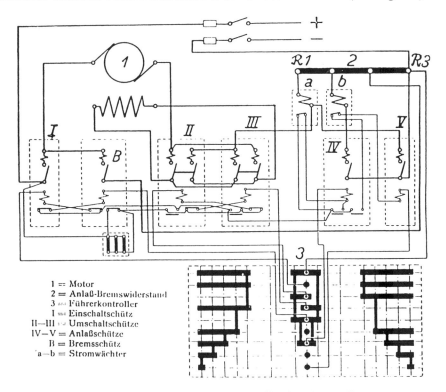

Figure 2. Wiring diagram of an automatic contactor controller for rolling mills. 1 = Motor–motor; 2 = Anlaß-Bremswiderstand–starting resistor (rheostatic starter); 3 = Führerkontroller–master controller; I = Einschaltschütz–starting contactor; II–III = Umshaltschütze–switching contactor; IV–V = Anlaßschütze–accelerating contactor; B = Bremsschütz–breaking contactor; a–b = Stromwächter–contactor.

automatic safeguard was too expensive for the small weaving-loom motors of 1/8 or 1/4 hp, but compared with the price of a several-horsepower tramway motor, the cost was bearable, and the almost foolproof motor won many markets other than street-cars. In a way it was an incomplete though sufficiently successful electric simulation of an ordinary steam engine. Steel managers were delighted that the great number of "little steam squanderers"[29] all over the vast areas of their steel mills could be replaced with something as rugged and easy to handle.

From Automatic Controls to Semiautomatic Drives

If the idea behind these automatic contactor controls was to protect the motor from fatal currents and still give the operator the feeling that he could get the motor's peak performance whenever he wanted, it also opened the electrical engineers' minds to the idea that the current could be used simultaneously as both a source of power and a carrier of information. This new insight led from using some form of automatic control to protect one motor to protecting a whole set of motors. For example, if the motor's own current could be used to protect it and control its power, why not use the current of another motor to control the speed and direction of the first? Life rollers usually transported steel blocks between roll stands, so motors in roll stands would always have to work close to or at their maximum output. This was as precarious with electric motors as it had been with gas motors, since both lack torque below their normal operating speed. The optimum solution was a life roller that fed steel only at the rate the motor of the roll stand could handle. This was achieved by controlling the life roller through the main motor of the roll stand (see Fig. 3[30]). A low current in the main motor would speed up the life roller; a high current would slow it down; a critical current would reverse the life roller and thus pull the steel out of the overloaded roll stand. The same control devices were used for many similar situations in industry, for example, in sawmills.

This semiautomatic roll-feed control both protected all the motors and still guaranteed best possible performance of the whole arrangement. This advance at last gave electric motors in rolling mills a clear advantage in productivity over steam engines while matching their reliability and ease of handling. Again, as with gearboxes, the crucial role of automation was not the creation of versatile and sophisticated engineering marvels, but the reduction of risks on the shop floor.

Spinning Motors

Automation or rather semiautomation, discussed in the second example below, was also a key to success. Spinning, like weaving or cutting metal, is a process that should be done at a single optimum speed, that is, the tension of the yarn to be spun has to be constant and close to the breaking point in order to get good quality and maximum output. An additional problem with spinning, however, is that the quickly produced yarn has to be wound onto a cop whose diameter changes rapidly and considerably in the process. To keep the speed of spinning—and with it the tension of the yarn—constant, the rotational speed of the cop has to vary. The same problem

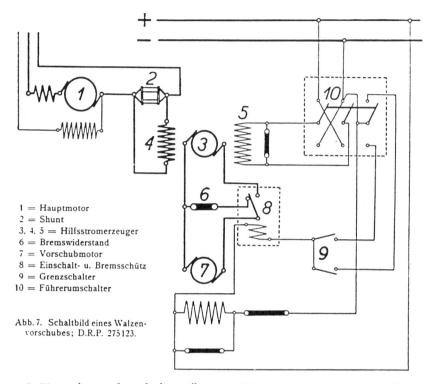

1 = Hauptmotor
2 = Shunt
3, 4, 5 = Hilfsstromerzeuger
6 = Bremswiderstand
7 = Vorschubmotor
8 = Einschalt- u. Bremsschütz
9 = Grenzschalter
10 = Führerumschalter

Abb. 7. Schaltbild eines Walzen-
vorschubes; D.R.P. 275123.

Figure 3. Wiring diagram for a feeding roller. 1 = Hauptmotor–main motor; 2 = Shunt–shunt; 3, 4, 5 = Hilfsstromerzeuger–auxiliary current device; 6 = Bremswiderstand–break resistor; 7 = Vorschubmotor–feeding motor; 8 = Einschalt-und Bremsschütz–starting and breaking contactor; 9 = limit (stop) switch; 10 = Führerumschalter–master controller.

occurs with papermaking, where the moist and soft paper has to be wound under constant and well-controlled tension. Since the motor characteristics required for these processes are the same,[31] I shall limit my short presentation to spinning motors.

The speed of the spinning machine is limited by the amount of tension the yarn can stand. At a given speed this tension is highest when the balloon is large, that is, when the bottom of the cop is built (see Figs. 4[32] and 5). With mechanical transmission and only one speed, the spinning frame would continue to run at the low starting speed for about 90 percent of the spinning time. A two-speed gear improved the situation, and was often used (see Fig. 6[33]).

But after the bottom of the cop was built, the tension of the yarn in the balloon was not constant, but changed with the level of the ring bank. This gives the curve in Fig. 7[34], which was impossible to achieve with mechanical gears.

A smooth curve for the spindle speed could only be achieved at a reasonable price with the electric motor. Once this was achieved, engineers asked why not go a step further and also allow for the speed variations in building every single layer of the cop? This curve would look like that in Figure 8.[35]

Summing up the productivity gains of these four steps measured in output per spindle would yield an additional output for a given machine of about 20 percent, 13 percent of which came from the speed variations of individual electric motors.

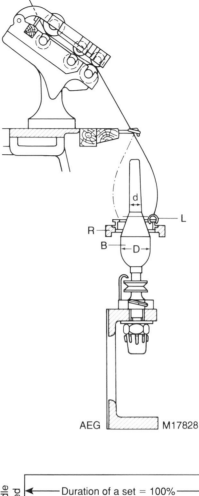

Figure 4. Diagram of a spinning machine. B = Kötzer–cop; D = Kötzerdurchmesser–cop diameter; L = Läufer–runner; R = Ringbank–ring bank; d = Hülsendurchmesser–tube diameter.

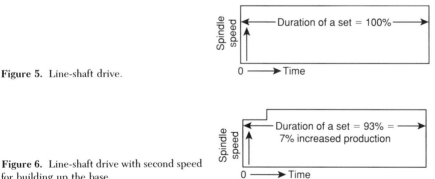

Figure 5. Line-shaft drive.

Figure 6. Line-shaft drive with second speed for building up the base.

The only problem left was how to govern the speed of the motor to follow this ideal curve. There had to be an additional element between the ring spindle and the motor to allow the position of the yarn on the cop to regulate the motor speed. And as with the back gear, in order to create a new market for their products, the elec-

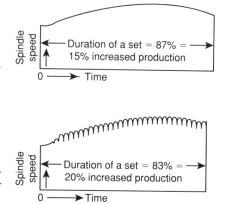

Figure 7. Electric individual drive with spinning regulator for the basic speed.

Figure 8 Electrical individual drive with regulator varying the spindle speed for each layer of the cop.

trical manufacturers were determined to find a solution to this problem. They tested dozens of ring-spindle machines, using stroboscopic light and sophisticated measuring equipment, which they had developed. The result of this R&D in the spinning process was the spinning regulator, a purely mechanical device that used the shifting level of the yarn, and consequently the shape of the cop, to adjust the rheostat that controlled the motor speed.[36]

Second Conclusion

The motors that were eventually designed for these spinning machines in the 1920s—like the papermaking machines, which had similar characteristics—were a combination of a dc and an ac motor, and were polyphase commutator motors (a polyphase stator with a dc rotor).[37] They were universally adopted in paper and textile mills, but not for machine tools, for which they were heavily advertised as an improved alternative to the ill-fated dc motor.[38] The reason for their success in the textile industry was that the ring-spindle machine had one single well-defined speed curve that could be governed by an automatic device, the spinning regulator. Speed regulation could be designed once and for all into the hardware, and was not left to the judgment of an unskilled or at best semiskilled worker who, for many reasons, might be tempted to act differently than foreseen by management, or might not even be able to assess and control the speed of his spinning machines as precisely as an automatic system could.

Where automatic devices, such as the spinning regulator, would not work because of the nonuniformity of the product and the frequent mounting of new workpieces, as in cutting metal, tables and written orders with specified speeds that came close to the optimum prevailed, rather than efforts to improve the skill or to increase the responsibility of the workers. Especially after the arrival of mass production, predictability was paramount among managements' concerns. Automation, tables, and "foolproof" machinery were ways of achieving it. A technology that required individual and spontaneous judgment on the part of the operators might have appealed to engineers, but it certainly did not to accountants.

Notes

1. Werner von Siemens, "Das naturwissenschaftliche Zeitalter," in Werner Siemens, *Wissenschaftliche Abhandlungen und Vorträge*, 2nd ed. (Berlin, 1889), pp. 491–499, especially pp. 498–499.

2. For a detailed account of this discussion and the introduction of electric motors in small workshops, see Ulrich Wengenroth, "Motoren für den Kleinbetrieb," in ed. Ulrich Wengenroth, *Prekäre Selbstandigkeit. Zur Standortbestimmung von Handwerk, Hausindustrie und Kleingewerbe im Industrialisierungsprozess* (Stuttgart: Steiner, 1989), pp. 177–205.

3. Sigfrid von Weiher and Herbert Goetzeler, *Weg und Wirken der Siemens-Werke im Fortschritt der Elektrotechnik 1847–1972* (München, 1972), p. 46.

4. On the various types of drives for small-scale industry, see J. O. Knoke, *Die Kraftmaschinen des Kleingewerbes* (Berlin 1887). (2. verbesserte und vermehrte Auflage, Berlin 1899)

5. Several examples from the early 1890s can be found in the Krupp archives, Essen, WA VII f 799, "Maschinenantriebe auf der Gußstahlfabrik."

6. Wilhelm Stiel, *Textile Electrification. A Treatise on the Application of Electricity in Textile Factories* (London: Routledge, 1933), pp. 124–125.

7. See the Siemens archives, Munich, SAA 35/30 Ls 223.

8. Karl Meller, *Einzelantrieb von Werkzeugmaschinen. Ein Hilfsbuch für alle Metall verarbeitenden Betriebe* (Leipzig: Hirzel, 1927), p. 5. On cottage weavers, see E. R. Lembcke, "Versuche zur Erheltung des Hausweberei-Betriebes im stadt- und Landbezirke Crefeld," in *Leipziger Monatschrift für Textil-Industrie*, Vol. 6, 1886, pp. 230–234; Vol. 7, 1886, pp. 280–281. For Switzerland, see Fritz Grieder, *Glanz und Niedergang der Baselbieter Heimposamenterei im 19. und 20. Jahrhundert* (Liestal: Kantonale Schul-und Büromaterialverwaltung, 1985), especially pp. 166–172.

9. See the documentation of the Berliner Gewerbeaufsicht for 1892, in Gerd Henninger, "Zu einigen Problemen der Elektrifizierung der Berliner Industriebetriebe von den Anfängen bis zum Beginn des 20. Jahrhunderts," in *Berliner Geschichte*, Vol. 2 (Berlin, 1981), pp. 46–51.

10. Georg Elten, "Einzelantrieb oder Gruppenantrieb?," *Maschinenbau—Betr.*, Vol. 12, No. 6, 1933, p. 164.

11. Texropes, or V-belts, which came from the United States, made their first appearance in Europe in Italy in 1929, where they were produced under license by the Soc. An. P. Alberzoni, Milano, which also supplied the German market. "Zeitschrift für die gesamte Textilindustrie," Vol. 32, No. 10, 1929, p. 175.

12. Allgemeine Elektrizitäts Gesellschaft, *Elektrischer Einzelantrieb in den Maschinenbauwerkstätten der A.E.G.* (Berlin: AEG, 1899), p. 85.

13. Ibid., p. 65.

14. Otto Lasche, "Elektrischer Antrieb mittels Zahnradübertragung," *Z. Ver. Dtsch. Ing.*, Vol. 33, 1899, pp. 1417–1422, 1487–1493, 1528–1533, 1563–1569.

15. See, for example, the sales documentation in AEG archives document number X.179, "Elektrischer Einzelantrieb von Webstühlen, Verzeichnis der ausgeführten Einzelantriebe." Also *AEG-Ztg.*, January 1911, p. 99; also Stiel, op. cit., p. 11.

16. W. Kübler, "Elektrische Einzelantriebe," *Z. Ver. Dtsch. Ing.*, Vol. 52, No. 22, 1908, p. 88.

17. Stiel, op. cit., p. 108.

18. Stiel, op. cit., p. 109.

19. Stiel, op. cit., p. 112.

20. For a more detailed discussion of early electric drives in the textile industry, see Ulrich Wengenroth, "L'électrification dans l'industrie textile," (forthcoming in a collection of articles to be edited by the Association pour l'histoire d'électricité, Paris, 1992).

21. J. Irtenkauf, "Die Drehzahlnormung. Anwendung und Auswirkung bei spanabhebenden Werkzeugmaschinen," *Maschinenbau–Betr.*, Vol. 12, No. 2, 1933, pp. 39–43.

22. P. Möller, "Die Weltausstellung in Lüttich 1905," *Z. Ver. Dtsch. Ing.*, Vol. 49, No. 36, 1905, p. 1457; also Henry Behrens, "Werkzeugmaschinen," *Maschinenbau–Betr.*, Vol. 8, No. 11, 1929, p. 348.

23. On the many shortcomings of early gearboxes during the first two decades of the twentieth century, see Friedrich Schwerd, *Spanenden Werkzeugmaschinen* (Berlin, 1956), p. 171; and "Elektromotorischer Einzelantrieb an Werkzeugmaschinen," *Loewe Not.*, Vol. 6, October–November 1921, p. 83.

24. Notably trams, for example, but also cranes and conveyor belts.

25. H. Hoffmann, "Maschinenwirtschaft in Hüttenwerken," *Z. Ver. Dtsch. Ing.*, Vol. 56, 1912, p. 508.

26. Early examples of up to 25,000 kW can be found in ibid., pp. 511–514.

27. Ulrich Wengenroth, "Die Elektrifizierung der Antriebe im Stahlwerk. Kräne und Walzwerksantriebe bis zum Ersten Weltkrieg," in ed. Horst A. Wessel *Elektrotechnik— Signale, Aufbruch, Perspektiven* (Berlin: VDE-Verlag, 1988), pp. 77–83.

28. Allegemeine Elektrizitäts Gesellschaft, *Elektrizität im Eisenhüttenwerk* (Berlin: AEG, 1922), p. 141.

29. H. Bonte, "Einfluβ der Groβgasmaschine auf die Entwicklung der Hüttenwerke," *Z. Ver. Dtsch. Ing.*, Vol. 52, 1908, p. 1914.

30. AEG, *Elektrizität im Eisenhüttenwerk*, op. cit., p. 142.

31. See "Drehstrom-Kommutatormotoren in der Papier- und Textilindustrie," AEG archives, document number G 4/1083, September 1932.

32. "Elektrischer Antrieb von Ringspinnmaschinen," AEG archives, document number G 4/2008, p. 3.

33. Stiel, op. cit., p. 208.

34. Ibid.

35. Ibid.

36. "Schablonen-Spinnregler," AEG archives, document number J 4/T 34a; see also Stiel, op. cit., pp. 251–256.

37. See "Drehstromnebenschluβ-Spinnkommutatormotoren—Ausgeführte Anlagen," AEG archives, document number J 4/T 11.

38. Meller, op. cit., pp. 102–103.

Competition and Consolidation in the Electrical Manufacturing Industry, 1889–1892

W. Bernard Carlson

Introduction

Competition and consolidation are the yin and yang of American business. On the one hand, we frequently celebrate the competitive aspects of the American economy, claiming that it is the spirit of competition that stirs men and women to devise new technology, marketing plans, and other innovations. And yet while we love to root for the heroic entrepreneur or inventor, citing their successes as a sign of the inherent goodness of American society, we often forget Joseph Schumpeter's point that competition is creative and wasteful. On the other hand, consolidation—the creation of large firms—is equally important to the success of the American economy. As many historians have argued, large complex corporations were essential in order to produce and distribute goods to large numbers of Americans. Without the rise of big business, Americans in the twentieth century would not have come to enjoy their high standard of living, whether it be measured in terms of the low cost of mass-produced goods, the variety of goods available, or the availability of low-cost energy. To be sure, big business has presented many challenges to American culture, in terms of the concentration of power, the standardization of products and experiences, or the exploitation of workers and consumers. Thus, consolidation is every bit as important in the shaping of American business as is competition.[1]

Despite the importance of both competition and consolidation in the American economy, how much do we know about how these two modes influence each other? How does competition give way to consolidation in certain industries at certain times? In particular, during the first three-quarters of the nineteenth century, much of American business was highly competitive, consisting of large numbers of small firms offering one or two products to local or regional markets. Yet between 1875 and

287

1900, the American economy witnessed the rise of large firms using high-speed, high-volume technology to distribute goods throughout the United States and overseas. How did this remarkable change come about?[2]

Historians have suggested that a wide number of factors contributed to the rise of big business in the United States in the last quarter of the nineteenth century. To be sure, a rapidly growing population meant ready markets and an ample low-cost labor force. Similarly, evolving legal doctrines concerning the corporation and a minimum of government regulation created a favorable environment for creating large firms. Yet the most persuasive argument has centered on technological change and national markets. As Alfred D. Chandler, Jr., has demonstrated in his seminal studies of American business, managers frequently created large complex organizations in order to exploit the economies of speed, scale, and scope inherent in the technologies they were using. In order to use new production processes effectively, businesspeople often had to coordinate several functions or activities within a single firm, thus leading them to create larger and more complex companies. In a similar fashion, as they produced larger quantities of goods, some managers were confronted by problems in distributing goods to the national market, and this led them to create extensive marketing organizations for handling advertising, distribution, and sales.[3]

While I believe that Chandler is correct in pointing to new technology and new national markets as two of the key factors shaping the creation of big business, the case of General Electric suggests that other factors were equally significant. First, I agree with Lance Davis that the undeveloped state of the capital markets in the United States exacerbated competition and favored consolidation in the electrical manufacturing industry.[4] Second, I think that Chandler and economist William Lazonick are correct in suggesting that entrepreneurs and managers often struggle to assemble the right combination of factories, distribution networks, and technological expertise—what they call organizational capability—and consequently they are loathe to let anyone or anything force them to dismantle this capability.[5] And third, I have found it interesting that the key figures in the rise of General Electric— Charles Coffin, Henry L. Higginson, George Westinghouse, and Thomas Edison— possessed differing views about competition and consolidation. Most significantly, Coffin and Higginson came to realize that competition would be undeniably wasteful of their organizational capability, while Edison and Westinghouse fought to the bitter end to maintain competition.

Consequently, in this chapter, I will use the story of General Electric to explore the interplay of competition and consolidation in the American electrical industry in the late nineteenth century. I will begin by sketching the key players in the industry and describing how they competed with one another. Next, I will discuss their needs for capital and how these firms struggled to find long-term financing. With this background in place, I will narrate the various attempts by Henry Villard, Coffin, and the banking interests to overcome competition and the problems of securing capital by consolidating the major firms in the industry. These attempts culminated in the creation of General Electric in 1892. In my conclusion, I will highlight what I think this case reveals about competition and consolidation in the American economy, and what lessons we might draw from it.

The First Movers

By 1889, three firms had emerged as dominant players in the industry: Thomson-Houston, Edison General Electric, and Westinghouse Electric. Each of these firms promoted central stations, and each had made the investment necessary to implement that strategy; they had developed large-scale production facilities, national and international distribution networks, and expertise in engineering and invention. Armed with such organization capability, each firm was determined to exploit its potential, through either economies of scale (such as utilizing their large factories) or economics of scope (such as expanding into related product areas).[6]

As I have discussed elsewhere, Thomson-Houston clearly had the capability to implement the central-station strategy. Founded in 1882 by a group of shoe manufacturers in Lynn, Massachusetts, this firm initially concentrated on manufacturing and marketing Elihu Thomson's arc-lighting system. Under Charles Coffin's leadership, Thomson-Houston perfected a new marketing strategy of selling lighting equipment to groups of local businesspeople who established central station utility companies. By 1889, Thomson-Houston had a large plant in Lynn producing a diversified product line of arc lighting, incandescent lighting, and street-railway systems. To market and distribute those systems, the firm had a sales and engineering force to help local businesspeople develop utility and traction companies. Likewise, to coordinate production and distribution, Coffin had developed a managerial staff organized along functional lines. And to provide a steady stream of new products and improvements, the firm employed Thomson, Charles Van Depoele, and Hermann Lemp.[7]

Although Edison and his associates had been major players in the electrical industry throughout the 1880s, it was only in April 1889 that their significant resources were brought together as the Edison General Electric Company. Organized by financier Henry Villard, Edison General was a consolidation of Edison's various electrical manufacturing concerns (Fig. 1). Drawing on his connections with major German banks, Villard capitalized the new company at $12 million. J. P. Morgan and his partners, Edison's bankers, also invested in the new company. Once established, Villard took the title of president, but left day-to-day management to Samuel Insull, Edison's personal secretary. With the help of Edison, Insull created a national sales organization with seven regional districts, all of which reported to a sales vice president. Insull also established an intelligence department at the company's New York headquarters that collected and analyzed sales data. For production, Edison General had the enormous machine works at Schenectady, a lamp factory at Harrison, New Jersey, and a plant in New York City. Although the company continued to focus on dc incandescent lighting systems, it contracted with Edison's new laboratory at West Orange, New Jersey, to develop better lamps, a multipolar dynamo, and a new meter. Insull hoped that Edison would develop an ac lighting system and a street railway, but Edison instead threw his energies into developing his phonograph and ore-milling ventures.[8] Edison General had access to the "wizard" and his laboratory, but it had no guarantee that Edison would put the needs of the company ahead of his own goals. Unlike Thomson-Houston, Edison General had not fully integrated the innovation function into its organization.

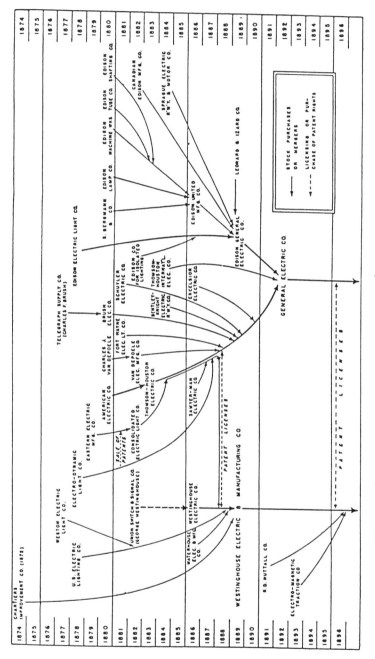

Figure 1. Evolution of General Electric and Westinghouse companies, 1872–96. Reprinted with permission of Macmillan Publishing company from *The Electric Lamp Industry: Technological Change and Economic Development from 1800 to 1947*, by Arthur A. Bright. Copyright 1949 The Macmillan Company; copyright renewed 1975 Evelyn F. Hitchcock.

By 1889 Westinghouse Electric Company had also emerged as a leading firm in the electrical manufacturing industry. Westinghouse had established its reputation by pioneering ac incandescent lighting, but the company had moved quickly into other product areas, including ac industrial motors and street railways. Through a patent-sharing agreement with Thomson-Houston, Westinghouse secured a foothold in the arc-lighting field. To develop its products, Westinghouse employed several inventors, including Nikola Tesla, William Stanley, and Oliver Shallenberger. In terms of production facilities, the company had plants in Pittsburgh (Garrison Alley) and Newark, New Jersey (formerly the United States Electric Lighting Company). For distribution, Westinghouse depended on a small sales force working on commission out of offices in six or seven major cities. Unlike its rivals, Westinghouse lacked a managerial hierarchy; instead, George Westinghouse supervised factory operations, participated in product design, and negotiated many of the major contracts.[9]

For all three firms, it required substantial capital, technical expertise, and entrepreneurial effort to become a major player in the electrical manufacturing industry. Consequently, once they had assembled their factories, sales forces, and inventors, they fought hard to maintain and expand their market shares. Even though the market for electric lighting and power was substantial in the United States, the need to sustain their established capabilities led those firms to keen competition in the early 1890s.

Competition

Competition among the three firms took several forms. First, they competed vigorously for contracts to supply complete lighting systems and street-railway systems to towns and cities. For example, in 1890, Thomson-Houston, Edison General, and Westinghouse bid $25,000, $60,000, and $70,000, respectively, to provide equipment to electric companies in Ironwood and Bessemer, Michigan.[10] Although Edison General cut prices on individual components, such as incandescent lamps and streetcar motors, the other two firms generally did not follow suit.[11] Instead, Thomson-Houston and Westinghouse offered utility companies low prices for complete systems, hoping that the profits would come by way of power plant expansion and sales of replacement equipment. As Coffin explained, "once we have [brought] our system into use [in a town or city], other companies may offer prices twenty-five percent lower, but the users willingly pay our price as they cannot afford to change the system."[12] However, as utility companies sought to lower the unit costs of lighting and power by expanding their service territories, they demanded larger generating plants and distribution networks from the electrical manufacturers. Although the manufacturers could reap handsome profits on a large installation, they also knew that they could lose a great deal if they had to submit an extremely low bid to secure the contract. Consequently, as systems grew in complexity and cost, the risk involved in competitive bidding became a mounting concern for the managers of the leading firms.

In competing for contracts for complete systems, Thomson-Houston and Edison General employed a second tactic of integrating forward into the construction and operation of central stations. Although Thomson-Houston had a large force of sales agents and field engineers who reported directly to headquarters, it established in 1887 a subsidiary, the Northwest Electric Construction and Supply Company (also known as Northwest Thomson-Houston), which specialized in the promotion and construction of central stations. Headquartered in Saint Paul, Minnesota, Northwest Thomson-Houston sold electrical equipment to the growing cities and towns of the upper Midwest and Pacific Northwest. With its own sales agents and construction engineers, Northwest Thomson-Houston could move into a city, organize a central-station company with local capital and management, market the company's bonds in Boston, sell a full line of equipment, and build a complete plant. In providing these services, Northwest Thomson-Houston took advantage of economies of scope to meet the vigorous competition for contracts. Northwest Thomson-Houston was a logical step in Thomson-Houston's overall strategy of central-station development, and that subsidiary captured a large portion of the market, at least in Wisconsin.[13]

In connection with Edison General, Villard established the North American Company in June 1890 to promote Edison central stations in the Midwest. North American was capitalized at $50 million, with backing from both the German banks and Morgan. With ample capital in hand, North American took over and enlarged the Edison lighting companies in Cincinnati, Saint Paul, and Minneapolis. In Milwaukee, Villard used North American to consolidate the existing street-railway and lighting companies into a single $5-million utility company. Unlike Thomson-Houston, which accepted only bonds as partial payment for equipment from utilities, North American accepted as much as four-fifths of the stock of an Edison utility as payment. Villard further insisted that Edison General sell central-station equipment only to North American "at factory prices, free of all royalty or profits, direct or indirect." By controlling large blocks of stock and being the sole source of Edison central-station equipment, Villard hoped to use the North American Company to gain complete control of incandescent lighting in the United States.[14]

Not only did the major firms integrate vertically and create subsidiaries, but as a third tactic they integrated horizontally and took over smaller firms in the field (Fig. 1). Between 1888 and 1891 Thomson-Houston spent $4 million purchasing control of seven firms in the arc-lighting and street-railway fields. At the same time, Westinghouse bought out the United States Electric Lighting Company and the Consolidated Electric Light Company for their incandescent-lamp patents and the Waterhouse Electric Light Company for its arc-lighting system. In creating Edison General, Villard brought in two non-Edison firms, Leonard & Izard (a small central-station construction firm) and the Sprague Electric Railway & Motor Company. In all cases, the leading firms absorbed minor concerns in order to gain market share and to prevent valuable patents from falling into the hands of the rivals. However, they were also anxious to secure the services of inventors, reminding us again that the knowledge of the new technology was embodied in individuals, not books or theories. Although Thomson-Houston continued to operate the large Brush factory in Cleveland, the smaller factories were closed, and their inventors were transferred to the major plants in Lynn, Schenectady, and Pittsburgh.[15]

As a fourth tactic, electrical manufacturers used patents in a variety of ways. Not only did they purchase smaller rivals to acquire their patents, but they used patents to shape their relationship with their customers, the central-station utilities. Patents allowed the manufacturer to exert influence over its customers; by requiring them to become licensees, the manufacturer could attempt to force its customers to buy equipment exclusively from it. At the same time, patents were necessary to attract central-station customers because they conveyed to central-station officials the hope of monopoly power. In order to convince local businesspeople to invest heavily in a new utility, frequently each electrical manufacturer would claim that it alone held the key patents for a particular type of system (arc, incandescent, or railway) and that it would prosecute all patent infringers. In making such promises, the manufacturer wanted the local businesspeople to believe that they would face little or no competition in the utility field.[16]

As competition increased in the late 1880s, the three leading firms did not hesitate to use patent litigation to attack each other. In 1887 Thomson-Houston launched a comprehensive attack against all who had infringed the patent for Thomson's dynamo regulator. That campaign helped wear down several of Thomson-Houston's major arc-lighting competitors and facilitated the acquisition of those firms by Thomson-Houston. Similarly, Westinghouse sued Thomson-Houston in 1887 for infringing its Gaulard–Gibbs transformer patent, leading to a patent-sharing agreement with Thomson-Houston.[17]

Of the major firms, the Edison organization was the most energetic in licensing its central-station customers and proclaiming the strength of its patents. As early as 1885 the Edison group began suing both nonlicensed utility companies and competing lamp manufacturers for patent infringement. As competition with Westinghouse and Thomson-Houston increased in the late 1880s, the Edison organization increased the intensity of its legal actions. Edison's lawyers instituted proceedings against a hundred or more infringers, but they devoted most of their energy to trying a single case against the United States Electric Lighting Company, concerned with incandescent-lamp filaments. (Because Westinghouse subsequently purchased U.S. Electric, this case was effectively against Westinghouse.) After a long and involved trial in federal court, in July 1891 Judge William Wallace ruled in favor of Edison, sustaining his claim to have invented the first incandescent lamp with a high-resistance carbon filament in a sealed bulb.[18]

It has been thought that the 1891 patent victory gave Edison General a decisive edge over Westinghouse and Thomson-Houston and permitted Edison General to force Thomson-Houston to submit to the merger that formed General Electric.[19] Yet the court decision had sustained only one claim of the original lamp patent, and both Westinghouse and Thomson-Houston found ways to work around that patent. Westinghouse avoided further infringement by developing a "stopper lamp," which was used in the elaborate incandescent-lighting displays at the 1893 Chicago World's Fair.[20] Thomson-Houston welcomed the decision, because Coffin was confident that he could negotiate a patent agreement with Edison General. As Coffin wrote to Henry L. Higginson:

> we believe the decision [sustaining Edison's patent] to be better for our interests than it would be to have the invention thrown open to the public, as we can far better afford to arrange with the Edison Co. than to compete with the fifty or more smaller manufacturers.[21]

Rather than giving one firm a decisive advantage over the others, patent litigation among the major firms served other purposes. It permitted them to weaken and absorb smaller firms, and it allowed one firm to force short-term changes on another. Most important, litigation demanded substantial amounts of time and money; by attacking Thomson-Houston and Westinghouse, the Edison organization hoped to force its competitors to divert resources away from further improvements in their organizational capabilities.

Along with patent litigation, the leading firms mounted publicity campaigns attacking each other. One example of this fifth tactic is how Westinghouse interfered with Thomson-Houston's efforts to secure a revised corporate charter. In late 1888, Thomson-Houston decided to amend its charter in order to enlarge its authorized capitalization and secure the right to manufacture and sell street-railway equipment. Because the company was chartered in Connecticut, Thomson-Houston had to petition the state legislature for a special act. In the course of all that effort, pro-Westinghouse interests vigorously opposed the bill, with the goal of preventing Thomson-Houston from entering the railway field and competing with Westinghouse. During the legislative struggle, Edward H. Johnson of the Edison organization wrote to Coffin, stating that he considered the Westinghouse action unfair and offering to help Thomson-Houston fight Westinghouse on the matter. With this assistance, Thomson-Houston secured its revised charter in 1889.[22] Clearly, this episode reveals the range of tactics that the major firms were willing to employ to prevent competitors from gaining any advantage.

By far the most significant publicity campaign was that mounted by the Edison organization attacking Westinghouse and alternating current.[23] Although Edison and his laboratory staff at West Orange were capable of designing ac lighting and power systems, Edison chose not to do so because he believed that power losses in the available transformers made such a system uneconomical.[24] Instead, Edison concentrated on improving the efficiency of his dc system, in the belief that the Edison organization would attract more customers as the cost of lighting decreased.[25] However, as both Westinghouse and Thomson-Houston began installing high-voltage ac plants, the Edison organization found itself unable to secure contracts in towns and cities with low population densities. (Because of the high cost of copper mains, the Edison system was economical only in populous urban districts where copper costs could be spread across a large customer base.) Edison managers became especially frustrated in the late 1880s when they came to believe that Westinghouse had beaten them on major contracts in Denver and Minneapolis by submitting unrealistically low bids.[26] Feeling that Westinghouse had already acted unethically, Francis S. Hastings, treasurer of the Edison Electric Light Company, launched a publicity campaign depicting ac and the "death current."[27] In doing so, he enlisted several allies who had already begun to question the safety of ac systems. Those allies included Harold P. Brown, a consulting electrical engineer who had already tangled with Westinghouse, and a group of New York City physicians who were investigating electrocution as an alternative form of capital punishment. Working through Brown and the physicians, the Edison organization whipped up public hysteria about the dangers of alternating current and surreptitiously arranged for it to be used in the first electrocution at Sing Sing prison in 1890. The Edison group also tried to convince several state legislatures to limit the maximum voltage of electrical systems to 300 volts, and they came very close to securing such legislation in Ohio and Virginia.[28]

The "battle of the systems" between Edison and Westinghouse gradually ended as Thomson, Charles Steinmetz, and other engineers improved the safety of ac systems, increased the efficiency of transformers, and introduced rotary converters to link ac and dc systems.[29] In addition, many central-station customers installed ac systems because it allowed them to distribute electricity over greater areas and thus serve more consumers. Yet the battle was significant as another facet of the struggle among leading firms to maintain their organizational capabilities.

Through these five tactics—competing for contracts, integrating forward into central-station development, absorbing minor firms, patent litigation, and publicity attacks—the major players struggled to sustain and improve their positions in the industry. Notably, when considered together, these five tactics suggest differences in the levels of organizational capability of the leading firms. Thomson-Houston and Westinghouse concentrated on improving their organizational capabilities by adding resources (such as buying minor firms or enlarging factories) and by making special efforts to coordinate these resources (such as arranging for in-house inventors to work on key products). Of course, Thomson-Houston went even further than Westinghouse in terms of organization building by developing a national sales network and a managerial hierarchy. In contrast, Edison General appears to have focused its efforts less on building its organizational capability and more on shaping the marketplace. Rather than improve the internal coordination of resources, Edison General chose to engage in price competition, patent litigation, and, ultimately, a major publicity attack on Westinghouse. To some extent, Edison General may have pursued these tactics because they appealed to Edison, but in general, the key decisions in this company were made by Insull, Hastings, and other professional managers. Although it may seem obvious to us that a policy of building organizational capability will lead to long-term growth, we must keep in mind that the Edison managers were among the first to be faced with the challenge of building a large, well-coordinated manufacturing firm, and they did not necessarily see what is obvious to us in hindsight. Instead, they framed a policy that made sense to them, based on their own business experience.[30]

Another important point is that these tactics required substantial amounts of capital, especially for the acquisition of small firms and patent litigation. Yet electrical manufacturing was already a capital-intensive business, requiring enormous amounts of money to develop full product lines, build major factories, and establish national sales networks. As Villard wrote to Drexel, Morgan & Co. in March 1890:

> the general business of the Edison General Electric Company is growing at a rate that is equally surprising and gratifying. This growth has rendered the provision for working capital made upon the organization of the Company entirely inadequate. Instead of one million, several millions are imperatively wanted to meet the current demands of the several manufacturing departments.[31]

Already a capital-intensive business, competition made the electrical industry even more unstable financially in the early 1890s.

The Search for Capital

The major electrical manufacturers found themselves in precarious positions because they had become capital-intensive enterprises prior to the development of capital markets suited to large-scale industrial expansion. Before 1890, individuals tended to invest surplus capital in real estate, and the stock exchanges in New York and other cities dealt only in railroad securities. Most manufacturing enterprises were private partnerships that did not offer stocks or bonds for sale to the general public. The exceptions to this pattern were the New England textile mills, which marketed securities through two Boston brokerage houses (Lee, Higginson & Co. and Kidder, Peabody). As a result, many manufacturers found it difficult to secure capital for expansion. Frequently, their only recourse was to borrow short-term money from commercial banks for long-term investment in plants and repay the loans out of large immediate earnings. Such a strategy was adequate in a period of economic expansion, but it often led to bankruptcy when business conditions worsened. Partly in response to the lack of available capital, firms in other capital-intensive industries (e.g., sugar refining, whiskey distilling, lead smelting) developed "trusts" in the late 1880s as a means of pooling capital and ownership.[32]

Thomson-Houston secured ample capital for expansion and competition by allying itself with the Boston brokerage house of Lee, Higginson & Co. Headed by Henry L. Higginson, this firm had made its fortune through the promotion of the Calumet & Hecla copper mines of northern Michigan. Building on that experience, Higginson specialized in the development of industrial securities. Higginson probably became associated with Thomson-Houston when the firm introduced its "trust series" for reselling central-station bonds. In 1889, Higginson helped Thomson-Houston offer one of the first industrial issues of preferred stock. (Preferred stock issues were popular with conservative investors, because dividends were paid on preferred shares before common shares.) By the early 1890s Higginson was assisting Thomson-Houston in raising money for takeovers, selling large blocks of Northwest Thomson-Houston stock, and financing street-railway companies. To facilitate these financial efforts, Coffin corresponded regularly with Higginson, sharing market data and consulting about strategy.[33]

Neither Edison General nor Westinghouse had a similar alliance with a powerful investment house that provided a steady flow of capital. In building up the Schenectady works for Edison General, Insull doubled the value of the plant from $750,000 to $1.5 million, but only by juggling numerous short-term loans and operating with a cash holding of less than $10,000. Drexel, Morgan & Co. did lend money to Edison General, but the Morgan partners were more interested in investing in Edison central stations in New York and Boston than in improving the factories.[34] Insull and Villard probably intended to expand operations by plowing back profits, but that proved difficult because Edison General accepted so much utility stock as payment for central-station equipment. In the fall of 1890, with the passage of the Sherman Silver Purchase Act and the failure of the London brokerage house of Baring Brothers, the German bankers lost confidence in Villard and recalled their loans to Edison General. These developments weakened Edison General and completely crippled the North American Company. In response, Villard ordered Insull to sell equipment only for cash or short-term credit, and in January 1891 he decided to raise $3 million through a new stock issue.[35]

Westinghouse also faced the problem of earning enough to pay off its short-term loans, and this problem nearly bankrupted the company. Thanks to the company's innovative ac equipment, Westinghouse annual sales jumped from $800,000 in 1887 to $4 million in 1890. As sales boomed, though, Westinghouse had to develop an engineering staff and enlarge its factories. At the same time, Westinghouse joined the other major firms in buying out smaller companies and engaging in vigorous patent litigation. Amazed by his rival's bold and rapid growth, Edison commented in 1889 that

> [George Westinghouse's] methods of doing business lately are such that it cannot be accounted for on any other grounds than the man has gone crazy over the sudden accession of wealth, or something unknown to me, and is flying a kite that will land him sooner or later in the mud.[36]

Westinghouse partly financed this expansion by advancing the company $1.2 million of his own money, but he also borrowed heavily. By mid-1890, the firm was carrying $3 million in short-term liabilities, when its total assets were $11 million and its current assets $2.5 million. As with Edison General, disaster struck in November 1890 with the failure of Baring Brothers, and Westinghouse's creditors called in their loans. In response, Westinghouse proposed to reorganize the company and double its capital stock, but investors failed to take up the new issue. Westinghouse next asked Pittsburgh bankers for an immediate loan of $500,000; however, they insisted that Westinghouse relinquish control of the company, and Westinghouse refused. In desperation, Westinghouse turned to the New York brokerage house of August Belmont. With the help of Higginson, Belmont set up a committee of powerful investors who reorganized the firm. Viewing Westinghouse as "a bright & fertile mechanic" who lacked both tact and an understanding of high finance, the committee initially tried to circumscribe his power. However, drawing on his friendship with committee member Charles Francis Adams, Jr., Westinghouse persuaded the committee to let him to continue as president.[37]

Cooperation and Consolidation

Concerned about their continuing problems in raising capital, the top management of the electrical companies concluded that relentless competition might well be fatal for all of their firms. Consequently, Villard early on investigated the possibility of cooperation among the three firms. Perhaps drawing on his extensive experience in Wall Street maneuvers, Villard shrewdly established relationships with both Westinghouse and Coffin. At first, Villard simply exchanged information on production, sales, and earnings with each man, but soon he was attempting to negotiate a patent agreement with Westinghouse and fix contract bids with Coffin. For instance, in February 1889, Villard and Coffin agreed that Sprague would not bid on a street-railway contract in Washington, D.C., provided that Thomson-Houston not compete for a railway contract in Richmond, Virginia. Similarly, in 1891, Villard sent an Edison General manager to meet with Coffin to negotiate the bids that Edison General and Thomson-Houston would submit for four street-railway contracts. Charles Fairchild, a Higginson partner, estimated that those negotiations saved the two companies $1.5 million, leading him to conclude that "the Co[mpanie]s in harmony get that much more than they would in Competition."[38] Although Villard had little success in cultivating a relationship with Westinghouse, such behind-the-scenes negotiations appealed to Coffin and helped establish rapport between Edison General and Thomson-Houston.

As Villard pursued a policy of cooperation, Coffin boldly proposed consolidation. In March 1889, just as Edison General was being organized, Coffin outlined a possible merger, arguing that continued competition and patent litigation would ruin both Edison General and Thomson-Houston. Coffin may have suggested that a larger consolidated company could work with Higginson to secure ample capital. Although Villard politely declined the proposal on the grounds it would be difficult to convert Edison General's stock to match that of Thomson-Houston, he let Edison demolish Coffin's plan. Enraged by the audacity that Thomson-Houston would even think of taking over his company, Edison attacked Thomson-Houston as "amateurs" who had "boldly appropriated and infringed every patent we use." As far as Edison was personally concerned, a merger would mean that "my usefulness as an inventor is gone. My services wouldn't be worth a penny. I can only invent under powerful incentive. No competition means no invention." Instead, Edison believed that the best policy for Edison General would be to reduce the cost of electric lighting through more efficient products and better manufacturing techniques.[39]

Although Edison still believed in competition, Higginson and the other investors came to agree with the managers that consolidation offered the only means of protecting their substantial investment in the electrical companies. J. P. Morgan was especially concerned with how much capital was required by the electrical manufacturers, but at the same time he was uncertain as to how Edison General and Thomson-Houston might be joined. As he observed to Higginson in February 1891:

> regarding Thomson-Houston, I do not think it worth while to run two establishments. The Edison system affords us all the use of time and capital that I think desirable to use in one channel. If, as would seem to be the case, you have the control of the Thomson-Houston, we will see which will make the best result. I do not see myself how the two things can be brought together, certainly not on any such basis as was talked about a year or more ago.[40]

Just as railroad leaders and financiers had concluded a few years earlier that competition and cooperation had to give way to consolidation, so the electrical manufacturers and their financiers were coming to realize that the competitive tactics of takeovers, patent litigation, and the creation of central-station subsidiaries were proving costly and ineffective. It seemed obvious to both the managers and bankers that they only way to manufacture and market electrical equipment profitably was to concentrate the necessary resources in a single firm. "What we all want," wrote Charles Fairchild, a Higginson partner, in July 1891, "is the union of the large Electrical Companies." Accordingly, during the reorganization of Westinghouse, Belmont and Fairchild attempted to arrange for Thomson-Houston to take control of the troubled Pittsburgh firm. That merger attempt failed not only because Westinghouse persuaded the committee that he should remain as president but also because Coffin antagonized the reorganization committee by letting it be known that he preferred to see Westinghouse fail.[41]

The Creation of General Electric

Unable to bring Thomson-Houston and Westinghouse together, Higginson and Fairchild encouraged Coffin and Villard to investigate combining their two companies. Villard and Coffin continued to exchange information on street-railway contracts and technology, and in February 1891 Villard visited the Thomson-Houston factory in Lynn. During the next eight months, little progress was made toward consolidation, perhaps because Villard may have felt more confident after winning a favorable decision in the litigation over the lamp patent in June. In the meantime, though, Thomson-Houston was beating Edison General in the marketplace, or, as Coffin boasted, "he is knocking the stuffing out of them all along the line." For 1891, Thomson-Houston had total sales of $10 million, and $2.7 million in profits, whereas Edison General had sales of $11 million and profits of only $1.4 million.[42]

Such marketplace performance may finally have brought Edison General to the bargaining table. Perhaps the major stockholders realized that although Edison General possessed substantial resources—large factories, a national sales network, and access to Edison's laboratory—Insull and the firm's top managers had not succeeded in creating an effective organization. Consequently, in early 1892, Coffin and Fish began negotiating a merger with Hamilton McKay Twombly, a Morgan associate who represented Edison General. The negotiations focused on the issue that Villard had raised in 1889, namely, the exchange of Edison and Thomson-Houston shares. Even though Thomson-Houston had earned 50 percent more per share than Edison General in 1891, Fairchild recommended that Coffin offer to assign a higher value to the Edison shares because "for the sake of union T-H can afford to give them a good trade." Coffin proposed that three common shares of Thomson-Houston be converted to five shares of the new company, with Edison General shares being converted one-to-one. That offer was accepted in February 1892, and a committee consisting of Twombly, J. P. Morgan, D. O. Mills, Frederick L. Ames, T. Jefferson Coolidge, and Higginson was organized to handle the exchange of stock and the creation of the new company. That committee met in March, and at Coffin's suggestion it secured a charter from the state of New York creating the General Electric Company (GE) on April 15, 1892[43] (Fig. 1).

General Electric was capitalized at $50 million; after U.S. Leather, it was the second largest merger prior to the financial panic of 1893. GE's board of directors consisted of six bankers, two Thomson-Houston men, and two Edison men, with Twombly as the chairman. The bankers included Morgan and his associates Charles H. Coster and Mills, and Higginson was joined by Boston financiers Coolidge and Ames. Representing Thomson-Houston were Coffin and Eugene Griffin, and they were balanced by Edison and Hastings. Thomson was also offered a directorship, but he declined it because he believed that it would keep him from his work as an inventor. Coffin was named president of the new company, and he selected most of his top managers from Thomson-Houston. The only Edison man to receive a major post was Insull, who was offered the position of second vice president; however, he chose to move to the presidency of Commonwealth Edison in Chicago.[44]

There were several reasons why GE was dominated by Coffin and Thomson-Houston men, not by Edison and his associates. First, at the time of the merger, Thomson-Houston was the more successful firm; in 1891, Thomson-Houston earned a return on capital of 26 percent, while Edison General earned only 11 percent. Anxious to see such profits continue, Higginson decided that Coffin and his associates should run the new company. Second, the other likely candidate for the presidency of GE, Villard, was not acceptable to the bankers. Involved in several business ventures (including the presidency of the Northern Pacific Railroad), Villard had had little to do with the management of Edison General. Moreover, his credibility had been severely damaged by the collapse of North American in the fall of 1890. Preoccupied with troubles on the Northern Pacific and campaigning for repeal of the Sherman Silver Purchase Act, Villard resigned as president of Edison General in February 1892. Thus, contrary to the claims of other historians, Villard played no part in the GE merger.[45] And finally, it had been Coffin, Higginson, and Fairchild—not Villard or Morgan—who had pushed through the merger. They had been seeking such a consolidation since 1889, and they took the lead in the negotiations. Consequently, Coffin and the Boston investors reaped the rewards of consolidation.

One might well ask why Westinghouse was not included in the merger of Edison General and Thomson-Houston. Higginson and Fairchild had participated in the reorganization of Westinghouse in 1891 and had hoped at that time to combine all three firms. It appears that such a merger was not possible because of the personal characteristics of George Westinghouse. Although the Boston bankers admired him as an engineer and entrepreneur, they questioned his understanding of finance and his ability to negotiate. As Fairchild explained:

> whatever power Westinghouse has, and I grant that it is great, is mechanical. His forte is the arrangement & control of a factory & in dealing with the practical problems. He is not a financier & he is not a negotiator. . . . What we all want is the union of the large Electrical Companies, and to bring this about will require skill & tact in the management of competing business as well as able negotiations when the time comes to trade. The final step will be to build up a disposition to trade—a willingness—Westinghouse cannot possibly do this. He irritates his rivals beyond endurance.[46]

Westinghouse particularly irritated his rival Coffin. Like the Edison managers, Coffin did not like the Westinghouse Company's "attitude of bitter and hostile competition"—an attitude reflected in the Pittsburgh firm's low bids on equipment contracts. Further, during the 1880s, when Thomson-Houston and Westinghouse shared the Sawyer–Man patents through the Consolidated Electric Light Company, Coffin felt that Westinghouse had been obstinate and difficult. At the same time, Westinghouse had little love for Coffin. Anecdotal evidence reveals that Westinghouse saw

Coffin as an aggressive wheeler-dealer who "will make a man about ten different propositions in ten minutes." Westinghouse had built up his business on the basis of engineering and manufacturing, and he had little respect for Coffin's understanding of marketing, finance, and organization building. Consequently, Westinghouse made it quite clear that he would not work with any electrical combination headed by Coffin.[47] Knowing of the animosity that had arisen between the two men, Higginson and Morgan probably decided that it was best not to attempt to include Westinghouse in the GE merger.

From another perspective, the Westinghouse Company may have been left out because it lacked a managerial hierarchy. Both the Edison and Thomson-Houston organizations had managerial and engineering staffs whose members could talk to each other. Ostensibly in competition, these staffs had been known to cooperate at times. As we have seen, Edison managers helped Thomson-Houston fight off Westinghouse and secure a revised corporate charter in 1888–1889. Under Villard's encouragement, Edison General and Thomson-Houston managers and salespeople had exchanged information about street-railway contracts. Although communications between the staffs of the two companies certainly did not cause the merger, such communications may have signaled to Higginson and Twombly that the combination of Edison General and Thomson-Houston would be feasible. In contrast, because George Westinghouse made most of the key decisions, the Westinghouse Company lacked a similar cadre of managers and engineers who might have interacted with their peers at Edison General or Thomson-Houston. Thus, there was no communications or managerial momentum to encourage the inclusion of Westinghouse in the merger.[48]

Conclusion

In his study of the electrical industry, Harold C. Passer argued that the formation of GE could be attributed to the patent situation and the desire of Thomson-Houston and Edison General to diversify their product lines.[49] As the foregoing narrative reveals, neither factor was as significant as Passer suggested. Although the ongoing patent litigation was costly, it had not created an impasse that could be resolved only by consolidation. Even though the court had found in favor of Edison in the incandescent-lamp case, both Westinghouse and Thomson-Houston had found ways to work around the Edison patent. Likewise, product diversification was not a major issue. To be sure, Edison General had focused on dc incandescent lights and motors, whereas Thomson-Houston had specialized in arc lighting and ac systems. However, through takeovers, patent agreements, and in-house research, both firms had taken steps to diversify their full product lines prior to the merger. Although it is not generally known, Edison's associates at West Orange experimented extensively with alternating current, high-voltage dc transmission, and rotary converters, all for the purpose of developing an alternative to their competitor's ac systems. Thus, neither patents nor incomplete product lines determined the creation of GE.

Instead, GE was the result of three other factors: the desire to eliminate competition, the problem of raising sufficient capital for a capital-intensive industry, and the efforts of managers and investors to maintain organizational capability. As we have seen, Thomson-Houston, Edison General, and Westinghouse competed fiercely between 1889 and 1892. Using a variety of tactics—new products, integrating forward into central-station construction and management, publicity campaigns, and patent litigation—each firm tried to expand its share of the market and increase its profits. However, whereas Edison and George Westinghouse firmly believed that such competition would lead to the survival of the fittest, Coffin, Villard, and their financial supporters soon realized that over the long run, competition was a poor use of resources and would lead to diminishing returns. Although the three firms could have continued to attack each other in the marketplace, the courts, and the technical and popular press, such attacks would have consumed capital and resources that could be better spent developing new products and improving manufacturing techniques. Well aware of the problems of competition. Coffin and Higginson chose to minimize it by merging with their chief rival, Edison General.[50]

The problem of competition in the electrical industry was compounded by the difficulties of raising capital for industrial enterprises in the late 1880s and early 1890s. The electrical manufacturing industry was created just as investors and bankers were developing the mechanisms for providing large amounts of risk capital for industry. Indeed, both Edison General and Westinghouse were caught in the trap of trying to build organizations appropriate for the scale and scope of electrical technology while employing the existing financial practice of borrowing short-term money. In my opinion, Higginson and Coffin saw this difficulty, solved it for Thomson-Houston, and then decided that the long-term solution was to create an even larger company. A large firm would be more profitable because it could take advantage of economies of scale (such as larger factories) and economies of scope (by manufacturing several closely related products). By exploiting such economies, the large firm should have a higher rate of return than several smaller firms and hence be more attractive to investors. Thus, the creation of GE was a response to the problems of raising sufficient capital in a capital-intensive industry.

Closely related to the problem of raising capital was the third factor of maintaining organizational capability. As the industry's pioneers, Coffin, Villard, and Westinghouse had struggled to build large factories, organize sales forces, develop full product lines, and create managerial hierarchies to coordinate production and distribution; in short, they had brought together the resources necessary to compete effectively. Once they had assembled their resources, those managers were loathe to let anyone or anything harm their organizational capability; indeed, they were anxious to utilize and expand their resources in pursuit of greater profits and market share. To build organizational capability, however, managers had to borrow heavily, and thus financiers such as Higginson and Morgan came to have a significant stake in those companies. Consequently, whereas the three firms competed and tried informal cooperation, eventually it became clear to both the managers and their bankers that the most promising way to sustain organizational capability was through consolidation.

The creation of General Electric in 1892 offers several lessons which we can use for thinking about competition, consolidation, and the American economy in the 1990s. First, while it is tempting to assume that impersonal market forces shape the course of competition and consolidation, the GE episode reveals that individuals and their personalities influence the level of competition and the timing of mergers. Clearly, both Westinghouse and Edison believed in fierce competition, and they actively encouraged their respective organizations to challenge each other in terms of price, product, and publicity. Likewise, Westinghouse's personality was a factor in the consolidation process, leading Coffin and Higginson to choose to leave his company out of the GE merger. In the contemporary setting, we still see individuals playing prominent roles in shaping events, whether it be Bill Gates at Microsoft or Frank Lorenzo at Texas Air. Hence any economic or social analysis of competition and consolidation must take the personalities of the entrepreneurs into account.

Second, not only do firms compete in terms of price and product, they also struggle to find sources of capital. As I have suggested in the preceding, Coffin and Thomson-Houston were victorious in the battle with Edison General and Westinghouse because they were able to raise more capital. Through their alliance with Higginson, Thomson-Houston was able to secure the capital needed to enlarge their factories, buy out their smaller competitors, set up a construction subsidiary, and extend credit to its customers. In contrast, Edison General and Westinghouse never secured the support of bankers who were able to supply them with the capital needed to undertake all of these activities. Looking at the history of electronics, we see that the need for capital continues to define the dual processes of competition and consolidation. In its early years, the challenge for the semiconductor industry was to find the capital needed to build high-volume production facilities, and the successful firms were those who could attract the necessary investment. Likewise, it has been suggested that the rapid development of high-tech firms on Route 128 outside Boston was as much the result of New England bankers willing to invest in electronics and computer firms as it was in the ready supply of engineers and scientists in the region. Hence, while it is obvious that the availability of capital shapes the level of competition in an industry, we seem to pay scant attention to this factor in both our historical and policy musings.[51]

Third, the case of GE also provides insight into what makes a firm a successful competitor. Of the three firms discussed here, Thomson-Houston was clearly the most effective, and I would argue that its strength came from doing two things well. First, this company worked to match its product line to the needs of its customers. Not only did Thomson-Houston offer a full range of lighting and streetcar systems to its customers but it also provided the necessary services of installation and credit. Second, in order to design, manufacture, and market these systems, the company developed the necessary organizational arrangements that allowed for the coordination of these functions. By creating a team of managers and engineers that could perform all of the tasks related to the production and marketing of central-station systems, Thomson-Houston was able to compete and surpass both Edison General and Westinghouse. For today, I think the lesson of Thomson-Houston's organizational strength should be quite clear; although we tend to think of the ideal competitor as a firm with a good product, low prices, or low production costs, we should pay more attention to those firms that have the right organizational structure for the tasks that need to be done.

In the final analysis, I would argue that any discussion of technology and competitiveness must consider the dual processes of competition and consolidation. Yes, at times, it is desirable for American industries to have numerous firms, competing in terms of product, process, and price. However, at other times, the success of American business is that competition gives way to firms capable of mass production and mass distribution, firms whose hallmark is the ability to achieve substantial economies of scale and scope. For both the historian and businessperson, the challenge is to understand how competition and consolidation are part of the heritage of American business and how both will continue to shape our future.

Acknowledgments

The research for this paper was undertaken with support of a Newcomen Fellowship in Business History at the Harvard Business School. My thanks to Alfred D. Chandler, Jr., Louis Galambos, Leonard Reich, and George Wise for their comments on earlier versions. A portion of this paper has been published in *Innovation as a Social Process: Elihu Thomson and the Rise of General Electric, 1870–1900* (New York: Cambridge Univ. Press, 1991).

Notes

1. For an indication of the significance of consolidation for the American economy in the 1990s, see "The age of consolidation," *Bus. Week*, October 14, 1991, pp. 86–94. This article was the cover story during the week of the IEEE Conference on Competitiveness.

2. For a concise overview of nineteenth-century American business, consult Louis Galambos and Joseph Pratt, *The Rise of the Corporate Commonwealth: United States Business and Public Policy in the 20th Century* (New York: Basic Books, 1988), pp. 17–37.

3. Alfred D. Chandler, Jr., *The Visible Hand: The Managerial Revolution in American Business* (Cambridge, Mass.: Harvard Univ. Press, 1977) and *Scale and Scope: The Dynamics of Industrial Capitalism* (Cambridge, Mass.: Harvard Univ. Press, 1990).

4. Lance Davis, "The capital markets and industrial concentration: The U.S. and U.K., a comparative study," *Econ. Hist. Rev.*, Vol. 19, 1966, pp. 255–272.

5. Chandler, *Scale and Scope*, op. cit., pp. 24–34, and William Lazonick, "Organizational capability and technological change in comparative perspective," paper presented to the Business History Seminar, Harvard Business School, Boston, March 1987.

6. My thinking about the key characteristics of the three leading firms has been influenced by Chandler's discussion of a first-mover firm in *Scale and Scope*, p. 34–35.

7. W. Bernard Carlson, *Innovation as a Social Process: Elihu Thomson and the Rise of General Electric, 1870–1900* (New York: Cambridge Univ. Press, 1991), pp. 203–270.

8. On the formation of Edison General Electric, see Forrest McDonald, *Insull* (Univ. of Chicago Press, 1962), pp. 39–42; Dietrich G. Buss, *Henry Villard: A Study of Transatlantic Investment and Interests 1870–1895* (New York: Arno, 1978), pp. 207–210; and Harold C. Passer, "Development of large-scale organization: Electrical manufacturing around 1900," *J. Econ. Hist.* Vol. 12, Fall 1952, pp. 378–395, especially pp. 380–381. Edison's role in organizing the management of Edison General is suggested by an undated list of

men, titles, and assignments in 1886 electric lighting, Edison United Manufacturing Co. folder, Edison National Historic Site, West Orange, N.J. (hereafter cited as ENHS). During the late 1880s, Edison raised the efficiency of his dc system by developing a new multipolar dynamo, a five-wire distribution network, high-voltage dc distribution using a rotary converter, a new meter, and a 200-volt incandescent lamp for street lighting. See Edison General Electric Company, "Central station lighting," February 1892, Trade Catalog Collection, Archives and Library, Henry Ford Museum, Dearborn, Mich.; Edison, [notes on multiwire systems], October 5, 1889, notebook N870902, ENHS; A. E. Kennelly, "Calculation for the dimensions of a commutating continuous transformer of 100 light capacity," notebook N880828, ENHS; Edison, "Induction-converter," U.S. Patent No. 534,28 (filed May 21, 1888, granted February 12, 1895); and "The new edison municipal lamp," *Electr. World*, Vol. 11, February 18, 1888, p. 74. On Edison's plans for a street railway, see J. C. Henderson to Villard, June 27, 1890, box 63, folder 473, Henry Villard Papers, Baker Library, Harvard University Graduate School of Business Administration, Boston.

9. Passer, "Development of large-scale organization," op. cit., pp. 389–392.

10. These bids came from a telegraph message Villard sent to Coffin. In that message, Villard accused Coffin of submitting an "unreasonably low" bid and proposed that if Thomson-Houston withdrew its bid, then Edison General would give it one-third of the contract's net profits. See Villard to Clark, Dodge & Co., May 21, 1890, box 127, Letterbook 167, p. 235, Villard Papers.

11. Edison was quite adamant that his manufacturing companies cut component prices in order to gain market share; see "Mr. Edison's reply to Thomson-Houston memoranda of March 23d, 1889," box 673, folder 472, Villard Papers. As examples, the Edison organization reduced the price of incandescent lamps from $1 in 1886 to $0.44 in 1891, and it sold streetcar motors for under $1500 when manufacturing costs would have dictated a price over $1600. See McDonald, *Insull*, op. cit., p. 42; and Arthur Pound and Samuel Taylor Moore, eds., *More They Told Barron: Conversations and Revelations of an American Pepys in Wall Street* (New York: Harper, 1931), p. 38.

12. Coffin's quotation is from Pound and Moore, *More They Told Barron*, p. 37. For an informed discussion of the economics of network technologies, see Paul A. David, "The hero and the herd in technological history: Reflections of Thomas Edison and the 'Battle of the Systems'," publication No. 100, July 1987, Center for Economic Policy Research, Stanford University, especially pp. 9–13.

13. Forrest McDonald, *Let There Be Light: The Electric Utility Industry in Wisconsin, 1881–1955* (Madison, Wis.: American History Research Center, 1957), pp. 21–22; T. Commerford Martin and Stephen Leidy Coles, *The Story of Electricity* (New York: Story of Electricity Company, 1919), p. 137.

14. On the formation of the North American Company, see Buss, *Villard*, pp. 215–217. The quotation is from McDonald, *Insull*, p. 42. For a description of its operations in Milwaukee, see McDonald, *Let There Be Light*, pp. 51–55.

15. Elihu Thomson to Charles A. Coffin, December 20, 1892, Letterbook 1/1/92–3/29/93, pp. 775–759, Thomson Papers; Harold C. Passer, *The Electrical Manufacturers: A Study in Competition, Entrepreneurship, Technical Change, and Economic Growth* (Cambridge, Mass.: Harvard Univ. Press, 1953), pp. 52–57, 103, 147; Arthur A. Bright, Jr., *The Electric-Lamp Industry: Technological Change and Economic Development from 1800 to 1947* (New York: Macmillan, 1949), pp. 80–83.

16. To the best of my knowledge, no historian has analyzed the role of patents in the relationship between electrical manufacturers and utility companies. In narrating the

problems GE encountered in the early 1890s with former Edison licensees, George Wise suggested that the licensees expected that the patents would convey monopoly power to them; see his "History of General Electric" (unpublished ms.), chap. 3, "Shoemakers," pp. 104–107. Additional information about the relationship between the Edison organization and its licensees can be found in A. Michal McMahon, *Reflections: A Centennial Essay on the Association of Edison Illuminating Companies* (New York: Association of Edison Illuminating Companies, 1985), pp. 13–17.

17. Bright, *The Electric-Lamp Industry*, op. cit., pp. 86–87; Passer, *The Electrical Manufacturers*, op. cit., p. 144.

18. Bright, *The Electric-Lamp Industry*, op. cit., pp. 87–88; John Winthrop Hammond, *Men and Volts: The Story of General Electric* (Philadelphia: Lippincott, 1941), pp. 180–187.

19. For examples of how historians have interpreted the lamp decision as giving Edison General the decisive edge, see McDonald, *Insull*, p. 48; and Hammond, *Men and Volts*, p. 192.

20. On the Westinghouse stopper lamp, see Passer, *The Electrical Manufacturers*, pp. 142–143. According to Thomson, although those lamps avoided conflict with the Edison patent, they worked very poorly, and Westinghouse used as few of them as possible in the lighting displays at the Chicago fair; see Elihu Thomson to Charles A. Coffin, June 19, 1893, Letterbook 3/93–4/95, pp. 132–133, Thomson Papers.

21. Charles A. Coffin to Henry L. Higginson, July 15, 1891, Henry L. Higginson Papers, Baker Library, Harvard University Graduate School of Business Administration, Boston, box XII-3, folder 1891, Charles A. Coffin.

22. Untitled lecture on the history of Thomson-Houston and General Electric, Hammond File, 6290–6392, especially 6350–1.

23. Among the more useful accounts of the "battle of the systems" are the following: Passer, *The Electrical Manufacturers*, op. cit., pp. 164–175; Thomas P. Hughes, *Networks of Power: Electrification in Western Society, 1880–1930* (Baltimore, Md.: John Hopkins Univ. Press, 1983), pp. 106–139; Paul A. David and Julie Ann Bunn, "The economics of gateway technologies and network evolution: Lessons from electricity supply history," *Inform. Econ. Policy*, Vol. 3, 1988, pp. 165–202; W. Bernard Carlson and A. J. Millard, "Defining risk within a business context: Thomas A. Edison, Elihu Thomson, and the AC-DC controversy, 1885–1900," in eds. V. Covello and B. B. Johnson, *The Social and Cultural Construction of Risk* (Boston: Reidel, 1987), pp. 275–293.

24. Despite the claims of various Edison biographers, Edison's notebooks and caveats reveal that he did understand alternating current and that he sketched a number of ac generators, transformers, and distribution networks. See Edison, "New idea—The whole system as a transformer" (sketch), November 22, 1887, notebook N87115, ENHS; and caveat No. 117, November 2, 1889 (Cat. 1141), ENHS. Edison also encouraged Arthur E. Kennelly and his other experimenters to test ac machinery at West Orange; see Kennelly Notebooks, Vol. 1, ENHS. On the basis of that research, Edison filed for several patents for ac systems, see "System of electrical distribution," U.S. Patent No. 438,308 (filed December 6, 1886, granted October 14, 1890); "System of electrical distribution," U.S. Patent No. 524,378 (filed December 6, 1886, granted August 14, 1894); "Alternating current generator," U.S. Patent No. 470,928 (filed August 25, 1891, granted March 15, 1892).

However, as Edison studied alternating current, he grew suspicious. He was troubled by power losses in transformers, which he found to be at minimum 7 to 12 percent.

"Evidently this results in a great diminution of the profits of the business," he observed in "System of electrical distribution," U.S. Patent No. 382,415 (filed December 27, 1887, granted May 8, 1888). See also Edison to Villard, February 8, 1890, box 63, folder 473, Villard Papers. Furthermore, Edison was concerned about the costs of building ac generating stations. Westinghouse claimed that a major advantage of ac was that one could erect a large plant that could generate cheap power on the outskirts of a city. Familiar with the difficulties of raising capital to build his own dc stations, Edison believed that large ac plants would cost too much money to construct and that the interest charges on the investment would eliminate any operating profits. See Edison to H. Villard, December 11, 1888, Letterbook 881112, p. 354, ENHS. Finally, Edison was distressed by the problem of properly insulating ac wires. He and his men were having enough difficulty finding good insulation for their low-voltage system, and he doubted that he could find insulation for a 1000-volt line and its transformers. See Edison, "Reasons against an alternating converter system," notebook N860428, pp. 261–265, ENHS. For all those reasons, Edison concluded that "the use of the alternating current is unworthy of practical men." See Edison to H. Villard, February 24, 1891, box 63, folder 475, Villard Papers.

25. Edison summed up his competitive philosophy when he advised a central-station manager: "Try everything you can towards economy. No one is safe in the cold commercial world that can't produce as low as his greatest competitor. No matter how much money you are making never for an instant let up on economizing." From Edison note, May 10, 1895, Meadowcroft Papers, box 84, ENHS.

26. For information suggesting that the Edison organization lost contracts in Denver and Minneapolis to Westinghouse, see "A Warning from the Edison Electric Light Company," circa 1888, Electricity, box E-5, Warshaw Collection of Business Americana, National Museum of American History, Washington, D.C. This is the famous red-covered pamphlet in which the Edison organization attacked the safety of ac systems. For a description of the technical and financial troubles of the Westinghouse plant in Denver, see W. P. Hancock, "Report on Westinghouse plant of Colorado Electric Company," 1888 Electric Light-Westinghouse folder, ENHS.

27. Documents in the Edison archives strongly suggest that it was Francis S. Hastings, not Edison himself, who mounted the attack on Westinghouse and ac systems; see Hasting's letters to A. E. Kennelly, August 6, 1888, November 20, 1888, and November 26, 1888, in 1888 Edison Electric Light Co., July–December, folder, and 1888 Electrocution folder, as well as Hastings to Edison, January 21, 1889, in 1889 Electricity-Use folder, ENHS.

28. On Harold P. Brown, see Thomas P. Hughes, "Harold P. Brown and the executioner's current: An incident in the AC-DC controversy," *Bus. Hist. Rev.*, Vol. 32, 1958, 143–165. On the role of the New York physicians in promoting ac electrocution as an alternative to hanging as capital punishment, see Roger Neustadter, "The murderer and the dynamo: Social response to the first legal electrocution in America," paper presented to the Popular Culture Association, Toronto, Ontario, April 1984.

29. Hughes, *Networks of Power*, op. cit., pp. 121–129.

30. Louis Galambos makes a similar point in his essay "The American economy and the reorganization of the sources of knowledge," in eds. A. Oleson and J. Voss, *The Organization of Knowledge in America, 1860–1920* (Baltimore, Md.: Johns Hopkins Univ. Press, 1979), pp. 269–284, especially p. 275.

31. Villard to Drexel, Morgan & Co., March 13, 1890, syndicate book 2, pp. 159–60, Archives of The Pierpont Morgan Library, New York.

32. Thomas R. Navin and Marian V. Sears, "The rise of a market for industrial securities, 1887–1902," *Bus. His. Rev.*, Vol. 29, June 1955, pp. 105–138, especially pp. 106–116, 125.

33. On the history of Lee, Higginson, see Navin and Sears, "The market for industrial securities," pp. 116, 125. The relationship between that brokerage house and Thomson-Houston is revealed in various letters in the Higginson Papers. In particular, see the following letters from Charles A. Coffin to Henry L. Higginson: April 18, and September 24, 1890, box XII-2, folder 1890 General; July 13, and October 5, 1891, box XII-3, folder 1891 Charles A. Coffin; February 25, 1892, box XII-3, folder 1892 Charles A. Coffin. See also the following letters between Charles Fairchild and Higginson: January 23, 1890, box XII-2, folder 1890 Fairchild; April 14, and December 28, 1891, box XII-3, folder 1891 Fairchild.

34. On Insull's efforts to juggle short-term loans, see McDonald, *Insull*, p. 38. In September 1891, Drexel, Morgan & Co. loaned Edison General $1 million by selling Edison General's six-month notes to a syndicate of a dozen banks and investors. See J. P. Morgan to H. Villard, September 9, 1891, and J. P. Morgan to Unger, Smithers & Co., September 11, 1891, Letterbook 1887–1893, pp. 600–602, the Pierpont Morgan Library, New York. See also Vincent P. Carosso, *The Morgans: Private International Bankers, 1854–1913* (Cambridge, Mass.: Harvard Univ. Press, 1987), no. 166, p. 775. Morgan's role in promoting Edison central stations is discussed in "Personal recollections. Edward H. Johnson. Mr. Morgan's contribution to the modern electrical era," November 1914, Herbert Satterlee Papers, box 3, folder A10, The Pierpont Morgan Library, New York.

35. On Villard's fall in 1890, see Henry Villard, *Memoirs of Henry Villard, Journalist and Financier, 1835–1900*, 2 vols. (Westminster: Archibald Constable, 1904), Vol. 2, pp. 342–343, 357–358; and Buss, *Villard*, p. 217. On the Baring crisis, see Charles P. Kindleberger, *Manias, Panics, and Crashes: A History of Financial Crises* (New York: Basic Books, 1978), pp. 153–156. On Villard's new policies for Edison General, see McDonald, *Insull*, p. 49. In response to the failure of North American, Fairchild recommended that Thomson-Houston "disregard the Edison Competition so far as to decline to give special credits in any shape or to take bonds & stocks of local [companies];" see Fairchild to Higginson, November 11, 1890, box XII-2, folder 1890 Fairchild, Higginson Papers.

36. Passer, *The Electrical Manufacturers*, p. 279. Quotation is from Edison note on Edward D. Adams to Edison, February 2, 1889, box 63, folder 472, Villard Papers.

37. For an overview of the financial difficulties encountered by Westinghouse, see Passer, *The Electrical Manufacturers*, p. 279; and Francis E. Leupp, *George Westinghouse: His Life and Achievements* (Boston: Little, Brown, 1918), pp. 157–161. The negotiations between Westinghouse and Belmont are described in letters sent by Charles Fairchild to Higginson; in particular, see letters dated December 30, 1890, February 4, 1891, and undated items in box XII-2, folder 1890 Fairchild, and box XII-3, folder 1891 Fairchild, Higginson Papers. Quotation is from Fairchild to Higginson, May 6, 1891, box XII-3, folder 1891 Charles A. Coffin, Higginson Papers. On the relationship between Charles Francis Adams, Jr., and Westinghouse, see Fairchild to Higginson, July 19, 24, and 26, 1891, box XII-3, folder 1891 Charles A. Coffin, Higginson Papers; and Edward C. Kirkland, *Charles Francis Adams, Jr., 1835–1915: The Patrician at Bay* (Cambridge, Mass.: Harvard Univ. Press, 1965), pp. 175–176.

38. Villard's efforts to cooperate with Coffin and Westinghouse are described in the following letters from Villard: to Westinghouse, December 16, 1889, box 126, Letterbook 64, p. 500; to Westinghouse, February 20, 1890; to Charles A. Coffin, March 5, 1890; to Westinghouse, March 10, 1890; and to Charles A. Coffin, March 25 and 28, 1890; all in

box 127, Letterbook 66, pp. 74, 111, 144, 299, and 341, respectively, Villard Papers. See also John Muir to Villard, March 31, 1890, box 12, Letterbook 66, pp. 360–362, Villard Papers; and Charles Fairchild to Higginson, n.d., box XII-3, folder 1891 Charles A. Coffin, Higginson Papers. On the Washington and Richmond deal, see Villard to Charles A. Coffin, February 18, 1889, box 126, Letterbook 61, p. 161, Villard Papers. In that deal, Villard got the better contract, because Thomson-Houston was unable to secure permission from the authorities in Washington to use overhead trolley wires and was forced to use expensive storage-battery cars; see Charles A. Coffin to Higginson, June 29, 1891, box XII-3, folder 1891 Charles A. Coffin, Higginson Papers. Quotation is from Charles Fairchild to Higginson, n.d., box XII-3, folder 1891 Charles A. Coffin, Higginson Papers.

39. I have not been able to find Coffin's 1889 merger proposal; consequently, the terms of his proposal must be inferred from "Mr. Edison's reply to Thomson-Houston memoranda of March 23d, 1889," April 1, 1889, box 63, folder 472, Villard Papers. See also Villard to Charles A. Coffin, March 15, 1889, Letterbook 76, p. 381, box 130; and Villard to Charles A. Coffin, April 3, 1889, Letterbook 62, pp. 3–4, box 12, Villard Papers.

40. Quotation is from J. P. Morgan to Higginson, February 3, 1891, Letterbook 1887–1893, pp. 532–533, the Pierpont Morgan Library, New York, I am grateful to Jean Strouse for calling this letter to my attention.

41. Alfred D. Chandler, Jr., provided an overview of the consolidation of American railroads in *The Visible Hand: The Managerial Revolution in American Business* (Cambridge, Mass.: Harvard Univ. Press, 1977), pp. 145–171. Quotation is from Fairchild to Higginson, July 24, 1891, box XII-3, folder 1891 Charles A. Coffin, Higginson Papers. On Coffin's antagonistic attitude toward Westinghouse, see Fairchild to Higginson, May 5, 1891; and Charles A. Coffin to Higginson, n.d.; both in box XII-3, folder 1891 Charles A. Coffin, Higginson Papers.

42. Fairchild to Villard, February 23 and 25, 1890, box 63, folder 473, Villard Papers; Passer, *The Electrical Manufacturers,* p. 322; McDonald, *Insull,* pp. 48–49. Quotation is from Fairchild to Higginson, December 29, 1891, box XII-3, folder 1891 Fairchild, Higginson Papers; profits and sales figures are from "Committee on stock list. New York Stock Exchange. General Electric Co. 31 May 1892," syndicate book 3, 1890–1892, p. 127, The Pierpont Morgan Library, New York.

43. Thomson recalled that Twombly was initially asked by the Morgan interests to reorganize Edison General and that in doing so he decided that Edison General and Thomson-Houston should be merged; see ET to John W. Howell, January 7, 1930, Woodbury's notes, Collected Letters, Elihu Thomson Papers, Library of the American Philosophical Society, Philadelphia. The course of the negotiations can be gleaned from letters from Charles A. Coffin to Higginson, February 1 and 7, 1892, and two undated notes, box XII-3, folder 1892 Charles A. Coffin, Higginson Papers. Quotation is from Fairchild to Higginson, January 29, 1892, box XII-3, folder 1892 Fairchild. J. P. Morgan does not appear to have played a significant direct role in the negotiations; his principal contribution was in securing the support of a majority of Edison General stockholders. See his letter to Higginson, March 1, 1892, box XII-3, folder 1892 General, H-Q, Higginson Papers. The terms of the stock trade and the organization committee are from "Stockholders' Agreement Appointing Committee," February 8, 1892, syndicate book 3, 1890–2, The Pierpont Morgan Library, New York. The March meeting of the organization committee is mentioned in J. P. Morgan to Higginson, March 1, 1892, folder 1892 General, H-Q; and C. H. Coster to Higginson, March 22, 1892, folder 1892 Coster; both in box XII-3, Higginson Papers. The charter is discussed in Charles A. Coffin to Higginson, March 2, 1892, box XII-3, folder 1892 Charles A. Coffin, Higginson Papers.

44. GE's board of directors and top management: Navin and Sears, "The market for industrial securities," p. 188; Passer, *The Electrical Manufacturers*, p. 322; David O. Woodbury, *Beloved Scientist: Elihu Thomson, A Guiding Spirit of the Electrical Age* (New York: Whittlesey House, 1944; reprinted Cambridge, Mass.: Harvard Univ. Press, 1960), p. 205; McDonald, *Insull*, pp. 51–54.

45. Perhaps impressed with how Villard had organized Edison General, several historians have assumed that he played a part in the creation of GE, only to be squeezed out at the last moment by Coffin and Morgan; see Matthew Josephson, *Edison: A Biography* (New York: McGraw-Hill, 1959), pp. 362–363; and McDonald, *Insull*, pp. 49–51. As evidence that Coffin and Morgan conspired to eliminate Villard, these scholars cited an unpublished Edison biography, "The Old Man," by Hugh Russell Fraser, in the Edison archives that described the Edison General and Thomson-Houston negotiations and a meeting between Coffin and Morgan. I have examined the relevant portion of this manuscript (pp. 362–372) and found that it does not mention the famous Coffin–Morgan meeting and that Fraser attributed a quotation to a Thomson-Houston executive (C. W. Dean) whom I have never seen mentioned anywhere else. A careful reading of letters in the Villard, Higginson, and Morgan papers reveals nothing to suggest that Villard was involved in the negotiations. In fact, according to the memoirs prepared by Villard's son, Villard advised his German banking friends to sell off their Edison General holdings in early 1892, and he strongly disapproved of the GE merger; see Villard, *Memoirs*, Vol. 2, p. 326. Both Morgan and Higginson were quite aware that Villard could be a stumbling block to creating a consolidated company; as Morgan wrote to fellow banker T. Jefferson Coolidge on March 24, 1892, "I entirely agree with you that it is desirable to bring about closer management between the two companies. Mr. Villard's resignation will take effect on the 1st [of] April, and I think the best way would be for Mr. Coffin to be then elected President of the Edison General Co." See Letterbook 87–93, p. 676, The Pierpont Morgan Library, New York. Villard's resignation can be found in his letter to the board of trustees of Edison General Electric, February 18, 1892, Letterbook 76, p. 318, box 130, Villard Papers. For a discussion of his activities in 1891–1892, see Villard, *Memoirs*, Vol. 2, pp. 358–363; and Buss, *Villard*, pp. 224–243.

46. Quotation is from Fairchild to Higginson, July 24, 1891, box XII-3, folder 1891 Charles A. Coffin, Higginson Papers.

47. First quotation is from Charles A. Coffin to Higginson, May 7, 1891, box XII-3, folder 1891 Charles A. Coffin, Higginson Papers. Second quotation is from Pound and Moor, *More They Told Barron*, p. 38.

48. I am grateful to Alfred D. Chandler, Jr., for suggesting this point about managerial hierarchies. He briefly discussed this problem for Westinghouse in *Scale and Scope*, pp. 215–216.

49. Passer, *The Electrical Manufacturers*, pp. 324–326.

50. In his study of the electrical industry, Passer is cautious about claiming that the desire to eliminate competition was a factor in the formation of GE. In his view, one could only draw this conclusion if the merger had included Westinghouse and thus completely eliminated competition. See *The Electrical Manufacturers*, pp. 326–327. However, as the many letters from Coffin, Higginson, and Fairchild reveal, these men believed that competition was problematic and that it should be minimized or eliminated. Furthermore, they had tried to merge all three firms during the Westinghouse reorganization, only to find it difficult to deal with Westinghouse personally. Consequently, given the

severity of the competition and the views expressed by the leading actors in their correspondence, I would conclude that the desire to eliminate competition contributed to the GE merger.

51. In fact, I would argue that historians and economists have failed to move beyond the conclusions made by Lance Davis twenty-five years ago; see Davis, "The capital markets and industrial concentration," op. cit.

PART VII

Electric Power in France

The final section considers electric power. Both papers in this section discuss French electric power companies which, like France's telecommunications companies, are publicly held and hence not subject to traditional forms of competitiveness among firms. In the first paper of this section Alain Beltran, a historian at the Institut d'histoire du temps present, examines the history of Electricité de France since 1946. He describes three kinds of competition that pertain to the French power industry: competition of nuclear technology with coal, oil, and natural gas; competition of French power companies with other power companies in the European Economic Community; and competition of France with other nations through industrial strength. Beltran shows how economic competition was simulated in a monopolistic environment, how tax laws shaped the competitive environment, and what sociological factors enabled nuclear power to succeed in France.

In the volume's final paper Gabrielle Hecht, a historian of technology at Stanford University, examines the relationship between engineering work and politics, economics, and culture in the French nuclear power industry between 1955 and 1969. She traces three stages of competitiveness: first a period characterized by competition between the government agencies for nuclear weapons and nuclear power rooted in their conflicting agendas, next a period of economic competition to deliver power from the monopolistic nuclear power industry at as low a price as possible and preferably at a competitive price with conventionally produced power, and finally a period in which the French industry competed against non-French firms and non-French technologies to construct power plants around the world.

Beltran's paper suggests several questions for further study. The theme of national competition he raises resonates with that discussed in Griset's paper on the French telephone system. It is clear that nations today keenly appreciate the importance of technology and technological infrastructure to national wealth, strength, and prestige, and that nations are not willing to leave these matters to the invisible hand of the marketplace. Beltran's paper introduces the timely question about the formation of a united Europe and what it may mean for French technological industry and French national competitiveness (and by extension for any other European nation). It might be profitable, as a comparison, to consider the effects on technological strength of major geopolitical changes in the past, e.g., in the context of the dissolution of the British empire, the unification of the German states in the nineteenth century, or the formation of the Unified Soviet Socialist Republics in the early twentieth century. It may also be instructive to extend to other countries Beltran's sociological analysis of the factors contributing to the French acceptance of nuclear technology, for the acceptance of this technology has varied widely across nations. The analysis might similarly be extended to other technologies, such as biotechnology or pesticides, which are widely regarded as presenting environmental or other human risks.

Hecht's paper raises many of the same themes as Beltran's about national competitiveness, especially once France became a player in a larger geopolitical environment through the formation of the Common Market in the 1950s. She shows how the French government did not speak with one voice because its agencies were pursuing conflicting objectives. This is the case today in the United States, where military and commercial competitiveness objectives clash over the development of high-tech materials, high-definition television, and other cutting-edge technologies. Hecht also demonstrates clearly the heavy influence more general political and economic goals and philosophies can have on a nation's technology policy. Only further research will tell us the degree to which these national goals effect energy developments in countries with less centralized decision-making than France.

Because of the heavy reliance on nuclear technology and the strong centralization of technological decision-making in France, the reader might question the representativeness of these two studies. It would be useful to compare these two studies with ones concerning the electric power industries in other European nations, the United States, Canada, and Japan.[1]

Note

1. There is a literature on electric power in other countries. Among the best studies are Thomas Hughes, *Networks of Power*, Baltimore: Johns Hopkins, 1983; Richard Hirsh, *Technology and Transformation in the American Electric Utility Industry*, Cambridge: Cambridge University Press, 1989; Leslie Hannah, *Electricity Before Nationalization: A Study of the Development of the Electricity Supply Industry in Britain to 1948*, Baltimore: Johns Hopkins, 1979; Hannah, *Engineers, Managers, and Politicians: The First Fifteen Years of Nationalized Electricity Supply in Britain*, Baltimore: Johns Hopkins, 1982.; and Timo Myllyntaus, *Electrifying Finland*, London: Macmillan, 1991.

Competitiveness and Electricity

Electricité de France Since 1946

Alain Beltran

Introduction

French electricity's ability to be competitive must be examined in a very specific historical and institutional context. The French monopoly did not remain isolated from outside events. The top management of this public enterprise also thought in terms of competitiveness. They adapted the means of production to market conditions, at the same time respecting the obligations of a "public service." Moving from a period of scarce electricity to one of relative abundance, from a closed France to an open European market (1992), Electricité de France (EDF) was repeatedly led to change the way it marketed its product.

A State-Owned Company: Electricité de France

Nationalization

All the French companies active in the production and distribution of electricity were nationalized in 1946. At the liberation of France, by voting to nationalize, the government was aiming at several objectives: return its "natural wealth" to the nation; increase the use of electricity, which in France was lagging; modernize the various means of production by enlarging the role of hydroelectric power. Some people, especially on the Left, did not want private trusts to control an essential element in reconstructing the country. Only the State seemed capable of reconstructing the country. Thus a large majority in the National Assembly voted to nationalize electrical production. If we take a look at the text of the 1946 law,

315

however, it becomes clear that it covered neither the ability to be competitive nor how to manage the company. The most urgent concern was reconstructing the war-ravaged country.

Electricité de France, for National Independence

The key term during this period—as it has been during the 45 years of EDF's existence—was *national independence*. France possesses few energy resources: no oil, no natural gas (not in 1946, anyway), and little coal (before the war one-third had to be imported). The great reliance placed on hydroelectric power after 1945 has to be understood in this context. Productivity, competitiveness, and the rational use of energy were overshadowed by the top priority of the time: reconstructing the country. The same imperatives largely influenced the launching of the nuclear electricity program in 1973/1974. National self-sufficiency in the field of energy justified this kind of effort; thus, as the minister Jean Auroux declared at a press conference on July 27, 1983: "The program for energy independence is aimed at once again endowing France with the capacity for autonomous action in the world." The main justification was therefore not competition with other energy sources.

A Strict Supervisory Authority

Electricité de France is not unique in the field of energy. Since 1946 the entire sector has been in the hands of the State: natural gas, electricity, and coal were also nationalized, and oil strictly regulated by a 1928 law. The government has the right to oversee practically all of EDF's activities, which means that EDF cannot set its rates without an authorization, because the State has a say-so about the price of electricity, just as it does about salaries and investments.

This dependence heavily influenced the evolution of electricity rates. In fact, when estimating the inflation rate in France—which is then used as a basis for salary hikes—a certain number of cost-of-living parameters are taken into account, including the price of the kilowatt-hour. So, any government eager to combat inflation or the perpetual price-and-wage spiral (a practically constant phenomenon in France since 1944) is compelled to restrict rises in the cost of electricity. The company's assets were often endangered by such a lack of freedom. Complete freedom in setting rates was enjoyed only rarely and under certain conditions. Moreover, the State, which dominates the energy sector, can favor one energy resource over another through taxes, forbidding advertising, limiting imports or exports, etc. In France the rules governing competition between the different energy sources are thus quite particular. The energy market is definitively not an example of unfettered competition!

Electricité de France in France

Controlled by the State, confident of captive markets, and, for a time, assured of healthy and regular growth (doubling of consumer demand every 10 years), EDF's sales policy during its first 20 years was characterized by mediocre dynamism. Producers of natural gas and oil were mostly preoccupied with how to market their products, while electricity producers were reproached for their unimaginativeness and even a certain "imperialism," their product seeming so sure of its strength. The slogan chosen at the end of the 1960s—"all electric, all nuclear"—is revealing. This kind of thinking became caricature when an executive of EDF, paraphrasing General Motors, declared "what is good for EDF is good for France. . . ."

The Factors Governing Adaptation to the Constraints of Competition

The Competition from Hydrocarbons

Within EDF, one circumstance concerning competition from natural gas must be pointed out. In 1946, electricity and natural gas were nationalized within the same company; a complex situation resolved through various compromises. More exactly, the same department became responsible for supplying both energies. This fact introduced an initial element of competition for EDF. More particularly, a natural gas deposit discovered in the South of France in the 1950s renewed this industry's vitality. Another source of competition was obviously oil, whose price fell very rapidly toward the end of the 1960s. A third competitor quickly disappeared: coal, actively relaunched just after the war, began its final decline after 1960.

The Importance of Economics at Electricité de France

In a corporation of national proportions, questions of investment choices, rates, or stock management automatically assume capital importance. Errors in analysis cost taxpayers dearly. The corporation's executives tried in several ways to introduce elements that could play the role of outside competition and increase the monopoly's ability to be competitive. In this respect, the quality of EDF's various executives was real: they were senior public servants or highly qualified engineers devoted to public service. They were aware of EDF's power, its size making it the world's leading electric company. It was essential to introduce, in one way or another, elements to safeguard flexibility in an organization that risked evolving into a gigantic bureaucracy.

An essential development was the gradual transfer of management power within EDF from engineers to economists. Men like Pierre Massé, Gabriel Dessus, Robert Gibrat, and Marcel Boiteux became the company's foremost executives. This shift from "engineer to economist" introduced new ways of reasoning, based on the search for an economic optimum.

The Search for an Optimum Rate

In the area of electric rates, the search for an optimum rate was based on the idea of marginalism. This theory was applied as early as 1957 through a "green" rate, which seemed the best way to translate costs and accommodate consumers (even if there is an *a posteriori* equalizing of the different residential rate levels). In this way, EDF demonstrated that it sought the optimum for the nation. This was a means of establishing EDF's legitimacy with respect to the State: "such a policy enables us to resist political pressures. It's a kind of safety rail and counterbalances the lack of competition."[1] Establishing rates according to different uses, which had ensured the prosperity of private companies before 1946, seemed discriminatory and complicated. One executive, Marcel Boiteux—a student of Marcel Allias (winner of the Nobel Prize for Economics), but above all, Manager and President of EDF—wanted to use economic calculations to find indications that are normally found in a free market. This goal was the reason behind the initiation of a new mode of calculation, the Productivité Globale des Facteurs (PGF), or Factor Global Productivity (FGP), which allowed one to compare the different electrical distribution centers. Management thus hoped to provide an incentive for those favoring more competition: "for this public service, the PGF makes size play the role that the profit plays in the private sector," an EDF economist declared.[2]

Contracts between the State and the Company

A shareholder whose presence is barely felt in terms of equity, the State exercises such strict control that a company like EDF has always wanted to attain the maximum amount of independence so it could act freely. This is particularly true during periods when competition becomes keener and when economic circumstances are favorable. EDF was twice able to obtain this kind of latitude from the government. In 1969/1970, EDF signed a "program contract" with the State, according to which the company committed itself to specific efforts to increase rates. With the unanimous support of the unions, this three-year period signaled the coming of age of this State-owned firm that had managed to loosen the State's stifling control. But the contract fell apart with the first oil shock in 1973, and the State resumed its firm control. This initial attempt nevertheless remained in everyone's memory, and in 1989, a new three-year "Plan Contract" was signed between these two parties (see below).

1989–1992 EDF–State Contract

EDF is committed:

1. to decrease its debt (minus 20 billion by 1992).
2. to lower its rates in terms of constant francs by 1.5 percent per year.
3. to improve the quality of its product and services (especially for hard-to-reach clients).

The State is committed:

1. to guarantee the level of rates, thus enabling the company to decrease its overall debt.
2. to grant the company more freedom, be it in respect to investments, salaries, new activities, or the means of transporting and supplying electricity.

An "Abundant and Competitive" Energy (The 1970s and 1980s)

The Development of Nuclear Energy

After hydroelectric power, nuclear energy was the most important project developed by EDF (and the atomic energy commission [CEA]). EDF's ability to be competitive had to be calculated with respect to coal and especially to fuel oil, whose price regularly dropped. Between 1964 and 1979, this role fell to the Production of Energy Origin is Nuclear (PEON) Commission.

During the 1960s, fuel oil's competitiveness (until 1975 comparisons were made of nuclear power with fuel oil and afterward with coal) was such that it was felt that the use of nuclear energy would only gain impetus over the long term. The 1970s and their two oil shocks wreaked havoc on these predictions. France became the country where nuclear power had the largest share (75 percent today). Some explanations for this are sociological (mild public resistance, strong central authority, a judiciary lacking independence, no counterstudies), but others, not including the lack of our own oil resources, are of an economic nature.

More particularly, nuclear power costs were relatively controlled in France. Between 1977 and 1991, the cost of constructing nuclear power stations practically doubled, but coal plants experienced a similar evolution. During the entire period from 1972 to 1982 "it can be noted that nuclear energy's competitiveness compared with coal's had not changed"[3] and that "nuclear power remains the economical way of producing electricity during periods of low and medium demand." During these ten years, "the cost of the kilowatt-hour rose more rapidly than expected, almost doubling,"[4] but nuclear energy had a large safety margin over fuel oil. Nuclear energy is more economical to use than coal, given the high level of yearly consumption, which seems to be the case in resource-poor France.

Among the advantages of the French nuclear energy program, one of the most significant is the speed at which the stations are built—6 years, against 11 in Germany. Positive roles were also played by the "series" effect (an average of 8 to 18 stations ordered) and by size (an increase from 900 to 1300 MW). Standardization was emphasized. Being its own prime contractor, EDF had at its disposal abundant engineering capacity through its Equipment Department. As a result, construction costs were contained (Table 1[5]).

TABLE I Average Increase in the Cost of the Nuclear Kilowatt (1970–1982), Ignoring Inflation

Country	Percent Increase
United States	+13
Japan	+11
Western Germany	+9
Canada	+6
France	+5

A Competitive Energy

Having become abundant, electricity also showed itself to be highly competitive. Energy prices remained stable from 1950 to 1973, and the real cost of energy steadily declined. From 1970 to 1973, energy prices stabilized before a spectacular rise (1978/1979). As for electricity, its price had largely fallen in terms of constant francs until 1973, then increased for high and medium voltage, while the cost of the low-voltage kilowatt-hour continued to decrease, albeit more slowly. In terms of competitiveness, it was electricity that benefitted the most from the increase in oil prices and the end of decreasing natural gas prices. In 1973 the cost of a kilowatt-hour was seven times that of thermal combustion; by 1983, the ratio had become 2 to 1, and sometimes less.

Percentage change in the prices of various energies from 1972 to 1982, in constant francs

Electricity 100-kWh low voltage, excluding taxes, business use	+117%
Electricity 100-kWh low voltage, excluding taxes, business use	+156%
Natural gas, 100 kWh, excluding taxes, residential use	+172%

Consumer price average +181%

Regular gasoline, 1 liter	+265%
Coal, French anthracite (50-kilo sack), 1 ton	+310%
Domestic fuel oil, delivered (2000- to 5000-liter delivery), taxes included, per hectoliter	+610%

Electric rates continued to decrease between 1983 and 1988 (an average of 12 percent in constant francs), although more rapidly for large industrial customers than for residential customers. The figures given by the National Utility Service (NUS)[6] establish that electric rates in France are in the medium range. By slowing price increases, the State favored consumers, but prevented EDF from significantly reducing its indebtedness (proportionately, EDF's level of indebtedness is nevertheless lower than it was during the period of the hydroelectric power program).

Electricity, an Answer to the Economic Crisis

To summarize, electricity fully profited from the fact that it enabled France to be mostly free from hydrocarbons. Other arguments in favor of electricity were that it represented a rational use of energy and that it was a substitute energy. In the 1980s, it was also claimed that electricity was "plentiful, not contingent on international politics, which consequently makes its price evolution mild and predictable."[7] The government's goal was three-pronged: to prevent certain businesses from leaving; to preserve labor-intensive industries; and to introduce new, competitive products. Electricity thus became an instrument of economic reconquest (the fight against unemployment and inflation, since the cost of electricity varies less than other products over the long term). But more important than its competitiveness was its capacity to open new markets.

New Opportunities

Electricity's competitiveness implied that its trajectory—energy "simultaneously old and new"[8]—would be from traditional mechanical uses to thermal uses. To industries, EDF stressed the adaptability of electricity and its attractive rates. Besides these points, it was increasingly argued that electricity was a clean energy, and consequently that it protected the environment.

The other decisive breakthrough of the 1980s was its adaptation for electric heating, which made it attractive for residential use. As a result, two out of every three new apartments are currently equipped with electric radiators. The cost to users is very low, since most of the money is spent "up-stream from the socket." Although the rates are attractive, they do not seem to reflect the costs. The increase over the ten years from 1979 to 1989 has been fairly spectacular (Table 2).

TABLE II Electricity's Share in Energy Utilization by Sector (%)

	1979	1986	1987	1988	1989
Industry	38	47	48.3	48	49
Residential	30	44	46	47	47.7

After having lagged seriously behind industrial use, residential use of electricity in France is now 2 points above the EEC average (31.3 percent compared to 29 percent), mainly because of electrical heating. The effect is perhaps perverse. Electrical heating is a big household expense and forces EDF to meet large winter peaks in demand (during which period fossil fuels are also used to ensure supply). Between 1973 and 1987, the maximum peak demand for electricity practically doubled in France! In the final analysis, however, France uses its nuclear power plants less than some of its European neighbors use theirs[9] (see the following table for 1987 averages, in hours):

West Germany	France	Great Britain	Belgium	Spain
6535	5090	6710	7230	6105

Opponents of an exaggerated use of nuclear power feel that this is not a very rational utilization of electricity, because it produces more kilowatt-hours than are absolutely necessary to maintain competition. Another sign of plenty is that EDF has become an electricity exporter. In January of 1990, the General Manager of EDF declared: "our major asset with respect to competition in Europe is, naturally, nuclear energy. The competitiveness of our production infrastructure has been confirmed. The proof of this lies in our ability to export, because the company's performance, in this field of enormous competition, has significantly improved." In answer to which it might be called to mind that "EDF's declared goal for the construction of nuclear power plants was to enable prices in France to drop substantially and not to enable France to export. . . ."[10]

Conclusion

At the end of the 1980s France found itself in a radically new situation vis-à-vis electricity. Its use now doubles every 25 years instead of every 10. And yet, there is a profusion of production processes. It has become necessary, as we stated, to find new outlets and opportunities. The achievement of European unity could offer new hope—or new dangers—for EDF. On January 1, 1993, Europe should become a single market, without obstacles, without national monopolies, so that the advantages of free trade can fully develop. For EDF, that means increased rivalry on the European level and a greater degree of competitiveness with similar companies in Europe and other service companies in France. Despite a certain vagueness, since the new rules set by Brussels (headquarters of the Common Market) are not yet precisely known, EDF is actively preparing itself for its new role. The 1989 Plan Contract states the following: "The development of consumer demand takes place more than ever in competitive markets. EDF must ensure its own ability, confronted with other energies in France and also on a European energy and electricity market destined to be completely open and subjected to increasing rivalry."

This statement presupposes, in particular, a change in the makeup of this company of engineers, where some voices deplored the lack of an energetic attitude about sales and marketing. Concerning the reforms that EDF is undertaking with an eye to the single European market, the General Manager declared in 1990: "This is a veritable cultural revolution for the company which will progressively change the mentality of its agents from the traditional one stressing means to one that is results-oriented." This new challenge also presumes the loss of uniquely French attitudes in favor of those emphasizing Great Europe. Being the two countries with the largest public enterprises, France and Italy (the share of the leading supplier in France, 94 percent; in West Germany, 18/20 percent; in Great Britain, 12 percent) are also the two countries with which the ad hoc committees in Brussels are the most concerned. Still unknown is whether, as in America, a common carrier will be the solution adopted. In any case, EDF has the advantage of being the leading European exporter of electricity, even if the quality of this electricity is often mediocre (problems with micro-power-cuts).

Defending themselves against European competition is a new challenge for French public firms. Legal upheavals (partial privatizations?) are predictable. People's attitudes will have to change. The notion of public service will increasingly have to be reconciled with the demands of competition and the ability to be competitive. Nevertheless, far from the rather bureaucratic image generally ascribed to monopolistic public corporations, EDF's history reveals that this giant—more than 100,000 agents—knows how to adapt to economic and technical challenges. EDF is a typically French model that will, after a half-century of existence, have to prove its viability.

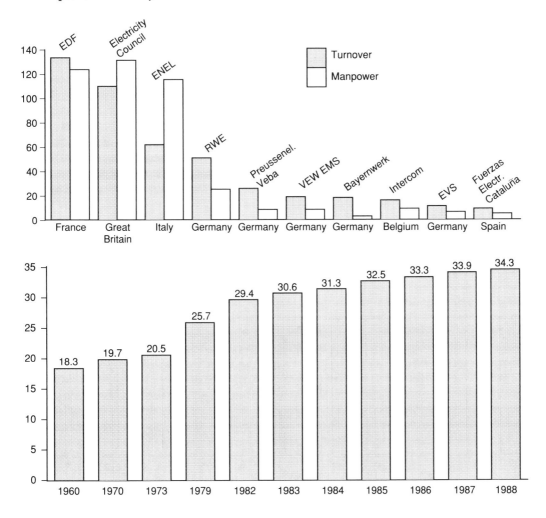

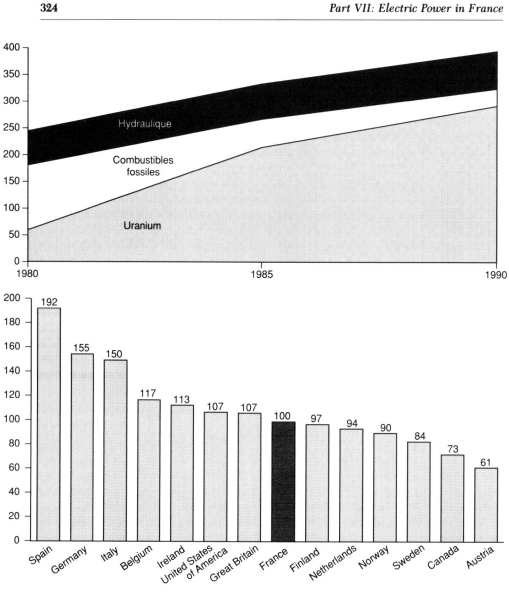

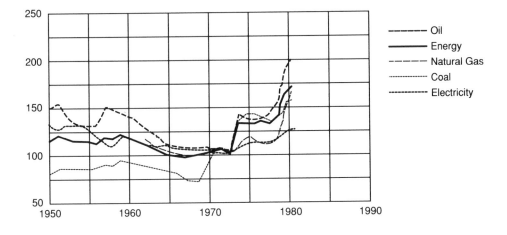

Notes

1. F. Picard, A. Beltran, and M. Bungener, *Histoire de l'EDF* (Paris: Dunod, 1985), p. 201. (The man speaking is Paul Questiaux, former Financial Manager of EDF.)

2. Louis Puiseux, *Histoire de l'EDF*, op. cit., p. 221.

3. *Rev. Energ.*, No. 364, May 1984, p. 249.

4. Ibid., p. 248.

5. C. Flavin, "Nuclear power: The market test" (Washington: Worldwatch Institute, 1983). Quoted by D. Finon, "Nuclear power between hope and resignation," in *Energie International* (Paris: Economica, 1987/1988) p. 163.

6. An international advisory company dealing with the purchase of electricity by enterprises (users whose monthly consumption is 450,000 kWh for a subscribed capacity of 1000 kW). This company was created in the United States in 1933. It is currently located on five continents, and has been in France since 1972.

7. *Rev. Energ.*, No. 344, May–June 1982, p. 602.

8. Ibid., p. 606.

9. United Nationals Bulletin (Electricity in Europe), quoted by Luigi de Paoli, *Energie Internationale* (Paris: Economica, 1989/1990), p. 165.

10. *Rev. Energ.*, No. 431, June 1991, p. 443.

Constructing Competitiveness

The Politics of Engineering Work in the French Nuclear Program, 1955–1969*

Gabrielle Hecht

Introduction

The term *technological competitiveness* invokes connections between technology and economics. But what precisely does it mean to say that one technology is "competitive" with another? Are judgments about competitiveness made on the basis of technical design? Of price? Do such judgments, along with the bases on which they are made, depend on political and economic agendas? In short, is this term immutable, as careless usage often implies? Or is it historically contingent, depending on the political, economic, and cultural climates surrounding the technology in question? Why and when do engineers, industry leaders, and politicians choose to label a particular technology "competitive"? What does such labeling imply for the development of that technology?

In this chapter, I examine French nuclear development from 1955 to 1969 to argue that we cannot assume that the term technological competitiveness has a fixed meaning. The notion of "competitiveness" acquired three different meanings over the course of these 15 years of French history. These meanings changed with the shifting political, economic, and cultural climates of French industrial development in general and the nuclear program in particular. Furthermore, each meaning was closely connected both to a distinctive kind of organization of technological work and to a particular vision of the role of nuclear technology in French economic and industrial development. The chapter begins with a brief discussion of the economic and political climate in France in the 1950s and 1960s. The body of the chapter is

*This work was supported by the National Science Foundation, the Mellon Foundation, and the IEEE Life Member Fund.

then divided into three parts in order to trace the shifting meanings of competitiveness in this time period. In the mid- to late 1950s, engineers in both the atomic energy commission (the Commissariat à l'Energie Atomique [CEA]) and the nationalized electric utility [Electricité de France (EDF)] used competitiveness to designate technological sophistication. Whether or not a reactor was competitive depended on its technical characteristics; in turn, how "advanced" these characteristics were provided a measure of institutional and national prestige. This use was accompanied by a form of engineering practice that was based on institutional traditions and that relied almost exclusively on trial and error. Between 1960 and 1964, competitiveness took on an economic dimension: the term referred to the cost of producing nuclear energy relative to that of producing conventional energy. This use of the term was paralleled by the introduction of various methods of formal economic analysis into engineering work. Engineers at EDF first used these analyses to defend their existing technological choices; subsequently, these methods became an integral part of their practice. In the mid- to late 1960s, competitiveness meant comparing the cost of the French gas–graphite reactor design with that of American light-water designs. This shift in meaning emerged from shifts in economic thinking within the government and ensuing debates between the CEA and EDF over issues of industrial policy and the organization of reactor contracting and construction.

Charles de Gaulle's return to power in 1958 brought drastic changes in the political and economic climate of France. Although the nation had undergone significant economic recovery during the Fourth Republic (1946–1958),[1] the frequent changes in political leadership had not encouraged confidence in government stability. In 1946, the postwar government had created the Commissariat Général au Plan (the Planning Commission), an independent state agency whose purpose was to draft multiyear plans intended to guide the recovery and development of the French economy. These plans represented the government's desire to follow an economic path between the free-market capitalism of the United States and the state-directed economy of the Soviet Union. Not intended to coerce industry into taking specific actions, these plans aimed rather at providing industrial leaders with suggestions for the production goals that would best enhance France's economic development. The First Plan had clearly stimulated reconstruction: in setting construction and production goals for all the major branches of industry, it gave company leaders sufficient confidence to make investments aimed at modernization. The Second and Third Plans, however, were less sector-oriented; furthermore, political turmoil delayed their approval by the government and their subsequent implementation. They were largely ignored by industrial leaders, who apparently did not see the point of paying attention to such plans when the government changed every few months.[2]

De Gaulle intended to disassociate himself and his gc   ...t from the political turmoil of the Fourth Republic. In order to emphasize the changes he intended to make, he rapidly proposed a new constitution and proclaimed the advent of the Fifth Republic. The new republic removed certain powers from the hands of Parliament and placed them squarely in the executive branch of government. De Gaulle strongly believed in the importance of the nation-state, seeing it as the "crystallization of social bonds."[3] He wanted France to become a modern country—as he put it, to "marry her century." For him, this meant that the country's leadership had to be both stable and decisive. Incorporated in these views was a strong sense of *dirigisme*, the notion that the State should have a strong hand in directing the economy. Weary of political upheaval, the French felt only too glad to support him in his endeavor and expressed confidence in the stability of the new government.[4] In this new political climate, the concept of economic planning regained both popularity and respect among industrial leaders.[5]

De Gaulle's position on nuclear issues exemplified his political stance. The governments of the Fourth Republic had consented to a national nuclear program, but the true policymakers in nuclear issues throughout most of the 1950s were the engineers, scientists, and administrators who headed the CEA and EDF.[6] By the end of the Fourth Republic, Parliament had approved a French atomic bomb project, but de Gaulle's vision of French nuclear development had far greater scope. He planned to bestow upon France a full-fledged nuclear arsenal: the *force de frappe*. Further, unlike the heads of the nation's nuclear efforts in the mid-1950s, he had no intention of keeping his plans secret. This unequivocal stance on the military atom had a twofold implication for the civilian nuclear program. First, it inspired great confidence in the future of the gas–graphite design. Clearly, the government had no plans to halt the reactor program. Second, it gave the CEA greater leverage over EDF in demanding the military plutonium that the utility was capable, albeit unwillingly, of producing in its reactors. As long as de Gaulle was in power, EDF could not outright refuse to perform this service.

The CEA and EDF were both state agencies created shortly after World War II. The CEA's purpose was to conduct nuclear research and, eventually, provide France with a nuclear program. EDF's goal was to give the nation a reliable and abundant supply of electricity. In the mid-1950s the two institutions began collaborating on the development of gas–graphite reactors. While the CEA wanted to use these reactors to produce weapons-grade plutonium for its (still secret) military program, EDF wanted them to generate electricity. The first four reactor projects— three run by the CEA, one by EDF—were thus fraught with tensions between the two agencies. Both considered themselves the guardians of the interests of the French state, and made or justified technological decisions accordingly. This attitude intensified in the late 1950s and throughout the 1960s. Between 1955 and 1967, the two institutions collaborated in the design of five more gas–graphite reactors. In chronological order of design and construction, these were: EDF2 (170 MW) and EDF3 (375 MW) on the Chinon site; EDF4 (480 MW), which was soon renamed Saint-Laurent 1 (or SL1), and SL2 (480 MW) on another site in the Loire valley in the town of Saint-Laurent-des-Eaux; and Bugey 1 (500 MW), on a site near Lyon at the foot of the French Alps.[7] EDF owned and operated all five of these reactors. In theory, the CEA was supposed to design the "nuclear" parts of these reactors and EDF the "conventional" parts; in practice, however, each institution tried to design most of each reactor.

Competitiveness and Prestige: Engineering by Trial and Error, 1955–1959

Since the inception of the nuclear program, the notion of prestige had dominated debates between the two institutions. Both argued that a nuclear program would increase their nation's international stature. Each pushed distinct technological and political agendas to enhance its institutional prestige. Notions of prestige continued to pervade quarrels between the two institutions until the end of the 1950s. Partly because of differences in institutional goals and work habits, and partly because each institution wanted to differentiate itself from the other, engineers in each developed elaborate technological notions of what it meant to enhance the prestige of the nuclear program. The next two gas–graphite reactors were EDF2 and EDF3, both to be built at EDF's Chinon site. The main argument over these reactors focused on the amount of power that each should be designed to produce. EDF engineers wanted to make big leaps in power with each new reactor. CEA designers preferred to build reactors similar to one another in technological design.

Ultimately, the nuclear adventure would only be worthwhile for EDF if it could eventually build a reasonably priced plant. This remained a distant goal in the mid-1950s. Unable to accurately analyze the cost of a reactor, EDF viewed this goal in technical rather than economic terms. Before the construction of EDF1 was even completed, utility engineers began considering design changes for EDF2. Based on their experience with conventional power plants and observations of their British counterparts who were building increasingly powerful reactors, EDF engineers decided that they first had to increase the reactor's power. They quickly drafted a preliminary proposal in September 1956. Using 150 tons of uranium arranged in a vertical empilement encased in a spherical metal pressure vessel, and pushing the carbon dioxide cooling gas through the core at a pressure of 35 kg/cm^2, they thought they could get 100 MW out of the reactor.[8] They presented this list of parameters to their CEA counterparts for review.

CEA engineers reacted favorably to this initial proposal. In May 1957, the CEA proposed a reactor that would use 258 tons of uranium, fashioned into fuel slugs identical to those of EDF1. These would be stacked in a vertical empilement encased in a cylindrical, rather than spherical, metal vessel, with carbon dioxide flowing through the core at the lower pressure of 18 kg/cm^2. This reactor would produce 114 MW of electricity.[9]

This suggestion went against everything the EDF team considered good engineering sense. If the CEA was willing and able to supply over 100 extra tons of uranium, EDF should get more than 14 MW extra in return. Furthermore, since drafting their preliminary design, utility engineers had had numerous discussions with their British counterparts. The British had developed a fuel slug for their gas–graphite reactors that was able to stay in the reactor longer and thereby produce more energy. Although fuel slug design was the province of the CEA, EDF engineers thought that the French should at least match the British in this domain. The next meeting with the CEA was a month away. The EDF team wanted desperately to produce a counterproposal by then. Working furiously, they arrived triumphantly at the meeting with a new reactor project. This reactor would use only two more tons of uranium than the CEA's version. With this uranium stacked vertically in a spherical vessel, and carbon dioxide flowing at a pressure of 25 kg/cm^2, this reactor could produce 167 MW of electricity. This design was predicated on the CEA's ability to design a fuel slug similar to the British one.[10]

CEA designers strongly objected to this counterproposal. Above all, they wanted a reliable reactor. Although also interested in building a "better" reactor than the British, they thought that a more effective way to do so would be with a series of less powerful, yet flawless, reactors, especially since the British had just experienced a fairly serious accident with their Windscale reactor. CEA designers feared that jumping to a larger reactor would increase the chance of running into construction and operational problems. They also feared the higher fuel slug performance posited by EDF's proposal. Should the CEA fail to design adequate slugs, the reactor would have to be stopped too often for reloading. CEA engineers would then take the blame for any resulting drop in availability, which translated into energy production.[11]

EDF engineers suspected an additional motive behind the CEA's reluctance to build a more powerful reactor. Running a reactor at higher power meant that the plutonium produced by the uranium fissioning inside the core would itself fission and produce additional energy. This in turn would make it nearly impossible to extract weapons-grade plutonium from the spent fuel.[12] If the CEA had thought about this in 1957–1958, it did not say so; it seemed content with the plutonium produced at Marcoule. But EDF's suspicions were confirmed after de Gaulle's return to power and his open support of the CEA's military program.

Debates between the two design teams continued for several months, as they countered each others' proposals and tried to achieve a compromise. The EDF team pushed the power threshold even higher. It began arguing for 250 MW, the current threshold for French conventional power plants, and closer to the British level. The final design parameters, settled in April 1958, incorporated many of EDF's proposals. Still, the CEA had managed to impose some of its own requirements. The reactor core, encased in a spherical metal pressure vessel, would contain 251 tons of uranium, cooled by carbon dioxide at a pressure of 27 kg/cm^2. The reactor would use two alternators, identical to those used in conventional power plants, of 125 MW each. The figure announced to the public, however, would be 175 MW. Thus EDF could get the prestige of building a powerful reactor, and the CEA would have an error margin should it experience difficulty designing new fuel slugs.

A CEA–EDF meeting the following month to discuss the design parameters of the next reactor reopened the question of power thresholds. The EDF team announced that it wanted EDF3 to run at 500 MW, using two alternators of 250 MW each. CEA designers resisted, arguing that a 250-MW reactor would suffice; they even felt willing to publicize this figure.[13] But utility engineers countered that if EDF3 ran at 500 MW, it would be the world's most powerful reactor—not a possibility to be discarded lightly. The CEA offered a compromise at 375 MW, noting that this level would still give EDF3 that distinction, and enable it to use three 125 MW alternators like those used for conventional plants.

Before engineers could settle the question, a technological mishap introduced a new hurdle into the discussions. Early in the morning of Friday, February 13, 1959, an explosive noise at the Chinon site signaled the sudden appearance of a 10-meter-long crack in EDF1's spherical containment vessel, then in the final stages of welding. The explanation for the crack soon became clear: a newly welded piece had not yet undergone the thermal treatment required to relax the internal stress produced as the metal cooled off. The fissure occurred when the metal suddenly released the internal energy it had thus accumulated.[14] It was easier to determine the cause of the accident than to fix the problem: the Société Levivier, builder of the containment structure, had no idea what to do next. The accident received extensive press coverage and took on national proportions, and for several weeks EDF and Levivier became the laughingstock of the CEA. A solution was eventually found, but the accident pushed back EDF1's start-up date by three years: it did not begin operation until September 1963.[15]

Of more immediate consequence to EDF, though, was the public humiliation it underwent after this incident. The CEA instantly blamed the mishap on EDF's stubbornness in picking a steel, rather than a prestressed concrete, containment vessel, and on the utility's insistence on being its own "industrial architect," rather than choosing a private company for that purpose, as the CEA had done for Marcoule and encouraged EDF to do for Chinon. Some industrial and economic leaders agreed with the CEA. But not everyone blamed the accident on EDF's industrial policy. Some CEA engineers thought only that insufficient metallurgical research had gone into the vessel design. Nor did the Ministry of Industry object to EDF's industrial policy, saying rather that the utility had not adequately organized itself to deal with the development of a nuclear program.[16]

After this initial flurry of blame-casting, questions about EDF's industrial contracting policy were dropped. Apparently, the time was not right (as it would be a few years later) to challenge the utility on this point. However, the incident did raise questions about EDF's judgment. In particular, Pierre Massé, the new head of the Planning Commission (and a former EDF manager), questioned the wisdom of increasing the power of each successive reactor so dramatically. He and some of the private companies that held contracts for previous reactors thought that EDF would do better to build greater numbers of smaller reactors in order to give the builders more experience with the technology. But EDF's upper-level managers did not trust the motives of the private companies. They suspected that companies merely wanted to build more reactors so as to make more money, without caring about the long-term future of the nuclear program.[17]

Until this moment, engineers both in the CEA and in EDF made their technological choices by relying on institutional traditions. For example, EDF used its experience with conventional power plants as a reference point, while the CEA wanted to build a series of reactors as it had done at Marcoule. They defended those choices by associating both institutional and national prestige with technological achievement and sophistication. No overarching theories of reactor design guided their work: engineers in both institutions learned by doing. This meant that much of their design work proceeded by trial and error. They had no idea whether they would like a component's design until they had actually built the component, and sometimes, as in the case of EDF1's pressure vessel, they ended up regretting their choices. But the pioneer spirit that pervaded the program kept them from feeling discouraged. And as long as their work remained unquestioned by the State or the public that they professed to serve, they felt no need to change their approach.[18]

De Gaulle's accession to power, the importance he attached to the military nuclear program, his fondness for the CEA, the fact that it had not committed any visible technological errors, and its unquestioned expertise in nuclear matters meant that the agency did not have to alter its positions. But the incident with EDF1's containment vessel and the shifting political and economic climate meant that EDF had to find another way to defend itself. In the late 1940s and early 1950s, the utility needed only to pay lip service to cost-effective energy. Its most important mission was to endow France with a reliable electric network, a mission now fulfilled in large part with conventional power plants. But in the France of the late 1950s, in which other government institutions were charged with implementing specific plans aimed at fortifying industry and the French economy, EDF, as a state agency, was expected to set both an industrial and an economic example for the rest of the nation. Engineers and managers involved in EDF's nuclear program could no longer argue that as employees of a nationalized company, they naturally tended toward solutions that best served the public interest and therefore that their desire to build ever more powerful reactors inevitably represented the best course of action. In order to control reactor development and minimize the influence of the CEA, they had to find a new rhetorical strategy.

Perhaps keeping in mind Massé's fondness for precise economic analysis—during his first tenure at EDF, Massé had created the Service des Etudes Economiques Générales to study the economics of energy supply—one EDF manager suggested that the utility generate an economic study comparing the cost of copying EDF1 with that of the proposed design of EDF2. Regardless of the results, he noted, "it is easy to justify our present policy by saying that we are building nuclear plants larger than those originally planned, but further apart [in time.]"[19] The study, completed a few months later, showed that the cost of reproducing EDF2 (30 billion francs) was less than twice that of reproducing EDF1 (16 billion francs). Considering that EDF2 would produce nearly three times as much electricity as would a copy of EDF1, reproducing EDF1 did not seem worthwhile.[20]

EDF promptly began a similar study for the various design options for EDF3. Launching requests for bids in industry for a reactor that used three 125-MW alternators and another that used two 250-MW alternators, it showed the CEA and the Planning Commission that the latter solution was cheaper. The two institutions reached a compromise: they would build EDF3 with two 250-MW alternators, but they would announce a figure of 375 MW. Again, this would give them an error margin as well as the capacity to push their technology to the limit.[21]

EDF's use of these economic studies to defend its technological choices signalled the beginning of a major transformation within the nuclear division of the utility. The success with which these studies had enabled engineers to have their choices accepted encouraged them to continue using such studies and to develop and refine their techniques. Rather than designing exclusively by trial and error, EDF engineers began using such studies in their design work as well. We shall now examine the increasing role of economic analysis in engineering work, and the role that this analysis played in helping EDF engineers change the terms of debate within the nuclear program.

"L'important C'est de Convaincre"[22]: Nuclear Power Competes with Conventional Power, 1960–1964

Engineers in EDF's nuclear teams began to use economic analysis both as a design tool and as part of their rhetorical strategy just as such analyses gained widespread national attention. De Gaulle's return engendered renewed enthusiasm toward economic planning. The Fourth Plan, intended to cover the years 1962–1965, was the first elaborated under the new regime. It benefitted not just from a political and economic climate more disposed to heed its recommendations, but also from a new Planning Commissioner, Pierre Massé.

Massé had spent much of his career in electric utilities and joined EDF at its inception. Renowned both within the utility and in political circles for his formidable intellect, he was one of the men responsible for introducing economic modeling, not just to EDF but to the French industrial world. During his first tenure at EDF, he elaborated theories of economic optimization to figure out how best to handle the electricity distribution network and regulate EDF's overall system of energy production. These models won the respect of engineers and managers throughout the utility, and recognition in French private industry as well as abroad. In his new capacity as Planning Commissioner, he used his theories to generate economic models of the nation's industrial development. The precepts of the Fourth Plan rested upon these models.[23] Meanwhile, back at EDF, Massé had left a solid legacy of economic analysis, concentrated in the Service des Etudes Economiques Générales.[24]

He left this division in the hands of Marcel Boiteux, a brilliant young economist from the Ecole Nationale Supérieure. The Service's main tasks were to forecast the nation's electricity demand, analyze external factors that would influence the cost and pricing of electricity production, and prepare the management and rationalization tools that corresponded to Massé and Boiteux's ideas about economic optimization. Typically, the division developed consumption forecasts for five to ten years in the future. These forecasts were then used to justify current construction of power plants. Prediction of France's overall energy demand would be based on the gross national product (GNP) forecasts publicized by the Planning Commission. At first, according to one of Boiteux's employees, the division used classic econometrics models that posited the growth of energy consumption to be a function of the expected rate of growth of the GNP.[25] When Pierre Ailleret, EDF's Directeur Général Adjoint, began to examine the question, he argued that uses for electric power were developing so rapidly that consumption would in fact increase geometrically rather than linearly; he predicted that it would double every ten years. This "doctrine," to use Ailleret's term, began to underlie the models generated by the division.[26]

Initially, these economic studies were directed less toward developing accurate forecasts of energy demand than toward convincing those outside EDF that demand would in fact rise. As Boiteux told one of his economists, "l'important c'est de

convaincre" ("What is important is to convince others."[27] The Service des Etudes
Economiques Générales thus provided EDF's project engineers with the tools they
needed to "sell" their work. And there was no question that these tools had persuasive power. Perhaps because it was headed by Massé, a primary architect of these
tools, the Planning Commission readily accepted the validity of EDF's analysis.
More important still, these analyses often persuaded the Ministry of Finance to up-
hold EDF's budget allocations—a crucial accomplishment, as the ministry had the
power to cut costs and slash programs when it deemed such actions necessary. A
high-ranking official of the Ministry of Industry later recalled that:

> EDF was . . . one of the first big enterprises to have done in-depth techno-economic
> [*sic*] studies. It is important to underscore this point, as they were very much appreci-
> ated by the [Ministry of] Finance. . . .[28]

Perhaps in part because of their persuasive power, the influence of such economic studies extended beyond the rhetorical spheres of ministerial politics into engineering practice. By 1960, the studies of the Service des Etudes Economiques
Générales comparing the price of different forms of electricity production had cir-
culated throughout the utility. Ailleret, known as a staunch advocate for nuclear energy since the early 1950s, became a great proponent of these studies as well. He
headed EDF's Comité d'Energie Nucléaire, a committee that met once a month to
discuss the utility's nuclear development policy and examine current technological
problems or choices in the reactor program. His background as an engineer of the
Corps des Ponts et Chaussées and his involvement in the CEA's Marcoule projects
doubtless gave him credibility. It seems likely that engineers in charge of EDF's nuclear program began using the techniques of economic analysis at least in part
through his influence.

Economic analysis, in the form of "optimization studies," had been used for
several years elsewhere at EDF in designing conventional power plants. These studies broke down the cost of a power plant into the cost of its individual components,
then minimized the overall cost either by finding ways to lower the cost of specific
components or by redesigning certain components so that the whole plant would
produce more power. These methods were not applied to reactor design until 1960,
however, partly, perhaps, because "optimization" did not become popular in EDF
until then, and partly because the number of variables to take into account when
analyzing reactors was so high that calculations were extremely difficult to perform
with mere adding machines. The arrival of computers in EDF's research facilities
changed the latter state of affairs.[29]

The first optimization study done for reactors covered the design of EDF3 and
was performed in the first half of 1960, before the final design parameters had been
set.[30] The principle guiding the optimization of EDF3's design was to maximize
power while minimizing the volume of the reactor core. Using reference costs provided by the Service des Etudes Economiques Générales and relationships between
various core dimensions, engineers could play with different core configurations to
calculate how to derive the most power from the least uranium. They could thus
"prove," for example, their assertion that increasing the unit power of a nuclear plant

decreased the overall cost of producing electricity. Using parameters provided by various CEA teams—such as the maximum temperature of the carbon dioxide cooling gas that the fuel slugs could withstand—they also played with the parameters of the thermal cycle. Whereas in earlier projects they had only tried to make the reactors thermodynamically efficient, they now began searching for economic efficiency as well.[31]

Using optimization studies thus changed the way in which EDF engineers did their work. In the words of one engineer who worked on EDF's nuclear project both before and after the introduction of these studies, before, "the whole trick . . . was to find the best compromise possible, without much economic data. We didn't do any optimizations. . . . It was a mixture of common sense, of intuition. . . ."[32] Once they began using optimization techniques and computers:

> Until then these calculations were done by hand. I had a young woman engineer with me [who did most of these calculations]. . . .
>
> At the time, the people behind the computers wore white coats. [They] took your calculations, a bit like a doctor would see you for a visit. . . . The machine put out for me in one run what the young woman engineer would have taken two years to do. . . . We could "play" in a much more sophisticated way. . . .[33]

Engineers soon began to plug technological options into economic models in order to test which option would best suit their purposes. Economic modeling, from optimization studies to energy consumption forecasts, became a trademark of EDF. Pioneered in the utility, these techniques became something that the whole institution grew proud of, and that marked the work done there, at least during the 1960s, as unique. Although these methods of working spread to a few other industries, EDF economists and engineers remained the acknowledged experts in the domain.[34]

Optimization studies did not set the goals of EDF's engineers, but their use influenced both those goals and the path that engineers took to attain them. As nuclear design teams began to use optimization studies in designing reactors and justifying their solutions, they became more caught up in the practice of economic comparisons. Initially, engineers compared the cost of their reactors with that of conventional power plants in order to show those outside EDF that they aimed to produce a technology that would soon be economically viable. But very quickly such comparisons began to dominate their work. In the words of one participant, "we lived in economic comparisons, in comparisons of the cost of the kilowatt-hour."[35] This comparison provided them with a new agenda, one as economic in nature as it was technological.

The use of economic optimization studies heightened the awareness of EDF's nuclear teams that their work had to fit into a larger system of electricity production. They had always wanted their plants to produce electricity at the minimum possible cost, but in the 1950s, the mere fact of building such a novel technology had provided them with a sufficient raison d'être. Furthermore, they had billed their reactors as "prototypes": no one had expected the first reactors to be economically viable. The government had even been willing to pay a *surprix*, a surplus cost for the reactors, on the chance that nuclear plants would eventually provide France with an independent energy source. Given their new tools, however, and given the political and economic climate of the early 1960s, these engineers began to realize that in order to survive, they not only had to compete with the CEA for jurisdiction over plant design, but also with their colleagues in conventional power—not just technologically, but also economically. They began furiously analyzing the "objective cost" of their projects, from EDF1 through EDF3, in order to get a sense of how close they were to producing a nuclear kilowatt-hour (kWh) that could "compete" with the conventional one.[36]

Their results indicated that they could achieve this goal with their next reactor, EDF4, destined for a new site in Saint-Laurent-des-Eaux. This time, however, they decided that rather than increase the power of the reactor, they would design a 480–500-MW reactor primarily geared toward "competitiveness" with conventional power plants.[37] They rejected the CEA's idea of copying EDF3's design, preferring instead what they called an "integrated" design. In this configuration, the heat exchangers sat inside the pressure vessel, right underneath the core. This new design, they felt, would save on construction costs and increase the safety and reliability of the reactor.[38] Because the reactor would probably last longer than the Chinon reactors, they planned to extend its amortization period, thereby reducing their initial payments.[39] And finally, they would design EDF4 solely for electricity production.[40] They had attempted to design EDF2 and EDF3 on these terms, but the CEA had managed to impose certain design features that facilitated the production of weapons-grade plutonium and reduced the amount of electricity that the reactors could generate.[41]

The debate over plutonium production in the early 1960s provides perhaps the most striking example of the increasing prevalence of economic reasoning and the change in ideas about competitiveness in the thinking and rhetoric of EDF engineers. In the 1950s, EDF engineers had cast their objections to plutonium production primarily in technological terms: this production would alter reactor design in a way undesirable for electricity production. But in 1960 they began casting their objections in economic terms as well, thereby changing the nature of the plutonium debate. In order to understand how this happened, we shall examine this debate in some detail.

The CEA did not dispute that nuclear plants should become "competitive" with conventional ones, even though it did not always agree with EDF's views on the best way to attain this goal. But it remained extremely interested in obtaining weapons-grade plutonium from EDF reactors, especially as de Gaulle's *force de frappe* agenda permitted the expansion of its military program. In 1960, it made its first official request for plutonium to EDF. Needless to say, engineers at the utility were less than thrilled by this request, but after extensive discussions between the Ministry of the Armies, the Ministry of Atomic and Space Affairs, the Ministry of Industry, and the CEA, the utility gave in. In December 1960, EDF told the CEA that it did not oppose providing the subirradiated fuel slugs necessary for plutonium production as long as the utility did not have to bear the extra expense of doing so, and as long as the experience that EDF hoped to gain out of operating the Chinon reactors was not impaired.[42]

As of February 1961, the official arrangement was that unless an unforseen incident took place at the Marcoule reactors, no more than one-sixth of the fuel capacity of the Chinon reactors would be used for military purposes, and this only as of 1966. In April 1961, however, the CEA asked for a higher limit: they wanted to use one-quarter the fuel capacity of the Chinon reactors for plutonium production. Both EDF and the Ministry of Industry protested this change, arguing that it would seriously impair EDF's ability to derive adequate operational experience from its own reactors. After further negotiations, the terms of the agreement were redrawn in April 1962. The CEA would give EDF a set number of specially designed fuel slugs reserved for plutonium production; it would pay for changes that EDF had to make in the fuel loading machines of both EDF1 and EDF3 to facilitate this production; the two institutions would agree on a definition of the maximum load destined for each type of fuel slug in each reactor; and finally, both institutions would evaluate the "inconveniences" caused in the operation of the reactors by plutonium production and come up with compensatory measures.[43]

Because the nature of those compensatory measures remained unclear, EDF engineers were able to use their newly found expertise in "technoeconomic" analysis to redefine the plutonium question in economic terms. EDF's Comité de l'Energie Nucléaire considered several ways of turning plutonium production into an economic problem. Initially, the CEA acknowledged that the plutonium was destined for weapons use. EDF would therefore derive no benefit from its production. Hence, concluded the Comité, it should calculate the financial loss EDF would suffer by figuring out the equivalent energy that a coal plant would produce.[44] But around 1962, the CEA began talking about civilian uses for plutonium. It had begun to work on Rapsodie, its first experimental breeder reactor, which ran on plutonium. The CEA argued that Chinon's plutonium could potentially go to Rapsodie, and eventually to future breeders. As these breeders would generate electricity, it was hence in EDF's financial interest to produce plutonium. Undeterred, EDF engineers calculated the financial benefit that the CEA would derive from treating the used fuel, arguing that this benefit had to be considered in the price that EDF might eventually pay for breeder fuel. The spent fuel went to CEA reprocessing centers, where the plutonium would be separated from the uranium for future use. The cost of this operation, EDF argued, was diminished by the monetary value of the plutonium. In response, the CEA noted that starting up a reactor, which EDF had to do no matter what, inevitably led to the production of certain amount of plutonium, known as "fatal" plutonium. This should be taken into account in any economic calculation made by EDF. EDF responded that it could easily devise a fuel loading cycle that would not produce "fatal" plutonium. Besides, the committee argued, "given the impossibility of predicting how the problem of military plutonium will be posed, right now it is not a question of proving anything, but of determining very objectively the different losses of information that could result from the presence of subirradiated fuel. . . ."[45] This determination was necessary both to facilitate the design of the next reactor, and to estimate the economics of future reactors. Engineers thus attached a specific financial value to their technological agenda.

This line of reasoning, together with the increased importance of producing a "competitive" kilowatt-hour, led the Comité to the idea of a plutonium credit as one possible way of making EDF's reactors more cost-effective:

> A plutonium credit with the CEA now appears possible. We would then go back to the formula of a "meter" according to which EDF would offer the CEA a recuperation price. This would be a function of the amount of plutonium present, EDF being free to operate [reactors] in the best economic conditions, which would result from the leeway involved in the "meter."[46]

Just as EDF could not outright squash the CEA's demands for military plutonium,[47] neither could the CEA deny the desirability of EDF's goal of a competitive nuclear kilowatt-hour. It did, however, argue that a plutonium credit would not help EDF attain this goal. The CEA had started a small division of economic studies whose economists appeared mainly concerned with refuting EDF's figures. They soon produced several reports directed at invalidating the concept of a plutonium credit. These studies concluded that a plutonium credit would in no way help the nuclear kilowatt-hour compete with the conventional one. On the contrary, such a credit might even set such an effort back. Rather, they argued, the concept of a plutonium credit should be set aside for a while and economic analyses should be devoted to studying the mechanisms of the creation and development of a worldwide plutonium market.[48]

In typical fashion the issue went back and forth between the two institutions for some time. The debate dragged on through 1964, when its terms were altered by a new definition of competitiveness that had begun to receive serious attention on the national political and economic front: the economic competitiveness of French technology on foreign markets. Once again, EDF tried to change the terms of the debate:

> The competition that our system is likely to encounter in the near future from the boiling water system leads us to reconsider the hopes of assigning a value to irradiated fuel [raised by] the prospect of breeder reactors.

> Despite the interest rates and the possibilities of liberating plutonium, it seems that preparing a bill for breeders gives an economic interest to the preparation of a stock of plutonium. This interest should translate commercially into a "plutonium credit" *on the order of magnitude of the differences in cost between the French system and the American system*[49] [emphasis added].

This new approach to economic competitiveness, which compared French technology with foreign technology rather than domestic nuclear plants with domestic conventional plants, soon began to dominate the debates between the two institutions, making them more acrimonious than ever. The dimensions taken on by new debates over exporting reactors eventually obscured the whole issue of the plutonium credit, as EDF's policies were called into question and the government's stake in the nuclear program rose yet higher.

The Organization of Industrial Contracting:
French Reactors Compete with Foreign Technology, 1964–1969

The arrival of the Common Market in the late 1950s focused the attention of government leaders on preparing their country for new economic conditions. They were especially concerned with French industrial structure and development. Many felt that, despite the intensive development of the reconstruction, French industry still lagged behind that of other developed nations. Some argued that French industry had spread itself too thin by trying to develop competence in too many different domains of technology. To remedy this, France should concentrate on specializing in a selected number of high-technology fields—of which nuclear energy was one.[50] Others argued that industry had spent too much time on product development and not enough time on long-range corporate strategies.[51] Georges Pompidou, de Gaulle's second prime minister, felt that the source of these problems lay in the protectionist policies and economic restrictions that had characterized French economic structure in the preceding decades. The solution lay in taking measures to decrease the hold of the state on French industry, thereby liberalizing the economy. In true French style, this attempt to open the economy was formalized in the State's Fifth Plan, elaborated by the Planning Commission in 1965. This plan aimed at combatting the inward focus of French industry and helping the French economy prepare for the competition it had already begun to face from foreign nations. Its biggest priority was "to establish the competitive capacity of French industry in the world."[52] But how should restructuring of French industry occur? Should French companies form large consortia that could compete on a European scale? Or would competitiveness on foreign markets work better if domestic competition were allowed to thrive? This national debate addressed issues at the heart of EDF's nuclear contracting policy.

Throughout the first half of the 1960s, EDF had smooth relations with the government. The only area in which the utility had any trouble was plutonium production. Otherwise, though, government institutions had supported its decisions and programs. The Ministry of Industry regularly defended EDF's interests; the Ministry of Finance had approved its plans; the Planning Commission, headed by a former EDF economist, appeared to hold a vision of France's economic future compatible with EDF's; and Comité pour la Production d'Energie d'Origine Nucléaire, or the PEON Commission, ostensibly in charge of elaborating programs for nuclear energy development, had approved EDF's proposals.[53]

EDF's easy relationship with the government would not continue. As the government's determination to look beyond the boundaries of the French state found echoes throughout the nuclear program, various issues once again challenged EDF's vision of nuclear development. In this round of debates, utility engineers had more difficulty defending their positions, partly because technological problems with EDF3 had damaged their credibility,[54] partly because the joint forces of private industry, the CEA, and various government institutions were arrayed against them, and partly because EDF engineers had lost the unconditional support of their managers.[55] Once again, aspects of the organization of technological work at the utility in the context of a new definition of competitiveness.

In 1964, exporting French reactors had begun to seem plausible to certain members of the nuclear establishment. How to build exportable reactors, however, remained an open question. Jules Horowitz, head of the CEA's Direction des Piles Atomiques argued that in order to export this technology, France would have to concentrate solely on building a reproducible product. Thus he tried to convince his EDF counterparts to copy EDF3's design in future reactors. Most EDF engineers strongly disagreed. One expostulated:

> What would be the position today of the CEA supporters of export if EDF had adopted Mr. Horowitz's point of view? EDF3 would be limited to 375-MW gross, [and] EDF4 would be a duplication of EDF3, which is to say a design completely surpassed by the British projects at Olbury and Wylfa.[56]

By the mid-1960s, though, not everyone at the CEA advocated building reactor series. In an effort to make peace between the two institutions so that they could work together more fruitfully, Robert Hirsch, the CEA's Administrateur Général, wrote to André Decelle, EDF's Directeur Général, that "the French efforts to export" led the CEA to consider the development of an improved version of EDF4 an urgent matter. The CEA, Hirsch wrote, was conscious of the increasing pressure of foreign competition and was willing to undertake the research necessary to push French reactor design as far as possible.[57] Decelle received this suggestion favorably, and the two leaders drew up informal cooperation guidelines. Thus the issue of international competition entered nuclear debates. It even seemed as though the two leaders agreed over both the need to conquer this new challenge and the means with which to do so. But this truce did not last long.

By mid-1965, engineers and managers had begun quarreling again. This time, their confrontations were not about how to design reactors; Hirsch and Decelle had at least managed to still those quarrels. Rather, the source of conflict was EDF's industrial contracting policy. The two institutions had argued briefly about this policy in the mid-1950s; the issue then lay dormant for nearly ten years. When it came up again in the mid-1960s, it was discussed with more venom, and, it seemed, with more at stake, for it related directly to questions about France's role in the international market.

The fundamental problem remained the same as before, only this time private industry had accumulated more construction experience with the nuclear program. Throughout the construction of its reactors, EDF had relied on a single, time-proven method of industrial contracting. One of several teams in the Direction de l'Equipement played the role of both *architecte industriel* and *maître d'œuvre* for a given reactor. Thus the team would devise an initial design for the entire reactor, subdivide various components into lots, launch requests for bids among private companies for each lot, pick the best bid, and supervise and coordinate the construction of the reactor. For its Marcoule reactors, the CEA had merely come up with the initial design; it then picked one industrial consortium to do all the rest, although of course the CEA teams followed the building process attentively and provided technical help to companies that ran into any problems. The CEA had raised strong objections when EDF proceeded differently.

EDF held that its method provided the best means of obtaining the lowest prices on components, and the debate subsided. In 1965, however, in the face of new questions about France's international "competitiveness," EDF's policy came under renewed attack. The companies that had been building EDF's reactors were unhappy because they felt that the policy did not allow them to get the experience they needed to successfully export reactors. Because no single company had had the opportunity to coordinate the construction of an entire reactor, none could actually sell a reactor to a foreign country. At best, they could put in bids for reactor parts. But the organization of nuclear programs in other countries differed substantially from that in France, and the opportunities to put in such bids were rare to nonexistent.

EDF defended itself by rephrasing its arguments in popular political terms. Its method would "make possible wider competition," as well as enable the utility to pay less surplus cost on its reactor. This, in turn, would "favor the competitiveness" of the gas–graphite design with other designs.[58] Realizing, however, the difficulties that its policy posed for companies wishing to export reactors, EDF engineers were willing to make slight changes. For the construction of the Saint-Laurent and the Bugey reactors, it encouraged private industry to create consortia that EDF could then contract to work on larger subdivisions of the reactor. For the case of Saint-Laurent 1, for example, this meant that only 17 orders were filled for over 80 percent of the reactor. Thus competition would continue to exist between two sets of consortia. But it also meant that EDF had to keep a closer watch on private industry to avoid cost overruns. This seemed as far as the engineers in the EDF teams were willing to go.[59]

Private industry and the CEA wanted to push EDF further. It wanted EDF to launch bids for what came to be termed "chaudières nucléaires," or "nuclear boilers." In this scenario, once an EDF team had drafted a preliminary design, it would accept bids from large consortia for the reactor core and attending machinery as a whole. This suggestion did not sit well with the engineers in the EDF teams. One wrote angrily:

> Increasingly one hears, and especially in high spheres, closer to Politics than to Industry, that EDF is not fulfilling its normal [*sic*] role with respect to French Industry, and in particular that the division of contracts that it passes prevents the birth, or impedes the growth, of powerful [industrial] Groups, the only ones capable, it appears, of exporting plants to foreign countries.

> This affirmation, so often repeated that it is taking on the allure of dogma, is but a vulgar untruth.[60]

The issue had arrived back on the level of the mission of a public institution to its State. EDF engineers, proud of their work, felt offended by attacks on their competence and judgment in fulfilling their mission. They argued that the division of labor between various companies had never posed a problem: the problem was, rather, with industry as a whole. On numerous occasions, EDF had had to help companies solve technological problems that they were incapable of dealing with independently. It was not fair, argued EDF engineers, to compare the "nuclear boilers" with the boilers in a conventional plant: "nuclear boilers" represented a full 70 percent of the entire plant, whereas conventional boilers made up only 25 percent of the plant.

One engineer pursued his defense of EDF's policy by noting that the utility's mission to the country was to provide the nation with electricity in the best possible cost and safety conditions. This could only occur if reactor construction could benefit from all the experience accumulated by the Direction de l'Equipement, and if engineers could continue to choose the best material at the lowest price. And the French reactor program would be in an even better position if industry would accept free-market competition rather than organizing itself into syndicates and lobbies whose power obstructed progress by killing any proposals that might jeopardize the existence of such entities. "The attitude of French industry," wrote this engineer, "despite a few rare and brilliant exceptions, is a defensive attitude, the role of its [leadership] being to build a 'Maginot line' around more or less sanely arrived-at positions."[61]

Currently, he continued, industry organized itself into loose associations of companies that became weakened rather than strengthened by such associations:

> . . . we think that the fusion of, or the understanding between, two Companies working in the same field can be worthwhile, while as the grouping, under the banner of a bank . . . is a grotesque effort and unfortunately dangerous, because, for many of our leaders, volume and power go together with intelligence, as if the diplodocus hadn't been dead since the secondary Era![62]

Such groupings diffused the technological knowledge and experience that resided in the companies rather than fusing such knowledge together. Rather than go along with such groupings, EDF should promote those that would make French industry strong on the international market. In conclusion, he wrote:

> The Commissariat à l'Energie Atomique, spokesman of the "Groups," reproaches EDF for a policy which, apparently prevents French Industrialists from exporting anything. . . .
>
> First, one must have something to export; whether one wishes it or not, as long as we cannot offer, in France, nuclear plants that function normally and give their user, that is EDF, full satisfaction, only political pressure or exhorbitant financial advantages can lead to the export of nuclear plants. . . .[63]

Many engineers in the Direction de l'Equipement felt the same way, even if none expressed himself quite so eloquently. Many sincerely believed that their method of working was truly the best one for the overall health of the French economy. But one of them expressed the most probable fundamental reason for their vehemence: if industry took over larger portions of the work of designing and building reactors, EDF engineers would not have much interesting work left.[64]

This time, unlike in the mid-1950s, the contracting issue reached the ministerial level. The whole issue of industrial competitiveness had become the single most important economic question in the nation. Furthermore, private industry had joined the CEA in attacking EDF's policy. And in the mid- to late 1960s, politicians felt less inclined to blindly trust EDF.[65]

EDF engineers fought hard to preserve their working methods, arguing that only thus could reactors become both technologically and economically suitable for export. For example, one engineer argued that even if industry formed two consortia, as it had done, the Direction de l'Equipement would not truly have a choice between them, since one of the consortia, Groupement Atomique Alsacienne Atomique (GAAA), had recently lost a contract with the Germans and would need a consolation prize in the form of a reactor contract. Furthermore, he argued, the CEA was unfairly balancing the odds to favor the policy advocated by industry. While the project costs were all that counted in the eyes of many, for EDF engineers the safety and reliability of the installations counted equally. Such concerns explained the surplus cost of EDF reactors. He continued:

> Who will decide between these two points of view? The CEA? I don't think so. I point out on this subject that EDF never got more than 445–450 degrees [centigrade] out of the CEA for the temperature of the fuel slug cans. But [the CEA] immediately gave Industry 465 degrees [centigrade] to make the system competitive for export.
>
> . . . When an accident or a breakdown occurs, if it occurs one day, ten or fifteen years may have gone by. GAAA and Schneider will have disappeared, and EDF will find itself alone before its judges.[66]

The top managers of EDF's Direction de l'Equipement, however, appeared unwilling or unable to decide in favor of their engineers. By the mid-1960s these managers were primarily career administrators or economists rather than engineers.[67] Perhaps the pressures put on EDF by the government and private industry were too strong to resist. In any event, at the end of December 1965 the Direction made a tentative decision in favor of a new contracting policy for the reactors at Fessenheim, the projected site for the next two gas–graphite reactors. EDF would launch two kinds of requests for bids: one set would follow the utility's traditional policy, and the other would call for bids on the "nuclear boilers."[68]

This proposal assuaged private industry, the government, and the CEA, but it angered the engineers at EDF. They continued to write memoranda and reports to persuade the Direction to reverse the decision.[69] The labor unions also expressed their objections. Claude Tourgeron, the Confédération Générale du Travail's (CGT)[70] representative to EDF's Conseil d'Administration (board of directors), argued that the new policy was bad for the nuclear program, bad for EDF, and bad for the nation. The companies submitting bids for the smaller sublots in the traditional request for bids, said Tourgeron, belonged to the consortia that would submit bids for the "nuclear boiler." They would play with the numbers so that the consortia bids would appear, artificially, lower than the sum of the individual bids. Were the Fessenheim decision merely an experiment in alternative bidding, that would be all right. But Tourgeron suspected that such was not the case: one thing would lead to another, this mode of bidding for nuclear plants would continue, and since the plants of the future would be predominantly nuclear, this policy would eventually put the vast majority of the Direction de l'Equipement's employees out of work. Finally, Tourgeron argued, it was unrealistic to think that France could ever really export gas–graphite reactors. Underdeveloped countries would not want nuclear plants because they were only profitable when they were very powerful, more powerful than such countries would ever need. And industrialized countries would clearly want American plants, as the figures showed these to be less expensive. Gas–graphite plants made sense for France because she had her own natural uranium supply, Tourgeron argued, but they did not make sense for anyone else. Thus the two consortia proposed would only have one customer: EDF. This situation would clearly accelerate the demise of the Direction de l'Equipement, and artificially affect the cost of nuclear power plants.[71]

The objections of the rank and file at the Direction de l'Equipement were to no avail. At a meeting of the Direction in mid-February 1966, director Jean Cabanius expressed his support for the concentration of industry into a few consortia, although he felt that the formation of a single French consortium for any given sector of industry should be avoided. Marcel Boiteux also favored industrial concentration, pointing out that if individual consortia did form, they could then compete more effectively on the international market. A few others had more reservations, but the final decision was made in favor of launching a twofold request for bids for Fessenheim.[72]

It appeared as though EDF's new leaders had, perhaps for the first time, surrendered to the position articulated in the Fifth Plan. Indeed, the plan's Rapport Général de la Commission des Industries de Transformation had emphasized "the need of pursuing the effort of . . . the concentration of French industry to increase its competitiveness and allow it to confront the powerful foreign companies as economic openings occur."[73]

In retrospect, some EDF managers have argued that the shift in emphasis within the nuclear program from competitiveness with conventional power plants to competitiveness on foreign markets and the bitter conflicts that ensued put the seal of death on the gas–graphite program. When the Fessenheim bids came in, EDF judged them all too expensive and refused to begin construction of the reactors. Its managers had been trying to escape the increasing interference of the CEA, to which end they had seriously considered abandoning gas–graphite reactors altogether, buying an American license, and pursuing the nuclear program with light-water reactors. The quarrel over this issue became known as the *guerre des filières* (the "war of the systems"). It was one that EDF eventually won, largely by biding its time and imposing its views on the government. That, however, is a different story entirely.[74]

Conclusion

Our story shows that the term *technological competitiveness* can take on different meanings depending on technological, political, economic, and cultural conditions. In the French nuclear program of the 1950s and 1960s, the term had three different meanings. In the 1950s, "competitiveness" had a technical meaning. Engineers in both the CEA and EDF mainly wanted to forge as "advanced" a technology as possible for their country. Both used the technological performance of the British nuclear program as a standard of comparison. For EDF, this meant building ever more powerful reactors; for the CEA, it meant building reactors similar to one another in design, but guaranteed to work. Each claimed that its agenda would reinforce the country's prestige through technology, and in both cases engineering methods of intuition and trial and error went hand in hand with the rhetorical and strategic emphasis on prestige.

These methods and strategies worked well for both institutions until the end of the decade, when technical mishaps and a changing political and economic climate combined to cast doubts on EDF's position. Utility managers recovered from their losses by changing the terms of the debate: they adopted economic modeling and forecasting techniques as a rhetorical strategy to convince government and industrial leaders of the worth of EDF's development strategy. Adopted and adapted by engineers in the nuclear program, these techniques changed the nature of engineering work in the utility. With the change in work methods and defense strategy came a change in goals. In the early 1960s utility engineers spoke primarily of making nuclear energy "competitive" with conventional power sources. The optimization techniques that engineers used, together with the economic reports that utility managers used to defend their program in ministerial and planning circles, gave the utility a unique institutional identity. Faced with this powerful array of technological, political, economic, and cultural resources, and the concomitant strength of this new definition of "competitiveness," engineers in the CEA could do little but accept the development strategy advocated by the utility. Because it had de Gaulle's backing, the CEA could insist that the utility produce plutonium, but the persuasive power of EDF's economic arguments in the early 1960s enabled the utility to change the terms even of the plutonium debates.

The rapidly changing political and economic climate soon posed a threat to the utility's newfound security, however. Economic planners, industrial leaders, and high-level government officials began to set their sights on opening the French economy to foreign competition. CEA engineers, who had not adapted their work methods to EDF's new emphasis on economic competitiveness, seized this opportunity to attack a different aspect of the organization of technological work in the utility: it charged that EDF's industrial contracting methods made the exportation of French nuclear technology impossible. Sticking to its own definition of competitiveness, the utility tried to argue that only *its* methods could make nuclear reactors competitive with conventional power plants, and therefore competitive for export. But this time, the array of forces ranged against EDF was too strong. The CEA had the backing of many of the private companies that had built reactor components, as well as of government planners and other leaders, and EDF managers, eager to maintain good relations with the government and extend the utility's purview, compromised on the contracting issue against the will of their engineers and technicians.

Elsewhere, I have explored links between technological design and the spheres of politics and economics in the French nuclear program.[75] Historians and sociologists of technology have shown that such links exist in all areas of technological development.[76] But as these same scholars would argue, technology is more than artifact, more than design: it includes entire systems of political, economic, and cultural networks. The story told in this chapter shows us that in order to understand technological development we should look even further than the links between design and politics, economics, and culture. Indeed, by looking at the organization and practice of technological work, we see that it is not just design and development that is influenced by and influences such networks, but also the way in which engineers work.

By looking at the ever-changing relationships between engineering work and the spheres of politics, economics, and culture, we can achieve a fuller understanding of the importance of and meaning attached to a technology in a given cultural context. In the particular case of the French nuclear program, the prestige of the project (a prestige conferred upon it by de Gaulle's ambitions, but also forged and reinforced by the rhetorical and cultural strategies of its architects), together with the close ties that existed between CEA and EDF leaders and government leaders (ties that grew out of both the structure of the engineering profession in France and the prestige of the project), meant that debates about the program's future became national debates. The importance of the nuclear program to the French government had political, economic, and industrial dimensions. The program had become symbolic of the nation's international stature. It was thought to ensure France's future energy independence, and hence have substantial influence on the nation's economy. And finally, the complexity of the technology meant that it required technological development in many different domains: mechanical engineering, electrical engineering, civil engineering, metallurgy, and more. The nuclear program therefore involved a wide cross section of French industry. Under such conditions, it was not just the function of the technology that was important—not just, for example, whether a reactor produced energy, or weapons-grade plutonium, or both—but also how engineers designing that technology worked. The structure of engineering work within the program was not only thought to set an example for the rest of French industry, it also became emblematic of French engineering as a whole. Thus the organization and practice of engineering work within the program became crucial, at least symbolically, to France's success in the emerging world of high technology.[77]

Acknowledgments

I am deeply grateful to the engineers and scientists of EDF and the CEA who so graciously granted me interviews and access to their personal archives; my thanks also to Jean-François Picard and Alain Beltran for giving me access to the research materials they collected for their history of EDF. Finally, for their suggestions throughout various stages of the preparation of this manuscript, I am indebted to Thomas P. Hughes, Nina Lerman, Arne Kaiser, Antonio Botelho, and Eric Schatzberg. This article is based on the third chapter of my dissertation, *The Reactor in the Vineyard: Technological Choice and Cultural Change in the French Nuclear Program.*

Notes

1. See Jean Bouvier *et al.*, *Histoire économique et sociale de la France. Tome IV: L'ère industrielle et la société d'aujourd'hui* (Paris: Presses Universitaires de France, 1982); also Jean-Claude Asselain, *Histoire économique de la France du XVIIIe siècle à nos jours. Tome 2: De 1919 à la fin des années 1970* (Seuil, 1984).

2. François Caron and Jean Bouvier, "Les agents: l'Etat," in Bouvier *et al.*, *Histoire économique et sociale de la France*, op. cit.; Bernard Cazes, "Un demi-siècle de planification indicative," in eds. Maurice Lévy-Leboyer et Jean-Claude Casanova, *Entre l'Etat et le marché: L'économie française des années 1880 à nos jours* (Paris: Editions Gallimard, 1991); John H. McArthur and Bruce R. Scott, *Industrial Planning in France* (Boston: Division of Research, Graduate School of Business Administration, Harvard University, 1969). The role of the plan in French economic policy and development has engendered much debate among social scientists since the 1960s. Some scholars, in emphasizing the distinction between the government and the State in France, argue that even during the Fourth Republic, the Planning Commission, as an agency of the State, provided political continuity despite frequent changes in government. Hence the plans should be understood as the true expression of French economic policy. Other scholars, in paying closer attention to economic practices than policies, argue that despite any continuity that the Planning Commission may have provided, government upheavals did influence the degree to which the plans were heeded. Hence it is the influence of the plans, rather than their content, that should be taken into account when analyzing their role. Although this chapter does not directly address these scholarly debates, I should note that my concern with industrial practice has led me to rely on the body of literature representing the latter position in these debates.

3. Maurice Larkin, *France Since the Popular Front: Government and People, 1936–1986* (Oxford: Oxford Univ. Press [Clarendon], 1986).

4. This is not to say that no one opposed his return, but in 1958 he had by far the strongest base of support of any politician. See Larkin, *France Since the Popular Front*, op. cit., also Philip M. Williams and Martin Harrison, *Politics and Society in De Gaulle's Republic* (London: Longman, 1971).

5. Cazes, "Un demi-siècle," op. cit., and McArthur and Scott, *Industrial Planning*, op. cit.

6. The early years of the nuclear program are discussed in more detail in Gabrielle Hecht, *The Reactor in the Vineyard: Technological Choice and Cultural Change in the French Nuclear Program, 1945–1969* (Ph.D. dissertation in History and Sociology of Science, University of Pennsylvania, Philadelphia, 1992).

7. The megawatt figures given are those announced by EDF for each reactor at the time of construction. In addition to these gas–graphite reactors, the two institutions designed another gas–graphite reactor, which they sold to Spain, and built one heavy-water reactor. The French also collaborated with the Belgians in building a light-water reactor at Chooz.

8. RETN1, BS/JCr, "Memento pour la réunion du 17.7.57 sur EDF2," July 15, 1957.

9. Ibid.

10. Ibid.; interview. The interviews referred to in this chapter are with EDF employees who worked on the nuclear program in the 1950s and 1960s. Most of them were conducted by the author in Paris between September 1989 and August 1990. Three of them are courtesy of Jean-François Picard and Alain Beltran, and were conducted by them between 1981 and 1984.

11. Georges Lamiral, *Chronique de 30 ans d'équipement nucléaire à EDF* (Paris: Association pour l'Histoire de l'Electricité en France, 1988), pp. 38–39.

12. Ibid., p. 120; interview. Weapons-grade plutonium was that element's 239 isotope. Pu-239 was produced in a reactor when a U-238 atom absorbed a neutron and decayed, first into U-239, then into Pu-239. If the Pu-239 stayed in the reactor long enough, it would absorb the neutrons produced by the fissioning of the uranium and decay into Pu-240 and

Pu-241. These isotopes were undesirable for weapons-grade plutonium, as they could cause the plutonium to spontaneously fission. They were also impossible to separate from the Pu-239 in the spent fuel. Therefore the CEA wanted to remove fuel from the reactor as quickly as possible, whereas EDF wanted to leave it in as long as possible in order to extract as much energy as possible from the spent fuel.

13. Interview.

14. Interviews; Lamiral, *Chronique*, op. cit., p. 47.

15. Interviews; Minutes of the meetings of EDF's Comité d'Energie Nucléaire, 1959; Lamiral, *Chronique*, op. cit., pp. 47–51.

16. Interviews. Jean-François Picard, Alain Beltran, and Martine Bungener, *Histoire(s) de l'EDF* (Dunod, 1985).

17. Minutes of meeting of EDF's Comité d'Energie Nucléaire, June 12, 1959.

18. Interviews.

19. Minutes of meeting of EDF's Comité d'Energie Nucléaire, June 12, 1959.

20. Minutes of meeting of EDF's Comité d'Energie Nucléaire, November 16, 1959

21. Minutes of the meetings of EDF's Comité d'Energie Nucléaire, 1958–1960; Lamiral, *Chronique*, op. cit., p. 41; interviews.

22. "What is important is to convince others": the words of Marcel Boiteux to one his employees. Interview.

23. Cazes, "Un demi-siècle," op. cit.; Caron and Bouvier, "Les agents," op. cit.

24. Massé created this division in 1955. It depended directly on the Direction Général (rather than on one of the three big Directions: Equipement, Etudes et Recherches, and Production et Transport). For more on Pierre Massé and his economic thought, see his autobiography: Pierre Massé, *Aléas et Progrès: Entre Candide et Cassandre* (Paris: Economica, 1984); Pierre Massé, *Le Plan ou l'anti-hasard* (Paris: 1965), a book on the Planning Commission that Massé wrote toward the end of his tenure as Planning Commissioner; Picard, Beltran, and Bungener, *Histoire(s)*, op. cit.; Robert L. Frost, *Alternating Currents: Nationalized Power in France, 1946–1970* (Ithaca, N.Y.: Cornell Univ. Press, 1991).

25. Interview. The elasticity coefficient, an expression of the ratio of energy use to the GNP, was set almost at 1. During the interview, this employee remarked that he had had no idea that this coefficient was artificially high in order to promote electricity production: at the time, he said, he had thought that this coefficient expressed a law of nature.

26. Interview. See also Pierre Ailleret, "Les besoins d'énergie à long terme et l'énergie atomique," *Énergie Nucléaire*, vol. 4, No. 1, January–February 1962.

27. Interview.

28. Interview. Translation mine. Another interviewee confirmed this point, adding that the Ministry of Finance people would even get irritated at the high quality of EDF's economic studies.

29. Interviews.

30. Minutes of meetings of EDF's *Comité de l'Energie Nucléaire*, January 18, 1960 and September 23, 1960.

31. Interviews; Minutes of meetings of EDF's Comité de l'Energie Nucléaire, October 21, 1960.

32. Interview. Translation mine.

33. Interview. Translation mine.

34. Interviews; Picard, Beltran, and Bungener, *Histoire(s)*, op. cit.; Massé, *Aléas et Progrès*, op. cit.

35. Interview.

36. Minutes of the meeting of EDF's Comité de l'Energie Nucléaire, July 7, 1961. By "objective cost," they meant the price of constructing the reactors not counting the interest rate or the amortization period.

37. Minutes of the meeting of EDF's Comité de l'Energie Nucléaire, February 7, 1962. At the meeting of the Comité de l'Energie Nucléaire on May 4, 1961, the committee concluded that EDF4 "must approach competitiveness by taking advantage of everything that will appear as a possible improvement during the construction of EDF3. One could very well envisage a solution in which the unloading is only done [when the reactor] is stopped, as long as this is not too slow" [translation mine]. This shows that unloading while the reactor was operating was not as favorable to electricity production as many afterwards claimed that it was: through EDF4, EDF engineers seriously doubted the appropriateness of this solution, and there seems to be no question that left to their own devices, they would never have picked this solution. It eventually did become appropriate because industry and EDF had to spend so much time ensuring that it would, but this would not have happened if it hadn't been for the insistence of the CEA on this point.

38. Minutes of the meeting of EDF's Comité de l'Energie Nucléaire, June 6, 1961.

39. Minutes of the meeting of EDF's Comité de l'Energie Nucléaire, March 7, 1962.

40. Minutes of the meeting of EDF's Comité de l'Energie Nucléaire, September, 28, 1962.

41. That the engineers explicitly designed EDF4 to be competitive with conventional plants is evident in "Element combustible EDF 4: Réflexions à la suite de la réunion du 5 Mars 1963; Service d'Etudes Générales Nucléaires, "Les appareils de chargement et de déchargement du combustible," for the CEA–EDF meeting program of September 17, 1963; EDF, Direction Production et Transport (Service de la Production Thermique), "Centrale Nucléaire à une tranche de 500 MW, réacteur graphite-gaz, Estimation des Frais d'Exploitation," December 27, 1963.

42. Lamiral, *Chronique*, op. cit., p. 56.

43. Ibid., p. 57.

44. Minutes of the meeting of EDF's Comité de l'Energie Nucléaire, June 15, 1960 and July 8, 1960; at the second meeting, the Comité concluded that it had to "study as of now what would be the loss in energy value . . . that would ensue from unloading [slugs] after a short irradiation [period] as a function of the average flow of fuel slugs that one would use in this fashion" [translation mine].

45. Minutes of the meeting of EDF's Comité de l'Energie Nucléaire, September 28, 1962.

46. Minutes of the meeting of EDF's Comité de l'Energie Nucléaire, March 29, 1963. Also "Esquisse d'un programme CEA-EDF de réacteurs de puissance," June 5, 1963, for the meeting of September 17, 1963.

47. And this is highlighted in "L'Evolution des Relations CEA-EDF," October 23, 1964: this memo notes that the CEA derives its power from "its scientific competence, its size (23,000 people), its direct dependence on the Prime Minister, [and] its role in the military program" [translation mine].

48. These studies were conducted in 1963, although their results were only published in 1964. See, for example, Jacques Gaussens, "Faut-il fixer un prix du plutonium?," *Bulletin d'Informations Scientifiques et Techniques*, No. 81, June 1964; also Jean Andriot and Jacques Gaussens, *Economie et Perspectives de l'Energie Atomique* (Paris: Dunod, 1964).

49. Minutes of the meeting of EDF's Comité de l'Energie Nucléaire, March 12, 1964 [translation mine].

50. Christian Stoffaës, "La restructuration industrielle, 1945–1990," in Lévy-Leboyer and Casanova, *Entre l'Etat et le marché* op. cit.

51. McArthur and Scott, *Industrial Planning*, op. cit., p. 179.

52. Ibid., p. 53.

53. According to several members of the commission interviewed by Picard *et al.*, PEON's significance and influence was primarily rhetorical: the commission had too many members, affiliated with too many different institutions (EDF, CEA, several private companies) to actually be able to decide anything concrete about the future direction of nuclear power in France. So even though the various controversies over nuclear development were played out in the PEON meetings, and formal plans for future development did emerge from the meetings, in practice decisions were taken within the institutions represented on the committee. Even the formal plans, it seems, were drawn from proposals put forth by EDF and/or the CEA. (See, for example, "Esquisse d'un programme CEA-EDF de réacteurs de puissance," June 5, 1963, for the meeting of September 17, 1963 [CB63.5]; "Préparation du Vème Plan Equipement Nucléaire," June 12, 1964; annule et remplace la note du June 11, 1964.

54. See Lamiral, *Chronique*, op. cit., for EDF3's problems.

55. On the shift of power within EDF from the engineers who directed much of the utility's development from its creation to the mid-1960s to the "economists–managers" who gradually took over planning and decision making as of the mid-1960s, see Frost, *Alternating Currents*, op. cit.

56. "L'Evolution des relations CEA-EDF," October 23, 1964. Translation mine.

57. Robert Hirsch, Administrateur Général, Délégué du Gouvernement, à Monsieur le Directeur Général d'EDF. Letter dated December 16, 1964.

58. "Filière graphite-gaz, Problème de répartition des commandes," October 19, 1965.

59. Ibid.

60. EDF, REN2, "La Politique Industrielle d'EDF," November 25, 1965. Translation mine.

61. Ibid.

62. Ibid.

63. Ibid.

64. EDF, REN2, "Complément à la note sur la Politique Industrielle d'EDF," December, 27, 1965. Examples of other engineers defending their contracting policy include: EDF, REN1, "La Chaudière Nucléaire," December 6, 1965; Memo from Yves Cordelle to Service d'Etudes Générales Nucléaires, EDF, re: "Marché d'ensemble 'clé en main'," December 20, 1965; EDF, Direction de l'Equipement, "Politique Industrielle EDF pour la filière gaz graphite," January 6, 1966.

65. For example, in a meeting of the Commissions des Finances in December 1965, Olivier-Martin had to defend EDF against accusations that engineers always wanted to build new things, and did not in fact pay all that much attention to cost. Minutes of the December 16, 1965 meeting of the Commission des Finances on "Dépenses d'Investissements."

66. EDF, REN2, "Complément à la note sur la Politique Industrielle d'EDF," op. cit.

67. Frost, *Alternating Currents*, op. cit., and Picard, Beltran, and Bungener, *Histoire(s)*, op. cit.

68. EDF, "Filière Gaz Graphite, Lotissement des Commandes," December 12, 1965. EDF, Direction de l'Equipement, "Politique Industrielle EDF pour la filière gaz graphite," January 6, 1966.

69. "Note sur Politique Industrielle d'EDF en matière de Centrales Nucléaires," March 1, 1966; EDF, REN2, "Répartition des Commandes," January 21, 1966.

70. The Communist labor union. This union included the majority of syndicated EDF workers.

71. Tourgeron declaration, February 1966.

72. "Extrait du Compte-Rendu de la Réunion de Direction du 17 Février 1966."

73. "Politique industrielle EDF dans les centrales de la filière gaz graphite," accompanied by a note from Roux to Bienvenu dated March 1, 1966 indicating that this was a draft of a note to be presented on March 24, 1966; also "Projet de rapport général (Ve Plan: Commission des Industries de Transformation): II: Objectifs et méthodes de l'amélioration des structures."

74. For more on the *guerre des filières*, see Frost, *Alternating Currents*, op. cit., Picard, Beltran, and Bungener, *Histoire(s)*, op. cit., and Lamiral, *Chronique*, op. cit.

75. Hecht, *The Reactor in the Vineyard*, op. cit.

76. For the best examples of such studies, see Thomas P. Hughes, *Networks of Power: Electrification in Western Society, 1880–1930* (Baltimore, Md.: Johns Hopkins Univ. Press, 1983); also Donald MacKenzie, *Inventing Accuracy: A Historical Sociology of Nuclear Missile Guidance* (Cambridge, Mass.: M.I.T. Press, 1990).

77. Nuclear technology was not the only field that took on such significance: another field was computer technology, and in this domain similar issues were also raised, particularly during the infamous "Affaire Bull" (see McArthur and Scott, *Industrial Planning*, op. cit.). It should be noted, though, that even the computer industry did not acquire the symbolic or economic prominence that the nuclear program did—perhaps in part because it did not have as blatant a military importance, and in part because it did not interact with the same variety of industries.

Lessons from History

What can historians possibly have to say about technological competitiveness that would matter to engineering managers or policy analysts? Although this study is only a first, tentative historical exploration of this subject, a number of lessons have emerged. As a conclusion, we have tried to distill these lessons into a set of thirty brief observations. These are the first (but, hopefully, not the last) lessons on technological competitiveness to be drawn from history:

1. The great success of Japanese government agencies, especially MITI, in choosing technologies and companies to support is attributed in the West to an uncanny omniscience; in practice, this success results from the knowledge transferred from industry to government through close personal relationships between business leaders and government officials.

2. Japanese industry, to a degree unmatched in America, benefits greatly from knowledge transfer created by close and continuing relationships between university professors and their students who work in industry.

3. Although the Japanese research system seems impregnable to Westerners, it contains considerable frailties, including rigidity and segmentation, which may eventually cause it to founder.

4. Japanese manufacturers have devoted substantial attention to components, materials, packaging, and manufacturing, which have been important in their ability to provide quality and reliable products.

5. By contrast, manufacturers in the United States have devoted greater attention to the production of finished systems and devices.

6. The orientation towards consumer rather than military markets has been a major factor in Japan's strong competitive showing.

7. Japanese manufacturers have significantly improved quality, reliability, and cost through mechanization of manufacturing.

8. Silicon Valley was shaped largely by Cold War defense policy, and taking it as a model for technological and economic development may be a mistake for other regions in a time when commercial markets are becoming more important than military ones.

9. A model commonly cited by proponents of Big Science hypothesizes that scientific advances lead directly to technological advances, which in turn lead directly to commercial and military applications. The fact that this model of the relation between science and technology has been discredited by historians of technology undermines this particular argument in favor of government support for Big Science.

10. Governments have a difficult time protecting indigenous industries. Efforts to rationalize industries, e.g. through forced mergers, to make them compete more effectively with foreign competition are particularly unsuccessful.

11. Perception and reality in national competitiveness are often at odds. For example, public pronouncements about the impending collapse of the American dominance in the supercomputing field have been widely overstated, partly because analysts have confined themselves to anecdotal evidence or a small number of technical indicators.

12. Contrary to popular belief, there is little solid evidence that America's national competitiveness is being threatened by lack of access to supercomputing resources.

13. Social factors can affect competitiveness in unforeseen ways. For example, strong social ties between users and manufacturers can create barriers to entry and retard the increase in technical specifications of products.

14. Competitiveness occurs in monopolistic and publicly regulated industries, but in these industries it is defined in terms of how technology should be employed, to what aims, and for what benefits, not in terms of competition over customers, profits, or markets. Government regulation can promote competition in monopolistic industries.

15. Two factors determining a nation's ability to compete, having the best technological infrastructure and supporting the country's indigenous suppliers of that infrastructure, are often at odds—especially in developing countries.

16. New technologies can frequently stimulate the pace and degree of competition among companies.

17. Industry and government may not be the only players in competitive fields; individuals and private groups can contend with establishment organizations over the uses of technologies and directions of technological development.

18. Technical performance, pricing, advertising, and political pressure all affect technological competitiveness. The relative importance of these factors varies from one case to the next.

19. In cases where cost and technical performance do not clearly decide a victor among competing technologies, other factors such as industry structure or perceptions about the progressiveness of the technology may prove decisive.

20. Business, technical, regulatory, and other factors all affect technologies chosen for a given application; there is no such thing as one ideal, correct, or appropriate technology for a given application. Frequently, the technology employed in a given application changes over time.

21. Versatility is a great asset of technologies; they can win out over competing technologies by being able to be used in many different settings and in new designs and applications.

22. Competition is not always good for an industry or a nation; it can lead to inefficiency, duplicative effort, and waste.

23. Contrary to widespread beliefs in technological determinism, individual firms and government agencies, or even people within them, often have a significant impact on the shaping of competitive environments.

24. The ability to compete successfully for capital can be decisive.

25. Having the right organizational structure can be as important or more important than having good products, low prices, and low production costs.

26. Tax laws can have a strong shaping force on competition.

27. Sociological factors are often critical in determining the reception of technologies, especially in cases where a technology is perceived as having some environmental or human risk.

28. The prevailing issues governing competitiveness for nations are highly temporal and are likely to change over time.

29. Winning technologies often win for reasons unknown at the outset of development; conditions of use frequently differ from those the inventor envisioned.

30. Many firms dislike protectionism either because they fear retaliatory protectionism from other countries or because they believe that they could create additional business through more competition.

Appendix

Technological Competitiveness in the Electrical and Electronics Industries: Historical and Contemporary Perspectives

A conference organized by the IEEE-Rutgers Center for the History of Electrical Engineering and supported by a grant from the Alfred P. Sloan Foundation.

This appendix lists the program of the conference, held in October 1991, from which this book arose.

Thursday, October 10

Keynote Session

Eric Sumner (IEEE), Introductory Remarks

Paul Leath (Rutgers), Introductory Remarks

Herbert Kleiman (Kleiman Associates), Keynote Address: Semiconductors in the Twentieth Century: Some Lessons for Today

Reception

Friday, October 11

Electrotechnology in Competition

Chair: Keith Nier (Edison Papers Historical Project)

Anne Millbrooke (United Technologies), Technological Systems Compete at Otis: Hydraulic versus Electric Elevators

Ulrich Wengenroth (Technical University, Munich), How They Won the Market: Electric Motors in Competition with Steam Engines, 1890–1925

Arne Kaijser (Stockholm), Lighting, Cooking, and Heating: Competing Energy Systems in Sweden, 1880–1990

William W. Weil (Computrol), Commentator

Power: Studies from France

Chair: Eric Schatzberg (Center for the History of Electrical Engineering)

Alain Beltran (Institut d'histoire du temps present), Electricity in Postwar France: Political Choices, Monopoly, and Competitiveness

Gabrielle Hecht (Pennsylvania), Constructing Competitiveness in Postwar France: The Case of Nuclear Power, 1955–1969

Steven Kline (Pacific Gas and Electric), Commentary

Power: Studies from the United States

Chair: Paul Israel (Edison Papers Historical Project)

Mark Rose (Florida Atlantic), Urbanizing Electrical Technology: The Political-Geography of Noncompetitiveness, 1880–1940

Richard Hirsh (Virginia Tech), Technological Stasis and Technological Reinvigoration in the American Electric Power Industry

Peter Kushkowski (Northeast Utilities), Commentator

Electrical Manufacturers

Chair: Reese V. Jenkins (Edison Papers Historical Project)

W. Bernard Carlson (Virginia), National Markets and Capital: Competition Among Electrical Manufacturers in the United States

Leonard Reich (Colby), Lighting the Path to Profit: GE's Control of the Electric Lamp Industry, 1892–1941

George Wise (General Electric), Commentary

Saturday, October 12

Military-Industry Interactions

Chair: William Aspray (Center for the History of Electrical Engineering)

Stuart W. Leslie (Johns Hopkins), How the West Was Won: The Military and the Making of Silicon Valley

Arthur L. Norberg and Judy E. O'Neill (Charles Babbage Institute), Military Funding for Research and Development: A Dual Role in Computing and Competitiveness

Robert Smith (National Air and Space Museum), Big Science and Competitiveness

Robert R. Everett (Mitre), Commentary

Electronics

Chair: Frederick Nebeker (Center for the History of Electrical Engineering)

John Peter Collett (Olso), Meeting the American Challenge—A Small Country Mobilizing its Resources to Create a Competitive Electronics Industry

Yuzo Takahashi (Tokyo University of Agriculture and Technology), Progress in the Electronic Components Industry in Japan after World War II

Lennart Stenberg (Lund), Technological Strength Needs and Feeds a New Research Infrastructure

James Gover (Sandia Laboratories), Commentator

Computing

Chair: Michael R. Williams (Calgary)

Martin Campbell-Kelly (Warwick), ICL and British Government Management of Key Industries Against Foreign Competition

Donald Mackenzie (Edinburgh) and Boelie Elzen (Twente), Supercomputing: The Dialectic of Autonomy and Network-Building

Emerson Pugh (IBM), Commentator

Sunday, October 13

Radio

Chair: Andrew Goldstein (Center for the History of Electrical Engineering)

Susan Douglas (Hampshire), Oppositional Uses of Technology and Corporate Competition: The Case of Radio Broadcasting

Open discussion

Communications

Chair: Sheldon Hochheiser (AT&T)

Frank Thomas (Max Planck Institute, Koln), The German Long-Distance Cable Company and the Restrictions of Competitiveness within a Closely Coupled Technology, 1921–1945

Kenneth Lipartito (Harvard), The Strategy of System Building: Bell Confronts the American South

Pascal Griset (Centre national de la recherche scientifique), The Centre national d'etude des telecommunications and the Competitiveness of the French Telephone Industry, 1945–1980s

Amos Joel (consultant), Commentator

About the Contributors

William Aspray is director of the IEEE-Rutgers Center for the History of Electrical Engineering and a member of the graduate faculty in history at Rutgers University. He has written extensively on the history of computing, including *John von Neumann and the Origins of Modern Computing* (MIT Press, 1990). He is currently writing a book on the history of computers with Martin Campbell-Kelly for the Sloan Foundation Technology Series and has recently begun research on the history of electric power, semiconductors, and telecommunications.

Alain Beltran is Chargé de Recherche, Institut d'Histoire du Temps Présent (CNRS, Paris) and Chargé de Cours à l'Université Paris, Sorbonne. He has published *Histoire d'Electricité de France depuis 1966* (Bordas, 1986), *Histoire économique de le France au XIX S*, (Colin, 1988), *Histoire des techniques XIX-XX S*, (Colin, 1988), and *La fée et la servante: la société française face à l'électricité XIX-XX S*, (Berlin, 1991).

Martin Campbell-Kelly graduated in computer science from the University of Manchester in 1968 and subsequently obtained a Ph.D. in the history of science. He is Senior Lecturer in computer science at the University of Warwick. He has written extensively on the British computer industry and government policy towards information technology. His book, *ICL: A Business and Technical History* (Oxford University Press), won the 1989 Wardworth Prize of the British Business Archives Council. He is currently writing a book with William Aspray on the history of computing for the Sloan Foundation Technology Series.

W. Bernard Carlson is an associate professor in the Humanities Division of the School of Engineering and Applied Science at the University of Virginia. His specialty is the history of American technology and business, where his research focuses on nineteenth century inventors and the electrical industry. He has published numerous articles as well as a book, *Innovation as a Social Process: Elihu Thomson and the Rise of the Electrical Industry* (Cambridge University Press, 1991). He is coeditor of a book series with MIT Press entitled "Inside Technology: New Approaches to the History and Sociology of Technology" and is pursuing research with Michael E. Gorman on the cognitive processes of American inventors.

Susan Douglas is the author of *Inventing American Broadcasting* and other essays on communications technology and the mass media. She teaches at Hampshire College and is currently writing a book on the history of television for the Sloan Foundation Technology Series.

Boelie Elzen is a researcher in environmental studies at the University of Nijmegen, where he is investigating why certain environmental technologies do not succeed in practice and how their chances for successful implementation can be enhanced. He graduated in electrical engineering from Twente University of Technology, the Netherlands in 1979 and then became a research assistant at Twente's Center for the Study of Science, Technology, and Society. In cooperation with the Stockholm International Peace Research Institute (SIPRI), he did technology assessment studies on the arms race. His dissertation covered "Scientists and Rotors—The Development of Biochemical Ultracentrifuges." In 1990 he collaborated with Donald MacKenzie on the historical and sociological analysis of the development of supercomputers. He is also engaged in studying the development of weapon innovation processes with the aim of developing schemes for the control of military research and development (R&D).

Pascal Griset is Charge de Recherches at the CNRS Institut d'histoire moderne et contemporaine. He holds a master's degree in history from, and is a These d'Universite candidate at, University Paris IV Sorbonne. He is the coauthor with Alain Beltran of *La crossance economique de la France au XIX eme siecle* (Paris, Colin, 1988) and *Historie des techniques XIX–XX siecles* (Paris: Colin, 1990), and author of *Genese de la civilisation de l'information* (Paris: Hatchette, 1990).

James Gover is supervisor of semiconductor programs at Sandia National Laboratories in New Mexico. He received his B.S. in electrical engineering from the University of Kentucky, M.S. in electrical engineering from the University of New Mexico, and Ph.D. in nuclear engineering from the University of New Mexico. He is an IEEE Fellow, awarded for work in radiation effects, and he has served as an IEEE Congressional Fellow. He has served as a member of the IEEE-USA Congressional Fellows Committee and was Vice-Chairman of the IEEE-USA Competitiveness Committee. He has also served IEEE's Nuclear and Plasma Science Society in a variety of conference positions including general chairman of the 1983 IEEE Nuclear and Space Radiation Effects Conference. He is currently the holder of a new IEEE Congressional Fellowship on competitiveness.

Gabrielle Hecht is an assistant professor of history of science at Stanford University. She received her Ph.D. in the Department of History and Sociology of Science at the University of Pennsylvania. Her dissertation was entitled "Technological Choice and Cultural Change: the Origins of the French Nuclear Program, 1945–1969."

Amos Joel is an executive consultant in telecommunications, following a distinguished career at Bell Telephone Laboratories. He is an authority on telephone switching and its history. One of his recent publications is a book written with Robert Chapuis, *Electronics, Computers, and Telephone Switching: A Book of Technological History* (North Holland, 1990). He is also the editor of the Bell Laboratories Technical History volume on switching technology. He is the holder of the Kyoto Prize, the IEEE Medal of Honor, and many other international awards.

Arne Kaijser (M.Sc. 1973, B.A. 1978, Ph.D. 1987) is a Senior Research Fellow at the Department of History of Technology at the Royal Institute of Technology in Stockholm. His research has mainly focused on the development of energy systems in Sweden, ranging from the establishment of the first Swedish gasworks in the mid-19th century to the challenge of phasing out nuclear power in the coming twenty years. He is comparing the development of energy systems in different countries, and also comparing energy systems with transportation and telecommunication systems.

Stuart W. Leslie teaches the history of science and technology at Johns Hopkins University. Among his publications are *Boss Kettering: The Wizard of General Motors* and a forthcoming study of the military's impact on postwar science and engineering education, *The Cold War and American Science*.

Kenneth Lipartito received his Ph.D. in history from the Johns Hopkins University in 1986 and in 1989 published *The Bell System and Regional Business: The Telephone in the South, 1877–1920* (Johns Hopkins Press, 1989). He is an associate professor of history at the University of Houston and is at work on a study of telecommunications technology and national policy in industrialized nations in the twentieth century. He was the Newcomen Fellow at the Harvard Business School in 1991–1992.

Donald MacKenzie is a professor of sociology at the University of Edinburgh. He has published widely in the history and sociology of science and technology, his most recently completed work being *Inventing Accuracy: A Historical Sociology of Nuclear Missile Guidance* (MIT Press, 1991). His current work includes a study of the development of high-performance computing and research on the social aspects of formal proof-of-program correctness.

Anne Millbrooke studied history at Boise State College (B.A., 1973), history of science at the University of Wisconsin, Madison (M.A., 1975), and the history and sociology of science at the University of Pennsylvania (Ph.D., 1981). While a student, she was a Mellon Fellow at the American Philosophical Society and a Smithsonian Fellow at the Smithsonian Institution. From 1981 until 1991, she worked for United Technologies as manager of the Archive and Historical Resource Center. The Otis Elevator company is a subsidiary of United Technologies. She is currently completing a book on the history of geology.

Eric Schatzberg is an assistant professor of history of science at the University of Wisconsin. At the time of the conference, he was a postdoctoral fellow with the IEEE-Rutgers Center for the History of Electrical Engineering. He holds the Ph.D. in history and sociology of science from the University of Pennsylvania and will soon publish a revised version of his doctoral dissertation on social and technical factors in the choice of materials for airplane design with Princeton University Press. He is also researching the social and technical history of the electric trolley.

Robert Smith is an historian at the National Air and Space Museum of the Smithsonian Institution and an associate professor in the Department of the History of Science at Johns Hopkins University. His latest book is *The Space Telescope: A Study of NASA, Science, Technology, and Politics* (Cambridge University Press, 1989), and among his current projects is a study of large-scale scientific enterprises.

Lennart Stenberg received a M.S. degree in engineering physics in 1969 from the University of Lund and a fellowship from the Swedish Board for Technical Development (STU) in 1971 to study international aspects of research policy. He was a Research Fellow in the System Dynamics Group at MIT in 1973 and worked as a researcher in the Resource Policy Group, Oslo, Norway, 1974–1978. He returned to STU in 1978 as a principal administrative officer in the agency's planning department, where he has since participated in the development of STU's overall policy and budget priorities. He has had major responsibility for studies of STU's programs on the structure and dynamics of Swedish industry and the Swedish R&D system, and on R&D policy in other countries. During the period 1988–90, as an associate research fellow at the Research Policy Institute, University of Lund, he made a comparative study of the research system dynamics in Japan and other countries. This study was done as a Visiting Researcher at the National Institute for Science and Technology Policy (NISTEP), Tokyo, the National Science Foundation in Washington, D.C., and the University of Tokyo.

Yuzo Takahashi received the bachelor of engineering degree in 1966, the master of engineering degree in 1968, and the doctor of engineering degree in 1971, all in electrical engineering from the University of Tokyo. He taught at Chuo University in Tokyo from 1971 to 1979. Since 1980 he has been an associate professor of the Tokyo University of Agriculture and Technology. He visited the Technical University of Munich from 1975 to 1977 as an Alexander Von Humboldt Research Fellow. His specialties are high-voltage engineering, electrical discharge, electrical insulation, and electrostatics. He is interested also in the history of electrical engineering, in particular in its institutional history. Dr. Takahashi is chairman of the IEE Japan Investigation Committee on the History and Future Prospect of Electrical Insulation Technology and active in other professional historical and engineering organizations.

Ulrich Wengenroth is professor of history of technology and director of the central institute for history of technology at the Technical University of Munich. He previously held academic positions at universities and research institutions in Darmstadt, Mainz, and Florence. His Ph.D. thesis on *Business Strategies and Technological Progress in the German and British Steel Industries, 1865–1895* (English edition, Cambridge University Press, 1991) won the German Association of Engineers Kellermann prize for the history of technology in 1982. He has published books and articles on the history of steel making, craft technology, and electrical engineering.